D0464612

IT'S NOT ALL ABOUT MONEY

IT'S NOT ALL ABOUT MONEY

Memoirs of a Private Banker

Hans J. Baer

BEAUFORT BOOKS

NEW YORK

FIRST EDITION

Library of Congress Cataloging-in-Publication Data

Bär, Hans J.
  [Seid umschlungen, Millionen. English]
  It's not all about money : memoirs of a private banker / Hans J. Baer.
    p. cm.
  ISBN 978-0-8253-0547-4 (alk. paper)
  1. Bär, Hans J. 2. Investment bankers — Biography. I. Title.
  HG1552.B367A313 2008
  332.1092—dc22
  [B]
                                    2007048181

Published in the United States by Beaufort Books, New York
www.beaufortbooks.com
Distributed by Midpoint Trade Books, New York
www.midpointtradebooks.com

10 9 8 7 6 5 4 3 2 1

PRINTED IN THE UNITED STATES OF AMERICA

To my life with Ilse Baer-Kaelin

CONTENTS

Acknowledgments

My ambition to publish an English version of my German language memoirs was marked by the difficulty of putting together an American publishing team. The daunting task of translating my Swiss-tainted German into my Swiss-tainted English was valiantly performed by Thomas Weyr — many thanks to him.

My editor in California, Gail M. Kearns, turned out to be a most gifted expert, not only as an editor but also as an e-mail communicator between Santa Barbara and Zurich. I cannot thank her enough for her untiring efforts to keep me in good humor with midnight telephone calls to clarify the written word.

Her proofreaders, Barbara Coster and Margaret Dodd, have done a great job, as has the genealogy consultant, Jayne Craven Caldwell. She was able to base her work on the excellent documentation put together by my sister Ruth Speiser, her daughter Irène Speiser, as well as my cousin Ray Baer. I hope that the genealogy charts, which should explain the complicated family relationships, have been further clarified.

Thanks go to my peer reviewers, Darrell and Kim Davis.

I should like to thank David C. Nelson, vice president and publisher, and Eric M. Kampmann, president, of Beaufort Books for the decision to publish what was after all a Swiss product in the United States.

Many thanks also to Margot Atwell, the associate publisher.

Last but not least, let me mention my friend Gail S. Kearney of the Lucerne Festival supporters in the United States. Her thorough understanding of globalized culture has provided me with the strength to carry on in a sometimes difficult task.

My thanks go, of course, once again to Ignatius Miller, who was my invaluable assistant in the German edition. His untiring support at all times cannot be overemphasized. My secretary, Esther Zoller, who was also part of the Swiss German venture, was of invaluable help.

The four mainstays of my life — Fritz Leutwiler, John Kenneth Galbraith, Isaac Stern, and Justin Thannhauser — are dead, and somehow I feel left behind. I hope that this updated version of my original memoirs will preserve the experiences essentially made during the period from Pearl Harbor to Ground Zero — two low points in a life that has however been blessed by good fortune.

I especially have reason to be thankful to my children, Monique and Raymond, my daughter-in-law Gabriele, and their four wonderful children.

HJB
Zurich, June 2007

It's Not All About Money

I

INTRODUCTION

From Pearl Harbor to Ground Zero

If music be the food of love, play on!
— *William Shakespeare, Twelfth Night*

When I began writing this book, I had every intention of showing how music dominated my life in many almost incredible ways. In the process of collecting my relevant thoughts, it suddenly occurred to me that two tragically low points in the world encompassed my career: the surprise attack on Pearl Harbor on December 7, 1941, and the terrorist attack on the World Trade Center on September 11, 2001.

On December 7, 1941, a Sunday, the New York Philharmonic Orchestra played its normal afternoon concert in Carnegie Hall. Arthur Rodzinski conducted Dimitri Shostakovich's First Symphony, and Arthur Rubinstein, who later became a good friend in Zurich, prepared himself to play the Brahms Second Piano Concerto in B major when CBS interrupted its broadcast with a terse bulletin: "Air raid on Pearl Harbor — this is no drill."

Sixty years later, on September 11, 2001, I sat at my desk at

Julius Baer & Co. on Bahnhofstrasse 36 in Zurich. I was looking forward to a memorial concert that night by the Chicago Symphony
Orchestra in Lucerne in honor of its late conductor, Sir Georg Solti.
His widow (he and his wife, Valerie, were my close friends) was due
to attend. Daniel Barenboim was to conduct Mahler's Seventh
Symphony. Suddenly, the Reuters news bulletin flickered across the
screen: "World Trade Center reported burning after a plane crashed
into it." Minutes later, at 3:05 p.m. European Time (9:05 a.m. in
New York), the agency reported: "Second plane reported to have
crashed into World Trade Center."

The second plane took care of any thought that the collision
might have been an accident. The United States had become victim of an apocalyptic attack every bit as dramatic and tragic as Pearl
Harbor. I telephoned the orchestra, which, on that sunny autumn
day, was cruising in a boat on Lake Lucerne. Contrary to my expectations, the musicians voted not to cancel the concert.

They opened with "The Star-Spangled Banner," and I felt myself back in the New York of the war years when no film, ball game,
opera, or concert began without playing the U.S. national anthem
and everybody stood up. In Lucerne, some of the audience rose,
others remained seated. A request to stand up would have been
appropriate.

I don't want to draw a parallel between the two events too
closely. (Given the infernal pictures of the collapsing World Trade
Center, we tend to overlook the attack on the Pentagon or the
fourth plane's attempt to hit the White House, which, fortunately,
was foiled. I find it strange that nobody thought to bury the passengers in Arlington.) Worlds separate the al-Qaeda people and
the commanders of the Japanese navy, and the gap between their
starting points is equally great. That is, the United States did not
react to Japan's expansionist policies, self-evident since the Russo-
Japanese war of 1904–05, until American interests were threatened

by the Japanese invasion of China; the subsequent oil embargo triggered the attack on Pearl Harbor.

The equally surprising al-Qaeda strike can only be understood as a desperate reaction to the uniformity of life brought on by global Americanization and the threat it poses to all cultural diversity. It is no accident that sons of wealthy families spearheaded the terrorist movement: they were aware of the impending loss of their cultural identity. In countries where women are expected to wear their traditional garments, the sight of women in uniform shocked them, and they saw this as a harbinger of Western modernism. They observed dramatic change and feared the destruction of their traditional world. My friend Samuel Huntington's book, *The Clash of Civilizations*, anticipated just such a development.

Nevertheless, American hegemony has been a fact of life since 1918 when many, though certainly not all, Europeans and Asians began to adjust to the new realities. My generation of Europeans saw the United States as a friend and a model to emulate, especially those who, like me, spent time there — in my case, ten years. Clearly, the next generations reacted differently to the United States and did so with greater caution as they focused, with sometimes reckless abandon, on their own interests. Hegemony ruins character, so I can only ask: Why should the United States receive better treatment than Napoleonic France?

The fact that rapid change became a constant in the second half of the twentieth century has turned into a cliché. Even Switzerland has changed. Switzerland doesn't make history; it only follows it. But as the case of the dormant accounts of the Holocaust victims demonstrated, the country needed tutoring until it learned to do so. It didn't recognize the dynamite these slumbering assets harbored, and it undoubtedly did not expect the representatives of the World Jewish Congress (WJC) to appear so forcefully on the global stage after their demands had been routinely dismissed for so many years.

The Swiss, therefore, could not possibly have been prepared for a discussion of an issue that would explode so violently in the nineties. Nor should anyone have been surprised that the country's banks so vastly underestimated its dimensions.

Looking back, I am again impressed to what extent music guided my life — even to the issuance of a bank license in New York City. With mild surprise, given everything I have done, I wonder how there was time left to manage a bank. I share my insight into management with Hamilton Jordan, President Jimmy Carter's chief of staff, who said, "If it ain't broke, don't fix it."

Charles de Gaulle wrote in his memoirs that throughout his life he had *une certaine idée de la France* (a certain idea of France). My idea of life is that we should not wait for the state to create something. Governmental institutions play too large a role in the daily affairs of business as it is. Collectively, we can only advance by supporting, not hindering, initiative. I have observed with great respect the activities of George Soros' and Bill Gates' foundations for the support of poor regions and peoples. Here too Europe limps far behind.

2

THE UNITED STATES AT WAR (1941)

No cuffs on shirts and trousers

I can't remember whether I was saddling my horse Action or cleaning out his hooves in the Van Cortland Park stables when I heard the news of the Japanese attack on Pearl Harbor. The radio was on as usual, so the interruption could not be missed.

Of course, I had no idea where Pearl Harbor was, and I couldn't grasp the meaning of the news when I heard it. We had only lived in the United States for five months; three months before, the family had settled in the Fieldstone area of Riverdale in the northwest Bronx section of New York City. It took us only a few minutes to walk to Van Cortland Park. The house that my mother had rented belonged to a prominent surgeon who trusted us with his entire belongings, including his very voluminous library.

My mother had a much clearer idea of the Pearl Harbor attack's consequences: "Forget about our trip to Florida," she told us. The trip we had planned for Christmas with our relative Ernst Radt became a casualty of threatened gasoline rationing. For me, this war began a lot more unfavorably than the war in Europe. News of the German attack on France on May 10, 1940, had occupied so much of my father's attention that he forgot to ask me about my

Latin grades. They were bad, and I was greatly relieved that the German offensive had diverted his attention.

The United States began rationing almost immediately, and this produced some odd quirks. Cuffs on trousers were banned, as were French cuffs on shirts. White shirts were difficult to find (and in those days white shirts were de rigueur). Textiles were at a premium. The army needed uniforms. You couldn't buy new cars or refrigerators. Industrial production was switched to wartime needs. But unlike Switzerland, cars in the States were not requisitioned.

Tires were subject to rationing because of rubber shortages. My mother felt the gasoline rationing most severely. She couldn't drive very far with three gallons of gas a week, given high-consumption engines, and dependence on the subways and commuter railroads wasn't much fun back then either, especially the Hudson Line that connected Riverdale to Manhattan via Harlem. My mother saved gas by rolling the gray Chrysler down the hill from Fieldstone to the train station, with the engine turned off. In the old-fashioned times of nonhydraulic steering and braking, this could be done without any problem, because the drum brakes were operated by cable.

Sugar and meat were rationed. I began my studies at Lehigh University in 1944, and part of my duties as kitchen head at Lehigh was collecting meat stamps from the other students. Nobody went hungry during the war, but the restrictions were noticeable; it was less so in Great Britain, where well-fed GIs were considered by the British to be "oversexed, overpaid, and over here."

The "inconveniences" did not end with VE Day, Germany's unconditional surrender. Only after VJ Day, Japan's capitulation on September 2, 1945, did the government end rationing that same night. To celebrate, a college friend and I drove all night in his luxurious car, for which he had gotten his gasoline coupons, in order to visit his parents in the Poconos.

During the war, phone calls to Switzerland were very restricted. Calls to our family in Zurich required notification several days in advance so that officials at the wiretap facility could transcribe our conversation fully. They took a lively interest in the health of our relatives. If we'd mentioned an illness in one conversation and hadn't come back to it in another, the official "listener" would regularly cut in and inquire about a sick aunt or uncle. The postal service was no different — they opened the mail and clearly indicated that the envelope had been opened.

Last but not least, the United States, as of June 14, 1941, blocked all Swiss accounts. The process of freezing was meant to weaken potential enemies in the United States. If my mother wanted to write a check to pay tuition for the children, she had to fill out an application at the bank. Repeal of the ordinance came on May 14, 1946, via individual licenses. Until December 1948, the treasury in Switzerland had freed up a total of SFr (Swiss francs) 4.3 billion ($1.02 billion). Why the "neutral" Swiss? The explanation went something like this: if the Germans were to march into Switzerland overnight, they couldn't take Swiss money because we already had it. Money for household expenses was exempted. But it was so tight that repairing a fur coat would break the budget. Anything beyond the strict minimum of the household budget would need a special authorization from the authorities.

President Franklin Roosevelt had begun steering the United States toward war in July 1941 in order to safeguard American interests — after he tried to postpone U.S. entry because of the isolationist mood in Congress and the population at large. But on July 9, 1941, Secretary of War Stimson and Secretary of the Navy Knox were told to determine how much war materiel the United States had to produce in order to outstrip all potential enemies. The so-called Victory Program was the result. The army and the navy built their planning on the assumption that Germany could only be defeated militarily (instead of through a naval blockade) and that U.S. help was needed to do so. Given the weakness of European colonial states in Asia, a military commitment against Japan also had to be included in their calculations. The war against Germany would have to be waged until the Third Reich was totally defeated. Accordingly, George Marshall and his chief planner, Albert C. Wedemeyer, calculated that an army of 8.8 million men would be needed — grouped into 215 divisions, with 61 of them being armored divisions. In fact, only 8.2 million men and 16 armored divisions were mobilized (in part because of limited shipping capacity), but that does not demean their enormous achievements. Before the war, in 1939, the army (including the air force, which was then part of the army) only had 255,000 men.

It took several weeks in October 1940 to recruit 16 million men capable of bearing arms, and that without a bureaucratic organization in place. Tank production rose from zero at the beginning of 1940 to 100 per month in a factory Chrysler had built in the spring. On the eve of the Japanese attack on Pearl Harbor, American generals had figured total armament costs through September 30, 1943, at $150 billion. Planners did not foresee major land operations against Japan nor the participation of the Red Army. They assumed that the Wehrmacht, the German armies, would defeat Russian forces by July 1942 and drive them behind a line that ran from the White Sea, in the north, to Moscow and the Volga. The United States only wanted to defeat Japan after victory in Europe (the "Germany-first strategy").

I cite all these details because Israel Singer, the secretary-general of the World Jewish Congress at the time, informed that I planned to open my memoirs with my reminiscences of Pearl Harbor, argued that the United States would never have waged war without that attack. Not without justification do historians complain that people scarcely take note of actual facts. In other words, Roosevelt was trying to help the Allies to the utmost possible extent without actually going to war, which implied a congressional approval. The Pearl Harbor attack merely pushed him over the brink.

3

A Family History (1890–1941)

The oldest son is always called Julius

The Swiss roots of our family do not reach very deeply. My mother's maiden name is Lohnstein. She hailed from Worms/Rhine, Germany, a city southeast of Frankfurt. Her father and his twin brother ran a porcelain business. They were court purveyors to the Grand Duke of Hesse-Darmstadt, an honorary title, and lived in a handsome house on Siegfriedstrasse in Worms.

My grandfather Ludwig Lohnstein and his brother Otto were identical twins who, in a double wedding, married the sisters Marie and Alice Kann. Their wedding trip became part of our family lore. One couple stayed at the same hotel in Engelberg shortly after the other. The manager lacked the imagination to think of identical twins and at first refused to give my great-uncle a room. His hotel was a decent establishment.

As children, we often spent our vacation with our grandparents, and ever since, I associate Germany with the smell of high sulfur-content lignite, which, in the seventies, still hovered over West Berlin. Worms has a famous Jewish cemetery (the oldest headstone is dated 1044) and one of the oldest synagogues in Europe. The "new" synagogue was erected in 1174–75, the predecessor 140 years earlier. My parents were married in the new synagogue on September 14, 1922, the year my father was appointed a university professor in Zurich.

After graduating from high school, my mother registered at the University of Heidelberg, majoring in chemistry, and then met my father six weeks later. It must have been a *coup de foudre*, because they became engaged a few days later. In traveling to see his bride-to-be through a Germany still starving in the aftermath of the wartime blockade, my father brought flour and milk instead of flowers.

Their first meeting was hardly accidental, because my parents were related. My father was a cousin of her mother, my grand-mother Marie Lohnstein, born Kann, who came from Stuttgart. My paternal grandmother, Marie Ulrich, had married my grandfather Julius Baer in 1891, and her sister Dorothea, twelve years older, had in turn married Heinrich Kann in Stuttgart.

Jacob Loew Ulrich, my paternal great-grandfather and my maternal great-great-grandfather, had been a draper in Harburg, a small town between Noerdlingen and Donauworth in the border country between Bavaria and Wurttemberg. My great-great-grandmother was thus Swabian. Today it's the eastern part of Wurttemberg, a county in the southwest of Germany. The two of them had thirteen children; three of the thirteen — Emil, Julie, and Otto — died weeks or months after their births. Dorothea, my maternal great-grandmother was, as the seventh child, right in the middle, and my grandmother Marie was the youngest.

The sum of my grandmother Marie's dowry is documented. It amounted to SFr 100,000, a considerable amount in those days. My grandfather signed the receipt for the money at the lawyer's office. In addition, as the marriage and inheritance contracts noted, she brought into the marriage a trousseau worth SFr 15,000 ($4,000) and silver worth SFr 8,000 ($2,000). Julius Baer's fortune at the time amounted to SFr 180,000 ($43,000), which he had invested as a capital asset with the Dukas and Co. bank in Basel.

Two of my grandmother Marie's sisters had married two important business partners of my grandfather Julius Baer: Bertha Ulrich
had wed the banker Ludwig Hirschhorn, who in 1890 founded the
bank of Hirschhorn & Grob (with the entry of my grandfather into
the partnership, it became Hirschhorn, Uhl, & Baer), and Anna
Ulrich married the banker August Gerstle, from whom my grandfather learned the banking business.

My cousin Peter Baer repeated my father's example when he
married Ray Salisbury. She is a great-granddaughter of August and
Anna Gerstle. My great-grandfather is her great-great-grandfather.
They met when Peter went to London to continue his training.

I must also mention Emma Ulrich, another sister of my grandmother. Born six years before Marie, Emma married the Zurich silk
manufacturer Iwan Sax. Her son Victor Sax was my father's first
cousin; he would become my fatherly mentor in New York. Victor
taught me how to handle a fishing rod, and he liked to invite me for
weekends of fishing off Long Island on a small houseboat where he
regularly played host to beautiful women. I'm sorry to say I was still
at an age where I hadn't a clue what to do with these lovely women.

Victor was a very worldly gentleman, as much at home in Paris
as in New York or Italy. He was married to the very beautiful Sylvia
Bauer, who was always accompanied by an ardent admirer and who
outlived Victor by twenty-five years. Uncle Victor was mildly
unhappy about the fact that the deposits of the Baer Custodian
Corporation, founded in 1940 in New York, were for all intents and
purposes not invested during the war. He would say later, "I'd like to
have 10 percent of the money you didn't make."

We know more about the Baer family tree than the other side of the
family. It can be traced back to the year 1650. The Baers come from
Heidelsheim, Germany, a community east of Bruchsal. The family
traded in animal skins and made small loans. The business was
empowered by a charter from the elector of the Palatinate. By

charter, the elector took part in the election of the king of Rome and emperor of Germany.

My great-grandfather married Rosina Dreyfuss in 1850 and expanded the inherited skin business as rigorously as he did the credit operation. My grandfather Julius was the eldest son, and his original name was Isaac. He and his brother Aaron secularized their first names in 1897. (Thereafter Aaron called himself Albert.)

My family thought very much in dynastic terms. After my grandfather Julius' death, my uncle Werner gave up his engineering studies in order to take over the bank with his brother Walter. At the same time, they made my father a limited partner.

My grandfather used to say occasionally, "What would I do with all the money that I have already lost?" He always lost money in speculations. From childhood on, he was more interested in his father's credit business than in the animal skin trade; as I said before, he learned the systematic side of banking from August Gerstle. The Augsburg banker was heavily engaged in financing industrial enterprises; for example, he invested in Maschinenfabrik Augsburg Nuernberg (MAN), a truck manufacturer the size of Freightliner, and Rudolf Diesel, the inventor of the diesel engine. In addition, Gerstle was one of the backers of an independent daily press. Two years later, Samuel Dukas offered my grandfather a partnership as co-owner in his Basel bank. Dukas was one of Gerstle's business colleagues. That's how Julius Baer came to Switzerland.

Ludwig Hirschhorn, my grandmother's brother-in-law, lured him from Basel to Zurich. The banker, who hailed from Friedberg in Hesse, had founded the Hirschhorn & Grob bank along the Limmat River in 1890. Grob left six years later, and consequently, Hirschhorn offered Julius Baer an equity interest. Industrial financing was the most important part of the business. That resulted in my grandfather joining the board of Switzerland's Southeast Railroad as well as the board of the Thunersee Railroad and the Oerlikon engineering factory (not to be confused with the arms manufacturer). Oerlikon's industrial fame rests on construction of the first alternate current generator, which made power transport across great distances possible. After Ludwig Hirschhorn's death, Julius Baer took over the bank and had it registered under the name of Julius Baer & Co.

My grandfather, a citizen of Zurich from 1907 on, died in 1922. After his death, my uncles Walter and Werner wanted to continue running the bank under the same name, but the canton's commercial register intervened, citing the regulation for partnerships that demanded company truth. In a partnership, the name of the company and the owner had to be identical. The matter ended, and Walter Baer added Julius as his second middle name. In the 1926 edition (the last one published) of the city of Zurich's civic book, Walter signed with the first names "Walter Jakob, Julius, banker," with the entry "two sons: Nicolas Julius, born 1924; Alfred, born 1926." Ever since, the family has made sure that the oldest son's middle name is Julius.

I was born as the second child on September 26, 1927, on Rigistrasse, a residential street on the gold coast, and I grew up in the Fluntern district, at Bergstrasse 27, a house not far from my grandparents and uncle Walter at Bergstrasse 54.

My parents drove identical automobiles, which made it less obvious that they had two cars. The body was custom manufactured in Langenthal, Switzerland, and mounted on a Chrysler chassis. The entire family, that is, my parents and my uncles, drove the "Langenthal ships." My parents cultivated a laid-back lifestyle, raising us in thrift and modesty and diligence. When we sat around with friends after school in Riverdale, my mother would ask, "What are you doing?" "We're sitting around" was our usual response. "You don't just sit around!" she would admonish. My mother expected us to be active.

Ours was essentially a classical education, true to the epigram of the baroque poet Angelus Silesius, "Eternal essence be," which my mother liked to quote and according to which she lived. "Distilled civility and unpresuming grace" is how the mathematician and Swiss Federal Institute of Technology (ETH) Professor K. Chandrasekharan described my mother in an homage written in 1976, in which he also called her an aesthete "for whom life is enjoyable when filtered through art. . . . Few carry as she does a faith in the lifelong validity of friendship, a hatred for the sordid, a willingness to stand engrossed and to make every friend of hers, young or old, a little happier."

In his obituary for my father, Edgar Meyer, professor of physics at the University of Zurich, stressed my father's sense for what is important "in science as well as in life." Material things were banned. Only intelligence, art, and music counted. My parents didn't know any businesspeople. Professionally, they associated with physicists and mathematicians, musicians, painters, and sculptors. Invitations that brought only a business group to our table were inconceivable. The arts and sciences were as mixed as possible. My father's fondest saying was, "I don't want to know anything about money." My mother too was totally disinterested in money. So I grew up in a world where nobody talked about money. Nor did I ever get an allowance. My pocket money was the loose change left over from my shopping. I never had to account for what I spent; even that didn't interest my mother. In my mother's later years, she only had two comments about business. If I said it was going badly, she replied, "It will get better." If I said business was good, she said, "It's bound to change." In general, she thought that people had too much money.

Richard Baer, my father, studied mathematics and then switched to physics after graduation. He became a university lecturer with a thesis proving the atomic structure of electricity. He did additional research about electric charges in gases. In 1933 he began to focus on ultrasonics.

By today's standards, my parents' villa on Bergstrasse was akin to running a small business. A maid in a light blue smock was responsible for the upstairs rooms. For the first floor we had a maid in a dark dress; she also served meals. In addition, we had a gardener,

Mr. Hotz, who, of course, had an assistant. There was also a cook, a laundress, a chauffeur, and a governess. They all had to be fed. In my case, the real governess was the chauffeur. I spent every free minute with him and amused myself washing the cars.

The personnel were housed modestly. Most of our servants came from Germany, except for Viktor Rusalem, the Swiss chauffeur. We hired our staff through a personnel agency, and they tended to stay with us for a long time. We never let anybody go. When we gave up the Zurich household and moved to the States, Frieda, the maid, went to work for my uncle. The chauffeur, without a car during the war, worked in the bank. The governess, who had a diploma as a baby nurse — she wore a uniform with a starched blouse that had a medal on it — threatened to quit every three or four years, whereupon my mother announced to her, "Well, then, we'll have to have another child." So Emma Schmidt stayed with our family for more than twenty years through the births of all of us four children.

The food in my parents' home was German: soup, main course, and dessert. The fare was heavy and without much variety. Cream desserts dominated. We had Bavarian cream, almond cream, vanilla cream with sour cherries, baked apple dumplings, or sometimes hard red groats. At night we were served a cold meal, which for us children meant sandwiches to be eaten in the kitchen. It would have been inconceivable to have us at the dinner table. The evenings when there were guests and when formal clothing, including tuxedos, was mandatory, lasted much longer than they do today. An invitation for a glass of wine after dinner, rather than to dinner itself, was common because it was less trouble. I still received such invitations in the fifties.

In the morning, we had rolls, croissants, and Ovomaltine (the original name for Ovaltine, which was developed in Switzerland). We ate breakfast together at 7:30 a.m. I had to leave at 7:45 a.m. to make it to the schoolhouse on the Fluntern on time. My father left for the institute then too. At 12:30 p.m. he returned for lunch, and around 2:00 he was back at his research. Then, around 4:00 in the afternoon, my parents and my uncles and their wives met for tea at the Chardon or Huguenin teahouse in the city. Daily tea was a sacred institution for the three brothers. My father strolled over from the university, my uncles came from the bank, and my mother and aunts all arrived from their houses. At 6:00 they were back at home. On Sundays, a joint dinner replaced the tea hour, usually at the Bahnhofsrestaurant, the main station restaurant, still a famous address today, or at the Hotel St. Gotthard.

Vacations aside, it was very rare that these daily rituals were not respected. My uncles never took business trips. Where should they have gone? Their world was too small, and Werner especially didn't enjoy traveling. When Werner visited me in New York during my apprenticeship at Brown Brothers Harriman, the trip had all the aura of a state visit. The brothers spent a lot of time together and were personally very close. Today the entire family lacks such contact.

My father was ill for as long as I remember him. He probably suffered from kidney cancer, but we never talked about his illness. His blood pressure was the depressing family drama. A doctor came into our home every few weeks to measure it. It's hard to imagine this now when people can take their own blood pressure. Fear hovered over the family. We always wondered how high the blood pressure would be when the doctor returned in two weeks. Dr. Erich Liebmann, the family physician who looked after my father, and Dr. Bruno Ricklin, the pediatrician who vaccinated the next generation, came and went on a regular basis. Today I think that my father's illness influenced my mother to concentrate her attention on him and to care less for us children.

Dr. Ricklin, a colonel in the Swiss militia army and commander of the military training area in Schwyz, usually appeared in uniform at our sickbed, an occurrence that heightened our fascination with him. As an educated man, Dr. Ricklin took care to speak High German with my parents instead of the local dialect, basically a medieval German comparable to Dutch.

During our childhood, guests never stayed in a hotel but rather at our house. We had two guest rooms. One was always occupied. Visitors, often scientists, would come with their wives and live for several weeks. A separate maid took care of their needs. She served breakfast in their rooms because my father didn't care to see visitors in the morning. Irene Joliot-Curie was surely among our best-known guests, but she didn't leave a lasting impression on us children. On the other hand, I still have lively memories of Chandrasekhara Raman, the Indian physicist and Nobel Prize winner. He had discovered the Raman effect (the change in the wavelength of light that occurs when a light beam is deflected by molecules), which was named for him, and this became one of my father's fields of research. Raman, a slim gentleman, wore a high-buttoned frock coat and was a good-looking man with dark skin, making him seem all the more exotic.

It was exciting when Armand Dreyfus, the head of the Swiss Bank Corporation (SBC), came to our house for dinner. You would think it too was a state visit. Only at one other time were we in such awe — when the president of the Schulrat (the board of the ETH) called on us. My father was nervous for three weeks before his scheduled arrival. Today it's hard to imagine getting nervous about the visit of the president of the educational board, and to me that says a lot about the decline of the academic world's social standing.

I also remember the mathematician David Hilbert. My father had been his assistant at Goettingen University. The Koenigsberg-born East Prussian used to say about his profession, "A scientist is nothing but envy, malevolence, and meanness." Great awe marked the meeting with this "God of Goettingen" who lives on in my memory, an old man, blind in one eye, and surrounded by a special aura.

Among my parents' good friends were Erwin and Annie Schroedinger. The Austrian physicist had a great liking for the female sex and consequently led an unconventional personal life. However, the Nobel Prize he received in 1933 was for his research in quantum mechanics. He taught in Zurich from 1921 to 1927. When Schroedinger was driven out of Graz after Austria's "Anschluss," he wanted to come back to Zurich but had to settle for a chair in Ireland. After the war, he taught in Vienna. On his own request, he was buried in Alpbach in the Tyrol. I always visited his grave whenever I attended the European Forum, an important annual seminar in that alpine village.

Gershon Scholem, an endlessly witty and entertaining man from a very bourgeois Berlin family — whose father threw him out of his house via a registered letter because of his Zionist convictions — was a postwar acquaintance of our family. He spent a guest semester in Zurich and then returned many times. In 1968, the University of Zurich awarded him an honorary doctorate. He first stayed at the university's guesthouse and then moved into a study in my mother's home. His best-known book, *Sabati Zevi: The Mystical Messiah*, published in 1973, was, to a large extent, written in our house on Bergstrasse. When my siblings and I put together a catalogue for my mother's seventy-fifth birthday, he contributed a few lines in which he lovingly described the spirit of the house: the bright study on the first floor with its view of the beautiful garden on two sides; Michele, the model, who floated around the studio and whom Scholem recognized in my mother's bronzes; the "indifferently organized" library with the large encyclopedias, the alphabetically listed authors, the biographies of Richard Baer and Hermann Weyl; and the "kinetically gifted mistress of the house."

Among my most thrilling childhood memories in Zurich were Chaim Weizmann and his Rolls Royce with its speakerphone to the chauffeur. We were allowed to ride in it around the Fluntern a few times, which made it especially exciting. Weizmann was a phenomenal personality. We would meet him again in New York. Surely one reason his presence made a deeper impression on me than anyone else in my life was that he was half blind. Weizmann's connection with my father had been made through science. In Zurich he didn't stay with us but with my uncle Walter. My uncle and my aunt cleared out their bedroom for him, a singular privilege.

One of my mother's best friends was Franca Pauli, the wife of Wolfgang Pauli, who taught at the ETH from 1930 until his death in 1958, except during the war years of 1940–46, when he was at Princeton. Fully aware of his intellectual superiority, Pauli, who won the Nobel Prize in physics in 1945, tended to show little respect for his fellow human beings, which didn't make his life in Zurich any easier. "Still so young and already so unknown" was his commentary on the performance of another scholar. Heinrich Rothmund, the chief of police in the federal Department of Justice, rejected Pauli's application for Swiss citizenship in 1938. Rothmund's reason: "It would be a major mistake . . . to naturalize foreigners who have not adjusted fully to our essence and our national traditions." The campaign against Pauli reached its absolute all-time low in 1942 with a note in the ETH board protocols that Pauli was "an eastern Jew who could not be assimilated." This was the reason given for turning down his second naturalization application. Actually, Pauli came from an upper-middle-class Viennese family, and his parents had already converted to Catholicism.

Among my family's close friends was Count Richard Nikolaus Coudenhove-Kalergi, the founder of the pan-European movement, who was born in Tokyo in 1894. He was good-looking, half European and half Japanese, and during the war lived in New York, as we did. He'd been married since 1915 to the actress Ida Roland, who amused us greatly in New York with her comment, "They're all Nazis," whenever she saw a motorized police patrol in jackboots. After the war, Nikolaus and Ida lived in a fabulous chalet in Gstaad with old doors and cupboards that they had collected from all over the Berner Highlands. My mother was a good friend of their some-what eccentric daughter, Erika Coudenhove-Kalergi.

In the thirties, Sunday visits were still made unannounced. If the residents were not at home, the visitor left a calling card with a bent corner. Before leaving on a longer trip, cards were left with the note "p.p.c." (*pour prendre congé* — to take leave). Relations with neighbors were only handled in writing. Our up-the-street neighbor at Bergstrasse 25 was the famous forensic physician Heinrich Zang-ger. He would correspond with my father about neighborhood matters, covering many pages, about such things as the overdue painting of the garden fence.

Music lessons were an integral part of our education. The first musical instrument I tried to play was the accordion; Miss Lenz-linger taught me the first melodies. My real introduction to music, however, came from Alexander and Irma Schaichet. The two of them played music with our whole family. My mother played the viola. She had studied musical theory in Mannheim with the com-poser Ernst Toch. In Zurich, she became Alexander Schaichet's student, played in his chamber orchestra and in a quartet, and took piano lessons from Irma Schaichet. My uncle Walter did too. He played the piano seriously all his life. Irma Schaichet also opened up the world of music to my cousins.

Our chauffeur drove my sisters and me to the Schaichets' home at Hadlaubsteig 6 once or twice a week. I was always a little afraid of those lessons. Irma was a strict teacher, and I was not a diligent student.

However, that didn't stop me from wanting to play the cello, an interest kindled at a children's concert at the Tonhalle Concert Hall. Frédéric Motier, the first cellist at the Zurich Tonhalle Orchestra, became my teacher; he too was a friend of the family. One time, I rode my bike to my lessons carrying the cello and promptly fell off, smashing the instrument. It was professionally repaired, and surprisingly, it sounded much better afterward. After my mother's death, we found that the most valuable part of my old cello was the French bow, "fait par Eugène Sartory à Paris." My parents had bought it in 1938 for SFr 100 ($25). I know this because I found the price tag stuck in the shaft. Several years ago the bow was sold for SFr 20,000 ($5,000). The best business deal of my life. The cello went to a children's home in Brazil.

Through Irma we met the young Georg Solti, who hailed from Budapest. Solti was stuck in Switzerland in 1939 and, as a refugee without a work permit, managed to survive only with the greatest deprivations. Irma had a special talent for bringing people together. As Solti remembered in his memoirs, the pianist arranged for his meeting with the unhappily married Hedi Gitermann-Oechsli. When Géza Anda, a pupil of Ernst von Dohnanyi (grandfather of the conductor Christoph von Dohnanyi), came to Zurich in 1943, Irma took the young pianist under her wing and introduced him to my uncle Walter. I met both Georg Solti and Géza Anda after my return to Switzerland. Anda was an especially charming man with strong opinions. I've remained on friendly terms with his wife, Hortense Buehrle-Anda, an extraordinarily gifted lady. She can be reached every morning at eight in her office, and has done a great deal for music in Switzerland, especially for the Lucerne Music Festival and the Anda International Piano Competition. Regrettably, her achievements haven't always been properly appreciated.

A fixed part of my childhood memories is the great poverty I encountered. When I took my obligatory Sunday walk with my father, we would always stumble over "beer corpses" who slept off their drunken stupor in the middle of the sidewalk. During lunch, beggars knocked at the front door and my father gave them vouchers good for the city's milk kitchens. "Why vouchers?" I asked my father. His answer: "Cash would be used for other purposes."

I learned about the help my father gave his persecuted colleagues in Germany from the Bergier Commission's Report (*Independent Expert Commission, Switzerland–World War II*). Twice he traveled to Istanbul, where there was, as the commission found, lively bank traffic between Zurich and Istanbul. Prompted by the anatomist Richard Schwarz, who launched the Aid Association of German Scientists Abroad, my father helped his anxious friends wherever he could. Istanbul was one possible destination for teaching because its universities, reorganized in the spirit of Kemal Ataturk, founder of modern Turkey, were ready to employ German professors. The physicist Edgar Meyer remembered in his obituary for my father that he had traveled with him and Professor Schwarz to Istanbul to pave the way for such employment. By the end of 1933, more than thirty German professors had been able to resume their teaching activities along the Bosporus. Among them was the economist Wilhelm Roepke, who was given a chair in Geneva in 1937. He gave the festive lecture celebrating the seventy-fifth anniversary of the Julius Baer bank in 1965 — an exciting event at the time. It was by no means a matter of course that the bank was able to win Roepke as a speaker or for a German to speak at a Swiss bank's anniversary.

The best-known scientist that my father got out of Germany was the surgeon Richard Niessen, a student of Ferdinand Sauerbruch and a famed professor at the Charité hospital in Berlin until the Nazi regime forced Niessen to resign his position and end his career in Germany. Niessen was the first doctor who succeeded in resectioning a whole lung. Until 1939, he worked in Istanbul and then went to the United States but could only find jobs at modest hospitals — where, among many others, he operated on me — before going to Basel in 1952. He died there in January of 1981. Turkey was one of the few countries that allowed persecuted Germans to enter, and for this the country should be honored.

My grandparents in Worms and their siblings were reluctant to leave Germany. I remember so well the nightly phone conversations in which my mother pleaded with her parents to leave before it was too late. My grandparents did not flee until after Kristallnacht, "The Night of Broken Glass," in 1938, and then they settled in Geneva.

My great-uncle Otto and his wife had used the last of their money — not exchangeable, of course — to book passage on a German liner for a world cruise, as had so many others. This was in 1937 and was the only legal way to use up the money. They had been attended to by Nazi personnel and had gotten off the boat in Brazil. Otto's son, August Lohnstein, born on July 3, 1904, and trained in the retail business at Macy's in New York, had arrived in Rio de Janeiro on August 21, 1936, and had founded ADAGA, an import business in eyeglasses and frames. When I visited August in 1950, business was flourishing. The brother of my mother, my uncle Fritz Lohnstein, born on May 6, 1908, had opted to escape to South Africa and arrived in Cape Town on January 3, 1937.

The grand tours taken in the family car were one of my mother's favorite pastimes. The most exotic tour was surely the voyage to the Middle East, which my parents undertook together with Walter and my aunt. They started in Zurich in 1934 with two convertibles, loaded the cars on a ship in Marseilles, and then drove from Alexandria to Jaffa. The chauffeurs were armed with revolvers. In Palestine, they inspected the Daniel Sieff Research Institute then under construction. It was named for a son of the founding families of the Marks & Spencer department stores who had died young.

Chaim Weizmann, who had close ties to the Sieff family, was the director. I don't remember if my parents attended the opening on April 3, 1934. Erich Mendelsohn, who had left Germany right after the National Socialists seized power, conceived the building. In 1949, this research facility was renamed the Weizmann Institute of Science.

I vividly remember the Swiss National Exhibition that opened in Zurich on May 6, 1939, just before the war. It attracted 10 million visitors, surely the most popular such show ever held in Switzerland. It had all the ingredients of a successful Swiss festival. It put together everything Switzerland was — its industrial perfomance as well as its cultural identity — and showed, as an idea, what Switzerland wanted to be. The "Landi" (its vernacular name) was a modern performance show; it involved folklore, Swiss-style wrestling, and history, and it sent a message of social integration. It also presented a technically creative Switzerland in such fields as energy output, aluminum manufacturing, the electronics industry, chemistry, watchmaking, traffic, and transport. And, of course, it was an arms show, something with which we had a very uncomplicated relationship. We found weapon demonstrations very exciting. We were taught about the importance of agriculture and discovered evidence for the beautiful landscape of the country. Every one of us Swiss left the exhibit a couple of inches taller than when we had gone in.

I belonged to the Flamberg scout troop and played in the symphony orchestra that gave at least two concerts at the exhibition. The staff of the exhibition grew scarce after the September 2, 1939, mobilization order, so bringing in the scouts made sense. And we were kept busy taking down street signs in order to complicate an invading enemy's orientation. Once we were even allowed to provide the bodyguards for General Guisan, the commander in chief of the army. That year, 1939, was really an exciting year. My Hauptfeldmeister (scout leader) was Hans ("Hansi") Hubacher, an architect and son of the sculptor Hermann Hubacher.

I learned the meaning of nervousness for the first time and up close when my older sister, Marianne, prepared for the entrance exam to the high school. She was three years ahead of me and gave me a feel for the stress that awaited me in the winter of 1939. My father could not imagine that I could go anywhere else but to a high school, which enabled access to a university. Another secondary school would simply have been impossible. So the academic and social pressures of my neighborhood on the gold coast weighed heavily on me. It was imperative to get into the high school; otherwise, social decline threatened.

The examination took two days for the written part and one day for the oral. But if your written effort was good enough, you didn't have to take the oral test. I had studied for the entrance exam for at least two years with the help of a tutor. A certain class distinction was hard to miss: if you didn't have ambitious parents or at least money for a private tutor, you didn't get in. It was that simple.

In the Fluntern elementary school, our class first had Miss Spielmann as teacher. We were especially proud of our second teacher, Ernst Attinger. He was an infantry major and thus a staff officer. When he was on vacation, we saw him in uniform. In 1940, our whole class rode out on bicycles to visit him in the positions he occupied with his battalion along the Rhine, somewhere between Kreuzlingen and Schaffhausen. He took us through the trenches, a very exciting experience for us. In later years, he would come to our class reunions, every inch an upstanding Swiss, and into old age he remained a very robust and interesting man.

War brought rationing and requisition. After mobilization, the army demanded all of the convertibles, including our Langenthal Chryslers; they were put at General Guisan's disposition. In the newsreels, we repeatedly saw the general ride in them during parades. I saw the car I had washed so often when the Flamberg scouts were his bodyguards and he drove by to inspect us. General Guisan was a very elegant man.

My sister and I were lucky during our mandatory agricultural service. Normally, one was assigned to a farm, and that could mean bad luck. It depended on the farmer. But we had good connections. Our governess, Emma Schmidt, had grown up on the large Trindler family farm in the Thurgau. My father made sure we were sent there, where I had to guard cows — a welcome change from our humdrum daily life. We're still in touch with the Trindler family today.

After the German attack on France on May 10, 1940, we took part in the evacuation to Montreux and Lausanne. In the event of an attack, Zurich was considered a primary target. Although the general staff did not rule out a deceptive maneuver, as Hans Senn noted in his history of the Swiss general staff, he had no firm evidence for that conclusion. But since the defense positions along the Limmat River were not fully manned, the military leadership probably did not count on an attack. Moreover, my family was convinced, as were so many others, that western Switzerland would not be occupied, probably in anticipation of French reinforcements. We slept with a packed knapsack on our beds and saw any potential evacuation as an exciting change from the boring everyday world. For us, it all seemed like a great scout exercise, and we children showed no fear.

Although few cars were around before the war, long lines of vehicles jammed the streets from Zurich to Lausanne in May of 1940. Parts of the gold coast establishment preferred to pass the critical days in the western part of Switzerland. Nor was the fact unnoticed that the families of the highest officers were also evacuated.

In 1940, conversation at the dinner table turned to the subject of emigration. We four children were strictly barred from talking about it to anyone else. My pessimistic father did not see a glimmer of hope in a Hitler-dominated Europe (and fearing Nazi Germany's destructive fury, had decreed that when he died, his urn should be placed in a modest corner of the central Zurich cemetery). As a noted experimental physicist, he had received an offer to work at the Institute for Advanced Study at Princeton, clearing our way for an untroubled entry into the United States, not easy for most people at the time. My parents saw the United States as a country free of discrimination. They had planned their emigration together with my two uncles, Walter and Werner, who ran the family bank in Zurich.

Walter had gone first, arriving in New York in the autumn of 1940 in order to open a U.S. branch of Julius Baer & Co. My father was to follow with the understanding that he would become the nonexecutive chairman. Werner was less interested in leaving home. He used to insist that he would emigrate only after "the German conquest of Alexandria." Alexandria was the key to the Suez Canal, the vital artery of the British Empire. Werner was confident that the Axis powers would never advance that far, and history would prove him right.

Our own plans were changed by my father's early death. He passed away on December 13, 1940, not entirely unexpectedly, due to his long illness. His invitation to work at Princeton was no longer an option, so my mother had to devise other ways of organizing our entry into the United States. She managed to do so on the German immigration quota rather than on the oversubscribed Swiss one. When my mother married my father, she lost her German citizenship and acquired a Swiss passport, but it was one's place of birth, not citizenship, that was recognized by the American immigration authorities. According to the 1924 National Origins Law, the place of birth determined a person's quota. The law allowed only a set number of persons from each country to enter the United States every year. The German quota was generous and, in the 1930s, not fully utilized. Since 1929, almost twenty-six thousand Germans were allowed to immigrate every year, but the average use of the German quota was only 36 percent, except in 1938, when it topped 85 percent.

Would-be immigrants needed an affidavit from an American who could pay for the living expenses of the new arrivals, should they be unable to do so themselves. In addition, a certificate about the family and its assets was required. Finally, in the 1940s, another bureaucratic obstacle was added: a second guarantor of the immigrant's support. All told, this was much more unpleasant than the signed declaration (without which a visa would not be issued) that

"I do not intend to kill the president of the United States." My father had removed one more problem before he died by procuring Swiss citizenship for our governess, a German orphan without proper documentation.

We left Zurich at the end of April 1941 for Estoril in Portugal, where we planned to board ship for the journey across the Atlantic. Our train rolled through Geneva and unoccupied France. We carried a well-filled picnic basket with us and traveled in the company of Edgar Meyer, who accompanied us to Lisbon and helped us survive unscathed a voyage that lasted several days. The whole ordeal has settled into my memory as a depressing experience. Customs and police controls were everywhere, as were postwar deprivation and the oppressed faces in neutral Spain, still ravaged from the effects of civil war.

To our horror, Madrid was full of German uniforms. The Hotel Ritz looked like a Nuremberg hotel during a Nazi party congress. Everybody wore brown uniforms, jackboots, and swastikas. Highly elegant, to be sure, but we were hardly in the mood to appreciate their appearance. We felt like the refugees in the film *Casablanca* and sighed with relief when we finally reached Estoril. At last we were in a country that was totally at peace. Fresh butter was plentiful. Almost everybody who wanted to leave occupied Europe passed through this Portuguese port.

Until we boarded ship, we spent several weeks at the beach, a marvelous stay for us children. The crossing on the *Excalibur*, an American Export Lines vessel, passed without incident, save an unexplained halt of the ship's engines on the high seas, which immediately triggered the rumor that a German U-boat had stopped our steamer. A layover in the Bermudas to pass the British quarantine extended the voyage. We four children slept in one cabin while my mother shared space with other passengers.

4

In the U.S.A. (1941)

Saddle sore, athlete's foot, and poison ivy

The *Excalibur* glided past the Statue of Liberty early on the morning of Memorial Day, May 30, 1941, a holiday that didn't mean much to me at the time, and docked on a Hoboken pier. It was hot, with the kind of heat we Europeans weren't used to, the first indication of how different this country would be from what we'd known at home. Sailors lugged the gangway into place, and the immigration official came on board. A large desk was set up for him in the ship's salon. With some trepidation, we showed him our entry papers. Our being allowed to land or not was entirely a matter of his discretion. A visa was nothing more than a consular recommendation, not an automatic entry right. Our mother had reminded us of this fact during the crossing after talking to several important personalities on board. I especially remember Minister Carl Bruggmann, the Swiss ambassador in Washington. He was married to the sister of Vice President Henry Wallace (1941–44). But everything went well, and we were spared from going to Ellis Island.

We made our way down the gangway to the street and were greeted by my uncle Walter and René Beyersdorf. René would become one of my New York mentors. He had fled to New York from Brussels, where he had managed a bank, and found a job in the United States with my uncle.

Born in La Chaux-de-Fonds (Le Corbusier and Chevrolet grew up in this town too), René had reached New York a year before us and had taken the same route. He'd survived a number of adventures during his escape from Brussels. He was the son of a watchmaker and a cantor, and at age seventeen had found a job with Cassell & Co. in Brussels. In 1937, when Baron Cassell quit the banking business, René and a partner had founded the Banque Beyersdorf, Terlinck & Cie. When the Germans attacked Belgium in 1940, René sent his wife and two children to Switzerland via Paris, closed his accounts, returned deposits to his clients, and drove his car to Bordeaux, where he was reunited with his family. They traveled on to Estoril, convinced that Switzerland was not safe from German attack.

In New York, René ran across Walter, whom he'd met in Europe. Walter gave him a job at half pay in our bank's modest offices at 67 Wall Street. After Walter returned to Switzerland, he entrusted our relative, Ernst Radt, a stockbroker with Halle & Stieglitz on Broad Street, with the supervision of our business, which was run by René.

Walter had put his wife and four children in the Hotel Croyden on the corner of Madison Avenue and 86th Street, where he found an apartment for us as well, without realizing that so large a number of children would soon overrun the hotel. There were, after all, eight of us children. But our youthful paradise ended with the construction of a kind of cable car from one flat to the other, commonly known as a dumbwaiter, which would transport food and wine and other items between floors of the hotel.

A month after our arrival, at the end of June 1941, my mother rented a summerhouse in Larchmont, New York, while Walter returned to Europe. He acted on the advice of Chaim Weizmann, who felt that after Germany's attack on Russia on June 21, 1941, America's entry into the war was only a matter of time and that Walter had better leave the United States and rejoin the Swiss Army as a cavalry officer. The future president of Israel was well informed. He had excellent contacts within the Roosevelt administration, and his guidance on behalf of my uncle was indeed accurate.

After a couple of weeks, my mother took me, barely fourteen years old, to Penn Station and sent me to Camp Susquehanna in Pennsylvania after shipping off my sister, Marianne, to Camp Fernwood in Poland, Maine. The matter-of-fact way in which our mother — thanks to the toughness of her German constitution — sent us to completely unknown institutions in a new country without our speaking a word of English truly amazed me, but only after I was grown and had children of my own. Her decision was a heroic one, and one for which I've always admired her. I never could have done it.

Summer camp was my first real American experience. Life resembled ads for the Marlboro man. We lived out of doors and slept in tents. Each camper had his own horse for the summer, which he had to feed, clean, groom, and rope in every morning. There was no stable help. Putting on a halter, bridling, and saddling demanded sporting ambition. Day rides took place with filled saddlebags. We washed in the nearby lake, which helped to promote the Marlboro man reality. After several days of riding, I — and many others — suffered from saddle sores that wouldn't heal until the camp doctor took mercy on us. And, of course, I rode my thighs raw. Athlete's foot and poison ivy were other camp discomforts. The former became so bad that I had to cut open the front of my boots in order to put them on. Poison ivy developed after I'd put my hand in a bush to grab a lost ball, and this put me into the sick bay with a temperature of 104 degrees. Toward the end of those two months, I was so exhausted that I was sent home to Larchmont a week early. But I had learned English. Mercifully, this summer camp remained the only crash course of my life.

By the time I got back to New York, my mother was getting ready to leave Larchmont and move into a spacious Georgian-style house on Greystone Avenue in Fieldstone, one of the tonier areas of upscale Riverdale. The day we moved, we received a lesson in American hospitality that was unknown in Europe. A neighbor rang the doorbell to welcome us into the neighborhood. When she left, she said she hoped to see us at church functions. My non-plussed mother said, "But you know we are Jewish." The neighbor's answer was somewhat disarming: "Oh, you know, that doesn't matter. We have a bazaar on Saturday with dancing afterwards. Perhaps you can bring a cake." Without having read Max Weber, regarded as one of the founders of modern sociology, we learned how important churches are in American social life.

The Sunday stroll, obligatory in Zurich, was only obligatory for Europeans in New York. Even back then, Americans played tennis or some other sport if they wanted to get any exercise. Our Sunday outing took us across the Westside highway, past Arturo Toscanini's villa on Palisades Avenue, and down to the Hudson River. The Sunday stroll had a deeper social purpose: it provided an opportunity for casual meetings and accidental reunions. Thus on the night we arrived in New York, May 30, 1941, my mother bumped into Justin and Kaethe Thannhauser, old friends from Munich. Today their names are immortalized in the Thannhauser Collection at the Guggenheim Museum with their seventy-three paintings, bronzes, and drawings, which include thirty-two Picassos. Thannhauser and his cousin, Siegfried Rosengart, were the most important Picasso dealers next to Kahnweiler. The art dealer had mounted the first major Picasso exhibit in Munich in 1913, displaying paintings from the Blue Period through Cubism (1901–12).

Thannhauser's father, Heinrich, a tailor and art dealer in his own right, had founded his gallery in 1904. In 1921, Justin

Thannhauser expanded the business with a gallery in Lucerne and, in 1928, moved on to Berlin. That year, Rosengart took over the Lucerne operation in his own name and created the basis for the Rosengart Foundation — a gift to the city of Lucerne from his daughter Angela Rosengart. The foundation's gallery officially opened its doors in March 2002. She also donated the Swiss National Bank building, which she had bought earlier, to Lucerne. The late Picasso pictures that Angela donated enriched the Swiss art landscape enormously. The origins of the gallery were not due to fleeing from Hitler, as a speaker at the opening maintained, but were based on the hope of clients with money and taste. "Knowledge may have its purposes, but guessing is much more fun than knowing," Wystan Auden had once written. In the 1928 elections to the Reichstag, the Nazis won a meager 2.6 percent of the vote. Hitler only became chancellor in 1933. Prewar Lucerne, with its grand hotels, was simply an elegant holiday address where gallery owners could find their customers — like Salzburg today.

Thannhauser and his wife left Berlin for Paris in 1937, after the Nazis had plundered his German collection. At the outbreak of the war, he went to Geneva, never dreaming the Germans would conquer Paris and plunder him once more. His only assets when he arrived in New York were nine major paintings that had been put on exhibit in Buenos Aires in 1939 and had never been returned to France.

The Thannhausers, together with their two sons, had traveled to New York along the same route we had and arrived in December 1940. The art dealer immediately acquired a brownstone on East 59th Street, which he used as living quarters and a gallery for his paintings. Invitations to his house were pretty amazing. It wasn't great luxury, but for us, splendid nevertheless. As children, we didn't really understand the paintings, but that did not in the least diminish our respect for them. Later, the small façade and the many stories of the house became too much for Thannhauser, and he moved to a house at 165 East 62nd Street, and from 1946 on, he lived at 12 East 67th Street.

Thannhauser had few illusions about the art world and could be quite cynical when talking about it. I remember him saying, "Signed pictures are sometimes genuine, unsigned ones always are." Otherwise, he was the most genial person in the world. His ties to musicians were as close as to painters. The Thannhausers regularly held Sunday concerts in their home, not so much to make music as to support the musicians. Even the Busch Trio played on 62nd Street, as the Thannhausers were close friends of Adolf Busch. We Baer children checked coats at the concerts, and my musical education received new impetus during these times. The Busch brothers opened up the greater world of music for me. Through them, I met Emanuel Feuermann months before he died, one of the greatest cellists of his age. I also met members of the Leventritt family, who were of utmost importance in New York's music life through their prestigious Leventritt Foundation awards. Eugene Ormandy and Vladimir Horowitz frequented the Thannhausers as did the Rockefeller family and the artist Louise Bourgeois.

To round out my relationship with the Busch Trio, Fritz Busch, the conductor, had led the Glyndebourne Festival from 1937 to 1939. He lived in New York during the war and remained somewhat distant, and I didn't know him well. He did not belong to the trio, but Rudolf Serkin did. He had married Adolf Busch's daughter. I could have built up the same relationship to the third brother, the cellist Hermann Busch, whose daughter I was asked to take out by my mother.

Thannhauser quickly became an important mentor to me. He asked how I was doing in school, gave me good advice, and, upon my graduation from high school, congratulated me with the gift of a Picasso graphic, a pony. I visited him regularly in New York until he moved to Berne in 1971. Usually, I appeared on Sunday afternoons for a frugal — and very German — cold supper, which we ate underneath his Picassos. On these evenings, he would warn me never to give loans for works of art. In such matters, he could be very suspicious. But for the most part, he was very wise. After he moved to Switzerland, he didn't think much of efforts to gather Giacometti's collected works for a donation to the Zurich Kunsthaus. It would provide no added value, he argued. For him, art was different than collecting stamps. In addition to an exclusive introduction to the world of music, Thannhauser also opened up the equally exciting world of the pictorial arts. I owe my collection of Picasso graphics to his initiative.

Most of the regulars at the Sunday concerts at the Thannhausers, a major social occasion for us, were other refugees, often personal friends who didn't have an easy time of it in New York but were happy, given the difficulties they encountered, to have gotten as far as they had. Without money or connections in the United States, few people had a chance of entering the country. In this respect, Americans were certainly no more humanitarian than the so often reviled Swiss.

To make matters worse, refugee medical doctors and other academics, who in Europe had all forged brilliant careers and enjoyed great reputations, had to repeat their exams in order to practice their professions in the United States, and most of them did so at advanced ages, which understandably made it more difficult for them. A family friend barely succeeded in establishing himself as an anesthesiologist, and Rudolf Nissen had to operate in a private gynecological clinic because he was not allowed to practice solo in New York. The clinic was across the street from where the Regency Hotel stands today. I know that so well because Dr. Nissen performed a hernia operation on me there.

Times in New York were tough in other ways too. Many housewives made a living by arranging a table d'hôte (a set lunch) in their own apartments. On occasion, my mother would take us to such lunches. I always found them uncomfortable affairs. The daughter served, the mother cooked, the husband would sit with us, and I felt like an intruder.

It wouldn't have embarrassed Thannhauser, I am sure, were I to mention his panicky fear of an air raid or U-boat attack on Manhattan. That's why some of his Impressionist paintings, wrapped in packing paper, were stored in our Riverdale cellar. Nor was he alone in fearing an attack on New York. The fear of German U-boats was triggered by a very real occurrence — dead sailors were repeatedly washed ashore on Long Island. One time, when we wanted to go on vacation to Long Island, my mother vetoed the idea. "That's out of the question. They've found a corpse," she told us.

Americans felt less engaged in a state of war against Germany than they did during the First World War, when Germany had lost U.S. sympathies after the sinking of the *Lusitania* and German composers were removed from the repertory, which was not the case in the Second World War. The Japanese were public enemy number one, largely because of the attack on Pearl Harbor but also because of the war hero General Douglas MacArthur, who received much public adulation, and because of a surprisingly early strategic turning point in June 1942 after the United States won the battle of Midway. Americans found the surprise Japanese attack particularly reprehensible. Given all the facts, the parallels to the World Trade Center tragedy are clear. American ideas about starting wars were based on the honorable ideas that launched their civil war. Pearl Harbor and the World Trade Center assaults violated the American public's highly developed feel for the right thing to do. If you wage war, you first put on white gloves and deliver a formal declaration commencing hostilities, which is what we were taught in our history lessons.

That feel, however, did not prevent the Americans from interning their fellow citizens of Japanese descent, with the loss of their assets and the ruin of their civil lives. Their sequestered assets were never returned, and that only because they had different-shaped eyes. Not until the 1980s were they given a lump sum payment. No U.S. president to date has asked for forgiveness. This arbitrary action is one of the darkest chapters in American history, I think.

The Japanese internment, rooted in racist thinking, is without a doubt the worst act of discrimination in, as I would later learn, this discriminating country. My former high opinion of John J. McCloy, the Chase Manhattan banker and high commissioner to the Federal Republic of Germany, was clouded by the role he played in the internment drama. But that's the way it is: the victors write history. McCloy is honored as a humane U.S. high commissioner who did so much to untangle German cartels and to speed reconstruction.

5

Horace Mann School (1941–44)

A green tie saved my Latin grade

Accustomed to the high quality of German and Swiss state-run education, my mother first sent me to a public school. The Bronx High School of Science had an excellent reputation, but its diversity would prove my second culture shock after summer camp. My mother learned quickly that American parents sent their offspring to private schools if they wanted to guarantee their future careers. Admission to a top college depended on a good high school or prep school education. Consequently, my mother quickly transferred me to Horace Mann School.

Even though the semester had already begun, I was admitted to Horace Mann, one of the top four high schools in the United States and, as it turned out, located right around the corner from our house. I didn't even have to take an entrance exam. Why the headmaster, Charles C. Tillinghast, accepted me, especially after school had already started, remains a mystery. Perhaps he simply liked the idea of having a European boy on board. Normally, youngsters were taken in only if their parents registered them before birth. Furthermore, I knew very little English when I arrived at Horace Mann. Nor were my grades that good. Academically, I had come in ninth out of a class of thirty in my first year at the Zurich high school, an achievement I found impressive. My father did not. "During your six years in the high school, two-thirds of the class will drop out. If you don't work harder and improve, you will end up at the bottom of the class," he told me at the time.

At Horace Mann I did improve. The school was demanding and strict and not that different, at least academically, from my school in Zurich; I had a lot of Latin, and French as my first foreign language, not to mention history. Happily, I was able to raise my Latin grades. William Nagle was an inspirational teacher with a passion for Latin. I always had the feeling he was in love with Julius Caesar, which was confirmed one day when I remarked that Caesar was a bad man. Mr. Nagle never spoke to me again. He was Irish, tough, and awe-inspiring. Every year on St. Patrick's Day, he would sell green neckties to make sure that everyone, at least those he sold his ties to, celebrated St. Patrick's Day in a seemly fashion.

At school, there were things I found very strange. In class, for example, the compulsory wearing of a jacket and tie was particularly hard in New York's summer heat and humidity, to which I was totally unaccustomed. This was before air-conditioning had arrived. The other was the compulsory attendance of morning prayers, where the headmaster would read the gospel of the day.

Another shock for a Swiss boy was the emphasis on sports. In Switzerland, a sport was regarded as an extracurricular activity. There were compulsory gymnastics, but nobody took them seriously. In the United States, sports were an essential component of the mainstream curriculum, football and basketball being the most important; swimming was also up there. Horace Mann had a large indoor pool, where we were expected to swim in the nude. Luckily, members of the swim team were allowed to wear silk trunks when competing with other schools at swim meets.

The success of the school sports teams in interschool competitions was essential. To my amazement, good athletes could win admission and scholarships to elite institutions, even if their scholastic achievements were well below average. Football was the king of sports. If you were no good at football, you had no chance with the girls, the saddest of fates for a teenager. Confronted with the alternative of being roughed up on the football field or to be ignored by the girls, I decided that tennis and swimming were the only face-saving solutions.

The stress on sports in Anglo-Saxon education recently inspired an author to coin the phrase "muscular Christianity." The late nineteenth and early twentieth centuries demanded a connection between athletic prowess and Protestant virtue. Rapid urbanization and extensive industrialization made educators fear an "overcivilization" — the kind of intellectualism that would neglect the body and lead to physical and cultural emasculation. Theodore Roosevelt's 1901 book, *The Strenuous Life,* is a typical example of a concern — prevalent in Europe as well — about a general decline that few have commented on so aptly as Ernest Renan: "It is not unpleasant to live in an age of decadence."

Sports, especially team sports, seemed the most suitable means of turning youth, spoiled by railroads and central heating, into the kind of robust Spartans for which the spirit of the age — stamped by an undigested survival of the fittest Darwinism with a strong racist streak — longed for. The most important drill grounds in the fight against decadence and emasculation were private schools like Horace Mann, which had all been modeled on British public schools. But part of the educational ideal of sports was the precept of fairness, respect for the rules of the game, and honorable treatment of opposing teams. Not much has remained of this kind of sporting spirit, as rampant drug problems in the sports arena attest. In business, the recent accounting scandals demonstrate the changes in a society that dismisses fairness and respect for rules with the sneering comment, "Nice guys finish last."

My own contribution to muscular Christianity remained swimming. But it is not true that our teachers and professors were only interested in the development of our muscles. Horace Mann had a school orchestra in which I played the cello.

Horace Mann was an all-day school. After a hasty lunch, instruction continued until three or four o'clock. The teachers were good, and they were used to the expectations of the paying parents, who wanted to see their children get into a good college. The war speeded up the educational process. High schools, colleges, and universities introduced an accelerated program with trimesters instead of semesters. Vacations no longer existed. The Roosevelt administration wanted to give young people as much education as possible before they were drafted.

The war was not discussed much in high school. Travel, however, was discouraged. Posters hung in train stations showing Uncle Sam, with pointing finger, asking, "Is this trip really necessary?"

With the shift of the school calendar from semesters to trimesters, my schooling effectively ended in the summer of 1944, at which point I visited my mother, who had fled New York's heat to Cape Cod in Massachusetts, where the Thannhausers and the Leventritt family spent their summers. The trip was hardly "really necessary," but it would become so on my return. On the train, I talked to a civil engineer who asked me about my plans for college and recommended that I take the engineering course at Lehigh University. I had never heard of this college before. But in 1944 I started attending classes at Lehigh in the small town of Bethlehem, Pennsylvania.

Since Horace Mann had close ties to Columbia, it made sense that I would study there. I could have continued living in Riverdale and helped my mother save money. Columbia is in the Ivy League, but my muscular Christianity obviously did not suffice. A registered letter came to the house with the laconic words "Not admitted." No explanation. Perhaps somebody meant well, because in the end it helped me in my development to leave home early and dive into an independent life.

I am still puzzled about how the Ivy League works. (I'm not alone, as I discovered in a *New Yorker* article on why college admissions have become unpredictable.) In my day, usually one wasn't admitted because one didn't bother applying to an Ivy League school, especially if one happened to come from a Jewish home, since Jews were excluded from half of them (with the exception of Columbia and to some extent Harvard).

The sociologist Jerome Karabel shed some light on this admissions jungle with his voluminous magnum opus, *The Chosen*. He describes in epic breadth the admission policies of Harvard, Princeton, and Yale over the last one hundred years, noting that they are not directed toward a selection of the best and the brightest but are oriented toward the ruling social climate and the ideas of the desired leadership class. I do not need to stress that in my youth, these were not philosemitic.

6

LIFE AT LEHIGH

You should become a diplomat

In the middle of a class examination, someone put his arm around my shoulder. "Baer, I have to talk to you," the professor said. My forehead began to perspire. Did he think I was cheating?

The professor didn't want to talk about cheating but about an upstart article in the student newspaper titled "Brown and White." I was the newspaper's editor-in-chief. It turned into a pleasant conversation. I had a column in the paper called Baer with Me, which I signed "Hans J. Baer," and it gave me some exposure on campus and helped me become editor-in-chief.

My range of interests drove me to a fuller life outside the classroom: I swam for Lehigh, played for Lehigh (the cello in the orchestra), debated in the various clubs, and held offices in my fraternity (Pi Lambda Phi) as well as the national journalism honorary fraternity, Pi Delta Epsilon. I was also treasurer of the student chapter of the American Society of Mechanical Engineers. In the end, I was proud of an entry in the *Who's Who among Students in American Colleges and Universities* in spite of the requirement to buy a copy of this expensive book.

Two or three times I participated as an usher in the Bach festival of the Bethlehem Bach choir, the oldest Bach choir in the United States. Founded in 1898, the festival goes back to 1900, and even today it is a great Pentecostal event. Bach's chorales were spiritually fulfilling, especially during the war, and as an usher I was able to attend the rehearsals and concerts without paying for the tickets. Ever since, I have considered myself an "expert" on the B-minor mass.

In the United States, not only do universities select their students, but fraternities too take a good look at their candidates. Membership in most of them was out of the question for me. A Jew only had a chance of entering a "nonsectarian fraternity," one that was not bound to any religion, at least in theory, but in practice it was a mostly Jewish fraternity. I am sure that no White Anglo-Saxon Protestant (WASP) ever lost his way into a "nonsectarian fraternity." For us, it was something of a paradox. We came from Europe to escape discrimination and ended up in a country that discriminated even more than we did at home.

College board examinations took place across the United States on the same day. Soon after Lehigh accepted me, we received a visit from the fraternity I was to join. The Lehigh alumni, three gentlemen living in New York, were obviously out to see if the candidate would fit in. Basically, I was being co-opted.

Fraternities are more than dormitories; they are also schools for living. I learned a great deal at Pi Lambda Phi, almost more than I did in school. As freshmen, we lived ten to twelve in a room, which meant very little privacy. We learned to do what we were told and how to integrate with the others. And the longer we stayed in school, the better our rooms became. My last residence was the "suicide room," named for a previous owner who had killed himself. It was located behind the kitchen and was the quietest room in the building, probably the reason why the suicide candidate had picked it.

Another story of my Lehigh times has to do with the way I communicated with my mother while at the same time trying to save money. Once a week, usually on Wednesday evening, I would place a collect call to our house in New York, which most often resulted in an open line between the operator and my mother. The operator would ask, "Do you accept a collect call from Mr. Hans Baer in Bethlehem, Pennsylvania?" If there was nothing new to relate, my mother replied no. For a nominal charge, I heard my mother's voice. She knew I was still alive because I had called. Only in the event that she had something important to tell me would she reply, "I accept the charge," and then we could talk. There were no ill feelings, but for probably a couple of cents, we had established that both sides to the phone conversation were in good shape. Today, of course, we could talk several times a day on a cell phone for practically no charge. That's how much the world has changed.

A college education in the countryside has one great advantage: there's not much in the way of distraction. So you suddenly discover how long a day can be and how much you can do in it. During the war, classes at Lehigh began at seven o'clock in the morning and all of them — lectures, seminars, and tutorials — usually ended at four in the afternoon. Swimming practice was next, every day. At seven in the evening, we arrived exhausted for supper, where we ate our own athlete's meal served in a separate dining hall. What was left of the day we used for studying. Saturdays we had swim meets with other colleges. I was on the swim team for a good two years and won a letter for the sport. Wearing that big L on my sweater helped impress the girls, important at that age. But Lehigh's real athletic prowess was in wrestling, still a surprise for a youth mired in the European view of sports being totally unacademic.

Army ROTC consumed a good deal of my time, even though, as a foreigner, I couldn't be commissioned as a second lieutenant. But officer training was as much a social "must do" activity as sports. I didn't suffer under the military drill. Indeed, I rather liked the sessions, which were held in one of the college's large courtyards. We practiced marching in formation and giving commands, the latter a useful skill later in life.

"Nonsectarian" may have meant "nonreligious" but not prayer-free. Grace was said before lunch, and if an alumnus attended, he was asked to deliver the Lord's Prayer: "Give us this day, our daily bread. And forgive us our trespasses as we forgive those who trespass against us . . ." After that, the speaker would continue with his own thoughts.

The fraternity house was located at 141 East Market Street in Bethlehem. Initiation rituals included several tests of our masculinity and night exercises involving special missions. The most notorious task was to acquire a woman's bra without using money and to have it signed by her. As a matter of honor, we wouldn't dare buy one from the only woman close by, the kitchen maid. The alternative to the kitchen maid? A nightclub in nearby Allentown. Only how was I supposed to get to Allentown without money, I wondered. And while the girls there did not mind playing along, they wouldn't do so without money. So the college allowed panty raids twice a year, and usually they were conducted at nearby girls' colleges, where boys snatched girls' underwear.

Today, Greek life, as we called it, has been put under stricter controls, with the university administration paying closer attention to any fraternity excess. Hazing was common in my day and it still is. As a personal experience, I remember having to write a couple of hundred times, "I am Lindbergh's baby. Hauptmann is innocent." (The famous flier's baby was kidnapped and murdered; Hauptmann was the culprit.)

As an upperclassman, one was expected to give his room to a fraternity brother who had a girl. One day I didn't do that, and I don't remember why. So the fraternity brother to whom I was supposed to give my room drove his car into the woods with the girl, got stuck in the mud, and had to find somebody who would pull him out. He unloaded his anger on me. Understandable. And because I had refused to give him my room, the fraternity punished me by having me pay for the towing service.

My career in the fraternity began with the duties of a treasurer, which, as I mentioned earlier, included collecting ration stamps for meat. Most of the time I gave my ration of meat to my dog. After that, I became secretary, and in 1946 I was elected president, a job that also taught me a great deal.

Alcohol and women were strictly forbidden in the fraternity house except on the formal ball dance weekends, the high points of student social life. The girls came in long ball gowns, and the boys wore tuxedos. We had to invite our mother or an aunt to act as chaperon and put them up at the fraternity house. That became a bit of a challenge when the GIs came back from the war and joined the fraternities. They had endured hardships and learned the reality of life in the field far more intensively than we had in the fraternity. They were twenty-three and twenty-four years old, and I was just seventeen or eighteen. And now, as president of the fraternity, I was to forbid them from drinking whiskey and taking girls up to their rooms?

We even had the first drug problems. Whoever took hard drugs was tossed out. As for me, I didn't even know what drugs were, but the college authorities made me throw out a fraternity brother.

I remember a young student who dated a girl from a non-Jewish home. When his outraged parents heard about this romantic liaison, they called the frat house. The telephone was out in the hall and rang during dinner. An unsuspecting soul picked up the receiver, listened to the outraged father, and then called me from the dinner table. I was faced with the father's fury when he yelled, "Tell our son that he dare not come home so long as he is dating that shiksa." I recommended that they tell him themselves. And this was supposed to be a nonsectarian fraternity. But only the by-laws of the fraternity specified that. In practice, it was a Jewish organization.

Another learning experience from my fraternity life was ordering a new garage door for the frat house. First we had to petition headquarters in New York for permission to place the order. No one should underestimate the learning experience of organizing either a new garage door or a dance. Much later, my friend Fritz Leutwiler, the longtime chairman of the Swiss National Bank, would note dryly, "If you can't organize a party, you can't run a bank." This was said after a bank's ball had flopped, and it's still true today.

Lehigh, which today ranks 37th among a total of 248 American universities, is located in Duchess County, Pennsylvania, where, not so long ago, the local population spoke Pennsylvania Dutch, which I understood better than most. "The cow is over the fence gejumped und hat den cabbage gedamaged" was not an untypical sentence.

On weekends when we looked for entertainment, we usually drove in a friend's car to New York City and came back on the last Lehigh Valley Railroad train to Bethlehem that left Penn Station on Sunday night. The trick was to order enough whiskey while the train rolled through New Jersey and the bartender intoned, "Last chance to order a drink." We usually lined up three or four glasses. In those days, Pennsylvania was dry on Sundays.

I studied mechanical engineering during my first four semesters. After that, I could pick a major. I chose industrial engineering. During the war, the usual eight semesters were squeezed into eight trimesters, with no time off for summer vacations. Classes continued even on New Year's Day. On the side, I got practical experience working in boiler construction for the Heilman Boiler Works in Bethlehem.

John J. Karakash, professor of electrical engineering, left the most lasting impression. He could fill a blackboard with both hands writing at the same time, from right to left and left to right. Absolutely amazing. Born to Greek parents in Istanbul, he came to the United States in 1936 and to Lehigh in 1946 as an assistant professor. His judgment about me was unerring: "Baer, you should not become an engineer, you should become a diplomat." At the time, I didn't like hearing that. I thought it was an insult. On the side, Professor Karakash translated texts into exotic languages and wrote music criticism. He still lives in Lehigh and visits the college daily. In recognition of his contribution, in 1981 the university named a wing of the renovated Packard Laboratory after him.

The economist Herbert Diamond was another noteworthy character at Lehigh. We students liked to tease him with "When the world's three leading economists got together, I said to the other two . . ." But he really was a man of national stature. We used to whisper that Hawaii's pineapple lobby had financed his chair. We found that mysterious. Today I don't find that mysterious at all. Hawaii's pineapple growers have a very influential lobby — back then and today.

I studied mechanical engineering because I wanted to, although to some extent it was a fashionable course of study and an obvious choice for the son of a physicist. Engineers were the standard bearers of progress just as information technology (IT) professionals are today. I graduated Lehigh with a bachelor of science in the early summer of 1947. The graduation ceremonies had an official and an unofficial role. The commencement speaker was Admiral William "Bull" Halsey, who took command of the Pacific fleet in 1942, covered MacArthur's landing in the Philippines in 1944, and whose flag flew on the USS *Missouri* when the Japanese delegation came aboard to sign the terms of surrender.

At the unofficial ceremonies, graduates had to drink glasses of beer equal to the numerical sum of their graduating year (four plus seven). Drinking was part of student life. If you didn't, you weren't a man. With four plus seven, our class came off fairly well. We had to down a mere eleven glasses of the brew.

The industrialist Asa Packer (1805–79) founded the university in 1865, a fact that I would register with relish, since it made Lehigh only a few years younger than the Swiss Federal Institute of Technology (ETH) in Zurich, which dates from 1857. The recently renovated neo-Gothic Packer Memorial Church with Tiffany-designed windows above the main entrance is his monument to the university. Lehigh is the product of the coal country, where leading families of Philadelphia made a lot of money. When I came to Lehigh, the war-curtailed student body numbered seventeen hundred, but after the war it quickly climbed back to the prewar level of three thousand. Today, Lehigh has seven thousand students, including two thousand in graduate school.

Although my years at Lehigh were perhaps the happiest years I spent in the United States, I didn't keep in close touch with my alma mater after graduation, that is, not until 1976, when Professor Carl R. Beidleman visited our New York offices. A colleague told him that I had studied at Lehigh, and this prompted an invitation to lecture there. A year later, in April 1977, I spoke at my old university about the Swiss financial system.

Months after this lecture, it happened that Lee Iacocca sat next to me at a luncheon of the Swiss-American Chamber of Commerce in Zurich. He had graduated from Lehigh in 1945 with an engineering degree, and he is surely the best-known graduate of that school worldwide and the second greatest automaker after James Ward Packard (Lehigh University Class of 1884). Together we signed the luncheon menu and sent it to Professor Beidleman.

Iacocca experienced the limits America sets in a different way than I did. He came from modest circumstances in neighboring Allentown and worked his way up into the executive suite at Ford, where he left his mark with the production of the legendary Ford Mustang. Yet he did not become president. When he asked Henry Ford why not, he received the famous answer: "Frankly, I don't like you." The cold verdict of a Detroit aristocrat about a successful upstart from the steel town of Bethlehem!

Ever since Professor Beidleman "discovered" me, the connection to Lehigh has remained unbroken. He invited me to deliver several lectures and gave me the pleasure of spending a few days as "executive in residence." About ten years ago, the university asked me to take over the chairmanship of the newly founded Global Council. The university thanked me for the very interesting work I did by bestowing an honorary doctorate in 1997.

The honor, however, had an eminently political component. It came at a time when the issue of the Holocaust victims' dormant accounts had damaged the image of Swiss banks in the United States. The New Year's Day 1998 edition of the *New York Times* demonstrated just how damaged that reputation had become. The lead story in the business section was a flattering Baer family portrait with a subtitle that said much about the mood in New York at the time: "A Human Face for Swiss Banks." A group photograph of my cousin Rudolf Baer, my brother Thomas, my son Raymond, and me accompanied the article.

I had a premonition of what the university expected of its new honoree. First, I helped endow the Lehigh International Scholarship Fund. The initial recipient was a very sympathetic Bulgarian student, Kalin Kolev, with whom I conducted a lively correspondence. In 2007, Pelin Seyhan holds the scholarship. She comes from Istanbul, is a trained ballerina, and wrote me a delightful three-page letter so that I know where she comes from and how she has adjusted to Lehigh.

On the occasion of a Global Council meeting in Vitznau in May 1998, I wrote a check for the Global Council Scholars. In the year 2000, finally, inspired by the ambitious plans for Professor Dr. Richard M. Durand's economics department (he left Lehigh in the summer of 2005), I endowed a Hans J. Baer Chair for International Finance — the Baer Chair. That allowed me to avoid the pressure of having a whole college named after me — at a cost of $25 million. The first holder of the chair is Professor Dr. Nandkumar (Nandu) Nayar, who began his teaching and research activities in the winter semester of 2001.

Curiously, Nandu Nayar is a trained engineer, as I am. He studied at the Indian Institute of Technology and taught at the University of Oklahoma before accepting the professorship at Lehigh. He comes from Malaysia and is married to the very pretty Chitra, whom he didn't know before the wedding. It was an arranged marriage but clearly a very successful choice, which I wouldn't have opposed for myself. Before he began teaching at Lehigh, Professor Nayar visited Switzerland in order to gain some insight into Zurich's institutes of higher learning. His investigation of the impact that part-time work has on stock prices was worth front-page coverage in the *Wall Street Journal* in early summer of 2002.

After careful deliberation, I gave up the chairmanship of the Global Council in the summer of 2001. I had gained the impression that Gregory (Greg) C. Farrington, president of the university since May 1998, really didn't want a Global Council. I understand his position. Experience has shown that self-confident alpha types, like the members of the council, don't like giving advice over the years, which the university management does not — or in truth cannot — follow.

Farrington was Lehigh's twelfth president. He came from the University of Pennsylvania, where he had been dean of the School of Engineering and Applied Science. During his tenure at Lehigh, he pioneered breaking down interdisciplinary walls and has proven an effective fundraiser.

But first of all, Greg Farrington is a scientist. He holds more than two dozen patents and has written several books, as well as more than one hundred technical publications. He earned a PhD in electrochemistry from Harvard in 1972, began his career at General Electric, and switched back to academe in 1979, when he joined the Penn faculty. On his trip to Europe in the autumn of 2005, he and his wife visited me at my home in Zurich to announce that he planned to retire.

In May 2006, the university announced with great pride the appointment of Professor Dr. Alice P. Gast of MIT as its thirteenth president. Professor Gast was vice president for research and associate provost at MIT. The search for a new dean of the College of Business and Economics was suspended until a president of the university was installed. In January 2007, the university announced that Dr. Paul Brown of the NYU Stern School of Business had been named the next dean of the Lehigh College of Business and Economics.

Dr. Brown is a highly regarded scholar who has successfully managed a very respected international alliance between NYU, the London School of Economics, and the Hautes Etudes Commerciales in Paris. This appointment fills a vacancy that was necessary to take Lehigh a big step further.

Since I gave up the chairmanship, my relationship with Lehigh has run along the usual lines of an alumnus. They were good times. A Tonhalle Orchestra concert on May 3, 2004, at the Zoellner Arts Center, with David Zinman as conductor, was the epilogue to a harmonious relationship. For all the stress on sports, no one should overlook the importance of cultural life at American universities. The Zoellner Arts Center, endowed by Robert and Vicky Zoellner, is home to a substantial art collection, with works by my Swiss friend Hermann Sigg, as well as a music academy, where the Metropolitan Opera gives guest performances. Today it is the most important cultural center between New York and Philadelphia. My friend Isaac Stern opened the center in 1997 with a recital and immediately afterward grouchily called me in Zurich. What was the matter, I wanted to know. "No toilet for the artists," the violinist griped.

7

A Swiss Interlude

I love Europe

On September 5, 1945, three days after Japan's surrender and at the end of my third trimester at Lehigh, we brought my mother to La Guardia airport for her flight to Europe. It was probably the first time a civilian without a government mission had been allowed to fly there. The reason she went to Zurich then was simple: she had to make an important decision she could no longer postpone once the war was over. Would we want to stay in the United States or go back to Zurich? We had lived in rented houses with other people's furniture. She had merely closed up our home on Bergstrasse, not given it up. We were not the usual immigrants, having made only provisional arrangements. Other questions begged for answers: What would happen to my father's limited partnership in the bank? Could my mother retain it? What would we live on?

After my father died, my uncles waited three years before notifying the commercial register, maintaining his limited partnership for his heirs. Walter and Werner wanted to keep my mother as a limited partner if I would join the bank. Just as the family had separated because of the war, it was now time to come back together again.

Mother's flight to Zurich took months to arrange. During that time, we moved from Greystone Avenue to 4546 Delafield Avenue, another Riverdale address. On August 30, when she cabled final flight plans to my uncle Walter, she noted, "Home very satisfactory," signaling she was happy with the move to Delafield Avenue. Although she had been booked on Pan Am to London, the difficulties of transiting through Great Britain made her change to an Air Transport Command (ATC) plane of the U.S. Air Force on which she was the only civilian, and the only woman. The flight was scheduled to go directly to Paris but instead stopped in Washington, D.C. to pick up eighteen officers, and then flew to Newfoundland. After landing in Iceland and an unplanned stop in London, my mother arrived at Le Bourget. When the Air France plane, a DC3, finally landed in Zurich, five days had passed since she left New York. Such was air travel in the immediate postwar world.

My mother's decision wouldn't be an easy one, as she noted in her diary on September 18 after taking tea with Edgar Meyer. "He too finds that my problems are almost unsolvable. I still hope for an intervention of fate." The next day she wrote, "Long conversation with the brothers [Walter and Werner] in their offices. Their generosity and love are staggering, but they only make my heart heavy and the decisions I must make more difficult. I insisted on two essential points: that I promised my children not to make any definitive decisions, and, if at all possible, to remain a partner in the firm, as they [Walter and Werner] so generously offered in accordance with our mutual interest."

Wherever she went, my mother found conflicting comments and advice. Friends and acquaintances were often pessimistic about the future in Europe or at least saw better opportunities for us children in the United States. Without dismissing America — as Thomas Mann, a generation older than she, had done — as a "gigantic mistake," my mother clung to the old continent. After visiting the sculptress Germaine Richier's studio on September 29, she noted, "We talked again about Europe and my future, and I realize more and more how much I love Europe." On October 1 she wrote about a lunch with the physicist Paul Scherrer and his wife: "He is totally enthusiastic about the United States. We reveled in our American reminiscences and he doesn't understand why we want to come back so quickly. To be sure, given the nature and the task of his travels, he has only seen the best." And two days later she wrote, "Went to the Poly [the Swiss Federal Institute of Technology] to inquire about entrance requirements for Hans." On her first visits to my uncles' homes, she wrote, "Am staggered about the totally unchanged lifestyles. The beauty, elegance, and refinement of the house with the many new works of art seem to me inconceivable; the same holds true for Werner's house. I realize with some horror how far we have declined, at least in the way we live. But America is different, and we were at war." And in another entry: "[Georg] Solti [the future conductor of the Chicago Symphony] visited in order to talk about his future. His experience as a foreigner and a Jew in Switzerland is sad."

My mother returned to the United States, still undecided, on a voyage even more adventurous and unpredictable than her flight to Europe. On October 10, 1945, we received a telegram that read, "Mother left this morning Zurich (for Claridge Paris) sailing New York still uncertain." Walter had made return arrangements well in advance and on August 17 had received a message from the American Embassy in Paris promising that our mother would encounter no difficulty in getting passage on another ATC flight. But that didn't happen. Instead of a couple of days, she spent three weeks in Paris before finally boarding a ship, not a plane, and arriving in New York in November. The problem of our future was still unsettled.

To the extent that I can reconstruct the course of events from the exchange of letters, my sister Marianne and I — as the two oldest siblings, we had been drawn into the decision-making process — wanted to complete our studies in the United States, no matter what the circumstances. Reluctantly, our uncles accepted that decision but only after much discussion via letters. On February 5, 1946, Walter wrote to my mother that "we hope that the decision taken was the right one, which only time will tell. . . . I can understand that if Hans and Marianne want to complete their studies over there, this would represent a major hurdle to their return. But perhaps Marianne will think it over and study one or two semesters over here in order to form an independent judgment about how she would like the old world again."

The correspondence continued indecisively through the first half of 1946, with pros and cons weighed carefully: giving up the house in Riverdale would save money, but would my mother be able to find equally good lodgings in case she decided to return? The limited partnership had been dissolved so that she would not have to pay Swiss taxes. If my sister and I interrupted our studies before graduation, would we be able to return to college to finish? "I have been assured," my uncle Walter wrote, "that Hans could study at the Polytechnic Institute or the university without taking any special exams."

I weighed in with my own letter to Werner, written in English on March 10, 1946, from Lehigh on fraternity stationery, which reflected my own uncertainty:

> Now I would definitely like to come to Switzerland for several reasons. My main reason is that I would like to talk to you about my personal future. I would like to talk to you about my possibilities in Switzerland compared to the ones here. I would like to find out about financial possibilities both with and without the firm and, of course, your plans for Baer custodian. . . . I assure you that I can make myself feel at home wherever it is economically the wisest to live. . . . The fact that Mother could never take care of her financial affairs herself is a much more

important factor in our decision. Louise (my college girl-friend) is, of course, an important factor in my life right now, yet I do not see why she should influence my decision to any great extent. . . . At this point, however, I would like to explain my dilemma. As I want to get my BS degree here, we must consider the following points. Colleges at the moment are extremely crowded due to the returning veterans. If I should leave Lehigh this June, I will get no guarantee whatsoever that they will take me back one or two semesters later. . . . Last but not least, an interrupted college education would spoil my chances for the different honorary societies that are rather important not only for reasons of prestige but also for getting a job later in life.

Subsequent letters continued to consider the advantages and disadvantages of our earlier or later return. Our uncles' concern? Failure to make a decision would result by default in a decision to stay in America. Business arrangements had to be considered, specifically my mother's role in the bank, which, Werner wrote her, would not be affected by any postponement.

8

Poor Georg Solti

I was sure I wouldn't see him again

By September 1946, it was clear that we wouldn't return to Zurich before the summer of 1947. Much of our family activities over the next ten months were focused on preparing for our journey. Even my proposal to bring an American car to Europe had Werner's approval, since purchase in Europe was hugely expensive. Car dealers calculated the foreign exchange rate at SFr 10 to the dollar, astronomically higher than the official rate. Werner suggested buying a lighter car, seeing as weight determined customs duties, and besides, we still had the family Chrysler in Switzerland.

Everything else was prepared with equal dispatch, including having five tons of coal to heat the Bergstrasse villa ready for us upon our return. Reservations on the *Queen Elizabeth* and the *America* were made and cancelled because the two ships could not take the new car aboard, so we ended up booked on a Holland-America line steamer whose crew had little trouble picking up our blue Dodge sedan from the pier in Hoboken and putting it into the hold.

The official name of the shipping company was Nederlands Amerika Steamship Maatschappij (NASM). The food aboard was so bad that my sister Marianne and I interpreted NASM as "Never a Square Meal." On our arrival in Rotterdam, I felt the first doubts: Was returning to Europe really a good idea? Rotterdam had been badly destroyed in 1940, and in 1947 it was still no place for a festive arrival. My mother and my younger siblings climbed into a plane and flew to Zurich. Marianne and I drove to Amsterdam, where it was not quite as bad; we looked at the art collection in the Rijksmuseum, visited the Hague, and then drove across Luxembourg, Metz, and Strasbourg in the direction of Switzerland. At every border crossing, customs officials stamped entry and exit dates into our passports and checked the engine number, to the extent that they could find it. We needed a special passport, or carnet, for the car.

On our arrival in Basel, we breathed as easy as we had six years before in Estoril; there were white tablecloths, fresh butter, and clean air to breathe. We enjoyed our first breakfast in Switzerland on the terrace of the Hotel Euler in front of the railroad station.

I hadn't been in Europe for long before I began to ask myself more seriously why I had come. A trip to Germany a few months after our arrival showed unparalleled devastation. It was one thing to hear about war-destroyed and famine-stricken Germany but quite another to see fields of ruins and the gaunt faces of the people. A blasted bridge hung in the Rhine, and in place of the proud cities we had admired during our childhood visits to Worms, we now saw only ruins.

I went to Frankfurt to find out what had happened to the house that my grandparents had bought in 1936 or 1937 in the mistaken belief that they would be safer from persecution in a large city like Frankfurt than in Worms. The previous owners, being Jewish, had emigrated and were happy to have found a buyer. But as I researched the ownership records, it turned out that the previous owners had put the property in trust, which meant that we no longer had control over the house. At the real estate registry office, the bureaucrats made no bones about what evil people my grandparents had been. For me, this was the classic irony of fate. I took legal action against the trust and agreed with the previous owners on a joint sale. In the end, the proceeds barely covered expenses.

Another of my early, and depressing, German experiences found resonance in the dormant accounts controversy half a century later. A month after my arrival in Switzerland, the bank received a call from the American Embassy. Could they send somebody to look at an International Refugee Organization (IRO) truck in Kreuzlingen, a Swiss town on the western end of Lake Constance across from Konstanz in Germany? I was sent and found the truck parked under a tree. It was so large that it couldn't turn around in the town's narrow streets. IRO was founded in 1946 as a successor to the United Nations Relief and Rehabilitation Administration (UNRRA) set up in 1943 to support victims of the Third Reich. It helped those who had survived the concentration camps. Among the tasks UNRRA bequeathed to the IRO in 1947 was the ownerless freight on the truck I was to examine: — small sacks the size of a handkerchief filled with bank notes and coins. Occasionally, I found a name scribbled on a piece of paper. Most likely, it was the last money taken from those dumped into a concentration camp: worthless German marks, French francs, quite a lot of pounds, Swiss banknotes no longer in circulation but exchangeable at a bank, and other currencies. My first experience with lost assets.

What did I do? After carefully sorting them, I gave the Reichsmarks to the truck driver in exchange for a receipt and then put the marketable money in my car. I sold the silver to be melted down and the other coins at scrap value and made out a dollar check to UNRRA or its representative, the U.S. Army. In light of the later debate about the dormant accounts, this episode was characteristic of the times. Given the needs of a starving Central Europe with its numerous deportees, refugees, bombed out homeless, and returning POWs, other matters were more pressing. Sums were small, and means of communication inadequate, so that nobody even thought of the idea of looking for heirs anywhere in the world. One great difference: the American army's procedure corresponded to wartime circumstances and was covered by occupation law. Lost assets and dormant accounts were actually not a topic.

In 1947 one could lose faith in a free economy. No Marshall Plan was in sight, but communists were represented in all the Western European parliaments. It only seemed a matter of time before they took over. Why should I look to my future in these circumstances?

I first asked myself that question in September when I drove our family friend Georg Solti, who was in Zurich for a visit, to Konstanz. The conductor had been named general music director at the Bavarian State Opera in 1946 and had thus become successor to the famed, but Nazi-tainted, conductor Clemens Krauss. Train connections did not exist beyond St. Margarethen. Instead, two American soldiers waited for him in a military jeep. That was the way he had reached Munich the year before.

We ate in Kreuzlingen, which borders Konstanz in Germany, in a fish restaurant with white tablecloths, and I began to feel deep pity for him. I was sure I wouldn't see the poor man again. I found it unbelievably selfless and brave that he was traveling into a destroyed country that he himself assumed would need fifty years to rise from the ruins, and that he would accept strict food rationing. During these times, one only traveled to Germany from Switzerland with a pack of sandwiches, a thermos, and a full-reserve gas tank. Solti and his wife lived on Maximilianstrasse in a ground-floor room of a half-destroyed house. And in the harsh winter of 1946, he was able to heat the room only once, after a music-loving coal dealer gave him a sack of briquettes.

Again I was confronted with questions: What am I doing in Europe where trains don't even run to Munich? Why and for what should I give up my luxurious life in the United States? Of course, Switzerland seemed like a paradise compared to Germany, but coming from the United States, it was hard to miss the poverty and general wretchedness. You only had to look at auto tires worn down to their lining. Still, our food was incomparably better than in England, where rationing of sugar and gasoline was finally lifted in 1953. When I visited a friend in London in 1948, we had the kind of dried eggs puddle that Evelyn Waugh wrote about in *Scott-King's Modern Europe* instead of the famed English breakfast. No wonder people kept repeating, "War never again."

At the same time, everybody counseled me to accept a career with the bank, especially my mentors Victor Sax, Edgar Meyer, Justin Thannhauser, and René Beyersdorf. They saw very clearly how tiresome it would be to start as an unknown civil engineer at General Electric or General Motors in lieu of a bank that belonged to the family. I rejected out of hand an offer made by an attorney, Dr. Ludwig Gutstein, a family friend, who lived from 1942 to 1947 in the United States and had excellent connections, to take over the representation of Volkswagen for Switzerland. One dinner with Gutstein and it was decided. "One can't do that." Even he agreed. Memories of the Third Reich were simply too strong.

My cousin Roger Baer recalled in his memoirs the unwritten family law that the oldest of each branch of the family was destined for a career in the bank. It was clear that my uncles wanted to plan for the succession and that 1947 would be the crucial year in which to hire young management. Dr. Hans Mayenfisch, the bank's non-family partner, was turning sixty-five and wanted to retire from the business. I had just finished my studies; my cousin Nicolas faced his final exams. Most important, my mother's plan to rejoin the bank as a limited partner depended on me. That I bowed to the pressure was a matter of tradition.

Having grown up in a dollar world with a large domestic market, I found it hard to envision a future in a country where every dollar transaction involved going to the Swiss National Bank. We had to pay twice for the fur coat my mother acquired in New York after the war. The purchase fell under the merchandise transactions and could only be settled officially through a Swiss National Bank clearing. Otherwise, we would have risked a very unpleasant judicial proceeding involving foreign exchange fraud. Everything was terribly complicated. If a car engine was damaged during a trip abroad and needed replacement, the owner could not pay the garage directly but had to deposit the sum in the merchandise transactions account of the Swiss National Bank. Until 1959.

No doubt my uncles led very civilized lives in large houses, with personnel and, due to the war, old automobiles. On the other hand, I asked myself about the substance of this kind of life. I saw the bank with its few employees as nothing more than a better class of money exchange and likewise its home at Bahnhofstrasse 36. Part of the bank's house was rented out. A reputable milliner had her studio on the second floor, and a well-known dermatologist, Dr. Hans Pfosi, a friend of C. G. Jung, had his practice on the third floor. Dr. Pfosi, a good-looking and pleasant man, treated every girl of easy virtue in the city, and his patients brought a colorful life into our stairwell. My idea to give our tenants notice and use the space for ourselves brought a reproach from my uncles: I must have "fôlie de grandeur."

I started working at the bank on August 21, 1947, with a monthly salary of SFr 320, less than $75, a sum that caused some ire, although SFr 320 was an absolutely typical salary for a beginner. I didn't much care, because I had few expenses. I lived at home and was forbidden to have a car.

Edgar Meyer, my father's friend who had accompanied us to Estoril, was especially outraged by my salary, which he found unacceptably low. My uncles, on the other hand, regarded a bachelor's degree only as an equivalent to a completed apprenticeship in Switzerland. And they were determined not to grant me any special privileges. For my part, I felt at times as if I belonged to a lesser part of the family and was treated as an outsider.

As for boosting my pay, there was always the Swiss National Bank and its policy of dollar management. At the official rate of SFr 4.30, the Swiss National Bank only bought dollars from the merchandise transactions. Nonresidents could sell $100 three times a month at the official rate. The bank would not buy what flowed back to Switzerland in terms of capital remission, interest, and foreign exchange. The result was the formation of a free market rate of exchange for finance dollars that fell to SFr 2.20 and offered nonresidents, such as students and interns, once they had $100, a chance to live comfortably. They only had to save SFr 430, and from that sum they could buy $100 for SFr 220. In 1947, one could live very well for ten days on SFr 210. Only after the dollar shortage of 1949 did the national bank give up dollar management.

I started in the accounting section of the Julius Baer bank, housed in one large hall on the second floor, and worked standing up. The standing desks were the hallmark of accounting. Some fifteen to twenty people stood in the hall. We worked on Saturday until three or four o'clock. The stock exchange was open Saturday morning, and we couldn't go home until everything had been accounted for.

I wrote transaction slips by hand with special purple copy ink and then put them in a press to make copies. If I didn't put them in carefully, the purple ink would smear, making the copies unusable, which meant I had to start over again. It just didn't work any other way. The copies were hung out to dry in the copy room overnight. Up until 1950, they hung on a laundry line. The staff took them down the next morning and then they were sent to the post office.

My first job in the accounting section was writing purchase and sales advices. And God help me if one of my uncles discovered a missing comma. Then I would have to start all over again. I always measured our state of grace by the number of our purchase and sales advices torn up in the evening. When Walter's son, my cousin Nicky Baer, wrote the advices, Werner would stand behind him, and upon discovery of a mistake, he would rip the page out of the machine and with great flamboyance tear it up. He was more forgiving with me. A few years later, Walter would show no mercy to my cousin Peter, Werner's son.

Everything that is handled electronically today I calculated by hand: ten shares at a rate of XY, plus commission and transaction tax. I remember my first foreign exchange transaction most vividly. A "huge" piece of business: I bought 10,000 blocked marks, in dollars a negligible amount.

A small bank offers a beginner some great advantages. You quickly learn all aspects of the business. Foreign exchange and security traders worked in the same office. Credit and asset management were the other pillars of the business that showed innate growth.

The year 1947 surely was not a year of great hope, but 1948 would be worse. On February 25, 1948, the Czech communists got rid of their bourgeois and socialist allies and ruled alone. The European Recovery Program, which George Marshall had announced the previous year, was still waiting for congressional approval, but the Czech government, following Moscow's orders, had already signaled that it did not want to participate.

In the spring of 1948, we toured once more with my mother in my parents' prewar style. My mother had planned an extensive trip, and our chauffeur steered the old Chrysler. Our companions were Wolfgang Pauli, who won a Nobel Prize for physics in 1945, and his wife, Franca, one of my mother's closest friends. The tour ended in Florence. Milan and the Emilia-Romagna, with their churches, museums, squares, and palaces, remain in my memory — even though I admired everything — as a strenuous experience. Not even the visit to a distillery near Parma could change that.

After Bologna, the road curved up to the Passo della Futa, once widely feared for its highway robbers, and at that time it was still a good idea to avoid the pass at night. We reached Florence safely but arrived in the middle of a general strike. The political climate had been tense before the parliamentary elections held on April 18 in which the Christian Democrats won a surprising 48 percent over the Popular Front with its 35 percent. Revolution and rebellion were in the air. The Italian carabinieri (police) blocked side streets. We traveled through the Medicis' city for two weeks and admired its beauties, from the Brunelleschi Cathedral to the Uffizi Gallery. We were spared the Stendhal syndrome — the impact of concentrated beauty provoking fits of fainting that Florentine doctors diagnose regularly.

My most important duty on this tour was to help Wolfgang Pauli light his pipe, no easy task, given the way his head wobbled back and forth.

Louise Metzner, my college girlfriend, visited me in the summer, and with the approval of my uncle Werner, who checked out all my girlfriends, we toured Switzerland. I will never forget our journey to the Jungfraujoch, because Louise and most of the other female passengers fainted from thin air once they reached the top at 10,000 feet. The train personnel, who were used to this, laid them out on the station platform and put them back in the coach before the train departed. They recovered on the ride back in the train.

9

RETURN TO NEW YORK

Brown Brothers Harriman and New York (1948–50; 1968)

Love is all right if you don't waste time.
— Lloyd George

At precisely 9 a.m. the clerk at 59 Wall Street exchanged the black sign-in pencil for a red one. A subtle way to promote punctual arrival. Staff who came late at Brown Brothers Harriman had to enter their name in red in the attendance list. It's a good thing the family had drilled punctuality into me. Werner always went over to the stock exchange at 11 a.m., and the chauffeur was told to roll up with the car at the strike of noon. My uncle's fringe benefit during his time as a stock exchange representative was a key that allowed him to call the elevator from any floor. He had the key made especially for this purpose.

I owe my decision to knock at Brown Brothers Harriman's door to my uncle Walter's business contacts and advice. For a while I had thought of trying the more imposing Chase bank. His comment:

"They're so big that even after three months you won't know where to find the toilet."

Brown Brothers Harriman was easier to survey. More important, however, the partners were men with a global outlook and a global reputation. Among them was Robert Lovett. He spent a long career shuttling back and forth between the Wall Street firm and the government, serving in key posts in the state and war departments and ending up as Harry Truman's last secretary of defense from 1951 to 1953. He remained a general partner for many years after moving "upstairs" in 1968. Robert Roosa came to the firm after serving as undersecretary of the treasury for monetary affairs. Prescott Bush, the father and grandfather of the two American Bush presidents, was one of the firm's managing partners before he spent a decade in the U.S. Senate. Averell Harriman's long diplomatic career — specialist for delicate missions at the State Department, ambassador in Moscow, and chief of the U.S. delegation to peace talks with North Vietnam in Paris in 1969 — was only interrupted by a term as governor of New York. Harriman, tall and very sensual, was an event in every sense of the word. The last time my wife and I saw him was at his wedding to Pamela Churchill at the Hotel Pierre in New York on September 27, 1971. His brother Roland Harriman was also a partner of Brown Brothers Harriman. He took over from George Marshall as president of the Red Cross in 1950 and stayed there until the end of the Johnson era.

I was, therefore, surrounded by the architects of containment politics, but in the two years I spent at the firm, the cold war was little noticed, at least not until the outbreak of the Korean War in the summer of 1950. Nor did Wall Street feel the impact of McCarthyism. Here, no one was suspected of communist sympathies. The most exciting event was Truman's unexpected reelection victory over New York's governor Thomas Dewey.

One enlightening experience about the collective spirit in America and its power over the individual has remained with me all my life: in addition to the strict dress code that demanded seer-sucker and other summer clothing after Memorial Day and certainly after Independence Day — and the equally prompt switch to winter clothing after Labor Day — was the water shortage in the winter of 1948. It was so dramatic that men were urged, if not exactly forbidden, not to shave. A patriot did not shave. So I flew unshaven to Switzerland, proud of my patriotic stubble. At home I found little sympathy for such collective Americanism. "He's off his rocker. Now he has become totally American," my uncles said. It was my first flight and my first trans-Atlantic flight — New York to Zurich via Paris and Geneva, with intermediate stops in Gander, Newfoundland, and Shannon, Ireland. TWA, which we called "Time Wasted Abroad," flew Constellations on that route, a plane passengers called derisively "Cancellation." If everything proceeded without "cancellation," the journey took twenty to twenty-five hours.

The tip to try Brown Brothers Harriman was all the support I received from my family. I applied for the job after I was already in New York. Bankers lacked the experience of sending their sons for advanced training at their correspondent banks. My cousin Nicky too had to find an internship with J. H. Schroder by himself and enlisted Ernest Meili's help. Next to Alfred Barth at Chase, Meili was surely the most influential Swiss on Wall Street.

Twenty-five years later, my son Raymond put great emphasis on arranging for his training at the Credit Commercial de France in Paris on his own. Toward the end of his stay, I was invited to Paris by a friend, and between fruit and cheese was asked what Raymond had done wrong.

"Nothing," I replied.

"Nothing?" My host looked up, slightly annoyed. "Then why wasn't he properly introduced?"

I arrived back in New York aboard ship in August of 1948. In Switzerland I had prearranged for the purchase of a car in the United States because they were still hard to get these. It was a Chevrolet convertible. The only thing I couldn't choose was the color. But dark red wasn't bad, and the convertible was waiting on the pier when I disembarked. To the utter amazement of my shipboard acquaintances, all I had to do was get in and drive off.

I was less lucky with the room I found at International House, a student residence on Riverside Drive near Columbia University, even if it was a Rockefeller institution. But Justin and Kaethe Thannhauser and Rosalie Leventritt helped me find a more pleasant place: in a lucky combination of art and music, they introduced me to Allie Walter at 1175 Park Avenue. Her grandfather, Heinrich Conried, was the last classical impresario of the Metropolitan Opera, which he ran from 1903 to 1906. He brought Caruso to the Met and performed *Parsifal* for the first time outside Bayreuth. It was the great time of German culture at the Metropolitan Opera. Allie's parents often spoiled me at their endless Sunday lunches and at the Century Country Club on mild Sunday evenings.

Interns at Brown Brothers Harriman, the "finishing school of Swiss bankers," were not spared. For a coffee break, we practically had to get on our knees, and no one who had the bad luck to be working in the credit division at Christmas plowing through its extensive documentation could think of celebrating the holiday. We consoled each other with comic anecdotes, one of which went something like this: Somebody called the switchboard and asked for an employee: "Do you have a Sexauer?" To which the stressed-out operator replied, "Hell, we don't even have a coffee break."

I was plunged into the firm's many activities where credit was a specialty — letters of credit, promissory notes, and bills of exchange for financing imports and exports (and the corresponding flood of documentation) — and for me very instructive. John Knox, who had been with Brown Brothers since 1925, and Arthur Nash, who would become chief credit officer, introduced me to the secrets of this profession.

With the exception of underwriting, which was left to the investment banking division and where I would have had to switch over to Harriman Ripley at the same address (because of the Glass-Steagall Banking Act), I ran through all the classic training stations of a banker. In addition to the credit information department, there were brokerage, research, asset management, securities (together with securities administration and their liquidation), as well as foreign exchange dealings. The partners examined my proposal to deal in blocked marks, a lively business in Zurich, and decided against it. "We don't deal in blocked currencies," was their response. Money under management at the firm totaled $15 billion.

Training was rudimentary. Interns had to manage their transfer from one division to the other themselves. No set program existed. Salary was marginal. But I was happy, as a letter I wrote to Walter on January 4, 1949, attests: "My work with Brown is very, very satisfactory. I am now on the export-paying end of the foreign department and am very happy. I have a regular job, a desk, a secretary, and lots of work and customer contact. I am learning a lot in the way of letters of credit, which I think is very useful to us in Switzerland." Above all, I learned how important an intimate knowledge of product was for a commercial banker. Harold D. Pennington, one of the bank's partners, for example, had an excellent reputation as a coffee expert.

The credit business fascinated me more than any other aspect of banking. My cousin Nicky, now at J. H. Schroder, developed a flair for securities and investments. Since our mutual cousin Peter had inherited from his father, my uncle Werner, a taste for trading, we would complement each other ideally later on.

Brown Brothers Harriman provided me with an incomparable

background in managerial skills and contributed a great deal to my future career. For all of its modest office décor, it was a remarkable house with an atmosphere all its own. The partners still work in one room, the "partners' room," a wood-paneled sanctuary, separated one from the other by giant, old-fashioned roll-top desks. During my tenure there, if a partner wanted to dictate a letter or other document, a secretary came into the room to take the dictation, and everybody could listen. Transparency certainly was the intention behind the institution of the partners' room, in which, for me, a superior kind of corporate governance culture found its expression.

The partners were all gentlemen, meaning men with a great sense of personal honor, a high degree of personal responsibility, and a profound respect for form and manners. That began with the sherry served as an aperitif before lunch. They proved to be caring bosses and will always remain in my memory as touchingly solicitous hosts.

It was forbidden to enter an elevator without a jacket and tie; not even the internal office lift was open to those in shirtsleeves. And in the tropical heat of a New York summer when it was so unbearably hot (this was in the days before air-conditioned office buildings) I breakfasted without a shirt on so that at least it wasn't drenched when I left the house. On one particularly sweltering day, Roland Harriman called me in before I departed on my coast-to-coast summer tour the bank had organized. I grew hotter than I already was. What could he want?

He wanted to see my summer hat. I didn't have one. "You need one. It's important for you to wear a Panama hat with a broad brim that protects your nose and your neck. Otherwise, you'll get bad sunburn," he told me, and wished me a good trip.

The hospitality the partners showed the interns outside of business hours was also unusual. Americans, I had learned in the years I lived in the United States, are generally fabulous hosts — a remnant, I suppose, of the frontier mentality. But the fact that the partners cared about us during the holidays touched me deeply. True, fifty years ago business and private lives were more deeply intertwined, and social homogeneity was stronger. It's hard to imagine bankers today inviting trainees to their homes. But instead of leaving us in our rooms, we were invited everywhere by everyone: for Christmas by Thomas McCance, who had worked in research and had been made a partner in 1945; or for Thanksgiving by Prescott Bush or Frederick H. Kingsbury, who only became a partner in 1949; or by Parks Shipley, who knew Switzerland well thanks to his close ties to the center for Moral Re-Armament (MRA) in Caux.

I only encountered a similar sense of hospitality much later with Berenberg-Gossler and Co. in Hamburg. It was no accident, by the way, that Parks Shipley's son, Walter, built his career at Chase Manhattan (he became president after the Chase merger with Chemical) and not at Brown Brothers Harriman. It was an ironclad rule among the partners not to take their sons into the business.

Whether Swiss or American, one tends to make one's best friends abroad. We had a Swiss table at one of the fish restaurants in the harbor, where, for example, I met Frank Bodmer, a partner at Rahn & Bodmer. At Brown Brothers Harriman I had a desk next to Alfred Sarasin, who was a star even back then (his grandfather had been president of the Swiss National Bank). In 1949, I undertook the mandatory coast-to-coast business trip with two colleagues from Geneva: François Barrelet, who hailed from the Barrelet et Pidoux family bank (unfortunately he died young), and François Chauvet, known as "Slowboat," an arch-conservative Protestant who did not appear at his sister's wedding because she married a Catholic. He would become a partner in Ferrier, Lullin & Cie, which is today part of Julius Baer. The three of us acquired a Buick convertible for the trip and sold it upon our return. That way we avoided arguing about whose car we were wearing out. We paid about $5,000 for the car, sold it for $3,000, and split the difference.

We traveled from bank to bank with a suitcase full of letters of introduction the partners had given us. Wherever we went, we were marvelously well-received, not because of who we were but because Brown Brothers Harriman was a name that opened every door.

Our itinerary took us — long before the United States had built a highway network — to California via Florida, New Orleans, and New Mexico and back through Chicago, Detroit, Toronto, Montreal, and on to New York. The purpose of the tour was simple enough: we really got to see the country and get a feel for it.

Among our memories of New Orleans was a visit to a house for which we did *not* have a letter of introduction. The girls were less interested in our reputation than in our money. I can't remember which one of my travel companions I sat with in the salon, but I can still hear the laconic remark of the Madam who came down from upstairs and announced, "Your friend is almost done." She could have learned her business from Lloyd George. Britain's World War I prime minister had a simple mantra: "Love is all right if you don't waste time."

New Orleans — where a meal at the well-known Galatoire with its Creole specialties rounded out our impressions — was not the only place I visited just once in my life. This trip was also the only time when I saw a film studio and lived through a guided tour of a slaughterhouse. In Chicago, of course. Not the kind of experience that demands an encore.

On this tour we once again experienced splendid hospitality. The gentlemen at Bank of America in San Francisco assigned us a vice president, took us out in grand style every night, and spoiled us all day long with programs that gave us an idea of the region's charm and attractions. During those two and a half months, we were smothered with attention and care and cheerfully lived modestly when we had to depend on ourselves, as we did in Los Angeles. Money was tight, but we didn't have that much opportunity to spend it. At the end of the trip, we had to write a report about our journey, which went off without a hitch until the very last second when I hit a hydrant backing into Wall Street. That too was a lesson.

Brown Brothers & Co. was founded in Philadelphia in 1818 and has been domiciled in New York since 1825. It is one of the oldest U.S. financial institutions. The Browns came from Belfast and settled in Baltimore in 1800 as importers of Irish linen. Just as Zurich silk merchants entered banking, the Browns entered overseas trade financing and set up as a viable alternative to the British Baring Brothers. From 1836 to 1917 they worked with partners in Liverpool — and later in London — on both sides of the Atlantic and thus developed into a leading overseas bank.

In contrast to Brown Brothers, Harriman Brothers & Co. was a young partnership founded in 1927, which emphasized bonds, foreign exchange, and brokerage. The younger partners at Brown Brothers arranged for the entry of the Harrimans in December 1930. They knew the Harriman brothers from Yale. The merger took place against the backdrop of the financial crisis that had followed the Wall Street crash in 1929. Brown Brothers sat on a large stack of securities and needed more capital for their business. But after the 1933 Glass-Steagall Banking Act, adopted in the wake of Black Friday in 1929, separating commercial banking (with the possibility of carrying individual accounts) and investment banking, most private banks opted for the investment side of the business. Brown Brothers Harriman, on the other hand, remained true to its traditional commercial banking business, delegating the investment end to Harriman-Ripley, a new firm.

The example of Harold D. Pennington taught me just how long it takes two companies to achieve true unity after such a merger — eighteen years later it was made clear to me that Pennington was one of Harriman's people. In 1930, he had organized the transfer of the securities business into the Brown Brothers building. Four men pulled a loaded hand wagon, and Pennington followed with a pistol in his pocket.

The invitation to the 150th anniversary celebration in 1968 of Brown Brothers Harriman presented me with one of the most fantastic journeys of my life among the most illustrious society. I remember Marcus Wallenberg, of Skandinaviska Enskilda Banken, Franz-Heinrich Ulrich of Deutsche Bank, Karl Blessing, chief of the Bundesbank, the German National Bank, and CBS founder William Paley with his wife, Babe, one of the fabulous Cushing sisters. Indeed, everybody who was anybody in the financial world attended that weekend. A high point was the rollout of the Boeing 747 in Seattle, the plane that brought a whole new dimension to aviation. Accustomed to using the DC-8 as a yardstick, we could not really imagine a plane of such size. "It'll never fly," we all agreed. A fundamental error on our part.

A private train took the festive group from Seattle to Sun Valley. Uniformed butlers who took care of the in-train mail spoiled us. William Paley had attached his private rail car to our train and invited my wife and me to dinner. In writing. A messenger in uniform delivered the invitation.

That our train was constantly guarded from the air irritated us. In that age of innocence, we were not used to security problems. In Sun Valley, which the Harrimans had founded in connection with their Southern Pacific Railroad, and whose best-looking façades fronted the railroad tracks, unlike all other cities in the world, we were lodged in spacious hotel apartments with their own fireplaces. All very sumptuous.

The only problem was how to get out of Sun Valley. But that was no problem for the chairmen of American corporations. They had all brought their corporate jets to the local airfield. The friendly relations we had developed over this extended weekend with

George Russell, General Motors' vice chairman, assured my wife and me of a memorable end of the trip. The plane he invited us to fly back on had a steward but no kitchen. The steward took our order and passed it on to the copilot, who radioed ahead to the next airfield. We landed. The steaks were loaded and on we went.

During my practical introduction into the international banking business in 1948–50, I also studied economics at New York University (NYU) in order to complete my master's degree. The program closer to my real interests, business administration, had not yet been introduced, even though the faculty called itself the "Graduate School of Business." It had come into being after the First World War, when the United States had morphed into a creditor nation. New York moved up into an international bond trading center, and bond issuers wanted to know more about overseas business. NYU is a private university that no one ever confuses with the City University of New York (CUNY), a public university in New York City. During the Second World War, when the number of students decreased dramatically, the university's administration thought seriously about closing the graduate school. But authorities like Marcus Nadler persuaded university administrators that the decline was only temporary.

Office hours at Brown Brothers Harriman ended at five o'clock, and at seven o'clock my lectures at NYU began in Washington Square. They usually lasted until ten. And that five days a week. A tough life. If seminars didn't last too long into the night, I would take a girlfriend out, often to listen to live music at a hotel or in a jazz club. The 92nd Street Y was an unusual address for a European to attend concerts. But it has remained one of New York's leading cultural attractions.

Where else did I go? René Beyersdorf, who ran our business in New York, liked to take me to Fraunces Tavern at 54 Pearl Street, where George Washington had given a farewell dinner for his officers in 1783. Occasionally, the bon vivant took me to the Brussels in midtown, at the time the best and certainly the most expensive restaurant in New York City. The money he tipped the maitre d' assured us of a warm welcome and an excellent table.

A German who almost became my father-in-law, a butcher by profession and often violent to his wife — she regularly greeted me with bandaged arms — took me to Luchow's on East 14th Street between Third and Fourth Avenues. It was founded by Guido Luchow in 1882, was renowned for its German cuisine and its historical façade, and certainly was an old Nazi hangout. After the war, the German and Swiss colonies frequented Luchow's. Venison was its major attraction and a rare delicacy in the United States where consumption of deer was restricted. I shared this gourmand paradise with my girlfriend Louise; it was one of the high points of 1949. Both the Brussels and Luchow's closed long ago.

During the summer, Tavern on the Green, with its outdoor dining in Central Park, was a pleasant alternative. It was tradition, after the theater, to go to Sardi's, just as people in Zurich go to the Kronenhalle after the opera. The menu was not terribly exciting, but the food didn't matter so much if you wanted to be seen. Vincent Sardi didn't take advantage of his customers. Table reservations, however, were essential; otherwise you had no chance of getting in.

As for my studies at NYU, the course differed radically from my Lehigh years. My fellow students now were very often war veterans who studied on the GI Bill of Rights. Most of them were out working, and many had families. Nobody thought about sports or having a good time. We tended to be so exhausted from our day at work that we often slept through the first lecture. One of my friends worked for customs and spent his days out on the pier in the fresh air. In the stuffy lecture hall, he inevitably fell fast asleep. But that doesn't matter when one studies for oneself and not to please a parent.

It took four semesters to earn a master's degree. I wrote my thesis on the Swiss banking system, because I expected this would be the most fulfilling exercise for me. *The Banking System of Switzerland* was printed in 1951 and sold out at once. Not a difficult feat with a first edition of 297 copies. The Swiss Bank Corporation in London ordered six copies, and Den Danske Landsmandsbank (today Danske Bank) wanted to know if my work was available in German. That would be unthinkable today, because German is no longer an important language in Europe and everything is available in English. A fourth edition of the book was published in 1972. Back then, the material could be published in ninety-nine pages, including the index. Today a thick manual covers the subject.

I learned something else in my night courses, and that is how common continuing education is in the United States — when Marcus Nadler lectured about interest rate policy, our seniors at Brown Brothers Harriman took the seats next to the Brown Brothers trainees. Nadler, a star, had to lecture in a capacious auditorium with room for five hundred students. When I hear students today complain about overcrowding, I can only say that in my day, it was worse. The hall was always jammed, but the excellent professors made up for the crowd with their fascinating lecture skills, which many had honed during the Hapsburg double monarchy and brought to New York with great success.

Marcus Nadler had grown up somewhere in the Carpathian Mountains of Middle Europe and had immigrated to the United States in 1920. In 1927, he founded the Institute of International Finance at NYU, which he managed up until the 1960s. Today it is known as the New York University Salomon Center. It was created to keep an eye on foreign dollar loans issued in New York (usually to public debtors). Their value sank rapidly during the global economic crisis.

Salomon Fabricant lectured about productivity, economic growth, and income. For a long time, he had also been study director of the National Bureau of Economic Research. The extremely courteous scholar died at the end of the seventies in a traffic accident.

Sipa Heller was another authority. No one could claim that he lacked practical experience. In the early twenties, he had earned his money in Vienna as a foreign exchange dealer. His lectures always drew at least 150 listeners. Finally, Walter Spahr was NYU's gold specialist. I wrote my thesis with him.

Had I now finished my education? Surely not. I still learn every day. But I didn't want to take the risk of staying in school too long. Although I came from an academic home, I never felt the need for postgraduate study. My early entry into business life was a great advantage, and I am vehemently opposed to young people starting work at twenty-six or, worse, as late as thirty. Instead, they should begin to experience the routine of daily work as early as possible.

10

AFTER MY STUDIES

The lack of alternatives concentrates the mind

Fifty years later, it seems incredible that I could have hesitated about settling in Zurich. My studies were completed, as was my apprenticeship at Brown Brothers. I had run out of excuses. My uncles' intentions were crystal clear. In a letter I wrote in 1949, I cited my education as a future benefit for the bank, adding, "provided you want me to come back." To which Walter replied, in his typical descriptive way, "Why shouldn't we want that? Quite the contrary. We are getting older day by day, grayer and balder, and have every interest in seeing that the younger generation bring new life into this old house — would almost say this wreck."

Dutifully, I returned to Europe in June of 1950, still not convinced that Switzerland would remain my professional base. The trip had an embarrassing beginning. My landlady's sister had taken a greater shine to me than I wanted in the long run, and suggested sweetening the journey by traveling with me. I didn't know how I could avoid her offer without offending her sensibility, until I came up with what I thought was a brilliant idea. "Okay," I said, "I'll get a ticket," only to tell her sadly a short time later that the ship — the *Statendam* of the Holland-America line — was booked solid.

She bore the disappointment with equanimity and proposed accompanying me to the farewell party on board. I liked that idea a lot. Shipboard parties were spirited affairs with several hundred passengers and lots of champagne. But when we went on board, we were pretty much by ourselves. The Korean War had started. Everybody feared a Russian attack on Western Europe, so the *Statendam* departed from Hoboken with only a handful of the fearless aboard, and I had one girlfriend less.

I spent the extremely hot summer in Zurich, fled into the mountains during the unbearable weeks, enjoyed my free time, worked in the bank, and was assigned to a small firm in which Julius Baer & Co. held a share. So for several months I invoiced bills in the Webag AG, a textile company in Basel, and became a member of the board of directors of the Solfix AG in Kreuzlingen, which the Lions family owned. My grandfather had already maintained business and friendly relations with the company. But my stay on the board would be a brief one. Quite unexpectedly, the customs authorities took an interest in the textile trade. My uncles realized that the enterprise wasn't as refined as they had thought and promptly withdrew me. Too bad. The Lionses gave extravagant evening parties where lots of pretty girls attended.

In the spring of 1951, I was still undecided about my future career plans and returned to the United States to look around. Back in 1948, I had toyed for a while with the idea of taking over a gas station in Maine or building a garage business. But wherever I looked, I didn't find much. And as a foreigner in the job market, I had the disadvantage of being considered as possibly only a short-term employee. The most attractive offer I had came from an oil company that wanted me to go to Venezuela as an exploration engineer. They offered me a then substantial salary of $10,000 a year. Enticing, but still I hesitated. The global political situation was everything else but clear.

With the outbreak of the Korean War on June 25, 1950, it appeared very likely that anyone with a permanent resident status like mine would be drafted into the armed forces. I wasn't particularly keen on an interlude in uniform, and neither were my American friends. I knew several Swiss who had been drafted without consideration of their citizenship.

So I decided to go on a tour of South America to visit clients of our bank — with letters of introduction from my uncles — but also to evaluate my career chances. When I arrived in New York in early April 1951, I looked into Baercustos, our Manhattan outlet. I had worked with them during my training at Brown Brothers Harriman. Then on May 3, I boarded the Clipper, which had given Pan Am the reputation as the world's best intercontinental airline, and flew to Rio de Janeiro. I had a visa good for a year and permission to work in the country. I found lodgings in the Copacabana Palace Hotel.

As I have already written, my uncle August Lohnstein had been in Brazil since 1936 and had built up ADAGA, a firm that imported frames for eyeglasses and optical instruments, which came from Japan before the war, and after the war from the Black Forest and the French Jura. He and his wife received me with great hospitality in their Copacabana home near the hotel.

In order to get a taste of the country and its customs, I worked a little in their business. But I don't remember much else than cafezinho, the ultra-strong Brazilian brew that is consumed all day long. Since my aunt and uncle didn't have children, I could figure on a good chance of being taken into the firm. Only I didn't find Brazil very promising, even though construction was going on everywhere. August, with his professional Jewish pessimism, did not discourage my doubts. He counted on being kicked out of the country again, as he had been out of Germany.

The political instability and the rate of inflation (short-term treasuries returned 10 percent interest) aside, everyday life in Rio took some getting used to. True, I did find the location of the hotel on the Copacabana as much of an enrichment of my life as the opportunity to swim with my cousin Vera Wohl and to be spoiled by the Lohnsteins in the evening. In a strange city, it is always a pleasure to know where you are expected in the evening. But water, for example, was so scarce that every morning my relatives filled the bathtub and every available pot and pan. Inevitably, the water pressure would collapse during the day.

Vera Wohl-Chown's mother Margaret, was born as a Lohnstein, who after Crystal Night fled from Nuremberg via France to Rio. At the time, Vera had barely started elementary school. Her father, Hans Wohl, a German margarine industrialist, had died of heart failure when she was three and a half years old.

From Rio I visited Sao Paulo, where I made the acquaintance of the pianist Leo Nadelmann, whose just as talented as good-looking daughter Noemi, born much later, today contributes so much to the Zurich Opera's flair with her coloratura soprano. But that meeting did not inspire me to remain in this rich country. Nor did I meet anybody else who was convinced that Brazil was the country of the future. On the contrary. Many families whom persecution and war had washed ashore in Brazil were planning their return to Europe.

On May 25, 1951, I flew on to Montevideo where I took up quarters in the Hotel Nogaro on the Plaza de la Constitucion and learned what it was like to stop in a place where you had no relatives or acquaintances. Pretty boring. My one great learning experience: in addition to their mother tongue, bankers in Montevideo only spoke French. Finally, I explored Buenos Aires on the other side of the Rio de la Plata. Peron was in power when I entered Argentina on June 14, and I had to hide *Time* magazine from the border police.

In Buenos Aires I lived very pleasantly at the famous "Plaza," the spiritual mother of all Plaza hotels. In addition to the Banco Holandes, I spoke at great length with Alejandro Shaw, the owner of the Banco Shaw & Cia, the leading private bank in the Argentine capital. The bank was housed in the "Edificio Shaw" at Sarmiento 355 and was managed by the Borchardt family — represented by Dietrich Borchardt — with whom our house was on friendly terms. Renate Borchardt, Dietrich's wife, today lives in Montagnola.

Undoubtedly, the Argentine lifestyle with the indispensable haciendas in the surroundings of the capital had great appeal. Looking back, however, I note that the owners of these magnificent residences spent most of their time in Europe and didn't seem to feel very much at home in Argentina. Perhaps they themselves could not bear the ostentatious wealth. On the whole, Argentina at the time impressed me as more stable and more European than Brazil. But neither was Buenos Aires an alternative to Europe.

The lack of alternatives concentrates the mind. After those two months, I returned to Zurich determined to start my career there. After a stop in Rio de Janeiro, KLM flew me via Recife, Dakar, Lisbon, and Geneva to Zurich, where I arrived on July 2. Back then, Swissair only flew to New York across the Atlantic, and Panair do Brasil would have landed in Madrid and Rome on the flight between Lisbon and Zurich.

On September 1, 1951, I joined the bank for good. Meeting Ilse Kaelin soon after — we would marry on September 16, 1954 — undoubtedly made it much easier to remain in Switzerland. The fact that I was the younger one and could hardly speak Swiss German anymore did not hinder her in accepting me, nor did the Lehigh T-shirt I wore on our first date, which was anything but acceptable in the early fifties. Even in the United States, it was unthinkable to show up in a T-shirt picked off a store counter. It had to be one with the name of one's own college or school on it. Even today it still hurts me to see someone in a Harvard sweater who has never set foot on the campus.

Ilse helped me return to Swiss German (*Schwyzer Deutsch*).

She did not like expressing herself in High German, for all her skills at languages. We met in the spring of 1952 when she was working as a secretary for Primateria, a trading firm that dealt in edible oils. Our bank had extended large credits to the company, which subsequently went bankrupt. Our 1949 audit report gave a detailed account of our extensive engagement with Primateria. The market had issued warnings. I wrote worried letters from New York and South America, but I was just a beginner, and my uncles reacted too late. That cost us a lot of money.

What had happened? Fritz Haller, now in his eighties and a director of the trading firm at the time, still remembers that Primateria went short on Philippine copra (the coconut basis for margarine). It had agreed to deliver product, which it did not have, assuming that by the agreed-upon delivery date, prices would have declined substantially. But copra was unavailable at any price — perhaps their competitors knew about their position and were wary of helping. Primateria tried to arbitrage with whale oil, because margarine can be made out of whale oil. But that didn't work out. And things being as they were, if one didn't deliver, one was forced into a compulsory settlement and then quickly went bankrupt. The old Wall Street maxim applied: those who sell what isn't theirs must buy it back or go to prison.

Dealing in raw materials, as they do in finance, arbitrage firms fail because of the margin. One of the better-known cases was the Frankfurt Metallgesellschaft, which went long on raw oil contracts and had to pump in more money when prices fell. When it ran out of money in 1993, it was all over. Long Term Capital Management, the hedge fund, was caught the same way on global markets.

My uncle Werner, generous by nature, demonstrated how such events should be handled. He combined the bad news with an invitation to a large dinner at his house and welcomed his guests, saying, "I would like you all to be in a good mood tonight." It turned into a fabulous garden party.

It was a major bust for our modest circumstances. The bank had to draw on earnings to cover our losses and to disband our undisclosed reserves. Later we used to say that my wife was the only asset we saved out of that disaster.

Ilse moved on to Interba, an international steel dealer that Ernst Englaender had built up. The adopted New Yorker was a banker before the war, worked in U.S. Air Corps intelligence during the war, interrogated Hermann Goering in Augsburg together with Eric Warburg, and spent a few weeks in Zurich every year. We became friends. Occasionally he would tell me, "I've known your bank longer than you have been alive."

Ilse was born in Bienne, where she grew up. Her father came from what we call "inner Switzerland." Because he couldn't stand local Catholicism, he converted to Protestantism and was elected a teacher at the grammar school in Bienne. After graduating from the high school, Ilse spent a year in London, spoke fluent English and French, her second mother tongue, and knew Italian well. She opened a new circle of friends and acquaintances for me, some of whom would become quite prominent in Switzerland. My friendship with Ambassador Charles Mueller and State Secretaries Raymond Probst and Klaus Jacobi developed via my wife. Mueller's wife, Marlise, was her closest friend. She knew Klaus Jacobi from her school days in Bienne. Hans Strasser, who would become president of the Swiss Bank Corporation, was another friend from Bienne. Through this Bienne and Berne-based circle, I also met the historian Walther Hofer.

My relationship to the family of her brother-in-law, her sister Yolanda's husband, grew especially close. Dr. Jean-Pierre Crosetti was head physician at the Cadolle, the cantonal hospital in Neuchâtel. Equally, my extended family accepted my wife wholeheartedly. That she came from a non-Jewish home was never a topic, nor was her father's profession as a teacher. The only thing that irritated my mother was that Ilse was a few years older than I was. While it can't have been very easy for Ilse to blend into the circle of my close relatives, she mastered that task with great skill.

As my emotional bonds to Switzerland grew stronger, my doubts about Europe's political future faded. My affinity for the United States remained. It could hardly have been otherwise. I was, after all, raised and educated in the United States, and many of my lifelong friends and acquaintances were made there, relationships nourished by my frequent visits to the country and the amount of business I did.

11

Intermezzo in Israel

Nordmann's most expensive night

The reason for our invitation to Israel in 1950 was not hard to guess. It was an invitation to subscribe low-interest treasury and construction bonds in order to support the young state. The drive from Tel Aviv airport to Jerusalem led us past burnt-out tanks. Since the armistice in the fall of 1948, nobody had had time to remove them, yet the exuberant mood of the people was infectious. The enthusiasm, the confidence, and the energy with which the country tackled building a modern state are hard to imagine today. A new society was in the process of formation — democratic and inspired by a deep humanism.

Israel was a radically modern state along the lines generally predicted after the war, with a largely government-steered economy, restricted individual ownership (which did not impose much of a burden since no one had much), and a high tax load, which offered Ephraim Kishon great material for satire. This fiscal policy had a simple purpose: the country urgently needed money. Most immigrants brought nothing but the rags on their backs and had often suffered through hell on earth. Given everything that we think about today, one must never forget that Israel commenced as a profoundly traumatized nation. The state had to be concerned about everything: industrialization, long-term financing, home building, roads, energy, ports, and airfields. Moreover, the country had to build itself up and assume the burden of national defense.

In the wake of Hitler Germany's annihilation policy, the need for an independent state was beyond doubt. So I came to represent the family on this trip, which brought together a number of Swiss bankers and businessmen from Jewish houses. We were lodged at the King David Hotel, from which we departed after a short stay at five or six o'clock in the morning for our flight back. The day begins early in Israel.

Robert Nordmann, from the Maus Frères department store concern, was a member of my group. When he asked for his bill on checking out of the hotel, he was told, "There is no bill, Mr. Nordmann. You are our guest."

"I've never spent a night so cheaply," he murmured spontaneously.

"No, Mr. Nordmann, this was the most expensive night of your life," was the quick-witted reply.

Without being the least bit Zionist, the Baer family felt close to Israel, thanks to our ties to Chaim Weizmann that dated back to the 1930s. Weizmann, Israel's first president, was a chemist, had taught in Manchester where he met the Marks & Spencer families, Marks and Sieff, and had made a fortune due to the founding shares Marks & Spencer assigned to him. The Zionists around David Ben-Gurion resented the fact that Weizmann was British and had earned his money in England as much as they resented his moderate views. He represented a classic liberalism and would have liked to see the Jewish state as part of the British commonwealth. Weizmann imagined Israel as a kind of Switzerland in the Middle East, with highly developed technology and research, divided into cantons, attractive to tourists, and politically neutral. His idea was to develop this state, founded out of dire need, pragmatically, from within existing society. The Zionists from continental Europe, on the other hand, insisted on a constitution for a sovereign state before worrying about society. The publisher George Weidenfeld reduced the contrast between Ben-Gurion and Weizmann to this formula: Weizmann was a pacifist at the core of his being, whereas Ben-Gurion was a man of the kibbutz movement, a fighter.

Weizmann retired as president of the Zionist World Organization at the 22nd Zionist Congress in Basel in 1946, after the majority around Ben-Gurion had rejected participation in it by a vote of 171 to 154 at a Jewish-Arab conference in London, and had decided on armed confrontation against the British mandate authority. Weizmann withdrew to Rehovot and excluded everyone he felt had betrayed him. Teddy Kollek, the future mayor of Jerusalem, for example, was no longer allowed to visit him. He would have to let guests off at Weizmann's door. After the founding of Israel, Weizmann was elected president but did not exercise any noteworthy political influence.

On this trip I also visited Vera Weizmann in her house in Rehovot. The elegant Erich Mendelsohn building is a beautiful example of Bauhaus architecture. The house is set in a splendid garden with a marvelous view of the Plain of Sharon and a large swimming pool where lunches would often be served in the summer. The Weizmann house was popularly known as the "White House." Today it's a museum.

Chaim and Vera Weizmann met as students in Geneva. She was the daughter of one of the few Jewish regimental doctors in the Czarist army and had retained a weakness for all things Russian. I really couldn't converse with her in Russian, but at least I brought her the fillet of smoked ham she had wished for.

Compared to the Israeli lifestyle, the two of them lived very grandly, even if their staff, with the exception of an aging English butler, consisted of uneducated Hungarian or Yemeni immigrants who only spoke their native dialect. Chaim himself suffered less from his inadequate staff than he did from his political isolation. Ben-Gurion and his people excluded him from every decision-making process.

In our family, my uncle Walter cultivated our relationship with Israel and its representatives most avidly. He belonged to the "Board of Governors" of the Weizmann Institute of Science and the founding committee of the Swiss-sponsored children's village, Kirjat Jearim, in Israel. His son, my cousin Alfred, was president of the Swiss branch of Keren Hayesod/United Israel Appeal and collected a great deal of money for Israel. Alfred was friendly with Yitzhak Rabin. He even took him on a hike through the Engadin, which was not at all to the great statesman's liking, with Yigal Allon, foreign minister from 1974 to 1977, and Moshe Dayan. Keren Hayesod collected money once a year. When their representative came to call, you had to contribute.

In Switzerland, we were by no means alone in our sympathy for Israel. Before the 1967 Six-Day War, nobody knew where Israel was; afterward, every second Swiss felt themselves as Israelis. Albert Mossdorf, for example, was a great friend. He was a man of liberal thought and from 1967 to 1979 a minister of the government of the canton of Zurich. He was not very tall but had a robust constitution, and he embodied the classic politician: he held his liquor well and had a great heart and an ironclad stomach.

My ties to Israel consisted of close personal relations with a number of people who were involved with the country for one reason or another. One time at the Zurich airport I accidentally ran into Isaac Stern. "So where are you coming from?" I asked. His answer: "From Israel. Yesterday I sat with Golda Meir in her kitchen. We had a great conversation."

I often had such chance meetings. Nahum Goldman, founder and president of the World Jewish Congress (WJC), crossed my path, as did Meyer Weisgal, one of the Weizmann Institute executives and the most talented schnorrer of all times. I got to know

Goldman in New York. He never occupied any official position in Israel for a very simple reason: he didn't want to give up his Nicaraguan passport, which he had acquired after fleeing Germany. In the final analysis, he made a greater contribution to Israel that way. Thus Goldman arranged the secret meeting between Konrad Adenauer and David Ben-Gurion at the Waldorf Astoria in New York. Teddy Kollek attended the meeting as Ben-Gurion's chief of staff. Later I would talk to Kollek a great deal. He believed in unity for Jerusalem, whereas I couldn't imagine it. The supporter of peaceful coexistence died in an Arab Jewish old age home.

Meyer Weisgal, a theatrical man with flowing white hair who liked to dress in white capes, had grown up on New York's Lower East Side, spoke a very common English spiced with obscenities, and was a talented fundraiser. With his charm and his inexhaustible persuasiveness, he gathered the means needed to expand the Weizmann Institute in Rehovot.

Weisgal liked to divide the life of a person into three phases: accumulative, contemplative, and distributive. For him, the idea was to make contact in the transition to the contemplative phase in order to be ready when the distribution began. One of his tricks was to show a potential donor a list of a dozen possible contributors, a list on which his name was missing. That provoked the question, "Why is my name missing?"

Weisgal's answer: "You are in another category, but I'll come back to you when you've reached the right level."

The reply from the potential donor was often mildly emotional: "What do you mean? Do you think I can't come up with a million in donations? Let me tell you something — that name on the list doesn't have a quarter of what I have. You know what, I'll pay for the whole thing . . ."

Goldman, Weisgal, and Kollek always stopped in Zurich on their way from Israel to Europe or the United States; without fail they had all talked to Levy Eshkol, Golda Meir, Shimon Peres, or

Yitzhak Rabin. So for a long time I always knew what was going on in Israel through these various individuals.

Collecting money for Israel goes back to the nineteenth century. Men like Baron Moritz von Hirsch — a cofounder of the Bavarian "Vereinsbank" (today a division of Unicredito) and, because he financed the Vienna-Istanbul railroad, also called the "Turk's Hirsch" — and Edmond de Rothschild donated substantial sums of money. Hirsch alone gave £8 million (at least $40 million) to the Jewish Colonization Committee. Before the war, Weizmann took Albert Einstein along on his money-raising tours of the United States, which Weisgal had organized. Evil tongues would claim that the scientist had only gone along to be near the beauteous Vera Weizmann.

Later, Moshe Dayan traveled around the world in order to collect money. His fame and popularity after the Six-Day War were immeasurable. The man with the eye patch had great magnetism and captivating charm — no Siegfried, but an intelligent hero and an exciting personality.

My appointment to the board of Bank Leumi le-Israel's (pronounced Le-umi) Swiss branch, founded in 1961, brought me in direct contact with Israel. (The bank's predecessor was Cifico Ltd., founded in 1953.) Board memberships basically have two pleasant aspects: you meet a lot of new people and you add to your learning. The appointment at Leumi gave me my first experience with a large organization: how to battle through the channels, how to fight for recognition, and all the other things that belong to the characteristics of a large company. The bank, after all, had had to make preparations for the two wars in the years 1967 and 1973 to ensure liquidity and to be armed for all possible events.

At first Heinz Gruenbaum was the head of Bank Leumi Switzerland. He understood the business very well, and his personality enriched those he knew and worked with. Board members included Rolf Bloch of the Chocolats Camille Bloch — later the head of the

Swiss Federation of Jewish Communities (SFJC) and a prudent spokesman of the Jewish community in the matter of the dormant accounts; my good friend, Paul Eisenring, deputy in parliament and president of the purchasing association of Swiss department stores; and last but not least, Victor Loeb, a good-looking man and, with his strong leadership personality, a classic alpha type. He taught me what to watch out for when looking for bank offices. I had found something suitable in Zurich's Loewenstrasse for the Leumi bank and, satisfied, telephoned Loeb in Berne. "You don't rent space in a house with storefronts. That's not first class," the boss of the department store company that bore his name lectured me.

All in all, the Leumi board was a prestigious committee. In Israel, the prime minister (Levy Eshkol until 1969 and then Golda Meir) regularly received us. On those board trips to Israel, I also learned how important it is not to have too many celebrities in your group. If you do, nobody arrives punctually and your whole travel schedule is thrown off.

For me, the high point of these travels was the concerts in Frederick Mann Hall in Tel Aviv. On his first visit to Israel in 1949, Isaac Stern had to play in cinemas, garages, and other provisional spaces. In 1957, Frederick Mann and his wife, Silvia, both great music lovers and good friends of Isaac Stern, endowed the fabulous concert hall, which has become an integral part of Israel's musical life.

Dr. Yeshayahu Foerder was president of Bank Leumi's board of directors from 1957 to 1970. He taught me something I have remembered all my life. I had been to Tehran on business without much success, stopped in Tel Aviv on my way home, and visited this man with the bushy, dark eyebrows that ended at his temples in a movie-ready curl. "What on earth did you do in Tehran?" he asked.

"Oh, Dr. Foerder, that's a long story," I began.

"Then it is already wrong," he objected.

He was right. The story was sad and involved large losses.

Dr. Foerder was born in Germany and had emigrated to Palestine in 1933, when he was thirty-two years old. The trained lawyer and economist belonged to the founders of the Rural and Suburban Settlement Company (RASCO). Politically, he was not close to the Socialists but to the Progressive Party, later the Independent Liberals, whom he represented in the Knesset for three terms. Dr. Foerder had a lively disposition — quite different from that of his predecessor, the legendary Eliezer Siegfried Hoofien, who came from the Netherlands — a strong desire to move the country forward, and the good luck to lead the bank during a phase of general growth.

When Dr. Foerder died in 1970, Dr. Ernst Lehmann took over as chairman. He too came from Germany but had emigrated before 1933 and in 1935 held his first top management job as managing director of the General Mortgage Bank. During his tenure, Leumi experienced incredible growth rates (1972: 38.7 percent, 1975: 60.6 percent), which even against a background of 30 to 40 percent inflation rates were substantial. Ernest Japhet became chairman in 1977 and at the same time remained CEO. At the end of the seventies, it was still unimaginable that merging the two jobs into one could remove the necessary checks and balances from the bank's operations.

Leumi always had to live with thin capitalization but from its earliest days had Swiss shareholders. In practice, my votes tended to represent the interests of those Swiss shareholders.

The history of Bank Leumi le-Israel (National Bank of Israel) is closely tied to the Zionist movement. It was founded on July 21, 1903, as a Jewish colonial bank known as the Jewish Colonial Trust. Theodor Herzl, the founder, insisted that all foundations in Palestine be constituted as companies under British law. He had the German model of a universal bank in mind for his bank, which, as an investment bank, would open up the country by creating companies whose shares would be sold to the public, while the commercial bank would be responsible for short-term financing. Raising capital among a broad public proved difficult. Herzl had angered major supporters of the Jewish cause with his insistent demand that charity and business remain separate.

Given its limited means, the bank focused on the short-term credit business and on the foreign exchange trade. Until the outbreak of the First World War, Zalman David Leontin, the first director, had opened four branches in Palestine and one in Beirut. In May 1914 he added a branch in Gaza. Some 20 percent of the credits went into agriculture, which, spurred by the example of the Knights Templar who had emigrated from Wuertenberg in the second half of the nineteenth century, had bloomed. Another 75 percent flowed into trade, services, and the crafts.

Leontin and other members of the bank also blazed a linguistic path. In 1903, they decided to use Hebrew as their business language and thus made a significant contribution toward the introduction of the biblical language into the workday. The final decision in favor of Hebrew wasn't made until the very controversial selection of the teaching language at the technical school, the Technion, in Haifa, in the years 1912 to 1913. The alternative was not English but German — beyond imagination today, in light of two world wars and fifty years of intellectual self-colonization. The Palestine bureau of the Zionist movement simply found German more practical than Hebrew.

The founding of Tel Aviv belongs to the rich and dramatic history of Bank Leumi. During the Ottoman rule, it often financed the purchase of "tax tenths," a medieval land tax, by the settler committees. So long as the medieval leaseholders could collect these payments, sensible agriculture was out of the question.

During the First World War, the bank was ordered to shut down. As an institution set up under British law, it was formally owned by an enemy power. But at the end of the war, the bank was still in business, because nobody was really interested in throttling further the already depressed economy. On the other hand, the bank profited from the opportunity to exchange the highly inflated

Turkish pound at the Deutsche Bank in Constantinople at the official rate, which, in turn, offered interesting arbitrage opportunities. And it acquired land at the foot of Mount Carmel, which the Knights Templar from Wuertenberg wished to sell. Today, the center of Haifa is spread across that terrain. The purchase was again financed with Turkish pounds, which the Templars accepted at the official rate of exchange.

A new era began with British Foreign Secretary Arthur Balfour's declaration, in a letter he sent to Lord Rothschild on November 2, 1917, assuring Jews of a national homeland in Palestine — a letter written at the instigation of Chaim Weizmann and Nahum Sokolow. Leontin wanted to increase the bank's capital by £2 million in order to make long-term investments. The Zionist World Organization created a committee that included Herbert Samuel, who later became the first high commissioner for Palestine, and John Maynard Keynes. It recommended the £2 million capital increase for the Jewish Colonization Committee (JCC) and another million pounds for the Anglo-Palestine Company (APC). But it determined that the APC should stay in the short-term business and suggested the creation of a mortgage bank for long-term transactions.

In the forefront of Israel's independence, the Anglo-Palestine Bank was given the task of preparing the new currency. It arranged for printing the money in the United States. Because time was short, several different plates were used — including ones that had been prepared for printing Chinese yuan. Another historical curiosity. In doing so, the Anglo-Palestine Bank assumed the role of a currency-issuing central bank. The real central bank was only created six years later. For now, the Israeli currency would be the Palestine pound.

The founding of the state of Israel did not change anything in the status of the Anglo-Palestine Bank. It remained a society under British law. How could such an institution be turned into an Israeli bank? An interesting assignment. Siegfried Eliezer Hoofien, Leontin's successor, founded a new company in September 1950, the Bank Leumi le-Israel B.M. (National Bank of Israel) with a capital of 3 million IL (Israeli pounds; the shekel was not introduced until 1980) and offered to exchange the holdings of shareholders in the Anglo-Palestine Bank for shares of the Bank Leumi.

I didn't leave the board until 1982, after my election as president of the Tonhalle Orchestra. My Israeli connections became particularly useful during the discussions about the dormant accounts of the Holocaust victims and how to get in touch with representatives of the World Jewish Congress in New York. Ernest Japhet had already retired but helped me when the campaign began in June 1995.

The relationship between the Julius Baer bank and the State of Israel is almost a footnote to the history of finance. In 1978, Fritz Leutwiler, a friend of Israel's, suggested — probably after the visit of his Israeli counterpart who wanted to obtain a picture of market conditions — a private placement of Israel notes. So we issued SFr 50 million ($25 million) worth of five-year notes carrying an interest rate of 5 percent for the Industrial Development Bank of Israel. After two years we suddenly had to buy back the notes. A lawyer in the Israeli Treasury had discovered that an antagonist with enough capital could buy up the notes and drive Israel into bankruptcy, in case outside circumstances, for example, a war, prevented timely payment of interest. After that, Israel didn't enter the international capital markets for a long time.

Of course, developments in the Middle East depressed me greatly. The disappearance of outstanding personalities in our world did not spare Israel. We grew up with Chaim Weizmann, we knew Golda Meir, just as we did Ben Gurion; we experienced Moshe Dayan, Yigal Allon, and Yitzhak and Lea Rabin, who liked to come to Switzerland and were exceptional representatives of Israel, giving a fundraising dinner in Zurich every six months or so. And remember that Israel had a steady representative in Zurich, the outstanding consul-general Moise Ofer, a worldly gentleman married to an American.

Today in Zurich we don't know any members of the Israeli cabinet; the current generation of leaders no longer comes to Switzerland. Among the talents a fundraiser like Mayer Weisgal brought with him was the ability to maintain ties to his donors even if he wasn't out to milk them. That tradition too has been broken off. Our bequests notwithstanding, even the relationship to the Weizmann Institute has withered away. My cousin Alfred remembers that he and his brothers were somewhat unhappy that Walter Baer's bequest was transferred into the general fund to finance a new building without first asking our family. On Walter's one-hundredth birthday, his four sons made another donation to the institute.

The Technion in Haifa, on the other hand, the only technical institute of higher learning with a medical school, cultivates much closer ties to Switzerland. It has an exchange agreement with the Swiss Federal Institute of Technology (ETH) in Zurich. Both schools have done pioneering work in computerizing the academic world. The Swiss Technion Society (STG), with Alfred Baer as president, endowed two chairs and a permanent guest professorship and pays for three laboratories and a student dormitory. There is a scholarship fund for Swiss students at the Technion, and the STG gives intensive support to the Institute for Mathematics as well as the Swiss Federal Laboratories for Materials Testing and Research. My cousin estimates that to date $20 million have flown from Switzerland to the Technion. The institute's leadership thanked Alfred for his commitment with his election in 1984 to the board of governors, and in 1995 they named him an honorary fellow.

What else? The Weizmann bureau in Zurich is orphaned, and Swiss sentiment toward Israel fluctuates. After the Six-Day War, the Swiss rejoiced with Israel. In the 1973 Yom Kippur War, Swiss sympathy was clearly with Israel too. Today, in contrast, Israeli ambassadors in Europe are forced to visit large and small newspaper offices in order to justify the security policies of their country. To win understanding for a policy of striking hard with an iron fist is no easy task. The Israelis must feel threatened, not from a Palestine state, but from the states behind it (a motive for the U.S. Iraq policy that should not be underestimated). Control of the West Bank, therefore, cannot be given up. Yitzhak Rabin saw it that way; he wanted a demilitarized Palestinian state. The Palestinians, based on their past experience, must assume that in a second-class state, they will have only limited freedom. Their desire for a sovereign state is legitimate but collides with Israel's security needs, which grow with every criminal attack. I doubt that this conflict can ever be solved. At best, a transitory solution could be found under the protective umbrella of the United States or the United Nations, assuming that the protectorate succeeds in convincing both sides that their very existence is not threatened. The protective wall Israel is building could, in that sense, be a beginning. But it could also be an expensive mistake.

Democracy does not mean that the greatest insight lies with the people, something we have known ever since Socrates was forced to empty the cup of hemlock. In Israel's case, given its high rate of immigration, the composition of the electorate changes markedly every four years. The most recent arrivals do have an unbroken will to self-assert themselves, but in practice they have minimal tolerance of others and, therefore, have the least amount of insight. The result has been a steady shift to the Right, and this in a country in which the Labor Party once ruled with a comfortable two-thirds majority and all the leading personalities in the economy and the military were at least close to the Labor Party. Today the country — which shares with Germany the tendency to overestimate its undoubted operative qualities and thus succumbs to the irrational belief that it can replace strategy with operations — is in a deep political crisis.

The majority is schizophrenic. It elected Ariel Sharon as well as Ehud Olmert and would elect Sharon again today, or if not him, Benjamin Netanyahu. On the other hand, public opinion polls show that the majority of the population is ready to give up the occupation of the West Bank and Gaza and to dissolve the settlements. The settlements are an impossible institution in the third millennium, a fact semantically so evident that it's hard to imagine how anyone could ever have had the idea of operating anything so historically obsolete. But the settlement policy was an awkward solution because the country had missed the chance after the two wars in 1967 and 1973 to reach a peaceful agreement. Typically, a replacement policy — moreover, one that has all the marks of a decision only half-made — is not enough to really penetrate the occupied territory, but it is enough to provoke the indigenous population every day.

Former Defense Minister Benjamin Ben-Elizier admitted as much: the settlements and the daily restrictions were a humiliation and provocation for the natives. Suicide attacks are the weapons of the little person and the most extreme measures at the disposal of the Palestinians. The logical response against terror is counterterror. Israel's general staff has certainly thought about this but also about the consequences. In the case of the suicide attacks, counterterror would mean introduction of a "family responsibility and arrest" policy. But Israel would only lose sympathy that way. Abba Eban once attested that the Palestinians "had never missed a chance to miss a chance."

But has Israel done any better?

My always "difficult" relationship with Israel has been rather unjustly rewarded with the Teddy Kollek Award for my contribution to the welfare of Jerusalem. A morning ceremony in the Knesset on May 7, 2006, was the background for my acceptance speech, which follows:

I stand before you to receive an award for my friendship with Jerusalem and essentially with Israel, an award that I must share with my family.

This friendship, in my mind, goes back to my youth and April 1934, when the Weizmann Institute of Science celebrated the completion of the headquarters building of the then Daniel Sieff Research Institute in Rehovot. My parents, who attended, were friendly with Vera and Chaim Weizmann, primarily because the men were both scientists — Weizmann a professor of chemistry in Manchester and my father a professor of physics in Zurich.

The names of all the well-known Jews who were associated with the birth of your nation come to mind again. The most prominent personality was, of course, Chaim Weizmann, who was also a close friend of my uncle, Walter Baer. He was a frequent visitor to Zurich also at the time of the 22nd Zionist Congress in Basel in 1946, during which Weizmann was not reelected as the head of the Zionist Congress. Weizmann saw Israel as the Switzerland of the Middle East, while Ben Gurion was in favor of a more militant policy, which the Congress ultimately followed.

We are reminded of good friends like Nahum Goldmann, the then president of the World Jewish Congress; Meyer Weisgal, the "Finance Minister" of the Weizmann Institute; Joseph Cohen, the European ambassador of the institute; and others. But it was not only the Weizmann Institute but also the Technion in Haifa, the Bank Leumi, and, above all, the Israel Bond Organization, which made for an ever closer relationship to Israel with my family.

Teddy Kollek, a world-famous name, which I would say is synonymous with Jerusalem and the State of Israel, served not only as an envoy to the United States but also headed the first fundraising campaign of the Israel Bonds Organization, in which capacity we got to know each other for the first time.

The Jerusalem Foundation has played an invaluable role in the development of your great city. The key areas being addressed today are educational quality, tolerance and coexistence, and the arts and culture, to name only a few. Isaac Stern, Arthur Rubinstein, and Zubin Mehta come to mind when we mention the arts. You will recognize that these are all fields of immense importance also to my country — Switzerland.

I stand here to accept your award as a representative of a nation that feels close to you and your endeavors to promote tolerance, a nation that wishes Israel every possible success in its efforts to promote peace in this historic part of the world.

History is never finished. Three months later, we faced a new war in the Middle East. It took the armed forces of Israel a considerable effort to weaken the Hezbollah so that a truce could be reached. In the end, the campaign has raised more questions than it has answered, and the Israeli government is in a weaker position than ever before.

12

WEIZMANN INSTITUTE OF SCIENCE AND PRINCETON INSTITUTE FOR ADVANCED STUDY (1947–52)

Beautiful minds

Without ever having studied at the Weizmann Institute of Science in Rehovot or at the Princeton Institute for Advanced Study, I nevertheless received invaluable guidance from both research centers during my life. After my father died, the idea came up of giving his library to the Weizmann Institute. To that end, Walter wrote to my mother on July 13, 1946:

> We have to apologize for not yet answering your inquiry about Richard's library as well as the research room at the institute. Indeed, it has been forgotten completely. I have just telephoned Edgar [Meyer] about the library. He thinks it is a very good idea, but points out that he believes he remembers that you had promised all or part of the library to Erwin Schroedinger. Edgar thinks that Schroedinger already has at his disposal a well-equipped institute, and that under the circumstances, Rehovot was

preferable. As far as the room is concerned, it seems to me that the budget is somewhat exaggerated for our means. If and when our funds are unblocked one day, we can see what we can do. However, $5,000 as contribution to this institute really will be the maximum we can manage.

On September 23, 1946, Walter reported to my mother:

The great event of last week was, as you must have read in the newspapers, Churchill's visit. For his speech on the Muensterplatz we had seats near the Leder-Locher and saw him from a distance of about twenty meters. Unfortunately, we did not hear very well because the loudspeakers killed the live language. . . . Speaking of visits, Josef Cohn [a close Weizmann associate and family friend from New York] was in Switzerland last week and told us a lot about all of you. For the Weizmann Institute, I agreed that once our assets are unblocked, I would urge the family to agree on paying for furnishing and equipping a room in Professor K. Chain's laboratory — it is supposed to consist of three rooms — devoted to the Raman effect, which should cost about $7,000, and that the room should then carry Richard's name. In addition, we have increased our annual contribution to the institute to $1,500. Cohn held discussions with other people here, Professor Reichstein, etc., which are said to have been quite positive. He flew to London today but expects to return here in the first half of October. A short while ago, I had a letter from Weizmann himself. He will have to undergo several cataract operations. The first one has already taken place, the next one is due in October, and after that, and before the Congress [the 22nd Zionist Congress where he resigned] plans to come to Switzerland for four weeks of rest and relaxation.

I suggested the Ticino. We're all looking forward to seeing him again.

Six months later, on March 15, 1947, Walter wrote to my mother:

You will remember that after further inquiry with you, and at Edgar's suggestions, we had decided to give dear Richard's library to the Weizmann Center in Rehovot. This, as I wrote to you at an earlier date, has already taken place, and Josef Cohn, who by the way will leave Europe in about ten days and should show up over there toward the end of the month or in mid-April at the latest, took a detailed inventory here and sent it on to Palestine. Now we are at the point where the books are ready for shipping, which will require export approval from Bern. That we will receive it is without any doubt. Before I take this last and therefore irrevocable step and ship the books, I would like for good order's sake to have your approval. So, if and when, please be good enough to give it to me.

A week later, on March 22, 1947, my mother wrote back:

I believe that as far as Richard's library is concerned, there can only be a mistake somewhere. First of all, from the very beginning, I had promised Erwin Schroedinger a part of the books for the new institute in Dublin. Secondly, last May, I had a discussion with Professor Mark before he went to Palestine about what would be of interest for the institute there. It turned out that what he wanted most were Richard's periodicals, all of them almost unavailable. I promised to give him an inventory of all the periodicals by late summer. I then wrote this whole report to you —

or perhaps to Edgar [Meyer] — with the request to catalogue them and send them on, and that was all; I have
never heard anything from you about it. I would urgently
plead with you — and in the name of the children as
well — to put aside the matter until our arrival. Under no
circumstances do I want the library given away without
prior selection. It included very beautiful and costly books
that cannot be obtained today and that perhaps will be
very valuable for Marianne [her daughter].

Walter replied on April 9, 1947: "Of course Richard's books
will remain where they are. I have told Josef [Cohn] about the complication and he received the news with composure."

I found a letter in the archives of the bank I had written on
January 30, 1949: "By now I am rather confused about the Weizmann deals myself. . . . I looked up the records and found out that
Baerbank contributed $1,500 in February as well as the final install-
ment from Mother of $2,000 for the room."

On November 2, 1949, with the agreement of the Sieff family,
which had financed the small organization in 1934, the institute
was renamed and formally dedicated as the Weizmann Institute of
Science.

For most of my life, the concept of "Rehovot" has been synonymous with Israel. The climax of my first trip to Israel, in addition to the lunch in the Weizmann villa, was a visit to the institute,
which housed the Richard Baer room. Today the institute has a
global reputation in applied research. The government, significantly, contributes only 45 percent of the necessary income. The
rest is covered by sponsors, foundations, and to a remarkable degree
through royalties of patent rights. In 2001, they amounted to a total of $60 million, a sum that ranks the Weizmann Institute behind
Columbia University with $90 million and ahead of Stanford with
$28 million. Without its own efforts and strong private support,

Israel could not afford the luxury of large research facilities like the universities of Tel Aviv and Jerusalem, the Technion in Haifa, and the Weizmann Institute. Seed money supports these endeavors. For example, the Casali family (it has since died out), which gave the world Stock Vermouth, sponsored a chemical institute at the university and provided a fund whose income maintains its operations. The scientists themselves have to come up with the rest. That forces them to practice a certain amount of efficiency and contributes to dismantling the barriers to the business world.

Today the personal contacts have of course disappeared, with the exception of Professor Eli Pollak, who holds the Zacks Professorial Chair in Chemical Physics.

The second institution that provided guidance for my life was the Institute for Advanced Study at Princeton. Indeed, had I not lived for so many years in the United States, Princeton would have been as synonymous for America in my life as Rehovot was for Israel. The reason for the Rockefeller Foundation's decision to make Princeton the international center for mathematics and physics was that John D. Rockefeller Jr., the son of the clan's patron who had died in 1937 at age ninety-seven, had studied there. Thanks to the sizable contributions to the university, mathematicians like John von Neumann and Eugen Igner had been brought to the university as early as 1930.

The formation of the autonomous Institute for Advanced Study provided added impetus to that development. Louis Bamberger and his sister Carolyn Bamberger Fuld had endowed the institute in 1930. They had made their money through the sale of their department store in 1929 to R. H. Macy & Co. in Newark, New Jersey. They didn't want to thank the United States but rather the State of New Jersey, and that's how the mathematician Oswald Veblen was able to win them over for Princeton. The foundation is managed by a board of trustees under the leadership of my friend

Jimmy Wolfensohn, the former president of the World Bank. Some thirty prominent names are on the board, including former Brazilian president Fernando Cardoso, Marina v. Neumann-Whitman, the daughter of the mathematician, and James Schiro, CEO of Zurich Financial Services.

Thanks to the Institute for Advanced Study, Albert Einstein, Kurt Goedel, and Hermann Weyl found their way to Princeton. John von Neumann switched from the university to the institute (and thus was saved from the terror of the students). Indirect assistance came — as it did in Rehovot — from a Germany infected by Nazi racial madness. As a result, Princeton quickly supplanted Goettingen as the leading center for the natural sciences.

My father was supposed to have done research at the institute, but it didn't turn out that way. However, the connections he had made remained because a number of my parents' friends and acquaintances taught there.

My mother enjoyed the academic milieu. During the war she often went to Princeton, a forty-five-minute train ride from New York, to further the friendly ties she had maintained from her Zurich days — to Wolfgang and Franca Pauli as well as Hermann and Helene Weyl, who had lived around the corner from us in Zurich on Schneckenmannstrasse and were frequent guests in our home.

I had wanted to attend Princeton because of Hermann Weyl, but that didn't happen because the university is oriented toward liberal arts. However, my brother-in-law, the physicist David Speiser, did his graduate work at Princeton. My sister met him through Wolfgang Pauli. David had been his assistant in Zurich.

At institute tea parties, which I began to attend in 1947, I made notable friends and acquaintances. I met the art historian Erwin Panofsky and the German economist Friedrich August Lutz, whose research was focused on money and currency theories. Lutz taught at Princeton from 1939 to 1953, when he moved to the University of Zurich. With his wife, Vera Smith, a British economist who wrote some well-regarded books of her own, they enriched Zurich's intellectual and social life. Because of him, the best American economists visited Zurich in the fifties. The presence of such a luminary would be good for Zurich even today.

In Princeton, I also got a close-up look at the Oppenheimer drama. My mother and I were regular guests at Neumann's and Oppenheimer's cocktail parties. I remember him as a worldly intellectual who had caseloads of champagne delivered to his house. (I did not only go to parties at Princeton, though. I completed writing my NYU master's thesis there.) Lewis Strauss, the chairman of the Atomic Energy Commission, was an institute trustee and in that function had, in 1946, offered Oppenheimer the job of institute director. Oppenheimer became its director in 1947. But for the cold war taste of the fifties, he had flirted too much with communists during his years in Berkeley. Moreover, he had the disadvantage of intellectual independence, with the disagreeable consequences that he thought about the political qualities of the atom bomb — he compared the two atomic powers to two scorpions in a bottle — and came to the conclusion that development costs for a hydrogen bomb didn't make sense. That led to his political persecution by Strauss, who made sure that in 1954 a special committee stripped Oppenheimer of his security clearance and thus isolated him from further atomic research. Oppenheimer was only rehabilitated in 1960, after John F. Kennedy succeeded President Eisenhower. In more than one way, the atomic physicist reminded me of my father. He was about the same age, had plunged into the same scientific discipline, had a broad spectrum of interests, had musical talent, took a passionate part in artistic and cultural life, and came, as we did, from a German-Jewish household.

Thanks to Hermann Weyl, I had the best contacts with the mathematicians. I met Oswald Veblen, born in 1880, who won renown for his vector theories, his groundbreaking work on objective geometry, and his reflections on the theory of relativity. His wife, May Veblen, was reputed to know every home in Princeton and all its inhabitants, no matter what their ethnicity or wealth.

I became quite friendly with John von Neumann, who was born in Budapest in 1903 as Baron Johann von Neumann and recognized early in his youth as a mathematical genius. After completing his studies in Zurich, he went to Berlin at age twenty-five and then on to Princeton in 1929. Neumann showed me the Electronic Numerical Integrator and Computer (ENIAC), for which he had invented the binary codes. ENIAC was the basis for the later Universal Automatic Computer (UNIVAC). It contained 17,468 tubes, 50,000 resisters, 10,000 condensers, 1,500 relay stations, and 6,000 switches, and weighed 30 tons. ENIAC was stored in forty-two cabinets that filled a whole house. Every operation required hundreds of new connections that had to be made manually. All this for a modest calculation of five thousand additions per second, an achievement the cheapest calculator easily exceeds today. The computer was officially, and festively, inaugurated in June 1952. Neumann and Oppenheimer, in his capacity as director of the Institute for Advanced Study, were the hosts. Perhaps not a coincidence, the house was located on the banks of the Milestone River. Tubes, condensers, and switches gave off a great deal of heat and had to be cooled with river water. When I realized what was involved and thought about a computer for our bank, I felt sick. We would never be able to afford one, and for that reason alone I thought we would never have a long-term perspective on our business.

In her book A Beautiful Mind, Sylvia Nasar describes the creative spirit, the daily exchange of thoughts, the lofty atmosphere, and the development from desire to brilliant achievement at the Institute of Advanced Study. The book is a biography of the economist and Nobel Prize winner John Forbes Nash. He was one of the elegant people at Princeton, well-dressed bon vivants. The only necessary correction to the text: the Rijksbank sponsors the Nobel Prize for economics. During Nobel's day, economics was not an academic discipline.

Among others at Princeton I remember well was Dorothy Morgenstern, the wife of Oskar Morgenstern, a famous Austrian economist who had been chased out of Austria in 1938 and had come straight to Princeton, where he and Neumann published the *Theory of Games and Economic Behavior* in 1944. (The 2005 economic Nobel Prize was awarded in this field.) She was a fascinating redhead, half her husband's age. My mother and I remained in touch with them even after we had moved back to Zurich. Morgenstern was a close friend of Friedrich A. Lutz.

After my mother married Hermann Weyl, she lived in Princeton and in Zurich, reason enough to combine my visits to New York with a trip to Princeton. Weyl was twenty-eight years old when he became a full professor at the Swiss Federal Institute of Technology (ETH) in Zurich, the youngest professor ever chosen in ETH's history, and he lived there about as long as he did in Princeton (1933–50), where he arrived via Goettingen. The decision to give up the chair previously held by his teacher David Hilbert and move to the Institute of Advanced Study was prompted by the fact that Helene Weyl, his first wife and a close friend of Arnold Zweig, came from a Jewish family.

Weyl was a typical product of the German genius cult. He thought in all seriousness that every scientist over the age of thirty should be shot, because nothing much could be expected from him or her after that. Weyl considered his work about compact groups in terms of matrix representations his most important contribution to mathematics.

I learned the news that my mother would remarry during my tour through the United States organized by Brown Brothers Harriman. At first, the news shocked me somewhat. But by the time of the wedding at the end of December 1949, I had recovered enough to deliver the toast. After the war, speeches often began with the flourish, "Unprepared as I am . . . ," which gave me the opportunity to say, "Unprepared as I am to speak at my mother's wedding . . ."

After 1950, when Weyl again lived in Zurich, he disliked paying church taxes. He wasn't used to doing so in the States. So he decided to quit the church, saying, "It is out of the question that I pay even one cent in church taxes."

This decision gave him a great deal of trouble, as leaving the church was close to treason, especially in the cold war atmosphere of the fifties. All the more surprising, therefore, that this special friend of elegant solutions — late in life a much celebrated man — should give such great importance to his appointment to the papal academy. Opposition to church and religion had become a habit, but he considered the invitation near the end of his life by Pope Pius XII to a private audience the highest of honors. We all had to admire the documents and pictures he brought back. My mother accompanied him to Rome and was astonished when the pope asked her about her sculptures.

The ETH honored the erudite man with a festive party for his seventieth birthday; the mathematician Beno Eckmann was master of ceremonies. But only a month later, Weyl died quite suddenly. The elaborate birthday festivities of his hometown Elmshorn (twenty-five miles west of Hamburg) must have exhausted him and provoked his sudden death. Days later, back in Zurich, he collapsed at the front door on his way back from the mailbox. For a long time, his urn was placed in a corner of the Sihlfeld Cemetery in Zurich. After my mother's death, the urn was transferred to Princeton at the request of his son Michael Weyl. But the Hermann Weyl room at the ETH remains in Zurich, housing the bronze bust that my mother had sculpted of the mathematician.

13

Bank and Family

One-third for each son

At the bank in Zurich, I felt like an outsider for a long time. My cousins Nicky and Peter Baer were the sons of the managing owners. My mother, on the other hand, as a limited partner, merely had a share, thanks to the grace of my uncles. For all their benevolence, I fully realized that I was not a son. They could have tossed me out at any time, just as after my father's death they could have thrown out his whole family. The world of private banking has enough examples of that, even in my immediate surroundings. When Theophil Speiser died in 1940 — posthumously he would become my sister Ruth Speiser's father-in-law — the capital participation in his bank was paid out at par and the family was excluded from the Speiser, Gutzwiler & Cie bank. No goodwill was paid, according to the custom of the times and the uncertainties of the war.

Among my uncles, I was a step closer to Werner than to Walter. He took a greater interest in me and always appraised my girlfriends. His marked affinity to the female sex did not permit any doubt about his competence. Of course, I brought Ilse around to meet him when we wanted to become engaged.

A prominent partner in the bank was Dr. Hans Mayenfisch. In

1914, my grandfather had brought the trained lawyer — he had a prominent saber cut on his right cheek and prepared the annual meeting of his dueling fraternity, Tigurinia, every year with great care — into the firm. Mayenfisch was born in 1882 and grew up in Zurich. He did his compulsory military service in the dragoons as a first lieutenant. After completing his studies in Zurich and Leipzig, he did an internship at the Swiss Bank Corporation (SBC) in London. After his stay in London, he deepened his knowledge of banking at Redmond & Co. in New York, a step that, at the time, was quite unusual for a Swiss.

It was Hermann Kurz, director-general of the Credit Suisse from 1905 to 1920, who brought him to my grandfather's attention. Jean Jacques Kurz, his son who died in 1990, was director general of the Credit Suisse from 1959 to 1965. His grandson, Jean-François Kurz, also a banker, is a friend and a great supporter of Swiss soccer, and was president of the National Soccer League.

Why was my grandfather looking for a partner? He wanted to turn management of the business over to a younger man, and my uncles weren't ready yet. Walter was twelve years younger and Werner seventeen years younger than Mayenfisch. When Mayenfisch began working in July 1913, Walter had not yet started his apprenticeship. He only began in the autumn of 1913. As of January 1, 1914, Mayenfisch became an unlimited partner, and a fruitful relationship developed on both sides. Mayenfisch learned the business from my grandfather, and thanks to Mayenfisch, the bank became creditworthy.

Because of his familial connections, my grandfather's new partner was also a vice president of the board of directors of the Rueti machine factory as well as the Rueti Silk Spinning Company. (When the machine factory went to Sulzer in 1963, we had to fight the raider Hans Bechtler, who had partnered with Credit Suisse, to make sure that Mayenfisch's widow was compensated on equal terms as other shareholders.) The capital Mayenfisch brought to our bank was several times more than our own contribution. That did not prevent him, however, from accepting only a 10 percent stake. He didn't draw a salary, any more than my grandfather or my uncles did. When, in 1947, he decided to withdraw from business, Walter and Werner had to think about evaluating his share in the building at Bahnhofstrasse 36 and the taxable consequences. He said he didn't much care and gave his share as a present to the Baer family.

My uncles, who tended to culinary frugality, were amused by the unfettered joy their partner took in life. Whenever he planned a trip, the choice of restaurants loomed large. During the Second World War, he knew several country inns that didn't demand ration stamps. These eateries liked to serve "spaghetti with" as a specialty of the house ("with" meant that a choice slab of beef was hidden underneath the noodles).

The First World War had limited the radius of the dragoon officer's travels, since he had to spend several hundred days in the Jura on the French-German border. Only after 1918 could he resume his foreign travels, cultivate business acquaintances, and develop contacts. His great skill lay in human relations; the actual business of the bank interested him much less.

It was hardly customary that someone from Zurich society, a university graduate, a member of a dueling fraternity, a cavalry officer, and a hunter — in short a pure cultural product of the establishment — should spend almost forty-five years as our trusted partner. Walter recalled all that in his funeral oration: "All members of the Baer family had in Hans Mayenfisch a truly sincere friend, who never left us in the lurch and, despite the most varied challenges, always remained true. I am thinking here especially about the fateful thirties of National Socialism and frontism." And my uncle mentioned something else in his memorial address: " . . . his love of country, nature, sport, art and artists, which he managed to transfer to us."

To keep all three branches of the family — Walter and his chil-

dren, Werner and his offspring, and my mother for my father's prog-
eny — as equal stakeholders in thè bank was Werner's decision. His
decision would prove immensely important for the future. It was also
a very generous decision, and I do not think that he had thought
about it for any length of time or discussed the details beforehand,
although he was critical by nature and tended to examine his decisions with care, often deciding only after he had looked at several
other options. He simply dictated it one afternoon. I was his secretary at the time and had to write down his "edict" in my homespun
shorthand. I don't know if Werner had discussed the matter with
Walter beforehand. Yet, the two men were together from morning to
evening. Their offices were next to each other, and since their doors
were always ajar, they heard everything the other had to say. Plus,
every day after lunch they walked into town together from their
houses on the Zurichberg overlooking the beautiful lake.

My own experience teaches that fundamental decisions are almost always made in passing and almost never at meetings. Fritz
Leutwiler floated the Swiss franc by himself, and Paul Volcker made
fundamental decisions in his pajamas. The American Bankers Association rang him out of bed at three in the morning, after a bank
had become illiquid, and he decided on the spot.

My uncles' decision that all offspring would become partners
cannot be valued highly enough for the future of the bank. It meant
that the money stayed together and thus laid the foundation for the
bank's growth. Nothing encumbers a company more than the obligation to pay off family members. Even Goldman Sachs had to fight
that battle. The Baers, on the other hand, stayed together, and that
was the whole secret of our success.

Werner and the family lawyer, Dr. Michael Meyer, the son of
the physicist and family friend Edgar Meyer, drew up the Baer family's contract for themselves and their heirs in order to satisfy the
legal requirements and the management of the bank. It was dated
October 5, 1958.

Every branch of the family held 133.33 out of 400 shares. Before consummating a marriage, every member had to sign a prenuptial agreement specifying separation of property and an inheritance contract in which the relative by marriage renounced their hereditary rights in favor of a pension.

After Mayenfisch's death in 1957, the Julius Baer & Co. general partnership was changed into a limited partnership, with Olga Mayenfisch as the only limited partner. She was given an 8 percent share in profit and loss but in exchange only held her limited partnership and had no share in the reserves of the business assets. The capital contribution paid 4 percent interest.

The tax office and the Social Security Administration were responsible for forcing the partners to draw a salary after they had been accustomed to living off earnings. The administration argued that part of the earnings were salary and therefore were subject to social security payments. When I started in 1950, my uncles deliberately divided my income into a salary of perhaps SFr 10,000 a year (roughly $2,500), which was subject to social security deductions and a share of the company's earnings.

Thursday's partner lunches became an ironclad habit of the house. We had launched the tradition after the acquisition of the house at Bahnhofstrasse 38. Until he died on October 23, 1970, Walter was the soul of the round table, with his infinite experience, cleverness, and skepticism but also with his humor and his talent for comic verse — and that in several languages. He transferred his great sense of family beyond his immediate next of kin to the family at large.

The close relationships my cousins and I developed with our uncles surely did the business no harm. In practice, the lunches were an informal reporting system, and they were always harmonious. We never fought. Peter often had a different opinion when Nicky and I agreed, but he wasn't obstinate, simply saying with charm and humor, "Why don't you do what you want to do."

Genetically and emotionally, Peter had inherited his parents' love of the arts. One result was that he could imagine unusual colors and shapes in decoration and ornaments. He didn't care what others said about him or the bank. In addition to artists, he cultivated a wide circle of acquaintances from the robust world of oarsmen and rescue pilots. He often flew his twin-engine Cessna for the Swiss Rescue Squad, of which he would become chairman in 1980. He was more at ease in the company of mountain guides than in the bank.

My cousins and I worked very hard in the business. In addition to Peter's other hobbies, he was an impassioned fisherman, but he only took leave of the banking sector he had inherited from his father — trading securities and other financial instruments — when the salmon began to run in Norway.

Nicky, whose passion for riding outlasted his service in the cavalry, did not take any seasonal absences. At night he cherished the club life. Friendly at a distance, but hard to approach, he was also very proper, and he represented authority and respect. The perfect CEO and chairman. I have always admired him for never re-examining a decision once it was made, while I, given my anxious personality, suffered the agonies of the damned if at first things did not develop in the desired fashion and tended to intervene at once. Nicky's self-imposed distance did not always protect him from his emotions. Thus he gave up the very work-intensive but honorary position as president of the stock exchange after a fit of rage. Ten years later he again agreed to take up the office.

Wistfully, I think back to how our uncles cultivated a closer relationship with us than we did with the next generation and that our predecessors had better luck integrating their successors. On the other hand, our lives were under permanent observation. A new car was never left uncommented upon: it was either too large, too bright, or too ostentatious. Naturally, Walter and Werner visited, individually, of course, our house while it was under construction. Werner grabbed the plans and examined in which direction, according to the architect's conceptions, the doors would open. Doors and the way they opened were his specialty. On an upper floor he made a few corrections in the blueprints.

Our predecessors, among whom I most definitely must count Hans Mayenfisch, treated us with great kindness. We were friends with Mayenfisch even though he was seventy years old at the time and we were barely twenty. My wife and I were often his guests without any obligation on his part to invite us.

The first and last outside partner after Hans Mayenfisch was Ernst Bieri. I thought we needed intellectual, not material, reinforcement. It wasn't easy to get the family to listen. In general, families don't like outsiders. In their eyes they undermine the pride of domestic tradition, and the relationship can easily become emotional. Bieri's appointment was almost shipwrecked, because he didn't offer his condolences to the sons of Walter who had died on October 23, 1970.

The family gatherings served to hold the larger family intact. In addition to the Buergenstock, we enjoyed meeting in St. Moritz (not at the Suvretta House but at the Kulm, where my brother was president of the board of directors), in Fextal (Engadin), on Mont Pelerin, or at the Park Hotel Vitznau, a splendid hotel of the old order at Lake Lucerne, which provides the catering to the Speisers' weekend home even today. Grandfather Speiser had built his vacation house next door, with a gate that opened directly into the hotel garden.

The days spent in these relaxing environments combined business with a sense of togetherness that marked peaceful family feasts. The children enjoyed playing together, and the adults did not like to spend time on serious subjects outside the daily agenda. When we held our family day in 1982 on the Buergenstock near Lucerne, the news that Roberto Calvi had been found underneath Blackfriars Bridge did not disturb our high spirits. Perhaps we touched upon the prickly subject briefly over cocktails. The evening program was light too.

The Savoy Club and the other circles where the business world in Zurich loved to spend its evenings interested me a lot less than the city's musical and cultural life. Early in our marriage, I had agreed with my wife that, whenever possible, evenings would belong to us. If I had to cultivate business friendships, perhaps with a correspondent banker, Ilse would share those duties with me. Often we had a drink at home and dinner elsewhere. I won't deny that I determined our weekly evening programs. But all in all, I think that the evenings we spent together stabilized our marriage. Until Ilse died on August 7, 2002, we lived together in harmony for forty-eight years.

14

CORPORATE GOVERNANCE AND THE WORKING DAY (1950–95)

The day has twenty-four hours . . .

"A real gentleman does not appear at the office before eleven o'clock and cannot be reached after four o'clock," Eric Warburg once preached. Our slogan at the bank was that "the day has twenty-four hours and then there is still the night." Many people apparently took offense at this, but I believe it served the bank well. Presence alone, of course, is not enough. The right spirit is essential. People must like to work and do so with enthusiasm. Obviously, some don't think it's much fun to commit head and heart and spend long hours in the office. The simplest way to counter such attitudes is by example. How did I make sure that someone didn't leave his desk at 6 p.m.? By making him believe that I could still telephone him.

I freely admit that my personal identification with the bank was stronger than that of the staff. I never took the trouble to differentiate between work and leisure. It was simply my life.

My wife always insisted that we have breakfast together — at seven in the morning. If she and I had nothing going on at night, I was home by seven in the evening. If we went to a concert, we often dined afterwards with the soloist or conductor and didn't get to bed until 1 a.m. As soon as one finds such a rhythm troublesome, one should stay home. No study about corporate cultural governance refers to this fact: one simply has to enjoy life or stay home.

Ilse's and my marriage motto was "for better or worse, but never for lunch." I left the house at 7:30 a.m. and drove down the Zurichberg to the office; in the summer I left at 7:15. At night around 10 p.m., after the TV news, I often spent a couple of hours at my desk taking care of the next day's mail. The day belonged exclusively to business. If the operator announced a call from my wife, I knew that something dramatic must have happened. Early in our marriage, Ilse once decided to pick me up at the bank and was startled to hear my rumbling voice all the way down at the reception desk. "Is that my husband?" she asked, and never entered the bank again. It by no means happened at home.

The strict rules of the game demanded that I be at work on Saturday, or at least Sunday. On Saturday mornings in Zurich, from ten to eleven, I used to see Helmuth Picard, my physician, who usually talked to me about the stock market more than my health. He obviously attached more importance to my psychological well-being than to my weight. Today, Dieter Wuersten, who cares more about my weight than about the stock market, holds this position.

Travel to any part of the world was routine. During the time our children were small, I traveled alone, and then later more often with my wife. The attention of the hosts and their social efforts increased significantly when Ilse and I traveled together. Traveling alone simply meant business. This is still true in the business world today.

We hardly knew leisure as it is defined today, not even on weekends, which is not to say that we had no private or family life. In my daughter's earliest childhood recollections, I was a man in a black-and-red-checkered flannel shirt with sunglasses on my nose sitting behind the wheel of a white American convertible. Otherwise, she had problems identifying me as her father.

Until the end of the sixties, the lunch hour was longer than it is today. In England, lunch could last three hours, usually accompanied by a grand cru wine, and it was never just one glass. Afterwards, people often showed up in their offices only to sign letters. These *déjeuners arrosés* (lunch with lots to drink) didn't just belong to the rituals of London. In Zurich too nobody would ever think of serving apple juice or drinking sparkling water.

Such meals served a serious purpose. Nobody took notes during lunch, so you could really find out what was going on in your business in London as well as in Zurich. My liver was the best witness of my devotion. Hepatitis led me to the doctor, who took some blood. The test results came back with the comment, "The patient is an alcoholic."

The doctor asked a concerned yet thoughtful question: "Are you an alcoholic?" My ingenuous confession was, "No, but I'll be happy to write down what I drink every day." It amounted to quite a bit: at lunch, an aperitif, white or red wine, and a brandy. In the evening, a martini, whiskey, and a beer. Over the course of the last thirty years, my consumption has substantially decreased.

Important dates in our annual agenda for over thirty years were the Christmas and New Year's holidays we spent at the Suvretta House hotel a mile or so outside St. Moritz. Our stay had tradition. My uncles had already lodged there in the past. The great thing at the hotel is not the outdated lobby with its large and dark sofas but the adjacent ski school for the children.

For me, the Suvretta House was a serious family hotel, which, however, did not prevent other guests from carrying out small escapades. One time, a Belgian manufacturer of toilet seats drove up with an attractive female chauffeur dressed in an elegant leather uniform. So far so good. But imagine my children's shock when they later found the two in the woods. Passing by in her Rolls Royce, the chauffeur would also hand out engraved cards with an invitation to call her at her home.

Rudolf Mueller was the hotel's director. He was definitely a man of the old school. In December 1984, as punishment for my high spirits behind the wheel, I landed on a rock while driving down from the snow-covered Julier Pass, almost seven thousand feet high. My wife did not think that was funny. Luckily, we were quickly saved from a tense situation when a car stopped and the driver asked if he could help. "Yes, if you'll take my wife," I said.

Back at the hotel, after midnight, Ilse ran into the director and told him of our misfortune. In black tie, Rudolf Mueller got into his car and drove out to rescue me. A hotel director who will go out at one in the morning wearing a thin tuxedo in order to help a guest stuck in the snow is tough to find.

In St. Moritz, we often met old friends, most often Hans and Walter Gerling, owners of the large Cologne-based insurance company, and later Karl Otto Poehl, then president of the German Bundesbank, who all stayed at the Suvretta House. We made new acquaintances, often through the children, who liked to escape from the contemplative family Christmas as quickly as possible and head for the ski school. Thanks to their knowledge of various languages, my children often worked as ski instructors themselves, frequently for some Hollywood great, who, to my great amusement, did not overwhelm them. One of these ski-pupil VIPs once asked my son where he could eat. Raymond's answer: "Only on the hotel terrace. If you like I'll reserve *us* a table."

My daughter, Monique, taught the Armour family at the hotel ski school. After graduating from high school, she knocked at the Armours' door in order to work on their ranch as part of her agriculture studies.

One time, my friend with the hotel director prompted me to give him some business advice. Given the demands for spacious living quarters made by our American friends, for whom one or several suites were not enough, I asked him why didn't he rebuild. Rudolf Mueller's reply was, "Really rich people don't come twice."

The reason that local police, reinforced by elite guards, focused their attention on the Suvretta House had nothing to do with the Armours or us, but with the Shah of Iran, who had bought the Suvretta's guesthouse. I can't say anything negative about Reza Pahlavi. On the contrary, he was extremely civilized. He did not demand special treatment in the swimming pool or in the hotel itself, and he swam with my children at five or six in the evening and with the rest of us in the early afternoon. When he or Farah Diba wanted to go skiing on the Corvatsch, they entered the cable car cabin along with everybody else.

In my memory, the only time the Shah was at all conspicuous was when his bodyguard hurried down from the villa to the pool carrying his suit. Indeed, his bodyguards were the only things conspicuous about him. During afternoon tea in the lobby, these gorillas, most of them resembling the French gangster actor Lino Ventura, down to the lead in their pockets, squeezed into the tables of other guests just to be sure they were close to him. Once in a while, we met former employees of the bank who decided to join the local police with the idea of guarding the Shah in order to make some extra money.

While my daughter remembers the Suvretta House as her "childhood terror" and was always relieved to have survived Christmas "in that horrible box," I remember the shocking realization that the host of a cocktail reception, a British manufacturer of staplers, was more interested in our children, whom he hoped to couple with his own, than he was in us. The manufacturer and his wife were really on the hunt. I found such calculating behavior insulting.

The Aga Khan, the current one at the time, owned the house next to the Suvretta, and he too was a seasonal friend. After we abandoned our Mediterranean sailing trips in 1976, his Hotel Cala di Volpe along Sardinia's Costa Smeralda became our summer destination. Our vacations there lasted for two weeks, and we saw many of the same faces we had seen in St. Moritz. They had basically exchanged their skis for yachts. Undoubtedly, the largest ship belonged to the Guinness family. I was fascinated watching sailors telephone the yacht from the docks with walkie-talkies, and this was long before the cell phone age that today sees mothers everywhere call their children in playgrounds. Soon after the call, a dinghy left the ship and tied up at the dock to bring the ladies and gentlemen, who had dined at the hotel, back to the yacht. In the afternoon, the children in the party played tennis accompanied by bodyguards, and once, in the dining room, I watched as a gun fell out of the handbag of an elegant lady at the next table. It was the time of the Red Brigades, when there was a lot of kidnapping in Italy and people generally felt insecure.

We owed our taste for sailing through the Aegean to our friend Heinz Lessing and his Alsen cement works. Lessing was the de-Nazified CEO and Alsen was later bought up by the Swiss Holcim. Later we chartered our own boat and, at times, followed a steamer of the Renaissance Music Cruises where Isaac Stern often played.

On one such trip we attended a nighttime banquet in an enchanting Greek village square. The stewards had put the ship's silver on the tables, decorated them with candelabras, and brought food and wine from the boat. A fabulous atmosphere. After the meal, we strolled to the amphitheater for a concert. It was still so warm at midnight that Isaac's sweat dropped onto his violin. Isaac liked to accept engagements on cruise ships. For him and for other artists who came aboard with their families, such perks were financially attractive. On this trip we unexpectedly met Nahum Goldman — he was a friend of Walter's. Goldman was the predecessor of Edgar Bronfman as president of the World Jewish Congress and a prominent Jewish personality.

My cultural ambition led me to visit the autonomous monks' republic on Mount Athos, a Greek peninsula that can be entered only by males. Entry was possible, provided one got a visa from the Greek embassy in one's country. I arranged with the captain of our chartered sailboat to accompany me and to act as interpreter. But when the rotund man saw the steep path up the mountain, he rebelled. He wouldn't think of climbing up that far. So I went up by myself. I didn't want to give up after I had gone to all the trouble of obtaining a visa. It turned out to be an experience that I wouldn't care to repeat. The "republic" had no restaurants. I would have had to knock on the door of one of the twenty large monasteries but decided not to, because I was certain that nobody spoke a living language besides Greek. What seemed like one of the most beautiful places on earth from a distance showed another side close up. The romantic little windows seen from below turned out to belong to the toilets.

For a long time, I traveled to the European Forum in Alpbach in August, and except for two times, I chose to not visit the Salzburg Festival. It isn't easy to drive from the Tyrolean alpine village of Alpbach to Salzburg, given the overcrowded roads. Moreover, Salzburg had always been a Karajan festival and for my taste had never lost a light Nazi ambiance. My son, child of another generation, is a lot less prejudiced. My wife and I tried Salzburg again when Georg Solti took over as musical director. But he was not happy either because he didn't meet with much success there.

Nevertheless, my friendship with Christoph von Dohnanyi, the eminent German conductor, goes back to a meeting in Salzburg, where I also met Sir Emmanuel Kaye, the British industrialist. He made his fortune manufacturing forklifts, but his passion was the world of music. My wife and I owe him thanks for the invitation to the Trooping the Colour on the queen's birthday, a custom dating back to the seventeenth century, which takes place each June on Horse Guards Parade, Whitehall, in front of thousands of spectators.

The late summer annual meeting of the World Bank was a permanent part of our itinerary. It takes place in Washington, D.C., and then every three years somewhere else, usually in Asia, South

America, Africa, or Europe. In Rio de Janeiro, the organizers had put my wife and me in a brothel — I had asked for a spacious room with air conditioning. Generally we added a week in order to see something of the country. After the World Bank conference in Manila, I collected a few impressions about the Philippines; and after the Nairobi conference, we went on a wonderful safari that took us across the border to Tanzania. To our great amusement, the customs officials strip-searched Othmar Emminger, the president of the German Bundesbank.

Ilse and I augmented the joint autumn meeting of the World Bank and International Monetary Fund in Washington with several private days in Mexico or the Caribbean. That became our yearly fall vacation.

We took music festivals very seriously. A week before the international Lucerne musical festival (August 15 to September 15), I began to worry about finding a parking space. Of course, it would never have occurred to me to take the train. The Buehrle family, especially Hortense Anda-Buehrle, were great sponsors and supporters of the festival. One of my Lucerne acquaintances was the chocolate manufacturer and art collector Peter Ludwig. And in Lucerne I met Lorin Maazel, music director of the New York Philharmonic, for the first time.

Few people recall that Montreux, famed today for its jazz festival, was originally renowned for classical concerts that drew large crowds. I can't remember what Isaac Stern played in 1960 with the Orchestre National de Paris with Georg Solti conducting, but I do remember that it was the evening before my birthday. After the concert, we all went to the Montreux Palace hotel — Georg Solti and his wife, Hedi Gitermann (they were divorced in 1964), Isaac Stern, Ilse, and I all gathered in Solti's sparsely furnished room. Nobody thought about taking a suite back then. The champagne flowed, and Hedi danced around the room in her undergarments; Solti, Ilse, and I sat on the bed. On the stroke of midnight, Isaac grabbed his violin and began playing "Happy Birthday." He had not finished his musical congratulations when a huge flowerpot crashed down on the balcony, accompanied by an outraged "Shut up!" — an anonymous morning greeting from a neighbor who needed his sleep.

Encouraged by Isaac, we traveled for many years to Evian, an enchanting little town on the French side of Lake Geneva. The late cellist Mstislav Rostropovich had inspired Antoine Riboud, the founder of the French Danone food group, to launch a classical music festival, and with his demanding extravagance, Riboud had helped the town build a magnificent concert hall made of Canadian oak. In the style of a Russian dacha no less! All that to keep Rostropovich happy. On our earlier visits, we had taken the bus, but with the concert hall built so near the hotel, the bus was no longer needed. The evenings ended with relaxed dinners that brought artists and public together. For me it was the most amicable festival and within easy driving distance from Zurich.

In Evian, insiders recognized each other through a special dress code that Riboud introduced. A draped sweater over one's jacket, a small concession to the advancing time of the year, indicated the connoisseurs. While Riboud, close friends with Rostropovich, always met the cellist's excessive demands, which left notable furrows in Danone's bookkeeping, his son Frank broke off the relationship with the demanding artist. Another thing I learned in Evian is that such festivals are only a modest business for the hotel industry. Music guests remain for only a short time, and in general it doesn't make sense to push out long-term customers. But clearly Evian doesn't depend on visitors as much as it does on mineral water. Commercial use of the water is tied to the obligation of operating the grand hotels.

Next to the joint meeting of the World Bank and International Monetary Fund in Washington, D.C., the two other highlights of the year were the Overseas Bankers Dinner and, very exclusively, the Lord Mayor's Dinner, both in London. I was invited in my capacity as head of a foreign bank domiciled in London. White tie and tails are obligatory for the Lord Mayor's Dinner at Guildhall, where the governor of the Bank of England is the main speaker. It's really not worthwhile owning a cutaway, which is seldom needed. So I rented the same cutaway I wore at the wedding of my cousin Vera Chown from Moss Bros in London. Given my somewhat unusual figure, it took two or three fittings. The charm of renting a cutaway from Moss Bros doesn't lie in saving money. Rather, in the front lines of a large wedding, it is an opportunity for meeting guests informally at the rental establishment. These are typical insider rituals. In Glyndebourne, for example, men change into their tuxedos in the toilet. After all, they're coming directly from the city.

I entered my first Glyndebourne party with butlers and roast beef during the intermission of the opera. The Reuters news agency had invited me to give several lectures in Zurich during the sixties and repaid me with an invitation to the opera. I like this form of societal intercourse a great deal. When Julius Baer International was still subject to foreign exchange restrictions, we became supporters of the Glyndebourne opera festival instead of paying dividends and friends of the Christie founding family.

The festival came about when John Christie, a great Wagnerian, decided to perform Wagner operas in his country house at Glyndebourne. At first he used an organ in his library for the instrumentation. The room, therefore, is called the organ room today. He met the soprano Audrey Mildmay there, whom he married several years later. The inspiration for the festival came from a meeting with Fritz Busch, one of the great conductors of the twentieth century, and Carl Ebert, the renowned German opera director. They had emigrated from Germany to England in 1935 and were looking for a stage.

My few board of directors' mandates carried travel obligations of their own. Thus I flew with other board members of Bank Leumi to Israel. The trip to Antwerp with the board of the Johnson & Johnson affiliate Janssen was equally instructive. On the side, I learned a good deal about the parent company Johnson & Johnson, founded by the inventive Colonel Johnson. The world owes him the Band-Aid. And why are they brown and not white? Because blacks might find white Band-Aids racially discriminating, we were told. We also owe the sensitive colonel the bone screw and other metal devices to patch up broken bones.

15

Ilse Baer-Kaelin (1952–2002)

The room waiter in bed

In 1950, when good friends of our bank and of our family used funds blocked in France to buy a house on the Côte d'Azur, my uncles issued this pronouncement: "You don't buy a house in the South of France; it makes a bad impression." De Gaulle's Prime Minister Georges Pompidou had similarly harsh words for a young Jacques Chirac, who had bought a château in Correze: "On n'a pas de château quand on fait de la politique." (If you're in politics, you don't have a castle.)

But it wasn't forbidden to travel to the Côte d'Azur. We always found our way to the French Mediterranean coast, sometimes to bring Isaac Stern to a concert and once because Bobby Greiff wanted to show us how to live a real life of luxury. It was much too strenuous for my wife and me. We couldn't take the nightlife.

Nevertheless, the charm of the landscape left traces, especially since my sister Marianne and her late husband, Jørgen Olsen, had an apartment in Antibes. They often sailed out to sea from there, in *Bjørnoya*, a lovely 42-foot-long sailing yacht made of wood. When we traveled to Marrakech in 1982 and stopped at the La Mamounia Hotel, my wife carried an envelope in her bag addressed to an anonymous post office box. I was not allowed to know what it was about. Embossed with Moroccan stamps, it finally ended up at the *Neue Zuercher Zeitung,* where she had seen an ad. Somehow I found out: a vacation house. I was always against the idea, knowing that buying one often foreshortens a marriage. The husband is in the office and the wife is bored in the mountains until the ski instructor rescues her from loneliness.

But why not? Ilse and I had traveled enough, and after shopping for ten years for a vacation home, Ilse had fallen in love with the house hidden behind the anonymous address: a charming place with a living room, two bedrooms, and a studio. The location on a ridge increased its charm. It had views of the Bay of St. Tropez on one side and of the Gulf of Toulon on the other. I was in agreement right away.

In furnishing the house, Ilse was careful to respect the genius loci and made sure that the gardens were laid out according to the design of a Provençal peasant garden. As far as I was concerned, it was her house, and she could do as she pleased. If we learned that the wind had knocked a tile off the roof or that a pack of boars had plowed through the garden, she got into the car with Isabel, our housekeeper, and drove down to the Mediterranean to make sure repairs were carried out properly.

Ilse was mobile and fearless, which made her life with me much easier. She had grown up bilingually (German and French) in Bienne and on top of that spoke English, Italian, and Spanish fluently. She had lived in London at the beginning of the war. Also, on occasion, she had no trouble flying alone to Mexico — we always planned for her to travel ahead in order to divide the risks. On one trip, when she arrived at the hotel late at night, she found that her suitcase was empty. It wasn't her suitcase. She grabbed a cab and roared back to the airport at midnight. By the time she got there, the suitcase was there as well. Someone else had taken her suitcase and brought it back.

The next morning, she found the room waiter in bed with her. Downstairs at the reception desk, no one took her seriously. Finally, she had a redeeming idea. She called Peter von Muralt in our office and declared, "Save me, there's a man in my bed."

No doubt a certain sense of humor helped Ilse through life. She only lost it once when an American she had never met before came up to her at the Hotel Danieli in Venice and said, "You must come from Iowa."

"I'm afraid I don't," she replied.

"You must, you look so corn-fed."

Not true — she really didn't look that well-nourished — and surely the comment was well-meant. But my wife could not do much with that kind of midwestern humor.

She stayed with me during my sabbatical at Harvard without complaint in a noisy two-room apartment. I found it more appropriate to use the assigned flat rather than live in a hotel.

Ilse also cheerfully accepted spending a night in a brothel in New York, courtesy of Swissair, whose representative said insolently afterwards, "Nobody forced you to stay there." And this in addition to the several days in the brothel in Brazil during the World Bank meeting.

Our last journey in 1993 led us to Romania. My siblings and I had decided to commemorate the hundredth birthday of our father with a gift. George Soros, a friend of our family and deeply committed to humanitarian causes in Eastern Europe, suggested the money be given to Dr. Sandu Bologa, the chief of a cancer clinic in Cluj, Romania. His first request was that it not be an award of money, because it would be taken away from him, but he urgently needed an up-to-date anesthetic apparatus so that he would no longer have to roll oxygen bottles around the hospital. We ordered the equipment from Germany, with local craftsmen commissioned to hook up the connecting cables made in Romania. For the inauguration of the project, my wife and I, along with my sister Ruth Speiser and my brother-in-law Professor Dr. David Speiser, were guests of the Romanian government for three days in Cluj, where we saw the sensational donor's plaque. We had asked that our name not be used on it, but only to say, "From friends in Switzerland." Instead, we discovered the following chiseled in stone: "A gift of the Swiss people and the Bank Julius Baer." Too beautiful to resist.

We ate marvelously well in Cluj. The doctors' wives had spent several days cooking the best recipes they had, and the mousse au chocolat was surely as good as in Zurich's Kronenhalle. The festivities lasted for three days. At the end, we attended a farewell lunch in Bucharest's famous Velvet restaurant.

Our lodgings were memorably modest, even as guests of the government. The mattresses in the overheated Hotel Viktoria were on the floor. Ilse didn't mind, or at least she didn't say anything. Nor had she declined to come along knowing full well that a trip to Romania would not be a luxury cruise and that afterwards we would have to fly directly to New York, where my cousin Nicky Baer and our son were being given farewell parties. Nicky was retiring, and Raymond was returning to Zurich. Ilse never said, "I'd rather stay home." Her sense of duty was only exceeded by her thirst for knowledge.

What helped keep us together was our shared taste. We designed and furnished our house together. We preferred the same colors, and both of us could not tolerate anything that seemed overly ornate. In that respect, we were avid students of the gallery owner Frank Lloyd, who thought that "a picture doesn't decorate a wall, a picture is the wall." Large, but alone.

I can recount many good examples of our identical taste. One in particular stands out. We had agreed to meet at the vernissage of the Vista Nova Gallery in Zurich; our tradition dictated that we buy something at an opening of an artist we knew. I came directly from the office into the jammed gallery, looked briefly at the pictures, was amply air-kissed by the gallery owner, took a deep breath and, pointing to a picture, told Helga Norych, "I'd like to buy that."

"I'm terribly sorry," she said, "but that picture has already been sold."

Ten minutes later I found my wife in the mob and she was beaming. "Hey, I bought a picture." Naturally it was the same one I had wanted to buy.

The painter Hermann Sigg, together with Thomas Wagner, at that time the mayor of Zurich, once determined that we had no paintings with a blue background. Yellow, maroon, and green were as much Ilse's favorite colors as mine. A green automobile would always get my wife's approval, even though it was always too expensive, too large, and too powerful. I chose my last convertible (green, of course) with care and with the determination not to talk about the new purchase at home. In the end, however, the joy of taking her on the new car's maiden voyage predominated. She didn't think it was much fun. She had never liked convertibles. The wind ruined her hairdo.

When met with the question, Do you love your wife? "Compared to whom?" is my answer to this. What can I say? It isn't only a jest. For me, my parents were people I respected, not love objects. It could well be that I transferred this attitude to my own generation. I cannot remember any *coup de foudre* or lightning bolt. We had been engaged for three or four years before our wedding. My car parked outside the home of my future wife on Kreuzplatz was well known to the police. They called my mother one day to ask about scratch marks on another car. I denied knowing anything, saying that I was never on Kreuzplatz. The outraged officer said, "What, you weren't there? You're there every night."

Ilse's mother was not pleased when she learned of her daughter's decision to marry me. Helen Kaelin-Tschantré, whose recipes remain in our kitchen library, thought that one doesn't marry a banker. It was not the thing to do. She would have accepted a lawyer or an engineer with the Swiss railroads — that was something solid. A doctor like her beau Gion Condrau was also okay. He would become a member of the Swiss parliament. In any event, someone with a real profession. But a banker? That's when I learned the deeper meaning of the nasty family joke that one should only marry orphans. No parent can object.

After our daughter was born, Ilse broke her shin skiing and suffered with the fracture for two years. During this time, her mother moved into our apartment with us. Finally, we consulted a famed surgeon in New York. Like a demigod, the specialist, followed by a large retinue, swept into the room and barked at Ilse, "Take off your sweater!"

"Yes, but my leg is broken."

At last the good doctor determined that the leg had not healed properly — and he even knew what to do. But his "take off your sweater" became a family standby in the humor department.

Ilse stabilized and strengthened me. I believe that I was in better form taking my wife on a business trip than traveling alone. Alone I could get stuck in the bar. And, as I've said before, business partners were more hospitable when you were in the company of your wife. Why should a partner at Brown Brothers Harriman invite me to dinner when I flew alone to New York? But when they heard that Ilse was coming along, they invited us both. A business trip with your (marriage) partner is worth more in every respect because it is much more stable. We had a rule in the bank that wives were allowed to travel at the house's expense once a year — that's what it said in our expense account rules. It was money well spent. Ilse contributed greatly to a pleasant atmosphere when we accompanied the Tonhalle Orchestra on its tour of China, at our own expense. I was the head of the delegation.

Unlike myself, she had no inhibitions about talking to strangers. By the time I arrived in a resort hotel, Ilse usually knew most of the people there. She was very open and was an exemplary friend to mankind.

It would be wrong to claim that she had been completely happy at my side. In the early years of our marriage, she had to adapt to the family. For us Baers it was simple: everybody who married one of us had to adapt to our behavior. But that's hard for the other side. And in her later years, she stood very much in the background. Ilse wasn't a dominant personality. On the other hand, she didn't find it amusing that over time all the honors were bestowed on me and she was only behind the scenes. Still, she accepted all that uncomplainingly. Today, however, I think she should have done more for herself.

Ilse was directly responsible for one personal tribute. A volume of my speeches that she published for my sixtieth birthday in 1987 received first prize for production and design at the Salon du Livre in Geneva. Ernst Hiestand was the graphic artist.

She was indifferent to most material possessions. You couldn't reach her with expensive gifts. She rarely wore jewelry. But unlike my mother, who all her life never wasted a moment thinking about money, Ilse in her last years worried about just how everything would continue. Would the children have enough money? Would our daughter get married?

No one at home ever badgered me about how business had gone that day. Ilse never asked, and there were many things I could not have told her. When somebody in the office said "Give my best to your wife," I often had to reply "I can't do that." For reasons of discretion.

Ilse managed the household, took care of the education of our children, and for a long time she did all the cooking herself. To remedy that, we hired Isabel, but when she arrived, we discovered that she couldn't even cook an egg. She came from a large Portuguese family and had been a maid in a hotel in the Ticino.

My children claim that we ate frugally. And it's true that as far as meals were concerned, we lived a Spartan life. At least once a week we had roasted hash. And I was never asked what I wanted to eat that night.

Death redeemed Ilse in August 2002, ten years after her first stroke. I had just come back from Portugal, and her night table was covered with travel literature about Portugal. She had joined me in spirit.

A touching scene comforted me at her funeral. My grandchildren came up after the burial of the urn and wanted to help cover it. Any normal cemetery gardener would have sent them away, but the good man on the Fluntern gave them a shovel and a cart and said, "And now you can finish the job."

As an impassioned reader, Ilse is certainly glad that she is buried in the immediate neighborhood of Elias Canetti and James Joyce.

16

THE BANK JULIUS BAER: THE YEARS BEFORE GOING PUBLIC (1946–74)

Let him run. We all started out small.

In 1947, when I stood at my desk writing transaction slips in purple copy ink, Swiss banks employed a total of 18,500 people; today, Union Bank of Switzerland (UBS) alone has roughly 85,000 employees. Then, the total assets of all banks amounted to SFr 23.77 billion ($5.66 billion), and there were ninety private banks. Today, the number of bank employees in Switzerland has risen to 115,000, and the number of private banks has shrunk to seventeen. The 369 banks operating today generate balance sheet totals of SFr 2,227 billion ($1.7 trillion), a hundredfold increase. Why did the private banks evaporate? Certainly because the regulatory environment has become much more daunting. Bruno Gehrig, chairman of the Swiss Life Group, and in the nineties a member of the National Bank's governing board, with whom I often discussed bank affairs, worries that the Basel II Accord released in June 2004 — a revision of the 1988 capital accord agreement setting new minimum capital requirements — which he thinks was written to fit commercial banks, will, in effect, force a minimum bank size.

In 1945, Julius Baer had forty-five employees (including the partners), total assets of SFr 12 million ($2.86 million), and capital resources of SFr 5 million ($1.19 million) with which it made a profit of SFr 100,000 ($24,000). The bank was tiny even for the modest postwar circumstances. During the war, the number of employees fell to thirty-five, including the partners. Some twenty of them were subject to military service, and four were assigned to auxiliary service, as Werner wrote to my mother on May 10, 1944. In 1947, the bank employed one woman — the telephone operator. Even the correspondence office, where dictated letters were typed, was an exclusively male domain — a total of five. Among them, I remember most vividly Emil Staerkle and Walter's private secretary, Heinz Tonnemacher, an excellent stylist and letter writer who was the grandson of one of the Reinharts of Winterthur and a close friend of the von Schumacher family. I learned my "non-German" from him.

The foreign exchange trading made a substantial contribution to every bank's results. In the days before direct dialing, it depended on who was given the first open line, a decision made by the national telephone operator at Poste, Telephone, & Telegramme. The lucky bank knew the rates in, say, Warsaw or Paris earlier than the others, and the day's business depended on that advantage.

Long before the war, my then unmarried uncles, knowing the importance of that first open line, came up with the idea of flirting with the operator. Werner was given the job of taking her out — in the interest of the bank, of course. Given his fondness for the fair sex, he didn't consider himself a victim of higher family interests. Armed with a bouquet of flowers, he marched to meet her on the Paradeplatz. But when he got a glimpse of her, all his flirting desires disappeared. He turned around and left the young lady standing there. Understandably, she was furious, and for several weeks served us badly. Since then, another family slogan has been, "The uncle did not do his duty."

Early in my career, we still traded bank notes, and the first foreign exchange transaction I carried out on my own was one such trade. I bought about $5,000 one day, sold them on the next, and earned about SFr 35 (approximately $10).

That was in 1947, when the National Bank still controlled the dollar. On the open market, the dollar rate was about SFr 2.70. When the dollar became scarce in 1949, it was only a matter of time before the National Bank would have to lift controls. The market must have known the date, because shortly beforehand, the dollar rose to SFr 4.20. Everybody had stocked up on the U.S. currency as heavily as they could.

Insider trading was not a problem. We thought it was great when a National Bank director came by a couple of days before a change in interest rates to adjust his portfolio. We were all proud of the connections we had. According to Swiss law, even today, insider crimes are only committed in cases where advance knowledge of changes in corporate structure is used. Taking advantage of advanced knowledge must be related to a corporation. Classic insider crimes were the buying and selling in the days leading up to ABB's takeover of the U.S. Combustion Engineering Company in 1989, an acquisition over which the talented and very sympathetic Christian Norgren stumbled. For the chief of the Bank in Liechtenstein A.G., it was the end of a meteoric career. Hermann Josef Abs, former head of the Deutsche Bank, had personally recommended him to Liechtenstein's ruling prince. A number of our employees had jumped to the Liechtenstein bank after Norgren took over. The handsome man, married to a very pretty journalist, like him from Sweden, lived splendidly in the "princely lodging" just below the castle, and he loved giving large parties.

His colleagues burst into tears when they heard the story of his wrongdoing — he was loved that much and had been an example for all of them. They couldn't believe that he had thoughtlessly used the knowledge he had obtained as a member of the ABB board. But clearly what he did was seen as quite normal. He was not sentenced in Switzerland, and in the United States he got away with paying a fine. He was thus saved from the "Club Fed."

Indicative of our childish innocence were the wild fluctuations of Maggi shares before its merger with Nestle on December 5, 1947. Only insiders stood behind the flux in the stock, and all of them used their information to achieve a handsome profit. For a long time it was customary for board members to rush out after a meeting where they learned news that could affect stock prices and place orders with their brokers.

Our know-how in the foreign exchange business didn't begin to really pay off until the Bretton Woods Agreements came apart in 1971. In those wild years, we made handsome profits thanks to Willy Himmelsbach and his crew. The opulent earnings from foreign exchange trading allowed us to accumulate the needed capital for going public in 1975.

Himmelsbach, who died in 1986, came from the Rhine Valley and was absolutely convinced that all famous Swiss originated there. The world-famous exchange trader used to lecture in-house that only Rhine Valley people were competent and smart. So it was no surprise that one Rhine Valley employee succeeded another and that Rhine Valley people controlled our foreign exchange business.

Himmelsbach had worked with us since 1931, was made executive vice president in 1938, and was remembered by our older employees as a great despot. In any event, he never thought about hiding his emotions. He once threw me out of his office because I had dared to lay out what I had learned at NYU. With some regret I note that in the early and middle years of my professional life, everything was much more personal and that strong personalities were still around.

Among my earliest professional memories are extended trips to Germany — in the convertible, sitting next to my mother's chauffeur. He complained bitterly because I liked to drive in an open car even in winter and he froze.

Hotels were rare in the beginning of the fifties. In Bremen, for example, I spent the night with a landlady in whose kitchen I cooked a couple of fried eggs. The unassuming modesty of the post-war years remains a pleasant memory. Everything had been shot to bits, but I thought the climate then more sympathetic than it was during my last German business trip in 1992, that is, after reunification. I can only hope that the huge rooms with a sofa lost in the distance and the exaggerated need for representation among the large German banks was a temporary sign of reunification euphoria.

My tours through a young federal republic led me to houses linked in friendship to our own, such as Sal. Oppenheim in Cologne, Warburg Brinkmann Wirtz in Hamburg, or the Berliner Handelsgesellschaft in Frankfurt, where Hans Fuerstenberg, son of the legendary Carl Fuerstenberg, and at the time someone who seemed to me to be an old man, became a role model, as did his bank. The connection was established through the good offices of Hans-Wilhelm von Tuempling, one of three liable partners.

The Berliner Handelsgesellschaft wrote a large chapter of German industrial history through financing the electrical industry, especially AEG, and its strong interest in the mining industry. But it also made history in developing the Grunewald housing colony in Berlin and in financing the city's transportation network. The long-suffering Serbia loans, which Carl Fuerstenberg saved with ingenious financial engineering, are part of the history of finance. Overall, he was a man famous for creative stock issues. Siegmund Warburg continued that tradition after the Second World War with the invention of the Eurodollar bonds.

The Nuremberg laws forced Hans Fuerstenberg to give up his supervisory board seat in 1938, and he emigrated to Geneva. His board colleague, Dr. Otto Jeidels, no Aryan either, emigrated to the United States, where he became a vice president of the Bank of America in

San Francisco (which received me with great kindness during my coast-to-coast tour while I was at Brown Brothers Harriman).

A joke about Jeidels made the rounds. During a supervisory board meeting in which a credit gone wrong was discussed, Jeidels insisted on pointing to his warning against making the loan, a warning recorded in the minutes of an earlier meeting. Fuerstenberg's reply: "Look, Jeidels, even a broken watch shows the correct time twice a day."

Despite his Jewish identity, of which he was very much aware, Fuerstenberg returned to Germany soon after the war. The Berliner Handelsgesellschaft, a classic investment bank without a branch business, had a problem in that its headquarters on the Franzoesische Strasse in central Berlin was located in the Soviet zone. The bank first relocated to West Berlin but in 1952, in a realistic assessment of Berlin's "island" position, moved to Frankfurt.

At the time, the bank — which would later merge with the Frankfurter Bank to become the German BHF — was the largest in the federal republic. Inauguration of the new corporate headquarters was celebrated with appropriate aplomb. In the country's rebuilding phase in the fifties, every new building was greeted with festive receptions. Therefore, I traveled often to Frankfurt or Cologne — to Gerling, one of Germany's leading industrial insurers based in Cologne, for example — took note of the refound optimism among German banks, and always met remarkable people. BHF's board had stars like Dr. Rudolf Brinkmann of Warburg, Brinkmann Wirtz & Co., Heinrich von Thyssen-Bornemisza, and Dr. Johannes Zahn, a partner in Duesseldorf's private bank CG Trinkaus, which merged in the seventies with Burkhardt & Co. in Essen. I knew Kurt Forberg, Trinkaus' CEO and an art-loving man, who in the course of his life assembled a considerable collection of contemporary art. His second wife, Bim Forberg, was a small, very energetic business journalist. They had a lovely house on the Suvretta hill in St. Moritz. His son, an actor, lives in Vienna today and is a neighbor of my second cousin, Sandra Baer Heuer, Alfred Baer's daughter.

The Berliner Handelsgesellschaft, founded in 1856 and closely connected to the Fuerstenberg name, had structured itself as a commercial partnership limited by shares; the owners were personally liable. The founders had deliberately chosen a form of partnership whereby "the legal framework was thus designed to keep top management away from speculative enterprises." The authors of the centenary jubilee volume wrote this of the successful form of corporate governance before there was such a concept.

Carl Fuerstenberg became a legend in large part because of his sharp wit. Walking on the street once, he heard someone yell, "Stop the pickpocket." Fuerstenberg reacted with the comment, "Oh, let him run. We all started out small."

Fuerstenberg avoided accepting titles, not easy for a successful businessman in imperial Germany. Why? "There's no amnesty for titles," he pointed out.

But neither the nicest anecdotes nor the best intentions helped solve the problem of creditworthiness under which the young republic suffered in 1950. My uncles stopped an approach by Sal. Oppenheim because the deal would have had a credit attached. Oppenheim was understandably annoyed. But the London agreement regulating German debt was not signed until 1951, and the settlement of the open "clearing billion" (the unpaid bills for delivery of Swiss goods) was still far off in the future. Germany's poor credit rating was only exceeded by Japan's. Until the late sixties, dealing with Japanese banks was considered to be risky.

At the start of the economic boom in 1951, the Bank Julius Baer began to flourish. With the know-how I had acquired at Brown Brothers Harriman, we built up our position in the credit business. We financed short-term trade and secured the credit with goods or commodities. As a result, we became a large customer of Surveillance, the specialty company for verifying products. To the extent that everything went well, we earned 3/16 percent of the total amount in the opening and 3/16 percent for the payout. Solid returns.

Financing the wheat trade fell into the credit business category. We worked together with the multinational Argentine wheat and seed oil trader Bunge y Born, which delivered grains to East Germany and Russia and accepted bills of exchange. The grain dealers thought they earned their money through sale of grain, when in fact they made their money through Russian bills of exchange. The Soviet bloc countries had no credit and depended on bills of exchange to finance their imports. The actual discounts of the individual Soviet bloc addresses or the South American countries were noted for a long time on over-the-counter sheets that banks could buy. For example, the list would state "Hungary, 13 percent."

It was not a distinguished business, which is why no one conducted it in their own name. You had discount firms for that, for example, Zilkha (a famous Syrian banking dynasty) and their Ufitec Company on Talstrasse in Zurich. If, in the fifties, a corporation, let us say Siemens, delivered a new telephone network to a country like Venezuela, it would be paid in bills of exchange with a term of three to six months, which in part it could sell to others.

South American or African states like the Ivory Coast all financed their infrastructure — harbors, transportation networks, telecommunications, and airports — with bills of exchange, which liquidity-hungry suppliers quickly pushed into the market. Zurich was the hub. Several small firms in business along the Limmat River lived from trading bills of exchange. Bobby Greiff was a prominent trader who grew rich in the business. The last time I met him at the Baur au Lac, he was over eighty and brought out champagne.

"What are we celebrating?" I asked him.

"I have a son," he replied, and proudly took a picture out of his pocket. However, he didn't say that he had become a father when pointing to the child, which a very pretty woman in the photograph held in her arms.

Greiff had a villa in Cap d'Antibes. He loved to introduce my wife and me to the nightlife there along the Riviera. Dinner at ten, a nightclub at midnight, and at 4 a.m. we fell exhausted into bed. Then the next afternoon a picnic on the ocean was on the calendar, complete with picnic basket. One time when we arrived on the beach, Bobby hungrily opened the basket and found it empty. No sign of the chicken. The outraged hostess (Greiff's wife) ran up the driveway to the villa, rushed into the kitchen, and found her staff peacefully sitting around the table eating chicken.

The major banks may have been too distinguished to trade bills of exchange under their own name, but they were not ready to let that piece of business get away from them. A big difference from the American houses. The Credit Suisse, for example, maintained its own very good credit company.

Cossacks watering their horses in Lake Constance, the lake along the border toward Germany, was seen, in the cold war anxiety of the fifties, as a real possibility, and one that I did not find far-out. We all still had Stalin's comments echoing in our ears when Averell Harriman, congratulating him on the conquest of Berlin, said, "Pfft, what do you want? Cossacks have already been in Paris."

During the Berlin blockade, I took care to fill up our automobiles' gas tanks every night. I still have a phobia of an empty gas tank. My housekeeper always laughs when the subject comes up.

On the other hand, we thought it exaggerated that Hans Gerling would travel from Cologne to Switzerland on every weekend when a political crisis threatened. My blunt question: "Are you crazy?"

"Live on my side for a while and then we can talk about who is crazy," he replied.

In the fifties, sixties, and seventies, everything was much more personal than it is today. With us, it was a matter of the bank's size and the fact that the bosses were also the owners. Most things depended on them. When my uncle Werner caused a traffic accident with his car and people were injured, he was very worried about losing his stock exchange license. If he had, the bank would have been finished. Here too times have changed. Today, if a Baer were to lose his or her personal admission to stock exchange trading, nothing would happen to the Bank Julius Baer.

The cohesion between the generations in the family was much stronger then, an indication of the personal relationships we had. Werner enjoyed inviting guests to his home. He was a generous host who liked to gather a group of disparate people (as did Walter) when he was not hosting a family gathering. Today I note with some regret that the changes in lifestyles, the endless recreational possibilities that are available, and surely the size of our expanding family, have loosened those familial ties. And gathering a really diverse group has become rare.

Business life too was much more personal. If, for example, I planned a trip to Hong Kong, I would tap into Willy Himmelsbach's global contacts and ask who I should look up in the crown colony. He always gave me a few names. When I met them, I determined that they all spoke Swiss-German. Since Himmelsbach's knowledge of English was limited, in his eyes Swiss-German traders were always the best. Friendships were forged through language.

Walter and Werner were quite different in dealing with people. Walter was always forthcoming. The curly-haired Werner — the more intellectual of the two — articulated his opinions vigorously and could react abruptly. When he died in 1960, many people in the bank asked, "Which one of the two was it?" "The man with the curly hair," we responded. "Oh, I was afraid it was the charming one" was often the reply.

Werner had the reputation of being a strict boss. But he brought paintings from his private collection and thus put art into the bank. At the same time, he was a caring patron who expanded pensions and old-age insurance. He was behind the decision in the fifties to introduce the five-day workweek. We were one of the first banks in Zurich to do so.

Werner was an active member of Zurich's rowing club (RIZ). In the summers, he rowed double sculls with his wife at least one morning a week to Obermeilen, about fourteen kilometers away, ate an expansive lunch at the Hirschen Restaurant, and then rowed the fourteen kilometers back to Zurich. He didn't forget business while out on the water. On one occasion, he ordered me to come to the Hirschen and brief him. I drove down to the lakeshore in my convertible. Isn't that poetic? It's something we have truly lost.

Werner had a sharp wit and used colorful language: "Jewish nanny bites German shepherd dog," was his metaphor for the popular Third Reich charge about "Jewish aggressiveness." Another saying I learned from this ironic man was "ubi penis ibi patria" (literally, where the penis is, there is your fatherland). A great bookworm and phrase maker, he was also the soul behind the bank's weekly reports, which he often wrote himself.

He readily accepted the fact that his always well-grounded points of view often rubbed people the wrong way. His suggestion made in November 1945, that an investigative commission examine National Bank policy during the Second World War, provoked the anger of the bank's president, Ernst Weber. He promptly struck the Bank Julius Baer from the list of those receiving monthly gold allotments at the official price. It took all of Walter's diplomatic skills to settle the issue ("I'm going down to the National Bank on Canossastreet . . ."). But on matters of substance, he saw eye to eye with his brother.

Several letters the brothers wrote to my mother illustrate this episode. On December 22, 1945, Werner noted:

Since we are already talking about the business, I want to tell you about our fight with the National Bank, which could have further repercussions. Once again the bank has objected to our weekly reports, the first time as president Weber told me, because of our un-objective criticism relating to the purchasing power argument, and another time because we suggested that an investigative commission look into the matter of Nazi gold [the gold the Germans had stolen during the war and sold to the Swiss National Bank]. He called the idea a vote of no confidence in our government and the National Bank. The National Bank does not want any criticism. During a very dramatic telephone conversation Herr Weber said that they do not want to have anything to do with us, after he had threatened us with sanctions in an earlier conversation. The National Bank, however, has carefully avoided burning all the bridges, but it refuses to give us any more gold and has struck us from the gold allotment list.

The whole thing is a great scandal. You can determine all kinds of constitutional and legal violations: (1) Violation of freedom of the press. (2) Criminal coercion. (3) Calumny, since Weber used the most insulting terminology about Dr. J. C. Meyer (a journalist who worked with the bank). (4) Credit damage. (5) Material damage. Of course all this should be taken with a grain of salt. Professor Guggenheim and I have consulted Federal Councilor Feldman in Bern. He is an expert on press law. He is about to work out an expert opinion, since in his view this whole thing is an outrage, which, if we cannot reach an agreement with the National Bank, should be placed before parliament. A first attempt to reach an understanding, made by Dr. Schucany-Calonder, a cunning and careful lawyer, has failed. We have tried to obtain a written statement from the National Bank, but they have avoided giving us one. Now we will have to roll up a heavier cannon. First of all, we will have to present the whole matter to Professor Bachmann, the president of the banking council, who, if he is willing, may persuade the board of directors that they have maneuvered themselves into a very awkward situation. Since all kinds of scandals have been uncovered recently, and it was after all President Weber who lunched with the vice-president of the German Reichsbank, Emil Puhl, one might recommend that the gentlemen reconsider.

On February 20, 1946, Werner wrote:

Perhaps some easements will be granted here too, even if the National Bank continues to act like a stupid fool (our fight over the weekly report still hasn't been settled).

On April 12, 1946, Walter reported to my mother about further developments:

In the meantime, I will have to pay a visit to President Weber of the National Bank, after the Treasury Department's director, Kellenberger, who spent an hour with me today, urged that I make such a gesture. That should take care of the gold matter to more or less everybody's satisfaction; after all, the concerned parties, us included, pulled back a bit. Representative Spuehler [he would become a member of various parliamentary houses and federal councilor, known as the Lord of Aussersihl, and someone whom I remember as a very sympathetic gentleman; the Social Democrats objected to his friendship with Walter] has already telephoned me about the possibility of such an intervention. In any event, the gentlemen on Bahnhofstrasse — when I told Director Kellenberger that I would visit Weber on Canossastreet he didn't believe it — should have noted by now that we will not allow us to be spat upon.

On May 23, 1946, Walter described the last act:

Finally the news has come that we have buried the hatchet with the National Bank and will now get our gold again. I don't know how well-informed you are about all this but just want to mention the visit by the Treasury Department's director, Kellenberger, whom Federal Councilor Nobs had dispatched to urge us to approach President Weber personally. I took on this mission, which can best be circumscribed by citing Schiller's verse from the "Buergschaft" (The Pledge) — "and both lie in each other's arms crying with pain and joy." Spuehler's intervention seems to have been the impulse to bring the gentlemen around because a parliamentary discussion of the matter would have been damned uncomfortable, and I had to assure Weber that from now on we would stop any other intervention. If I had not done this, the affair would have been brought before a parliamentary commission.

By the way, people here think that the position of Weber's colleague, who went to Washington with him, has been undermined as a result of the gold affair. Personally, I assume that the consequences will be drawn in a matter of weeks or months because otherwise Switzerland's bona fides would be weakened.

And that's how it was.

On October 16, 1946, Werner reported to my mother about the latest developments:

Apropos the National Bank, you will doubtless have read that Weber had to resign as National Bank president and Professor Bachmann as head of the banking council, which gives me no small joy (which pleases me greatly). We'll have to wait and see if things will get any better.

Given all the differences in their temperaments, Walter and Werner shared a strong inclination toward thriftiness. Privately, Werner wasn't at all stingy; otherwise he couldn't have amassed his important art collection and we would not have taken part in so many memorable family feasts. But he was very miserly when it came to business. I can remember that once, as a victim of purple copy ink, I wanted to purchase a photocopier, at the time an expensive piece of equipment. Both uncles came to look it over. Afterwards they both said no.

Werner said no over and over again. I once ordered a new elevator, and the contract had already been signed. At the last second, Werner came around and asked why we needed it. I argued that the new lift was faster. His response: "The seconds you save would cost us SFr 1,000. Your time isn't worth that much."

Thriftiness went hand in hand with discretion, usual in the banking business. "The name of the house does not belong on the door," Walter and Werner agreed. For a long time, the sign above the entrance to Bahnhofstrasse 36 read JB & Co. Every effort to win them over to a greater public presence met their determined resistance and failed. Today we have come full circle for fear of terrorism and too much publicity.

Yet for my cousins and me it was clear that the large investments we had made in electronic data processing could only be compensated through expansion of our business. With ornate initials above the door of our house as the ultimate in public relations, we would not get very far. We needed a more open attitude toward publicity and the role of the corporation in society.

Wiener & Deville became our first advertising agency. Rodolphe Deville was a divinely gifted advertiser, and Max Wiener our "house doctor." It turned into eight fruitful years with long lunchtime discussions that in the end pushed us into the modern era. Nobody ate during our first lunch, as Wiener remembers. My cousins and I bombarded him with so many questions that at our second meeting he insisted on eating first and then talking.

Wiener & Deville brought us the slogan "The Fine Art of Banking" and ran exciting ads in the *Neue Zuercher Zeitung*. Full-page ads provoked the heads of the major banks into making irritating inquiries, such as, "Why do you run such expensive advertisements?" Once, their reaction was very nettled. We had run an ad with a somewhat subversive headline: "At least you know who owns our bank." Today, the major banks advertise as if they were producers of laundry detergent.

At Ernst Bieri's suggestion, we started to hold press conferences and to inform the public of our performance in a very direct manner. That too drew sneers from the banking world. We argued that we gave press conferences to prepare the way for going public. The real reason, however, was that Ernst Bieri, an old journalist, liked to hold press briefings.

My uncles' overall aversion to publicity reflected the views of their generation of customers. One of the customers made his position unmistakably clear when he said, "I don't wish to read my banker's name in the newspapers." My uncles lived strictly according to the maxim, "A bank is like a young girl. The best thing is not to talk about her."

It was not possible, however, always to avoid doing so. One time Walter had me come to St. Moritz; it was in the sixties. An important customer had been quoted in a newspaper and referred to Julius Baer as "my bank," and Walter was afraid that his use of the possessive pronoun could be misunderstood, especially since we didn't like reading that particular client's name in the paper.

Today, anybody who wants to open a bank account must provide a personal ID plus many other documents. In the early years of my career, I had quite different experiences. It could happen that a client introduced himself or herself by presenting the label on a bottle of cognac. "My name is Hennessy. I don't want to say any more. Here is $300,000." We accepted the money gladly, thankful for the trust placed in us.

The banking world was divided into two categories: the major banks on one side and everybody else on the other. That's hard to imagine today. If a major bank had capital problems, it simply increased its own capital whenever it thought the time was right. But regulators didn't wait five minutes if a small bank was involved. National Bank President Fritz Leutwiler's decision to give Credit Suisse a disguised guarantee after the billion-plus Texon scandal in 1977 was indicative of the time. It led to an exchange of letters with Ernst Bieri, who wanted to know if in a worst-case scenario we too could count on such a declaration. Leutwiler replied that if institutes of our size got into trouble, they could always turn to the major banks for help. Every bank, therefore, had a standby bank.

Our customers were speculators pure and simple; nobody talked about asset or wealth management. And no wonder, it simply didn't exist, and my uncles were right to protest when the first ads placed by our media agency showed up proclaiming, "We have been active in wealth management for [so and so] many hundreds of years." The term was unknown. The business didn't exist. On the contrary, our customers bought, let us say, a hundred shares of Interhandel to sell them the next day. They were day traders who paid full brokerage fees.

Traders would arrive at their desks at 9 a.m. after having had their coffee. Werner used to maintain that traders first went to the café, where then and there they decided if the day's exchange would be strong or weak. Upon leaving the café, the traders went to their offices and called clients for half an hour. "Today you have to sell Interhandel." Or buy some other stock. At around ten they went over to the stock exchange. The café theory is not wrong. Zurich had twenty stockbrokers. If you talked to ten of them in a café, you knew the market's direction that day.

Our first asset manager was Ferdinand Lips, who would become our gold guru. When Lips arrived in 1960, Walter was still alive and resisted his advent. "I don't want an asset manager. People who deposit their securities here know what they are doing. Let's leave them in peace." Here my uncles were in accord with Siegmund Warburg, who thought that portfolio management was a sure way of annoying your best customers. (That aside, Warburg's Mercury Asset Management became one of the biggest in the field.)

After asset management had become an integral part of banking practice, a customer called up. In reading her statement, she discovered that she was holding shares of the Volksbank (the people's bank), and now she wanted to sell them. In reply to my somewhat nonplussed question as to why she wanted to get rid of this particular stock, I received her informative answer: "I don't want a stock with that name in my portfolio." So be it.

The bank's business with its stock-trading customers was based much more heavily on margin transactions than it is today. Take Interhandel — a holding company registered in Basel in 1928, which was contractually bound to IG Farben — whose shares were actively traded as a hot stock tip and almost exclusively only on margin. Before the computer came along, calculating margins during crisis times grew into an all-night undertaking. Calculating margins for nights on end was my idea of a banking crisis. During the Cuba crisis, the bank hardly did anything else. And we were far less interested in the question of "Is our customer bankrupt?" than we were in "Is the bank bankrupt?"

During the dramatic days when Russian freighters carrying

missiles were steering toward Cuba, we had a company party in Buesingen. While the chauffeur drove me to the restaurant, I wasn't at all sure that I would still be alive the next day. The market fell into a black hole during the 1963 Cuban crisis. The price of American shares halved in Europe. Albert Merz stood in the pit and decided when prices had dropped into the cellar and then shouted, "Now I'll buy two million shares for the book." Prices were so low that Merz took the risk to buy. When the missile ships turned around the next day, share prices doubled. It took five years before we again approached our 1961 earnings level. The next crisis hit very quickly: the assassination of John F. Kennedy. At first nobody knew if it was a plot.

Getting back to Interhandel. Bank Vontobel made its money with that stock, but the UBS, under the leadership of Alfred Schafer, made even more. Schaefer bought Interhandel for UBS and managed to unfreeze the last enemy asset still blocked in the United States. Thanks to his personal relationship with the Kennedy clan — he knew Jacqueline Kennedy's brother-in-law Prince Stanislas Radziwill very well — he succeeded in persuading Attorney General Robert Kennedy to unblock the assets. There was one condition: UBS had to take over the company. UBS formally merged with Interhandel. Shareholders were given the option of swapping their stock for UBS shares. Until very recently, UBS faced a plethora of lawsuits, all of them without success. It is surely no accident that Interhandel files have remained sealed, even for the Bergier Commission (also known as ICE — the Independent Commission of Experts) that investigated Swiss conduct in the Second World War.

Today we live in a world of electronic markets where everybody can read supply and demand on the screen. In the archaic times of violent course fluctuations, the world was quite different. An executive would come back from lunch at two-thirty with the announcement, "I'll start making the allocation now." And Carl

Kuenzler, the CEO of Julius Bear at the time, would then decide who got his shares and at what price. And if customers complained that they couldn't find the price in the newspaper, they were told, "If you don't like the price, why don't you do your business with the newspaper."

In his memoirs, Walter Eberstadt, a distant relative and a former Lazard Frères partner, describes how, while he worked for Model Roland and Stone, he lived off persuading California banks to have their customers buy well-priced European stocks:

> The Californian houses liked over-the-counter ideas, which were more profitable to sell to their customers than listed securities. The European brokers from whom we bought the stocks earned a commission and in return gave Model business on the New York Stock Exchange. The Model firm made a good profit buying the securities before we sold them to the Californian houses, which marked them up further before they retailed them to their clients. Fortunately, the stocks went up so much in price that even the retail customers made a profit.

From his time at Lazard Frères, Eberstadt reported that in 1971, André Meyer wanted to handle the IPO of the *Washington Post* and outbid all his competitors, and afterwards faced the problem of finding buyers for the shares:

> We left no stone unturned to find purchasers for the stock. It was put into accounts over which we had discretion, something that would not be tolerated nowadays. Inevitably the shares did not do well, and our clients started to sell once the shares had recovered their purchase price. The buyer for the shares sold by the irritated Lazard clients turned out to be largely the famed Warren Buffet,

who has kept the stock ever since. He made a fortune on his holdings and became Katharine Graham's [publisher of the *Washington Post*] business mentor.

Foreign exchange was a difficult business as well. We only knew price cuts, especially among the more exotic currencies. No newspaper recorded interim rates, only the closing price. Nobody knew the dollar rate during the day except for professional traders. I wouldn't dare to claim that things have gotten any better today. As the trade became more internal, the banks evaded all efforts to improve market transparency.

Our business lived off the fact that we did not wait for customers. Instead, we visited them — in South America, South Africa, Italy, and Mexico. Our Latin American business was managed out of New York. South Americans will fly to the Big Apple over the weekend but certainly not to Switzerland. The importance of Switzerland as a banking center was pretty relative.

During the fifties we had our largest client business in Chile. My cousin Nicky looked after that region, including Venezuela. Our success always depended on the man we had in place. In addition to Argentina, where we had been active since my uncles were young, Brazil was important, particularly Sao Paulo. And we were successful in Mexico too, where we had a serious commercial business, notwithstanding a branch office as a nonbank (a serious commercial business doesn't meet a private client's desire for discretion). Moreover, Mexicans can park their overseas money more comfortably in Texas.

The need for overseas banking connections was a function of the ban many countries imposed on ownership of foreign bank accounts. Only rarely, therefore, did we approach natives directly. Most of our clients had fled Europe and made their fortunes abroad.

Early in the fifties it was suggested that we take over the Bank Leu. I was young and enterprising, found the idea a good one, and we buckled down to running the numbers. So I personally bought a few hundred shares. But then Werner came round and announced, "I wouldn't dream of working for someone else." This was something he believed in all sincerity. I got rid of the Leu stock and used the proceeds to buy a Marino Marini painting. I didn't make enough on the deal to afford one of his sculptures.

We were approached about taking over the Bank Leu over and over again. If we had done so, we might possibly have faced some difficulties after an embezzlement case was uncovered in one of the bank's branches. The embezzled SFr 60 million (approximately $43 million) would have been hard to make up. Chairman Rainer Gut and the Credit Suisse were used to quite different amounts.

We were lucky in that nothing bad ever happened. God was good to us. We were spared embezzlement and money laundering in our house. The worst that happened was that someone paid his dental bill out of the bank's own account. Juerg Heer, who later would create problems for Rothschild in Zurich and who in the late phase of his career banned employee cars from his bank's garage in order to park his collection of vintage automobiles, was supposed to come aboard as our credit chief, but his exaggerated salary demands prevented it.

One time in our credit business we came into a memorable collateral: a large farm south of Washington, D.C. The client, an American who lived in Zurich and dealt with industrial alcohol, had gone bankrupt, which wasn't funny, but we thought his offer of the farm was a pleasant change. I agreed to keep the place until it came to buying a breeding bull. I knew from Peggy Rockefeller, the Chase's David Rockefeller's wife, how expensive such a bull could be. She raised Simmentaler cattle as a pastime and sold such bulls for more than a million dollars each.

We never received a South African gold trading license, a good thing, given the class action suit against all companies doing business in the apartheid state. The major gold pool bank for South

Africa was Rothschild in London; they set the price. The daily fixing took fifteen minutes. The five or six largest gold traders sat around a table and determined that day's price.

Because Werner never thought about working for anybody else, the idea of going public was anathema for a long time. He lacked the imagination to realize that the advantages in opening up the ownership structure outweighed any negative aspects. An initial public offering is not necessarily a "turbo charge," as Tove Maria Söiland, one of Peter Baer's nieces, put it, but undoubtedly the requirements of a public company to boost performance. I felt that myself. I was not happy in the beginning when the Bank Julius Baer became a public company. One lives much more pleasantly without the duty to publish one's results. I only had to justify my actions to the family. Typically, family-owned enterprises must often endure critical questions from stock exchange supervisors. They are not used to confronting harsh realities.

When we became a joint stock company, we had to introduce titles to the bank. Until then, I had been a Bankprokurist, a general title for executives that has no real equivalent in English, but there was nothing else. During a phase of rapid growth, we hadn't thought much about the structure of our business. But with the founding of the corporation, my cousin Nicky became president of the board of directors and I was the "working stiff."

Without my cousins and me having consciously worked toward that goal, the employees of our house developed a style that they themselves called "baerlike." If we made a contribution, it was through a civilized style reflected in our "corporate guidelines." I still have the 1962 version in front of me. One example: "Suggestions, wishes, and complaints, as you surely know, should be taken to your superiors openly and personally. . . . Unlike other banks it is not forbidden, but rather desired, that our associates read the newspapers."

Leo Loretan, for a long time in charge of bond sales, remembers that in 1958 the bank had exactly one hundred employees on the company outing to the Buergenstock, because Walter used the occasion to introduce the hundredth member of our crew. Everybody knew everybody else by name. Every young Baer knew the entire staff, because the head of personnel took him or her on a tour of the house. Our uncles told my cousins and me to wish every employee a Happy New Year.

However, our style also required that requests for a pay raise be made in person. When, after the birth of his first son, Loretan could no longer make ends meet, he knocked on Walter's door. He needed SFr 50 more per month. Walter understood. Werner, in the office next to his with the door ajar, listened and cleared his throat in a significant manner. Whereupon Walter said, "I'll have to think about it." But the raise went through. When, however, Ernst Gall, who was paid much more than Loretan, wanted more money, with the argument that he couldn't afford his apartment without it, he was told dryly, "Then move into a smaller flat."

Looking back, I think our style was as much a product of our modest beginnings as it was a patriarchal structure that didn't want "subordinates" but instead valued those who thought for themselves and accepted responsibility. Part of our style was to approach people first instead of waiting for them and, in the event of differing opinions, grab the telephone and talk together rather than call for a judge, meaning not mounting a high horse but letting a certain amount of humanity rule. Many things can be straightened out that way, and not the least important, you save money. But when the concept of baerlike began to be cloned and gave way to smugness, I abolished it.

Part of the patriarchal style demanded that the partners eat lunch together once a week and that they always take a personal look at new hires. I had the candidates read aloud from the *Financial Times*, the *Herald Tribune*, or some other English language paper in order to get a first impression. Nobody was prepared for that, and so I heard how the candidate spoke, if he or she understood the reading, and if he or she could make a good presentation and deal with a new situation. Ten minutes says everything. In that time I could look over the candidate. I freely admit to not hiring someone who wore a leather tie. I also pulled the emergency brake with women who were too elegantly dressed.

Walter once received an application addressed to Bahnhofstrasse 35 instead of 36. The wrong number took care of the applicant. Another time a candidate interrupted the conversation and said, "Excuse me, it's raining. I have to go out and close the roof of my car." "Then you'd better stay with your car," Walter ended the interview.

Leo Loretan, who died in 2007, remembered that his interview lasted forty-five minutes. That was in 1957, and he became the ninetieth employee — with a monthly salary of SFr 800 ($190). My uncles examined all applicants for apprenticeship personally. Werner spent half an hour testing their language skills while Walter examined mathematical savoir-faire and logical thinking for another thirty minutes.

Such was the case of Juergen Luethi, whose teacher knew that the bank had accepted him before he came back to school. According to him, the future head of our management operations had three finest hours in his younger years. The first came when after nine months of his apprenticeship, he typed faster than anybody else. The second came when Curtis Lowell recognized who he was by his writing style while the two men were conversing by telex. And the third came after his apprenticeship: stock exchange invoicing was handled by Computronics, which required a small engineering education. One day when the man who handled it was sick, Luethi jumped in and completed the invoicing of stock orders. The next day Walter had him come into his office. Luethi walked in highly nervous and walked out beaming. He'd gotten a 10 percent raise (SFr 50).

I often think of the importance of playing soccer for the

solidarity of the staff. During sports, people tend to talk about what moves them, and colleagues at work often become friends. The soccer players often arranged for large competitions and played against crews from Berenberg in Hamburg, Bordier in Geneva, Dreyfus in Basel, and even against Julius Baer in London. Somewhere along the line, the Londoners no longer wanted to play. They kept losing against Zurich. Wild stories were told about one game against Berenberg in Hamburg, but one thing was sure: at two in the morning, the whole team was in the police station of the Reeperbahn, Hamburg's "entertainment, gastronomy, and sex mile," and they weren't there for drinking green tea or swapping pictures of saints. Whatever. But nobody can deny that this bit of extracurricular activity helped the camaraderie. Spending times together at a police station are ties that bind. And that is the point of the exercise.

I was always present when the bankers played in Zurich. Hans Guth, married to Katja Dreyfus and originally a professor of statistics in Zurich, did the same thing. At age ninety-plus, he is still president of Dreyfus' board of directors and since 2002 its honorary president.

It doesn't have to be sports to create team spirit. What counts is doing something to boost the inner bond. When my son Raymond worked at Salomon Brothers, a weekly cocktail party was the rule — a rule Salomon CEO John Gutfreund himself had promulgated. The reason for these parties was beside the point. The pretext could be a cleaning lady becoming a grandmother or retiring. The social side was important.

Leo Loretan, our bond dealer and a good skier, organized the first bond dealer ski race in Klosters in 1975. It turned into a very prestigious affair. Even the *Wall Street Journal* carried a story about it. In the first year, 60 people took part. A year later in Verbier, the number had climbed to 200, and it eventually grew to 450 participants. Only those who were registered with the Association of International Bond Dealers could take part. Traders from New York flew in for the weekend race, and on Monday morning, red-eyed, they were back at their desks in New York. Before the debut of the race, Loretan and Peter Hangartner realized they would need a trophy. They bought the cup with their own money instead of asking the bank. Since Loretan won the race, he could keep the trophy. (Pedro Hangartner, our chief trader, finished number 23.) Today the event is a solidly established major race.

When on September 12, 1985, Julius Baer shares rose above SFr 10,000 for the first time, I sent a small bottle of Veuve Cliquot with a message of thanks to every desk. Alcohol was forbidden in the workplace.

The bank's Easter present to its employees was introduced because Walter's wife was president of the Women's International Zionist Organization for Switzerland and was looking for buyers for her oranges and grapefruits, which she sold at charity prices. Here too you can observe the decline of personal ties. If the Zionists called today, someone who has never heard of that organization is sure to answer the phone. So now we hand out eggs with candy inside.

When times were good, we considered giving bonuses at the company picnic before Easter. During a bank employee dinner, I persuaded Nicky, the more thrifty and conservative of the two of us, to do so, and we made the announcement during dessert — much to the joy of those who attended.

I always got along well with people who worked with me — at least I think so. I only intervened when danger threatened. For the rest, I let everything happen. For example, I wouldn't have dreamed of editing a newspaper article I received for vetting before it was published. My attitude astonished Edi Estermann, who accompanied me to Minsk for the *Schweizer Illustrierte* (the *Swiss Illustrated* magazine). I had gone there in the spring of 1999 to visit the Jewish community. He faxed me his story on a Saturday, only hours before his paper closed, and was surprised when I called him ten minutes later to say that everything was okay. You tend to ease your fellow humans' life considerably if you allow them the greatest creative freedom possible.

I do not deny the concern I feel for others, a concern that sometimes leads to amusing situations. My two housekeepers took their dog on vacation to Croatia. For once I didn't want to become hysterical, so I decided not to call at night to make sure they had arrived safely. So what happened? At 1 a.m. the phone rang. My two "pearls" were at the other end. "We are hurt that you did not call us and ask how we were doing."

It has not hurt me that people try harder in my presence. Creativity inspires me. In the end, I live off the fact that I can build a creative climate. I don't believe that fear and uncertainty are leadership principles that promise success. Who wants to be feared rather than loved?

Are employee shares a motivational method? Hardly, if you look at share prices over the previous years. We examined the idea when the bank became a public company but wisely opted against it. My cousins and I decided in 1982 that in times of massive price fluctuations on the stock exchanges, shares were not an adequate means for employees to participate in corporate success. We reached the conclusion that factors like interest rates, shifts in exchange rates, and politics have a greater influence on the valuation than the course of business, and we were concerned — with a look at the taxable discount's impact on the issue price of employee shares — that in a weak stock market the shares could become a nightmare for our employees. As one of our employees put it not long ago when he came to say good-bye upon retirement, "As long as prices rise, everybody can play the market."

"Our strategy is that we have no strategy" was our slogan while everybody else was talking about strategy. But we did have a concept about our business. Over time, after the war, we had decided that we would cultivate all aspects of the banking business while maintaining our focus on the portfolio business. We also built in a risk equalizer through our credit operations: a good interest rate account when rates are high and stock prices are low, and vice versa. For the most part, our income rested on three pillars: interest rates (they work on Sundays), commission fees, and the profits we made with our own trades in stocks, foreign exchange, and precious metals. In the seventies, the credit business accounted for up to 40 percent of our total profits. In the nineties, we gave it up because it was no longer profitable.

The Christmas season of 2005, for no apparent reason, brought on far-reaching discussions among the family shareholders. The shareholder agreement itself still had decades to run, which in itself may have been a reason for restlessness. The question of why the breakup of the family pool finally took place naturally comes up frequently. A big and rather obvious reason is the number of partners in the pool — about forty at the time. A group of that size and all ages is most unlikely to function successfully. A more philosophical reason is perhaps the fact that the elder generation in our family never really accorded the necessary trust to the younger generation. It is a fact that grooming for succession was never taken seriously and that a real discussion of the abilities of the various younger family members never took place. The fact that the top positions of chairman, deputy chairman, and CEO were occupied by Baers was surely not conducive to attracting first-class talent to our organization.

The result of the discussions was the immediate dissolution of the shareholder agreement — a step that was accomplished within hours. My son, Raymond, saw himself as the only family representative in a leading position and naturally was on the lookout for a viable future strategy. Embroiled in rumors of an imminent takeover of our bank, he wisely decided on the opposite strategy.

The proposition that UBS might be willing to sell their private banks against the consideration of a large cash payment, plus a participation of about 20 percent in the form of nonvoting shares in the capital of the new Julius Baer Group, was attractive. The group is now the largest independent money manager in Switzerland, the staff having roughly doubled in size through this transaction.

The initial doubts about whether such a large group could in time be merged into one efficient entity were soon dispelled, and within a rather short time, the share price of Baer Holding doubled and the money under management multiplied. At present, a shareholder wants a focused operation, and the very large banks in the world that offer various services realize a significantly lower valuation of their shares than what resulted in the metamorphosis of Julius Baer Holding.

17

On the Way to Going Public
(1970–81)

Our charming disorganization

Ernst Bieri, who died in 2003, was a talented and multifaceted man and would have become a member of the Swiss Cabinet if God had given him less intelligence and greater ability in handling people. That God denied such a gift to the theology graduate but showered him with intellectual powers proved to be our good fortune. He decided on theology for economic reasons — he didn't come from a wealthy home — given that the course of study could be completed in seven semesters, a story he liked to tell over and over again. But he preferred a newspaper office to the pulpit and started work at the *Neue Zuercher Zeitung* in 1946. At the same time, he joined the Liberal Party. In 1966 he was elected to the Zurich City Council, and from 1967 to 1971 he represented his city in parliament. His military career was also impressive. Ernst left the service with the rank of colonel in the motor transport service. This wiry and erect man started in the antiaircraft corps before transferring to the mechanized troops, where he became a specialist in the AMX-13 tank. His final assignment was on the staff of the 4th Army Corps, serving, in his own words, as "political officer." With his theological background and his sharp mind, he was the Swiss answer to Leon Trotsky. I owe Bieri a great bon mot. When asked after a lecture how one could thank him, he answered, "No problem since the invention of money."

Our common friend Fritz Leutwiler brought us together — he was a man I had wanted to win over to Julius Baer since the early sixties. But our exploratory talks never got far enough so that I could have presented his name to a family council. At the time, Leutwiler was only one of several Swiss National Bank (SNB) directors and, given his forceful manner, not universally loved. But he knew our situation: the bank had grown and its payroll had increased tenfold, all without structural preparation for our new size. To cite Bieri: "The patriarchal small business had become a mid-size bank." It was clear that "our charming disorganization" would sooner or later lead us into trouble.

Even though I only enjoyed qualified support from the family, I felt strongly that after Werner's death in 1960, we needed greater backup. And where would we get it if not from an outside partner? We could move forward only by professionalizing our management. The discussion between us cousins was congenial, if emotional. Nicky Baer, the first among equals, always a little distant, was open to the idea of bringing somebody from the outside to succeed Walter. At first, Peter resisted and said in his sometimes rather drastic manner, a result of his membership in a rowing club, "Then I won't be able to pick my nose anymore." The answer to this metaphor was at hand: "Perhaps we shouldn't pick our noses any longer."

I thought we badly needed a nanny, someone who could put corset bones in our dress. Fritz Leutwiler felt that Bieri would be the right man. Bieri still had hopes of joining the Swiss cabinet but saw little hope of succeeding Hans Schaffner, who resigned on December 31, 1969.

As our future partner would tell us, Leutwiler called him during a session of parliament in Bern. He had a new task for him. The two men met in the Veltliner Keller restaurant, where Leutwiler gave Bieri his marching orders. All I had to do was confirm them. Thus a member of the city council became our second outside partner after Hans Mayenfisch. The partners approved his nomination on July 5, 1970 — much to the later distress of the Liberals, who lost their second seat in the city council in a special election held on December 13, 1970.

No capital contribution was required, nor did we follow the custom of other banks to have partners without money of their own take on a credit at another bank, accept liability for it, and book the money as a capital deposit. Instead, we offered him a share of the profits. On the other hand, the partner, according to the law, was liable for everything he owned. However, until the collapse of Arthur Andersen in the wake of the Enron scandal, nobody had taken this liability seriously.

With Bieri on board, everything became much more formal. He brought with him the experiences he had gathered in the administration of the Zurich city finance department. The first result of his activity was a new partnership agreement we signed on March 18, 1972, which stipulated an official set of business rules for the bank. The long-time journalist gave us valuable advice about maintaining good relations with the media, to report offensively, and never wait until pressure mounted to the point where truth filtered out bit by bit.

What became more formal? As an example, Bieri saw that our management had no rules and did not record minutes — not at the annual meeting or at the weekly management conference. We met once a week, ate lunch together, and talked about business. We were by no means alone. Even the top management of the Credit Suisse (CS) — even though it was a joint stock company and a major bank — met without minutes until the Texon scandal. (The Banca Commerciale Italiana, however, recorded minutes from the day of its founding. Amusingly, CS had been one of its founding banks.) "It was Bieri's thankless task to persuade the partners and the staff to act less informally, meaning to record decisions in writing, to introduce controls, to oversee management and investment policy, and to hold meetings," Nicholas Faith wrote in *Euromoney* in 1976, describing Bieri's activities.

On his to-do list, Bieri always had an item titled Special Events. Why? So that nobody could claim to have forgotten to report something or other. Under Special Events we treated cases of a personal nature, for example, if someone had problems with a client.

Life became more serious with Bieri aboard, and not everybody was happy about the advent of more orderly conditions. Our team members loved the informal patriarchal milieu. Moreover, Bieri tended to ensure control over his areas of responsibilities with brute force if need be. Right at the beginning I was chided in no uncertain terms for having ordered presentation folders from a neighbor and friend. The house was shaken to its foundation because of this nonchalant violation of the new purchasing policy.

Bieri also introduced the daily information meeting, the so-called early mass. Many of our cadre found it was a waste of time to keep everybody informed, but as an officer, Bieri knew all about the motivational impact of early morning reports from the noncoms.

Ernst Kilgus, professor at the Swiss Banking Institute and one of the early proponents of operational accounting in the banking industry, remembers that Bieri had "tortured me until I had completed my concept." Over two lunches he had scribbled across ten menus in order to prepare himself mentally about the until now unplowed field of internal cost accounting in banks.

Bieri's social instincts, however, were underdeveloped. From Brown Brothers Harriman I had brought back the habit of distributing notes about our luncheon guests in the expectation that those in our bank who were to attend would read them. Our partner, who

1. The wedding picture of my grandparents Julius and Marie Baer. "The sum of my grandmother Marie's dowry is documented. It amounted to SFr 100,000, a considerable amount in those days. My grandfather signed the receipt for the money at the lawyer's office."

2. My grandmother Marie Baer-Ulrich (1869–1917), my grandfather Julius Baer (1857–1922), my great-grandmother Sofie Ulrich-Schwab (1827–1910). In front on the chair is my father, Richard Baer, born in 1892. The child on my grandmother's lap is my uncle Walter Baer, born in 1895.

3. My grandfather Ludwig Lohnstein (*right*) and his brother Otto, identical twins and owners of a porcelain shop in Worms. The birthmark on Otto's head was for me the only distinguishing feature. Born in 1872, they died barely a year apart — my great-uncle in 1942 in Rio de Janeiro, my grandfather in 1943 in Geneva.

4. "His hotel was a decent establishment." On his honeymoon, my great-uncle wanted to stay at the same hotel where, a short time before, his brother had spent the night on his honeymoon. At first the owner refused. Otto and Ludwig Lohnstein had married in a double wedding the sisters Alice and Marie Kann.

5. A regular holiday destination: the villa of the two Lohnsteins on Siegfriedstrasse in Worms. In order to make sure that justice was done, Grandfather and his brother regularly exchanged apartments. The late nineteenth-century neoclassic building survived the war intact.

6. My father, Richard Baer (*right*), with his friend and colleague Edgar Meyer, physicist and professor at the University of Zurich. In the background, the university's Institute of Physics on Schoenberggasse. Meyer accompanied us to Estoril when we emigrated in 1941. (Photo ca. early 1920s)

7. My father's colleague and house guest on Bergstrasse, the physicist Irene Joliot-Curie, with my father. Irene, together with her husband, Frederic, won the Nobel Prize for chemistry in 1935.

8. By today's measure, a small- to medium-sized enterprise: gardener and assistant, chauffeur, cook, two maids, and a governess were an integral part of the house on Bergstrasse in Zurich-Fluntern.

9. "I realize with some horror how far we have declined, at least in the way we live." The Georgian-style house, in the Fieldstone section of Riverdale, very close to Van Cortland Park, which my mother had rented furnished. Today my mother's comment is a puzzlement.

10. "Dependence on the subways and commuter railroads wasn't much fun back then either, especially the Hudson Line that connected Riverdale to Manhattan via Harlem." The Broadway railhead in Riverdale, which has not changed since my youth except for a new coat of paint.

11. "Maharuto," the family acronym for us four siblings: With Marianne (*right*) and Ruth (*left*), and in the foreground, Thomas. (Picture ca. 1950)

12.

"After mobilization, the army demanded all of the convertibles, including our Langenthal Chryslers; they were put at General Guisan's disposition. In the newsreels, we repeatedly saw the general ride in them during parades." General Guisan enters a "Langenthal ship" outside the Jegensdorf Palace. The plate ("GENERAL") and the spurs on the officers' boots are unbeatable.

13. "An eastern Jew who could not be assimilated." In reality, Wolfgang Pauli was a Catholic and came from the Viennese bourgeoisie. Franca Pauli was his second wife. The couple accompanied my mother and me in 1948 on our great summer trip to Florence. My most important duty was to light Pauli's pipe while his head shook back and forth.

14. In cap and gown. Admiral William "Bull" Halsey spoke at the official part of the graduation ceremony in 1947. During the unofficial part, we were to consume the numerical sum of our graduation year (4 + 7) in glasses of beer.

15, A neo-Gothic creation of the late nineteenth century: the renovated Packer Memorial Church at the entrance to the Lehigh University campus.

16. "Why the headmaster, Charles C. Tillinghast, accepted me, especially after school had already started, remains a mystery." The main tract of the Horace Mann School, a private high school in Riverdale.

17. "Unprepared as I am to speak at my mother's wedding . . ." In 1950 Ellen Baer married the mathematician Hermann Weyl (1885–1955). The two of them lived alternately in Princeton and Zurich.

18. "Your friend is almost done." In the United States with two Geneva bankers "from coast to coast" in the summer of 1949. On the left, François Chauvet (called "Slowboat" — he would become a partner in Ferrier, Lullin & Cie), and on the right, François Barrelet (of Barrelet et Pidoux), who died young.

19. "They are so innocent, and we are so decadent." My sabbatical at Christ Church, Oxford, in 1975. I was lodged — without a telephone — in a late-medieval tower that was locked every night from the outside at 10 p.m.

20. Donald Bardsley. He drilled me with the slightly sadistic zeal of a sergeant. His resignation from the board of the London and County Securities triggered the secondary banking crisis.

21. "He [Wilhelm Roepke] gave the festive lecture celebrating the seventy-fifth anniversary of the Julius Baer bank in 1965 — an exciting event at the time." (*Left*) Alfred Sarasin, president of the Swiss Bankers Association and my co-trainee at Brown Brothers Harriman, and (*right*) my uncle Walter Baer.

22. René Beyersdorf, son of a watchmaker and cantor from la Chaux-de-Fonds, and his wife, Madeleine. He was one of my mentors in the United States and a man of never-flagging optimism. At the outbreak of the Second World War, he sent his family from Brussels to Switzerland, started out anew in the United States, and, as our representative in New York, discovered the business with Mexican promissory notes. (Photo ca. early sixties)

23. With Peter Baer and Walter Baer, (*left*), and Nicolas Baer, (*right*). "Until he died on October 23, 1970, Walter was the soul of the round table, with his infinite experience, cleverness, and skepticism but also with his humor and his talent for comic verse — and that in several languages."

24. " 'The name of the house does not belong on the door,' Walter and Werner agreed. For a long time, the sign above the entrance to Bahnhofstrasse 36 read JB & Co." Discretion went along with extreme parsimony. With the exception of my uncles, nobody had his own office. The upper floors were rented to a dermatologist and a milliner.

25. Cartoon in the Sunday edition of the *New York Times*: "Swiss Knights Take New York." A reference to the accreditation in 1976 of the Baer American Banking Corporation as an "investment company," according to paragraph 12 of the New York State Banking Law.

26. (*From left*) Marie-Blanche Baer-Halperine, Walter's wife, known as "Doucia"; Walter, who wore his pocket-handkerchief flopped over as a kind of trademark; and Ellen Baer-Weyl. In the back, a bust of Walter by Charles Otto Baenninger. (Photo ca. late 1960s)

27. Nelly Baer-Theilheimer (Werner's wife) and Werner. Both of them combined a deep knowledge of the arts with a convivial nature. They themselves were active sculptors and built up a large art collection, housed in the Kunthaus today.

28. "Lived happily removed from all art until his fortieth year." Hans Mayenfisch, partner of the bank. Mayenfisch persuaded the Baer family to take an interest in the visual arts. (Portrait by Ernst Morgenthaler)

29. Ernst Bieri. National Bank president Fritz Leutwiler recommended the former *Neue Zuercher Zeitung* editor and city councilor as a partner. Bieri brought structure to our "charming disorganization," accustomed us to orderly administration, took care of the new buildings, and in 1978 replaced the old telephone switchboards with a modern trading platform, just in time for the precious metals boom.

30. Chaim Weizmann, elected as Israel's first president in 1948, rolled up in a Rolls Royce with a speakerphone to the chauffeur. The Baer children were allowed to ride in it around the Fluntern. Siblings and cousins (*from left*): Beatrice, Marianne, Sonja, Peter, Hans, Roger, Alfred and Nicolas. (Photo ca. 1935)

31. The Weizmann Institute in Rehovoth. My parents and my uncle Walter left Zurich in two convertibles and traveled to Jaffa via Marseilles. The chauffeurs were armed with revolvers. The Berlin architect Erich Mendelsohn conceived the building. (Photo 1934)

32. The Weizmann Institute today, for me for a long time "synonymous with Israel." The institute has specialized in applied research and thanks to its research achievements is able to cover more than half its outlays.

33. Heinz "Heio" Lessing. Went to school in Salem, learned the banking business with Max Warburg in Hamburg, and after the war worked first in the cement industry before he became a partner at the Hamburg Berenberg-Gossler private bank.

34. "The ABCs of banking," as Hermann Josef Abs determined after looking at the nameplates. Every August the "European Forum" in Alpbach — with its simple framework — made possible informal meetings and easy exchanges of views among colleagues.

35. Without him nothing serious happened in the world. Alfred Schaefer, Switzerland's first classic investment banker and long-time head of the Union Bank of Switzerland. He arranged the Interhandel deal for UBS.

36. Enormously gifted, Gershon Scholem lived in the university's guesthouse and had a study at my mother's home. His standard work, *Sabati Zevi: The Mystical Messiah*, was written to a large extent in our house on Bergstrasse.

37. Her return to Paris "tears a sizeable hole into the circle of our friends," wrote Werner Baer: the sculptress Germaine Richier, who introduced Werner, Nelly, and my mother to their higher level of sculpture.

38. My mother and Rudolf Serkin in the 1960s. The attraction of the house on Bergstrasse was the large Bechstein piano. Whenever he was in Zurich, Serkin practiced on it.

39. (*From left*) Ellen Baer-Weyl, the sculptor Charles Otto Baenninger, and Marie-Blanche "Doucia" Baer.

40. The pillars of Zurich's musical life. (*From left*) Irma Schaichet, strict piano teacher for the whole extended family; Alexander Schaichet; and Geza Anda, whom Irma Schaichet took under her wing when the Dohnanyi student came to Zurich from Budapest in 1943. (Photo ca. 1970)

41. "Signed pictures are sometimes genuine, unsigned ones always are." Justin Thannhauser (1892–1976) in conversation with my mother. When talk turned to art, the gallery owner could easily become cynical. Otherwise, my mentor was the most charming person in the world.

42. With Hermann Sigg at the opening of Sigg's show at Lehigh. The artist painted a portrait of Marie-Blanche Baer and painted Werner and Nelly Baer's dining room.

43. "Undoubtedly an important catalyst for Zurich's musical life." Alexander Pereira, the opera's managing director and impresario of the music festival, is also an impassioned breeder of racehorses. This photo, which shows him with one of his four-legged darlings, was taken in Ireland in the autumn of 2003.

44. Szymon Goldberg. When the shirt of his tailcoat hung on a laundry line in our garden, we were ordered to ride our bicycles around it at some distance. During his internment by the Japanese, he gave the camp commandant violin lessons, and after the war he married a Japanese.

45. Homage for the savior of Carnegie Hall. The city council named the street crossing outside the concert hall after Isaac Stern. It was the posthumous recognition of the other life's work the great violinist left behind.

46. "As Marta Istomin remembers, the sequence of Istomin-Stern-Rose arose like this: pianist Eugene Istomin and violinist Isaac Stern were the youngest soloists at the first Casals Festival at Prades in 1950, where they enjoyed playing trios with the legendary cellist. This inspired the idea of Istomin and Stern forming their own trio, choosing Leonard Rose as cellist." (From left) Leonard Rose, Eugene Istomin, Isaac Stern, and Arthur Rubenstein. (Photo ca. late 1950s)

47. With Isaac Stern. Enjoying a glass of champagne in the Restaurant Kronenhalle in Zurich.

48. Recording session in Switzerland. (*From left*) Eugene Istomin, unidentified sound engineer, Isaac Stern (with his glasses shoved on the back of his head as he did so often), and Leonard Rose.

49. January 1997: With Isaac Stern on the way from the Baur au Lac to the "fiddlefest" in the Tonhalle. Isaac searched New York for a neurosurgeon for me (who, in turn, recommended a colleague in St. Gall).

50. With Cecilia Bartoli, during a dinner Alexander Pereira gave on the stage of the opera house.

52. With Lorin Maazel, a friend since the early fifties. "I'd like to have hired Lorin for the Tonhalle Orchestra and wanted to negotiate with him. But he didn't bother himself with material things. 'Talk to my attorney.' The attorney's ideas, however, were too absurd for Zurich's limited means. So Lorin went to Vienna."

52. I owe Christoph von Dohnanyi the bon mot that a conductor is a kind of animal tamer. His prescription for training: he doesn't interrupt rehearsal but lets the orchestra play.

53. "I would prescribe Zinman (*above*) for Zurich," Isaac Stern advised abruptly, but the conductor only came fifteen years later. By then I had turned over the presidency to Peter Stueber.

54. "Be embraced, you millions!" With (*from left*) Ilse, Lady Valerie Solti, and Sir Georg Solti after the jubilee concert. After that concert, Solti became reconciled with Zurich. (Photo 1990)

55. "A college education in the countryside has one great advantage: there's not much in the way of distraction. So you suddenly discover how long a day can be and how much you can do in it." Professor Peter Likins, president of Lehigh University, confers my honorary Doctor of Laws degree, June 1, 1997.

56. "You're all so nice so I'll let you all in." Before takeoff from Zurich for the Tonhalle Orchestra's great tour of China. With (*from left*) Juerg Keller, Irene Keller, Richard Baechi, Christoph Eschenbach, and concertmaster Anton Fietz.

57. "Well then, I'll fly you to Geneva." With Jean Tinguely. Through an accidental meeting at the airport between Peter Baer and Tinguely came the idea for the lighting fixtures installed in 1987 at the Café Muenz, which found great resonance and became somewhat legendary in Tinguely's career. Naoharu Nomura, president of N. Nomura & Co. Ltd. Kyoto, also wanted such lamps for his café.

58. Silvio Mattioli. The only iron-working sculptor who forges his "synthetic materials" in a smith's hearth. He learned how from his family; his ancestors were all blacksmiths. Mattioli forged the bank's latticed gate.

59. "A dead mouse in the red wine." (*From left*) Vreni Imfeld (half-covered), Hildi Hess, Hermann Sigg, Yoshida Frueh, and in the foreground, Nelly Baer. At one of those extended teas at my mother's house on Bergstrasse, it happened that a dead mouse splashed from the bottle into the glass.

60. My mother liked to gather people from the arts and sciences, and of course the family: (*Clockwise*) Karin Sautter, "Doucia" Baer, Walter Sautter, Richard Olsen, Igna Baltensperger, and Res Jost.

61. With Paul A. Volcker. With his godlike authority, Volcker simply operated from the motto, "If you want the truth, you have to pay for it." (Photo taken during an IMF meeting in Washington ca. late 1980s)

62. "Zvi Barak was not far from the truth with his suspicion that an American chairman believed he was the committee." The Volcker Committee in 1999 in Zurich during delivery of the report to the Swiss Banking Commission.

63. "If you can't organize a party, you can't run a bank." Fritz Leutwiler spoke excellent English and did not spare with biting comments.

64. "Keep the dignity of your organization." John Kenneth Galbraith. I owe him my sabbatical as a visiting fellow at Harvard.

65. An arranged marriage I would not have resisted: Nandu Nayar, "my professor" in the Baer Chair at Lehigh, and his wife, Chitra. Nayar studied mechanical engineering and found his way to finance.

66. Monique and Raymond Baer. My children give my life its personal content, which for a long time was given short shrift.

67. "Her sense of duty was only exceeded by her thirst for knowledge." Ilse stabilized and strengthened me. With Ilse (*right*) and Katja Maurer at the jubilee concert of the bank in 1990.

had not run into that custom at the city administration, regularly ignored them and, to our mild horror, would go up to our guests, hand outstretched, and say unabashedly, "My name is Bieri, are you a customer?"

His historic achievement remains taking the bank public. We'd played with the idea for quite some time. A first written indication came in the contract we signed on October 31, 1969, purchasing the Augustinerhof building, where we noted: "The buyer [the bank] declares that it is acting in the name of a stock corporation in the process of formation."

The impulse to think seriously about changing our corporate structure came indirectly from the Swiss tax authorities. They had inquired why silent partners were not taxed. After the introduction of the AHV (the Swiss Social Security System), my uncles had arranged to avoid taxing silent partners through a gentlemen's agreement. Suddenly that didn't help us much. On December 28, 1965, we were slapped with social security contributions from the year 1960 to 1965.

The edict spoiled the family's holiday spirit. The partners paid the full AHV tariff of 10.5 percent. The authority then demanded from the silent partners practically half their annual income — after taxes had been paid on it — within thirty days.

In addition to the AHV campaign, there was another reason to think about a different legal status for the bank. Whenever for some technical reason the bank had to change its books, the fourteen silent partners had to correct fourteen tax returns, much to the chagrin of the tax collectors. They would have liked nothing better than to see our transformation into a public company in order to encompass the earnings of the bank independent of the income and wealth circumstances of the owners.

At first we doubted whether a stock corporation and the double taxation it involved in Switzerland really was the best form of a public company for us. In the meantime, the number of general partners had grown to sixteen, and therefore the four active partners ordered another expert opinion, this time about the most suitable legal construct. We learned from our attorneys that a limited commercial partnership based on shares would not be a viable alternative. The optimal solution would be a stock corporation within a holding structure — an innovation on the Swiss banking landscape that decades later the Credit Suisse copied without, however, putting the holding company under the supervision of bank regulators so that the chairman of the board could assume operational control. On October 27, 1973, the meeting of the general partners unanimously opted for the form of a joint stock company.

That we decided relatively early to take the bank public helped our future development tremendously. It is self-evident that winning unanimity between twenty partners was not easy. Not everybody's interest was identical, and at the same time, emotions foamed and frothed in face of this so decisive step. On the other hand, we were looking for unanimity for financial reasons.

We were concerned — and with reason — that several of the silent partners might sell their shares and that others would face a difficult financial situation. At the beginning of 1972, our equity capital amounted to a meager SFr 28 million ($7.36 million), but we wanted 50 million ($13 million) to launch the joint stock company. I found even that sum degradingly low. Happily, the disintegration of the Bretton Woods Agreements brought us hefty foreign exchange trading profits and therefore markedly better overall results, so that we were able to make up the missing millions relatively quickly. Formally, the money was a family loan to the bank, which, on Bieri's advice, we converted into equity capital in order not to begin in debt. But that still didn't give us any reserves, and we were not at all sure at first if we should open our balance sheet without reserves.

Our tight funds forced us to begin building taxable reserves only after the foundation of a joint stock company. After five years, we had accumulated some SFr 18.4 million ($7.4 million). In addition, we increased our own capital by SFr 4 million a year ($1.6 million).

Without Bieri as our outside partner, we certainly would not have been able to change the bank into a public company. He succeeded in bridging internal differences and to explain the historical necessity of our transformation. True to his Hegelian worldview, he described this phase: "The spirit of historical necessity hovers above the past; it gives meaning to the course of events and raises the actor to creator and executor of a program hidden under the everyday rubble." And he continued: "At the moment of an epic event those involved have no idea what the future will look like."

In fourteen commission meetings, held between 1972 and 1974, the will of the family had crystallized to maintain its influence even in a joint stock company. The result was a shareholder contract that limited capital mobility, at least theoretically. Reality would be different, as we discovered in the wake of the Ambrosiano affair.

At the end of 1974, the designated executors of this historical necessity had worked out all contracts. On January 1, 1975, Julius Baer & Co. began life as a public company.

Outside circumstances were not particularly propitious. In June 1974, German regulatory authorities had closed the Herstatt Bank in Cologne at midday and thus triggered a large earthquake in the banking world. Subsequently, all credit facilities in the interbank business were closed to us, except for a few trusted friends of the house like the Deutsche Bank. At the same time, we were caught up in the secondary banking crisis, thanks to our London subsidiary. On top of that, we faced a severe recession. Times were anything but simple, but given the risks involved, they justified our decision. We had no other choice but to run the bank with limited means and "bake smaller rolls."

The development of the young stock company, therefore, was slow. On the other hand, our new legal entity gave us a unique opportunity to become better known in the banking world, where as a private bank, we were only known to a few. Juergen Luethi and a colleague hit the road for twelve weeks, explained who we were, showed our halfway-confidential opening balance, of which only a few numbered copies existed, and our first annual report, and came back with new foreign exchange and money lines.

After the five-year holding period — a change in the owner-ship, such as issuing or selling shares, within that period is seen in tax terms as a partial liquidation and triggers taxes for real estate ap-preciation — our shares could be listed on the stock exchange. As a first start, the family gave up 10 percent of their securities at SFr 3,000 per share. The market saw the initial price as high, and as a result, the stock meandered for a while at a price of around SFr 3,300 ($1,300).

The young stock company had gathered such speed that until 1980 we depended on outside capital in order to develop further. We decided to issue bearer shares. On July 6, 1981, bearer shares of the Baer Holding AG were introduced on the main Zurich stock exchange. Registered shares were reserved for the family and for our best customers. We issued the first bearer shares at SFr 3,000; at their introduction on the exchange, they were quoted at SFr 4,825. The future price development absolutely justified our decision.

"What does this festive seriousness — 'feierlicher Ernst' — portend for me?" Ernst Bieri wrote on the invitations for his sixtieth birthday, alluding to his first name by citing from Friedrich Schiller. I should have taken him at his word, because on my sixtieth birth-day he described me in our internal bulletin as the incarnate execu-tor of progress, and dedicated the kind of homage to me that everybody likes to read. Bieri — trained equally in theology, philos-ophy, and history, very well-read, a sharp thinker, brilliant speaker, and a good observer — confirmed about me, in addition to my sense of reality and of possibilities, a tendency to play the outsider, a weakness for unconventional points of view, and surprising theses.

At the same time, he said I demonstrated respect for social convention as well as a highly developed readiness to take action —
simultaneously recognizing that it doesn't make sense to clear up every detail before a decision is made. Summing up, he extolled my drive for the new and my fear of torpor. I can only say yes and no. Inside, I do wish everything to remain as it is; on the other hand, I know only too well about the dangers of smugness and torpor.

"Only nascent truth exists; the world itself is a nascent world, a never-ending process," Bieri also said. He's right, and when he told me that this is my philosophy, I can only reply that it was his too, just as Victor Hugo's words he meant for me applied to him: "Ce n'est pas assez d'être heureux, il faut être content" (It is not enough to be happy, you must also be satisfied). The leap we took at the bank to reach our current level was very much his achievement. I don't know if he was happy, but he could certainly be satisfied.

18

REAL ESTATE (1952–89)

Bieri's simple and functional building

My uncle Walter's frugality was exemplified in the following incidents. Once, when the noon edition of the *Neue Zuercher Zeitung* — until 1969 the paper had three daily editions — didn't arrive on time, he sent a messenger to the newsstand on Paradeplatz. By the time he came back with the requested paper, the subscription issue had appeared. So Walter sent the messenger back to the Paradeplatz to return the newspaper and collect the 50 centimes. Frugality was in his bones. Sent to look over a bride in Paris, Walter cabled back only a single word to save money: "KNIF" (for "Kommt nicht in Frage," meaning Out of the question). To this day, the acronym has remained with the family.

It was in this spirit of extreme thriftiness that the bank managed its real estate holdings at Bahnhofstrasse 36. The number of Baer employees rose from 52 in 1950 to 82 in 1957. By 1960 their number had grown to 125. That exhausted all our space reserves, with the exception of the storefronts on Bahnhofstrasse, which the Boehny glove shop and, since 1952, the Lucerne jeweler Guebelin had rented. Guebelin had first rented space at Bahnhofstrasse 37 and was eager to move to number 36 across the street. But the

Schelhaas Company — a smaller version of today's Meister Silber for silverware and gifts — had rented the premises. Werner pointed out that Schelhaas had a long-term lease and suggested that Guebelin simply buy the business, which they did. In 1957, Guebelin also took over the glove shop.

In 1947, Walter and Werner called me a megalomaniac when I suggested urging the dermatologist upstairs to find new quarters and to do without the rent he was paying. But over time they realized that space was tight in the desirable building Georg Lasius had conceived in 1873–74 in the style of the second empire. The newly founded National Bank had moved into the building in 1906 and remained there until 1920. Lasius had been Gottfried Semper's successor as head of architecture at the ETH.

Walter and Werner had the only two single offices on the second floor above the Guebelin establishment. The stock payment office was in the corner room overlooking St. Peterstrasse/Bahnhofstrasse, and then came the trading floor, with Walter's and Werner's offices adjoining and overlooking Bahnhofstrasse. It was normal for up to ten people to be squeezed into one room. At least half of them smoked incessantly. You could cut the air with a knife, and the window, seen from the door, disappeared in a blue haze. For years, my workstation was a desk between foreign exchange and securities trading. It had the advantage of letting me know what was going on every minute of the day. After Jean Neidhart, one of our senior managers, had settled into the building next door, I took over the office of Dr. Pfosi, the dermatologist, from him. It had the extra luxury of a private toilet.

The opportunity to build up a real estate reserve first presented itself in 1954 when the house on Muenzplatz 3, the northern part of the old university, was up for sale. The building had been erected in the years 1835 to 1838 and operated as a school of higher learning. The playwright Georg Buechner, author of *Wozzek* and *Danton's Death*, and a trained medical doctor, held his lectures on comparative anatomy there. Until 1940, the northern wing belonged to the Christ Catholic Church community, which handed it on to an "AG zur Muenz." The property housed a café, and on the upper floors it had day rooms with foot baths, harking back to a time when the rural population marched into town and rented a room in order to wash their feet.

In 1954, my cautious uncles — perhaps still under the influence of the Primateria bankruptcy — showed no interest. Their own house had room enough. So the Niedermann butcher acquired the property. Ten years later, when Niedermann took over the Ruf butcher, we sensed the opportunity of coaxing them into selling us the north wing. We were thinking of paying between SFr 2 million and SFr 3 million, until we got a call the Wednesday before Easter in 1964. The house was being offered at SFr 4.4 million ($1.04 million). Shocked, we decided not to bother. After we had calmed down, we returned that same day to our buying decision and bargained Niedermann down to SFr 4.1 million.

We had better luck in buying the southern wing of the old university. To give an idea, the whole building lay parallel to the Bahnhofstrasse and reached from St. Peterstrasse No. 10 (the southern wing) to St. Augustine church on the Muenzplatz (the northern wing). In 1959, the City-Druck AG sold us the southern tract. A local paper, *Die Tat*, was printed in that house for a while, and the editorial offices of *Finanz und Wirtschaft*, a financial biweekly, were also located there. The opportunity for buying the building arose when City-Druck lost the contract for printing the *Textil-Revue* magazine.

Toward the end of the fifties, we had to rent additional office space. It became clearer every year that provisional housing was not enough. In 1963, the bank employed 163 people; in 1968 it was 280. Our dynamic growth was unmistakable. Our next opportunity to buy arose after Dr. Oskar Zuppinger's death. The bachelor had owned the house on Bahnhostrasse 38 as his residence. The Blumen

Kraemer flower shop had rented the street space in front since 1905. Dr. Zuppinger, who lived in the house, would not dream of selling out but did provide us with office space. His heirs, however, sold us the property for SFr 9.2 million ($2.2 million) in 1968, and Mrs. Bendel, the housekeeper of the deceased, cooked for the top management that had set up shop on the third floor. Mrs. Bendel later on gave us a lot of work to do — after she had retired and bought into a German retirement community. Our drama: two years later she had had enough of her chosen hell. We had to get her out and salvage at least some of her savings. Escaping from a German old age home while still alive and with some assets intact is not that simple. It turned into a high-carat financial exercise.

At the end of 1969, we were finally able to purchase the Augustinerhof at the corner of St. Peterstrasse. The building belonged to the Protestant Society of the canton Zurich and was a hostel and hospice, which offered wandering workmen food and shelter and provided local apprentices and laborers with an opportunity for prayer, evensong, and courses of instruction. At times, it was managed under the name Hotel Widder. But the name — UBS would use it later for its hotel on the Rennweg — was not a success. So it was renamed again as the Augustinerhof/Protestant Hospice. Until 1949 it housed a café that I still remember.

At the end of the fifties, we began talking to the Protestant Society about office space and discussed common plans for adding to the existing building. Finally, they preferred a sale and asked for SFr 16.75 million ($4 million). We settled on SFr 15 million ($3.6 million).

On August 14, 1970, when the *Neue Zuercher Zeitung* published a story about our building expansion plans, which we had revealed in an innocent press briefing, an avalanche of protest cascaded down upon us. To begin with, we had wanted to tear down the newly acquired old buildings and in a first stage build anew on the lot and then replace the houses on Bahnhofstrasse and build a circle-shaped complex with a two-story shopping center with adjoining offices. We had already reached an agreement on this with the owners of number 40.

The city council liked the project, but the public and our own family less so. The expansion, let's state it carefully, was not to their taste. The deciding factor was that Ernst Bieri, who had just joined us, thought the building impractical. Jacques Schader, the architect, had been satisfied with conceiving a beautiful shell. But nobody had evaluated the space needs of the bank business — for example, the trading floor. As an experienced politician, Bieri went to the city of Zurich's building commissioner in order to determine the city's official position about the new construction on Bahnhofstrasse. A mixed committee made up of representatives from the building commission and the monument preservation commission quickly evaluated the buildings on Bahnhofstrasse, categorized the properties at numbers 36, 38, and 40 as "especially worthy" of protection, and in doing so signaled that permission to go ahead with the project was unlikely. For a short while we played with the idea of demanding damages for infringement of our property rights by the monument protection commission and to have a court rule on the rejection of our building application. But we wouldn't have done our image any good. After extensive discussions during our general partners' meeting in October 1974, we decided not to seek our rights in court.

As an alternative to the ambitious circular construction, or building on the green meadow outside of Zurich, which we had also considered, we had, since 1972, thought about leaving the old buildings intact on Bahnhofstrasse and limiting the new construction to the properties in back. Our readiness to build depended somewhat on the course of business. The year 1974, with the secondary banking crisis and the Herstatt bankruptcy, dampened our mood considerably. Bieri suggested a compromise: "Let's do it real small." And that's how we came to the botched entrance on St. Peterstrasse, which we've lived with ever since. A door had not been intended there, and it was only put into place with the completion of the second new building in 1983. Until then, the bank could only be reached through the small entrance next to Guebelin.

We had chosen Alfred Baer and Jacques Schader as our architects. I can attest that my cousin was never a builder's nightmare. His bills never exceeded his estimate. He brought in the new building on St. Peterstrasse, which Bieri always conceived as a "simple, functional building," at a million Swiss francs below the estimate. In addition, he turned out to be an exemplary team player who focused only on the project. Back in 1960 he had designed and built the house in which I still live. It combines simple cubic forms with a carefully thought out, comfortable spatial distribution.

The Oerlikon-Buehrle Immobilien AG, the Buehrle family's construction business, which had developed in the 1930s from the construction office of the machine tool factory, took over the actual construction. They submitted the best bid. Work on the new building began in May 1977, and the rooms were ready for occupancy in July 1979. The only bad luck we had was with Jacques Schader. He abandoned us halfway through the project. Thus we were faced with the uncomfortable necessity of finding somebody who could quickly obtain a construction permit for the second building with which we would replace the old university on the Muenzplatz all the way to St. Augustine's church. Given the complex building code for the old city with its endless special ordinances, Bieri asked the city building inspector who we could work with to get a building permit quickly. His answer: Tilla Theus, the later architect of the FIFA building, the new headquarters of the International Soccer Association. Bieri got along with her very well. The second new building with its superimposed bay sections over the Muenzhof was completed in July 1983. The city did not spare praise and contributed a plaque with the words "Award for excellence in building" next to the Cafe Muenz's entrance.

To a large extent, the city of Zurich is responsible for the way our new buildings look. The building inspector, the construction committee, and the preservation office largely determined materials, color, window axis, and the architectural design. The city also *wished*, which in practice is the same as a decree, that a Café Muenz be installed and that the courtyard, accessible from the Bahnhofstrasse only through the café, be paved with cobblestones. On its own, the city saved this expense by paving the much more frequented Paradeplatz with hideous asphalt.

Most of the money did not flow into the new buildings but into the bank's houses on Bahnhofstrasse. Our building commission sank SFr 20 million ($8 million) into number 38 and its flower shop alone. Not a single square meter of space was added; all the money went into technical installations and renovation. All in all, since 1977, the renewal of the three houses on Bahnhofstrasse cost us SFr 55 million ($22 million) without changing its appearance.

The "simple functional building" turned out to be a much more expensive proposition because air-conditioning had to be installed after the fact and the whole technical infrastructure needed to be vastly improved.

After the two new buildings were completed, we went almost seamlessly into the planning for an operational center in Zurich-Altstetten, which every railroad passenger sees today before the train rolls into the central station. We assigned the project to the Buehrle Company, which owned the real estate via the Allreal firm, as general contractor. Although we did not develop any great aesthetic ambitions in Altstetten, the building is surely our handsomest. Josef Burri, Buehrle's house architect, and my cousin Alfred conceived it. We had begun planning with great enthusiasm in 1981 but became more careful after the Mexico crisis in 1982. I even wanted to cancel the whole project. Bieri was told to start looking into renting and to conceive an advertising campaign with this final instruction: "Total purchase or acquisition of a floor possible." That all real estate experts praised the location did not quiet my concerns. When I confessed my fears to our coshareholder, Robert Studer, head of UBS and a tank colonel, I was given unforgettable marching orders: "Get your ass moving, and do it."

Future developments confirmed Robert Studer's assessment. By the next year, the crisis had been forgotten. We badly needed space for our backroom operations. Construction began in May 1984 with a tremendous inflow of water. In order to remove the mass of water, we had to install large industrial pumps capable of removing 21,000 liters per minute and flush it into an abandoned Swiss railroad canal, until we had the situation well enough under control to allow installation of the concrete slab.

When the house was ready in April 1987, the bank occupied the entire space of 7,500 square meters. The number of our employees had increased from 445 in 1983 to 770. A last festive occasion for Bieri, who loved ceremonial openings, came in 1993 with the superstructure on Brandschenkestrasse 38/40. My cousin Rudolf had accidentally discovered the architect and construction entrepreneur Bernhard Gerwer and his Sumatra Bau AG. On his way to the office, he drove past a construction site of the Sumatra Bau AG and made inquiries about the purchase of the site. Again, Alfred Baer became one of the architects and took care of the bank's technical requirements.

I constructed buildings for almost twenty years as a sideline. Nobody who dared to build in the inner city during the last quarter of the twentieth century made himself or herself popular with the preservationists. Certainly no one will thank us for the fifty million we sank into the houses on Bahnhofstrasse. Today they belong to the visual identity of the Bahnhofstrasse and of the bank. Others, in a desperate search for identity, spent a lot more.

19

In the Age of IT (1966–95)

It's easier to follow the crowd

Werner was an engineer and as such open to innovation in the banking business. Given his lively temperament, however, he was perfectly capable of saying, "If this machine doesn't work by tomorrow, I'll throw it out of the window."

In the time that I shared with him (1947–60), the purchase of an electric bookkeeping machine was a major investment. On December 3, 1949, Werner wrote to me in New York:

> There are some very good machines in America — the national line of NCR, or perhaps a German manufacturer, which, at the moment though, are hard to get. There is one catch. One machine would meet our needs, but if it broke down, our whole bookkeeping operation would come to a halt. Currently, no representative office would be in a position to provide a substitute machine, anyway not right away. Perhaps you could find out which company's system would best suit our needs and also have an adequate representation in Europe. The question of price plays a role, of course: if a machine costs SFr 20,000, the

annual depreciation amounts to half an employee's annual salary, i.e., instead of depreciation we could pay for generous overtime.

Finding the right model was no problem; obtaining the machine, however, was something else. The National Cash Register (NCR) bookkeeping machine had a twelve-month waiting period. But through my friends at Brown Brothers Harriman, I was able to acquire a machine for about SFr 12,000 ($3,000) in an acceptable period of time. The inherent problem with such a machine was that the bank then not only depended on the machine, but it also depended on the operator. If there was no substitute, he or she could never afford to fall ill.

It was already obvious in the early sixties that electronic data processing was coming into the banking industry. In 1964, I had the opportunity, in a self-critical lecture, to warn of private banks' lack of initiative. Increasing pressure to rationalize business and the need to automate, due to rising personnel costs and competition from foreign as well as major Swiss banks, would force private banks to adopt electronic data processing — otherwise they risked being pushed out of the market.

Our colleagues in Geneva had plunged into the electronic adventure well before we did. When we visited Lombard Odier in 1964, we saw that they were managing securities on an IBM 360. We were amazed at how far they had come and how much money they had invested. The fact that we followed developments rather than spearheading them saved us money and nerves. The one negative was that we failed to arouse the curiosity of our employees. Handling the most modern equipment — and forced to learn how to use it — creates the kind of goodwill that should not be underestimated.

In order to evaluate electronic data processing, we formed a technical committee in 1966 with my cousin Peter, our manager

Jean Neidhart, and myself as members. The final acquisition discussion lasted long into the night. Finally we told the waiting competitors, "The choice is IBM." A consulting German engineer sighed, "I know, Mr. Baer, it's easier to die in company than to die alone." In other words, it's easier to follow the crowd than to expose oneself by making an unusual decision.

In order to obtain delivery, I had to spend a week at the IBM academy in the Dutch town of Blarikum learning how a computer functions. After that I had to lecture at the bank about the workings of the binary numbers system.

The IBM 360, with its central console, a central unit, printer, and tape unit, took up a hundred square meters and was fed punched cards, which the "input office" managed. The computer was situated on a rented floor in the ATAG building at Bleicherweg. The installation was unveiled on August 1, 1968, but the first computerized stock market transactions took place earlier, in March of that year.

Jules Frener and Peter Demuth handled the day-to-day operations, and Hansjoerg Huber was our first data processing manager, no doubt a talented man but unhappily cursed with a difficult personality. We lived with him as if he were a temperamental super chef running a grand household: he didn't keep his employees breathless but rather kept them in a stranglehold.

These were exciting times for my cousin Peter and me. Peter, Ray (his wife), and I spent half the night in the computer center, bought sandwiches at night at the Moevenpick shop around the corner, and brought them to the office so that poor Huber wouldn't suffer from hunger pangs while he worked. Once, when he scratched his arm during a bank handball game, I drove him to the hospital with the panicked thought: God forbid that anything happens to our data processing chief. For years we lived in fear that the bank would be endangered should he leave. That is, until Bieri, more accustomed to leadership than we were, found the courage to dismiss our difficult colleague. This dependence on personnel was only one of many risks we had not thought about when deciding to make the investment into the computer age.

Between 1964 and 1971 our capital investments increased fourfold, much to the displeasure of our silent partners who had to accept smaller earnings. But information technology (IT) remained our problem child. On the one hand, we were appalled at how expensive it was; on the other hand, we were equally appalled at how far we still had to go. During our transition to data processing, we had largely failed to modernize the fifty-year-old structure of bank data, and that would prove a major handicap — our costs were persistently higher than those of our competitors.

How we arrived at this insight is characteristic for a Switzerland that no longer exists. Dr. Fritz Laager, who moved from the ETH in 1968 as a bank adviser and succeeded Ernst Bieri as chief of our central services, used maneuvers and other military exercises to exchange operational efficiency figures with colleagues from banks similar to our own, with everything done on the basis of personal trust. With his retirement, those connections broke. Today, for a lot of money, outside service providers try to plug the gap, conduct confidential conversations with chief accountants and other management personnel, and then come up with an evaluation of the individual deviation from the calculated standard. But that doesn't bring us up to the level of knowledge we had in Laager's time.

Part of the data processing history of our house was our temporary jump to Siemens technology in 1974. It set us back a decade. Add to this an ideological conflict over whether we should work with a central system or a decentralized one. In practice, the issue revolved around running our SWIFT traffic through our central computer or through a separate machine. The man who pushed through the decentralized solution left the bank after a relatively short time.

We introduced the first database in 1976 and began to computerize our offices in 1983. Since then, our IT costs have grown exponentially — from SFr 6.2 million ($3.65 million) in 1980 to SFr 42.4 million ($25 million) in 1989 (in 1990 we added a third supercomputer). We avoided any major breakdowns thanks to a good working environment and an excellent team spirit. Everybody thought proactively and acted independently in concert with the task set for them.

Our lease on the ATAG building was limited to ten years, which influenced our decision to risk a second building in the suburb of Altstetten. The move was eased through the modernization of Zurich's infrastructure. Until the introduction of the Swiss Interbank Clearing System in 1987, the payments transactions of Zurich banks ran through a pneumatic tube connection to the SNB. All data had to arrive at the SNB by 2:30 p.m. in order to be processed that day. Thanks to the electronic clearing system and the availability of fiber optic cables, we could set up our second central office in Altstetten without sacrificing daily updates.

For a long time, telecommunications (telephone, telex, and fax) were separate from data processing. In 1978, Bieri had a communications concept developed that would replace the old phone system with a separate trading platform. It became operational in September 1979, just in time for the precious metals boom in 1980, and allowed us to finance the building in Altstetten with the windfall profits.

In 1989, for the first time we examined the possibility of a logistical merger of our data processing with that of a neighboring bank. Thanks to Paul Erni, it turned out that we had a superior securities processing system, a fact that persuaded our neighbor to keep going it alone. Whoever has the processing system gets to know the customers — one reason why even today all private banks hesitate in using common platforms.

In my time, we made two half-hearted efforts to free ourselves from the expensive decentralized system. Fritz Laager's suggestion of founding a new, parallel bank from scratch, which would then take over the old bank, seems in retrospect to have been the smartest idea. But when he presented it in 1992, it was shot down quickly.

After our bank doubled its size in 2005, because of the acquisition of several private banks owned by UBS, the decision to install a new platform was reversed, and considerable write-offs resulted.

20

Baer Custodian Corporation (1940–84)

Foreign affairs

Our U.S. business started modestly in 1940 when my uncle Walter set up the Baer Custodian Corporation and picked René Beyersdorf as manager. Baer Custodian Corporation dissolved in 1968 and ramified into Baer Securities Corporation, which had been founded in 1962 and was renamed Julius Baer Securities Inc. in 1981. It then merged into Baer Credit Corporation, which had been constituted in 1959. Baer Credit Corporation was succeeded in 1976 by Baer American Banking Corporation.

A further step led to a separate asset management entity, established in 1983, as Julius Baer Investment Management Inc.

Finally, Julius Baer (Switzerland) New York branch took over the Baer American Banking Corporation. That was in 1984.

The umbrella company for the whole group is Julius Baer Holding, which is the quoted entity on the Zurich Stock Exchange. Bank Julius Baer is the largest subsidiary, but obviously there are many. Taken as a group, we are today the largest independent money manager in Switzerland. All in all, it is quite a complex story, notwithstanding its modest beginnings.

Werner had sentenced me to reading *Foreign Affairs*, which is rarely written in a fluid or entertaining style and where George Kennan wrote under the pseudonym Mr. X for many years out of a sense of duty toward my uncle. Reading it, I learned to differentiate between the rich Council on Foreign Relations, which publishes *Foreign Affairs*, and the poor-as-a-church-mouse National Committee on American Foreign Policy, to which Kennan had belonged and whose executive vice president is my friend William M. Rudolf, the son of the conductor, Max Rudolf. William worked for Salomon Brothers. The obligatory reading Walter had insisted upon was *The Economist*, to which I have also remained faithful.

Back in Switzerland, I still felt part of the Swiss community that had spent the war years in New York. Traveling to New York became part of my daily life, even if going by plane in those days took much more time. Business, friends, and the arts inspired me to fly to New York as often as possible. Although after 1950 I was no longer a U.S. resident, I have remained true throughout my life to the Anglo-Saxon world and especially to New York, even if Switzerland was always a presence in the background. Thus I've never forgotten the Swiss compatriot who during the war tooled down Fifth Avenue in a cream-colored Rolls Royce with Lucerne plates. Paul Alther was a very prominent Swiss, an executive of the global reinsurance giant Swiss Re. Also a bon vivant. He was a daily customer at the Brussels Restaurant, at the time New York's most expensive eatery. He lived at the Plaza Hotel. After the war, Swiss Re scrupulously examined Paul's expense account and demanded that he repay some of the money.

Keeping leading executives in New York during the war was

part of the corporate strategy all large Swiss concerns followed. Thus the SBC founded the Swiss Bank Corporation New York Agency on July 4, 1939. Two of its top managers, Albert Nuss-baumer and Armand Dreyfus (he died in 1942), lived in New York during the war years.

Members of the Bloch-Sulzberger textile family, who in Zurich resided in the building that today houses the Bellerive Museum, lived at the Plaza as well. In the early postwar years, I often visited their home on the lakefront, with its inviting entry hall and stair-case, not to mention their two beautiful daughters.

Bringing your own car to the United States may seem a little strange today, but fifty years ago it was not at all unusual. When my cousin Alfred began his architectural internship at Emery Roth in New York, he took his MG-TF along and certainly impressed many girls with it.

New York restaurants are a world apart. Their cycle runs much faster than it does in Europe. Yesterday's restaurant is gone today, usually because quite suddenly it is no longer a favorite with the in crowd. I always liked going to Reuben's on 58th Street — it too closed a long time ago — even after I discovered Israeli Foreign Minister Abba Eban at the next table. I found this proximity dan-gerous and moved to another, more distant table. Even today I think that was a smart decision. Reuben's was an institution for Jew-ish breakfasts: bagels, lox, and cream cheese.

Sol Hurok, the Russian impresario, was a fixture at the Brus-sels, where René Beyersdorf had taken me. Hurok sat alone, unap-proachable. Among many others he represented Isaac Stern. Hurok's funeral ceremony took place in Carnegie Hall with the cof-fin on stage. The privilege of a great impresario. Stern, by the way, introduced me to the world of New York's Chinese restaurants, where he knew his way around very well. Isaac liked informal din-ing and avoided the showy décor of the classic restaurants.

The Russian Tea Room near Carnegie Hall was another obligatory stop on my New York itinerary. Nor were my ties to Carnegie Hall only musical. In this Temple of the Muses, I was introduced to the American art of giving. Thanks to Isaac Stern, my name is on the wall of Carnegie Hall. The savior and patron of this unique concert hall was a talented fundraiser. It is a tribute to his finesse that he did not invite me to open my purse the first time. He only knocked the second time — during a center stage dinner. No heart is so hard that it can say no under those circumstances. But it was bloody serious. That dinner was arranged to raise the means for the structural maintenance of the building, and it cost me a lot of money. I remember it very well: for one thing, I had not yet started to earn money; for another, at the time, the pledged sum for incomes in Swiss francs had to be multiplied by 4.25, the then current rate of exchange. I signed the pledge program and agreed to pay off the donation in four annual installments.

The American way of giving is quite foreign to a European sensibility; the public way of donation is especially unknown in Europe, where people would just as soon not talk about it and rarely make a contribution anyway. Of course, public giving promotes the desire to give more than your neighbor, much to Carnegie Hall's blessing. You don't dare attend a dinner — to exaggerate the situation just a bit — if you're not ready to contribute $100,000. Otherwise, you just don't belong. Charity in America, which has a much, much higher social importance than in Europe, is a matter of giving and taking.

This is how it goes. People organize a charitable event for a museum, a hospital, or a concert hall and round up their friends by selling them each a table for $100,000. The friends accept in order to cultivate their business relationships or to satisfy the social climbing ambitions of their wives. On the next occasion, the friends organize an event of their own and in turn sell a table for $100,000. A while back, a perfect example landed on my desk — an invitation to the "10th Anniversary of Midori & Friends." A decade ago, the Japanese violinist Midori had launched a music education program at New York public schools in order to discover and promote young talents from poor households. Tables for the evening event on April 29, 2003, at the St. Regis Roof on 55th Street, cost $25,000. The executive committee included Zubin Mehta and Barbara Knowles Debs, wife of the former deputy chairman of the New York Federal Reserve, Richard Debs.

This big money charity society arose against the background of a benevolent tax code, which in effect does not contain any limits on deductions. So long as incomes are high enough, this charity costs nothing below the line. Sandy Weill's $2.5 million contribution for the restoration of Carnegie Hall was a good investment. He outspent Brooke Astor, the doyenne of New York society, by $500,000. In exchange, Isaac Stern asked him to come on stage during the gala and thanked him before the eyes of the assembled Rockefellers, Vanderbilts, Astors, and Kennedys. This kind of social charity is seen in England, in contrast, as a form of social climbing.

Several years ago, I received an invitation from the then Citigroup chief and Carnegie Hall president to purchase an "honor table." The price tag: $1 million. It provided me with a wonderful opportunity to shock my son with the announcement that I had booked two tables. He needed a couple of seconds to get the joke. He received a second shock days later when he learned that indeed a dozen honor tables had been booked. By the way, Sandy Weill had pledged to match each contribution out of his own pocket.

World Bank President James Wolfensohn was Weill's predecessor at Carnegie Hall and of course occupied that office by the grace of Isaac Stern. Stern was a power broker who used his sense of where power could be found to good effect. As a hobby cellist, Wolfensohn could at least claim to have some knowledge of music. Weill, on the other hand, just focused on giving millions to Carnegie Hall. Stern had enticed him with the argument that "Carnegie Hall is the 57th Street version of a golf course," a good place to talk business outside the office. The Club Room, where champagne and canapés are presented during intermissions, serves this purpose. Weill learned that supporting a concert hall made it far easier to engage in serious negotiations by talking about culture rather than about business. And he found a supportive friend in the artistic director, Judith Arron, who unfortunately died early. The present head is Sir Clive Gillinson.

Isaac was never embarrassed about using financial and economic arguments to persuade donors. A concert hall, he would contend, raises the overall value of a neighborhood and therefore boosts local real estate prices. His arguments, however, were not always rational. I remember that in my Zurich dining room, he once negotiated with a real estate broker in New York about a new office two blocks from his home on Central Park West, among the most expensive real estate in the city. "I'll save the money in taxi fares," he reasoned.

Travel to the United States during the first decades of my professional life was more hopping than flying. Right after the war, only TWA had mercy for the trans-Atlantic-oriented Swiss. TWA Constellations flew the New York-Paris-Geneva-Rome-Cairo route. Swissair only began flights to the United States a year later (May 2, 1947) and only if required from Geneva. Regular Swissair service was not established until April 1949.

I needed a visa to enter the United States and a good conduct pass from the police. One could only leave the country with a confirmation in writing that one didn't owe American taxes. Even after a short visit, no one was spared a trip to the IRS inspector to attest to his or her tax-free status, but the assessor was usually an understanding man.

My Christmas 1948 flight on a TWA Constellation took me first to Gander in Newfoundland and Shannon in Ireland. These landings were routine in both directions. I had hardly fallen asleep after dinner when the plane landed in Shannon in the middle of the night. Passengers had nothing else to do but wander through the halls with glaring neon lights, past enormous PX stores for American army personnel, and endless stores that sold duty-free items. Gander was no different.

These stopover rituals continued on the trans-Atlantic routes after propeller-driven planes stopped flying. The DC-8's, Swissair's first jetliners, were not allowed to fly without stopovers to check the engines. Only after retrofitting the engines toward the end of the DC-8's life was Switzerland linked directly and nonstop to the United States.

The journey took a good twenty hours even with the DC-8. Passengers flew five hours from Zurich to Shannon at the western tip of Ireland, spent two hours on the ground, and then continued on to America, another five to six hours, depending on the wind. The stopover added two hours, and it took another four hours to reach New York. Planes generally left Zurich at four in the afternoon and arrived in New York the next morning. TWA's return flight landed in Paris at 8 a.m. and we arrived in Zurich later that morning.

Flying was a different kind of adventure compared to what's happening with flights today. Passengers did well to prepare themselves for surprises. After a trans-Atlantic flight, a day's rest was mandatory, not only because of the strain during the flight or the inefficiency of the air-conditioning, but also because passengers had to be prepared for massive delays at all times, even assuming that they would arrive at their planned destination at all. It happened that I was bumped off the plane in Geneva instead of in Zurich, even on a flight from Israel. After circling above Zurich for two hours in glorious weather — ground fog made landing impossible — the plane touched down in Geneva. On a flight from London, the other passengers and I had to disembark in Geneva. The pilot didn't even feel it necessary to inform us about the changed flight plan.

Landing in Geneva instead of in Zurich didn't seem worth talking about, because it happened so often. Also landing in Paris or Frankfurt. As a passenger, you didn't take it very seriously. My wife and I once boarded a flight to New York (it now left at nine o'clock in the evening, real progress) that landed in Cologne two hours later. Why? The pilot decided the luggage had been badly stowed.

On one flight to New York, the DC-8 ran into a snowstorm and had to circle overhead prior to landing. However, it started to run out of gas, so the pilot landed in Connecticut and used his personal credit card to pay for the fuel. The passengers were then faced with the question of whether to fly on or not. The issue was clear for the pilot: "I have a date with a young lady. I have to go to New York," he announced. So the plane took off again and got back in the circling waiting line.

As long as the Concorde existed, I flew Air France. Three hours and ten minutes and arriving at your destination before you departed is a striking difference from twenty hours and arrival for breakfast the next day. Airport connoisseurs noticed the early arrival time in New York. Usually only flights from Latin America landed at JFK in the morning. Early in the Concorde's history, my early arrival earned me the attention of a taxi driver. Once he realized that I had not come in from South America, he said, "Oh, you came on the Concorde. Would you allow me a personal question?" I said, "Of course." So he asked, "Are you really so important?"

Part of the convenience of the Concorde were the lounges in Paris and New York. Especially on Saturdays, it was a great pleasure to breakfast in the lounge and to experience *tout le monde* with its lady friends, often really quite beautiful women, on their way to a Paris weekend.

Before the Concorde era, you could easily spot the workaholics — they took Swissair's SR-100 route on a Sunday, instead of the Monday flight. First class was like a cocktail party. Everybody knew everybody else. It was no accident, therefore, that the

Palestinians kidnapped the Sunday plane after the Yom Kippur War and landed it in the desert. The most prominent victim of this zealous act was Ernest Meili, the Swiss chief of the J. Henry Schroder Banking Corporation.

I knew Meili and Alfred Barth of Chase from my stint at Brown Brothers Harriman. Both were good business friends. A third friend was Ernst Schneider, whom I met in New York when he was head of the International Division at Irving Trust. In 1979, the Credit Suisse, one of the major Swiss banks, brought him to Zurich as a senior vice president. Alfred Barth, a Catholic from Zurich who grew up in one of the city's poorer districts and had close ties to Opus Dei, made his career at Chase Manhattan. He used to come to brunch on Sundays when he was in Zurich. As head of the foreign division, Barth was the highest-ranking Swiss on Wall Street. Thanks to the large postwar credits he granted to impoverished Western European states, he became a much honored man, including the (French) Legion of Honor. When he retired (it must be more than twenty years ago now) I wrote an appreciation about him for the *Neue Zuercher Zeitung*.

Thanks to Alfred Barth, Julius Baer was Chase Manhattan's correspondent bank in Zurich for a long time, the reason too why I met George Champion on a stopover in Zurich on his way to a World Bank meeting in Vienna. And one time I was "travel agent" for David Rockefeller, Champion's colleague and successor at Chase Manhattan.

Rockefeller traveled like the president of a country. His entourage sent advance word where he was and where he was going every step of the way. Incredible for a time before cell phones. We knew about his arrival three minutes after he landed. The Chase Manhattan president stayed at the Baur au Lac, the prestigious hotel in Zurich located right on the lakefront. On his first night, he probably went to see Alfred Schaefer, the head of Union Bank of Switzerland (UBS), one of the major Swiss banks at the time; the next day he lunched at the National Bank, and so on. I had reserved Rockefeller's last evening to be at my home. Everything went smoothly except for the fact that I had not checked the dinner menu. Soon I received an excited phone call: "For God's sake, change the menu. Otherwise he'll run right out if he has to eat *Geschnetzlets mit Roesti* [minced veal Zurich style] one more time."

Rockefeller was the most charming man with a refreshingly common touch. One time when we had made a date in New York, he arrived very late and admitted quite freely, "I couldn't find the restaurant." The father of six would open his speeches with the cliché, "I'm glad to have you here, and Peggy sends her greetings." In some respects, he resembled Walter Baer. Both were even better diplomats than bankers.

Until I discovered the Sherry Netherland on the corner of Fifth Avenue and 58th Street, I usually stayed at the Drake, where my mother had been a frequent guest.

Among my assignments in the Big Apple was the care of the bank's international relations and the Baer Custodian Corporation and its successors under various names. My uncles founded the Custodian Corporation in 1940 in New York, expecting that their dollar accounts in a Swiss name would be blocked. They assumed that the United States would not block accounts of an American company and thus parked the dollar holdings of the bank and its clients in the Baer Custodian Corporation. But in doing so, they overlooked a legal concept unknown in Europe and not uncontroversial in the United States — the "beneficial owner." American regulators argue that deposits of a foreign bank, let's say Julius Baer, in an American bank, for example, Chase Manhattan, do not belong to Julius Baer & Co. but to an individual (or several of them) who has a dollar account with Julius Baer. To that extent, the attempt to avoid blocking via a local entity was doomed from the outset.

Walter picked René Beyersdorf to run the Custodian Corporation and had Werner's cousin, Ernst Radt, look over his shoulder. Radt was a partner at Halle & Stieglitz, a Wall Street brokerage. The blocking did not leave Beyersdorf or his factotum Frederick Stone out of work; Beyersdorf only worked half days in the beginning anyway. You could actively administer blocked assets. For foreign customers, Baer Custodian held sizable amounts of cash.

But what did we do with it? Nothing. We didn't even buy short-term General Motors promissory notes, even though at that time GM had a better reputation than the treasury. My uncles, unfamiliar with conditions in the United States, found that too risky. Against this background, my uncle Victor Sax remarked, "I wish I had 10 percent of the money you didn't make."

For a long time, my uncles didn't know exactly what they wanted to do with the Baer Custodian Corporation. Walter wrote to my mother on April 24, 1946, "At least we can say that he [René Beyersdorf] is well paid with $350 a month." And three weeks later, May 13, 1946, he wrote, "He has not asked us for a raise and of course we have not brought up the subject either. On the other hand, if the BCC [Baer Custodian Corporation] continues to exist in the future and to flourish, he will get an appropriate share of the net profits. I like him very well; Werner thinks he talks too much."

Finally, Werner wrote to my mother on February 22, 1947: "We have recently done some good business in the Baercustos [Baer Custodian Corporation]. Beyersdorf has proved himself in concluding licensing arrangements for payments out of blocked accounts. On the other hand, we are not quite on the same page in the arbitrage field."

So-called license procedures proved to be big business after the war. Deposits were not freed wholesale the way they had been frozen, but individually, and through licenses issued by the Enemy Property Custodian. That opened up some possibilities for arbitrage. You could assign blocked accounts to those who had died in the meantime and free up others in exchange. Another approach was to trade blocked assets at a discount. Several lawyers specialized in this field and corresponded with the Enemy Property Custodian in Washington, whose representatives proved very cooperative. Irving Moskovitz (Graubard & Moskovitz in New York), for example, became legal adviser for Hoffmann-La Roche in the United States in the early fifties. We became good friends with him and his wife, Adele.

Baer Custodian was located at 67 Wall Street. Most of the offices in the building belonged to Brown Brothers Harriman. We stayed there until we followed the general trend to move uptown to 42nd Street, of course East. Publishers are West, bankers East. "I only go West when I sail for Europe" is the text of an old song that plays on the snobbism of the old East Side when ocean liners docked on West Side piers or in Hoboken.

But not even the East Side of Manhattan was always as safe as one might like to think. Paul Jolles, a passionate collector of modern art and a high-ranking Swiss diplomat of imposing height and size, faced a jolt of fear one evening when he sent his limousine off in front of a brownstone where some billionaire had invited him to an artists' party. Suddenly he saw a "black panther" arise out of the darkness. *Now it's happened*, the art-loving diplomat thought as he already saw himself lying in the gutter with a smashed skull. Then he had a second thought, *Oh, I'll try and talk to him first*. It turned out that both were going to the same party.

The move uptown to 42nd Street and Fifth Avenue was a big step for our firm. The crucial factor for the new address was not the public library across the street but the proximity of Grand Central Station. Most of our employees came to work by train. Under David Rockefeller, Chase Manhattan once tried to reverse the flow with construction of a new headquarters in Battery Park City, but it didn't work. Today the bank's headquarters is located on Madison Avenue.

As a Francophone Swiss, René Beyersdorf liked to move in the

French camp on Wall Street. His most important business acquaintance, however, was Edgar Paltzer, from 1946 to 1961 head of SBC in New York and dean of the Swiss bankers. (His son George Paltzer married my niece Annette Olsen in 1984.) In addition to dealing with Mexican promissory notes, Beyersdorf built up a successful commercial finance operation for Baer Custodian's successor, the Baer Credit Corporation, founded in 1959.

What were we poor Europeans to do on Wall Street? As a newcomer on the market, the Baer Credit Corporation had to be satisfied with the crumbs of the commercial business that the large houses disdained. In practice, that meant finance companies, of which New York had many. They bought foreign credits and issued notes for refinancing, not at a prime rate, because the paper was not first class, but the business, in part, was very big. You could make good money off these notes.

Another not very noble business were the so-called factoring companies who bought receivables from textile firms and who then took over their credit risk. (That way, textile producers could save bookkeeping costs.) We were represented in these factoring companies through buying "silent" equity interests from our good friends. We conducted this business for a pretty long time, and it still exists today, even if it dies each time there is a financial crisis.

Talcott was certainly the largest factoring company. Herbert Silverman was the owner, a good friend and adviser of our family. He died in August 2003, well over ninety years old. Herb Silverman also worked for Leona Helmsley, the notorious Queen of Mean, who became a victim of her greed and told a judge that "only the little people pay taxes." The judge put her in jail. Later, Silverman sold Talcott to Franklin National, which paid him in stock. Franklin National collapsed before he could sell his shares, and that's how he lost his fortune.

And one more example of how small and entangled the world is: Herb Silverman's son-in-law, Daniel K. Mayer, is a senior partner at the well-known law firm Wilmer, Cutler & Pickering in Washington, D.C. He earned his first spurs as a clerk for Supreme Court Justice Felix Frankfurter and accompanied me to the D'Amato hearings about the dormant accounts on April 23, 1996.

Sandy Weill's Commercial Credit Corporation (CCC) is another example of a factoring company, and one I remember so well because we received an offer to merge our U.S. operations with CCC. But we found that CCC was not good enough and thus missed a rare opportunity to be a partner in his coming successes. We actually missed a rare opportunity twice. Our friends at Chase Manhattan wanted to hook us up with Hank Greenberg's AIG, today the largest insurance company worldwide. Again, we felt the company was beneath us, even though it was a good customer of Baer Securities in the underwriting business. In both cases, we would have drawn a winning ticket. On the other hand, we had entered in partnership with UDT (United Dominions Trust London) and inherited a lot of headaches. So much for the subject of risks with partners.

Shortly before dissolving the Baer Custodian Corporation on April 30, 1968, we were caught in the whirlpool of the back office crisis, which was actually more of a clearing crisis, with which all New York institutions had to battle as a result of the explosive growth in the Euromarket. Brown Brothers Harriman, our depository, was hopelessly snowed under. Much more unpleasant was the cancellation of the Baer Credit Corporation's Banker's Blanket Bond, an insurance against fraud and embezzlement, a cancellation that hit all financial institutions of our size. The insurance companies acted because such crimes and misdemeanors had begun to mount dangerously. Loss of this protection forced us to look for alternatives and to search for a partner together with our joint venture UDT. Chase Manhattan helped us. But instead of picking CCC in Baltimore, from whom we had even bought debt issues (and which later, thanks to Sandy Weill, were incorporated into the empire of Citigroup), we tried a joint venture with the Rochester-based Lincoln First Bank. On January 7, 1972, we founded Lincoln First/Baer Corporation, headquartered in New York. Lincoln First owned 51 percent. We held 49 percent and ran the business. A year and a half later, Lincoln First acquired our share, including René Beyersdorf's pension payment. Why? They had no feel for international business and found it strange. They also had no interest in learning more about it.

As a result, we once again faced the daunting task of directing our activity in New York toward the dollar market and at least reducing our credit costs, since we could no longer insure our business risks. For the Baer Credit Corporation, by statute a financial company, costs for obtaining money were substantially higher than a bank's. When we started to think about it, Julius Baer & Co. in Zurich was still a partnership, which excluded the idea of a branch. We would have risked major problems with the IRS had we opened one. Nor could we consider a bank license for a New York–based stock corporation. But we figured we had a chance of receiving a license for a merchant bank — formally known as an "investment company" — according to Article XII of the New York State banking law, even if so far only four foreign banks held such a license. (Henry J. Schroder, London, as well as a French, Swedish, and Dutch bank.)

At first, however, the New York Federal Reserve was not inclined to give us one, even though I knew John Heiman, the banking commissioner. The negotiations dragged on so much that one day I let off steam at Isaac Stern's house. The compassionate violinist asked with what institution I was negotiating.

"With the Federal Reserve," I told him.

Isaac replied, "I know the deputy chairman very well. Richard Debs is a good friend of mine. I'll call him and he should listen to you directly."

This he did, and that was how a meeting with Richard Debs

came about. He wasn't directly responsible but had great influence in issuing such licenses. Once again in my life, music came to my aid.

Isaac and Debs knew each other from Carnegie Hall. He blamed the fact that he did not become chairman of the New York Fed after his boss retired because of the socially acceptable anti-Semitism then still prevalent in New York. He quit, went to Morgan Stanley, and joined our board of directors.

Our receipt on April 26, 1976, of a license for the Baer American Banking Corporation caused a sensation in New York. The *New York Times* ran a cartoon on page 1 of the Sunday business section titled "Swiss Knights Take New York." I arrived with my wife in New York from Zurich on that day and was somewhat surprised when I picked up the newspaper at the airport and discovered the cartoon. Nobody had expected that anyone would take notice of us, and certainly not so prominently. We used the cartoon as an illustration on our next Christmas card.

The new corporation (with total assets in 1981 of $136.8 million) focused on commercial business. In addition to trade financing, our major activities were foreign exchange, money market instruments, and credit. No one would claim that we were excessively successful. René Beyersdorf had led the bank under the motto that no equivalent personality could be found to follow him, and therefore he had not bothered grooming a successor. The man we found, with the help of a prominent headhunter, turned out to be an alcoholic. For a while, I thought seriously of suing the headhunter. The successor we sent from Zurich had to clean the house, but he wasn't always on top of things. We would find after the collapse of the Italian Banco Ambrosiano that the Baer American Banking Corporation had given a line of credit for an Ambrosiano subsidiary shortly before the breakdown.

In 1984, the New York branch of the Bank Julius Baer took over the business of the banking corporation. David E. Bodner, a cultivated and very respected man, became chairman of the board. Under Richard Debs he had been in charge of foreign exchange trading at the New York Federal Reserve. As the man in charge of international relations, he knew everybody worth knowing and worked at Chemical Bank before I brought him over to us.

Bodner's predecessor on the board of the corporation was Tom Wage, a man widely respected in New York's financial community and a great opera lover. He died during a Metropolitan Opera performance. The very next day, the auditors at the New York Fed asked me who I planned to nominate as successor and ombudsman. I hadn't thought beyond "a senior city figure." But the auditors would prove very helpful: "Why don't you take David Bodner?"

I had my doubts. "Do you think he would come?" I asked.

"We know he will."

For me, David Bodner — of average height, slim to gaunt, dark blond — is an example of what can happen when you fall into doctors' clutches. After he retired, he went skiing, suffered a heart attack, and had an operation during which the surgeon scratched his vocal cords. A minor error. David couldn't talk for months. A terrible drama. He has recently died.

In 1962, we founded the Baer Security Corporation to handle the securities business. Asset management came much later. Don Williams was the first head of Baer Securities, a very entertaining gentleman whose aphorisms became part of our house's treasury of quotes: "The noise you hear is not the overhead, it's the air-conditioning."

In 1981, Baer Securities Corporation mutated to Julius Baer Securities Incorporated. The impetus came from an extraordinarily dynamic man named Morris Offit, who told us that "there are many Baers but there is only one Julius Baer." We would have preferred the name to be Baer Securities in order to stand higher in the alphabetic ranking.

Offit was senior partner and chief analyst at Salomon Brothers when he showed up one day in Zurich in 1980 and surprised me with the proposal, "I want to become your partner."

My reply was simple, "Why don't you buy the bank?"

But he was serious, and that flattered us greatly. Naive as we were, we followed our emotions. It was as if Michael Schumacher, the Grand Prix racing champion, had applied for a job as family chauffeur. Back then, we saw his offer as "finally somebody who knows what he is doing and has discovered how good we are."

Morris Offit — slender, of medium height, good-looking, a workaholic — worked at a rate and speed that proved too much even for me. I fought with him on the phone through many a night. He thought nothing of calling at eleven at night or midnight to say he urgently needed ten stock analysts, when at the time we only had two in Zurich. It was Offit too who said that a bank without an office in Tokyo was not a bank. So we opened an office in Tokyo.

This high-pressure man — you really couldn't push any harder than he — used his immense energy to catapult us into the upper league of the banking world. At Julius Baer, only Pedro Hangartner could stand up to him. Offit was also a member of the holding's board of directors, which was only conditionally successful, since not everybody spoke fluent English. He insisted, to cite one detail, on determining the page in the annual report on which his picture was to appear, arguing, "I can't travel with an annual report in which my picture is not properly placed."

You could learn from him, and from the way he left us. He had only penciled us in as a transit stop on his way from Salomon Brothers to his own bank. But he gave us a lot — for example, our friendship with Salomon Brothers.

Offit was also the man who championed founding subsidiaries. Whoever wants to do business with the large pension funds and foundations has to fill out forms detailing what they do. If they have several businesses — let's say securities administration, credit, brokerage, and asset management — that's bad, because it isn't focused enough. But having the names of several firms at the same address does not bother Americans. Offit himself was only interested in asset management. So in 1983, he founded Julius Baer Asset Management Inc. domiciled in New York. But after he had collected the first few hundred millions in asset management, Offit left us in 1986 and founded the Offit Bank, taking many clients with him.

He hooked other clients very cleverly through his pro bono work for large foundations. He was president of several Jewish museums and chairman of the board of trustees of Johns Hopkins University. When he had enough, he sold his Offit Bank to Wachovia, and this at a time when his bank was in full bloom. Here too he showed an excellent sense for the right decision at the right time, since he also sold his management contract, which did not expire until the end of 2002.

An illustrious member of our board in New York, a good personal friend and adviser, was the lawyer Robert Herzstein. Jimmy Carter brought him into his administration as undersecretary of commerce. Herzstein called me that night. I congratulated him and said, "You are exchanging one sinking ship for another," to which he replied, "Yes, but mine is larger and sinking slower."

Before and after his government service, Herzstein was a partner at the prestigious Washington law firm of Arnold and Porter. Abe Fortas, who would become a Supreme Court justice and stumble over a $10,000 bribe, was the senior partner. And as another example of how small the world can be, Fortas was Isaac Stern's best friend and had been the lawyer for the Swiss watch industry in the great antitrust trial of the early sixties.

An essential part of my trans-Atlantic experiences was the Three Days in the White House event arranged by *Time* magazine. Without our bank ever having run an ad, I was often invited, together with ten or twelve other "leaders of the world" from Europe, to talk to the president of the United States.

On the first tour, I met with President Jimmy Carter, together with Renault head Raymond Levy, BMW chairman Eberhard von Kuenheim, and the president of the British bank J. Henry Schroder, as well as the heads of other large British institutions. After lunch, the president sat across from us in the living room and asked us straight out, "What am I doing wrong?" A very intelligent man who had a lot of bad luck during his term of office. I remember his reputation for micro-management. Word was that he assigned the parking spaces of the White House.

Ronald Reagan, on the other hand, made everything seem laughable or ridiculous and avoided any serious conversation. When the head of Alitalia asked him about the airline imbroglio that was in the headlines at the time, Reagan gave some sort of answer along the lines of, If my grandmother had wings, she would fly. Carter left quite a different impression.

These meetings demonstrated the great influence of *Time*, whose editor-in-chief was, of course, a member of our party. The schedule was tough starting at seven in the morning for breakfast with a senator and continuing with meetings with Washington names throughout the day. These were certainly the choicest invitations I have ever received, and I can only praise my fellow guests: BMW president Kuenheim was especially nice and so was Renault head Levy.

Later, the PR agencies would copy this idea. Without White House access, however. But you could buy breakfast with a senator. I almost fell into that trap during a study tour in 2001 for the Baer-Kaelin foundation, which the Swiss embassy had arranged. The agency wanted an insane amount of money for dinner with a senator. I pulled the emergency brake and said, "Thanks, I don't need a PR agency to get an appointment with a senator."

Among my trans-Atlantic acquaintances was the best-selling author Arthur Hailey, who acquired his financial savoir faire for his 1975 thriller *The Money Changers* at our bank. He specializes in researching the professional environment he is writing about. How does it work? How does it influence people? He and his amusing wife stayed at the Dolder, one of Zurich's five-star hotels, and we often ate dinner together at the Kronenhalle. Hailey was born in England, grew up in Canada, and lives in California. Over Wiener schnitzel and roesti he used to instruct me on how to write successful books: "One year's sabbatical, a year to learn the business you are writing about, and another year to write." His iron discipline is one of the reasons for his many successes.

Dust-collecting Steuben apples made of heavy crystal and manufactured by Corning Incorporated, where my cousin Rudi Baer had worked occasionally, are the visible proof of my trans-Atlantic labors. These crystal apples, which symbolize New York, are sometimes given in the United States to thank speakers for their remarks. Since I was often the host of visiting firemen — traveling board members of foreign firms — I occasionally had to make a mealtime speech, and so my collection of crystal apples has grown apace.

It was most amusing to watch the behavior of the various members of boards. If a board of directors meeting was scheduled for Zurich, it could happen that a private secretary would arrive beforehand for a "test" sleep at the Dolder. These people gave themselves such airs that they would fly in their own beds. As a matter of course, the directors would arrive in three or more planes. Risk has to be divided. In the past, directors were not given much in compensation but took advantage of all kinds of luxuries, including handmade tie tacks to commemorate a board meeting in Zurich.

21

The Euro Market (1957–85)

Siegmund Warburg's ingenious idea

Without warning, in March 1952, the U.S. Treasury blocked all our deposits at American banks. The reason: the Foreign Assets Control Regulations and the Trading with the Enemy Act.

What had happened? The Schweizerische Volksbank (Swiss People's Bank — Credit Suisse took it over in the nineties) had moved a smallish sum, about half a million dollars, from an account in the United States to an account at our bank in New York. The Treasury had noted the transfer and immediately ordered the freeze, on the assumption that the money had come from trade with the enemy. China, which had become an enemy of the United States during the Korean War, was under suspicion.

That same night, we checked on our correspondent banks in the United States not yet hit by the freeze in order to remove as much liquidity as we could from the Treasury's grasp. Walter flew to Washington and assigned Adam Yarmolinsky to protect our interests. The attorney was a leading member of Washington's intellectual elite, but he did not succeed in freeing up our money. It took four years before everything was cleared up. We still have no idea what the Treasury thought the payment had to do with North Korea or China.

Given the American tendency to block foreign deposits, banks in the Eastern Bloc (and everybody else who feared such a freeze) began, after the outbreak of the Korean War, to deposit their dollar accounts outside the United States. Julius Baer maintained an account for its dollar holdings at the Deutsche Bank in Frankfurt (known until 1957 as the South German or Sueddeutsche Bank). Government banks on the other side of the Iron Curtain preferred depositing their holdings with the Russian-owned Banque Commericale pour l'Europe du Nord in Paris, whose telex address was, significantly, Eurobank. The name Eurodollar was soon adopted for the offshore dollars that led, by the end of the 1950s, to the Euromarket. It is somewhat amusing that Theo Waigl, a German minister of the Christian conservative CSU party, would succeed in adopting the term "euro," coined by a communist banker, rather than the planned "ecu," for the common European currency.

Offshore dollars have a long history. At the beginning of the Second World War, when the United States was still neutral, the German Reichsbank, recalling its experiences during the First World War, decided to dissolve its account at the National City Bank and transfer the balance to the Swiss Bank Corporation (SBC), which had already enthusiastically recommended itself. The Reichsbank had first queried the Union Bank of Switzerland (UBS), which, knowing the risks, suggested a subsidiary, the Lombard Bank. The German consul wrote back, "We cannot recommend the Lombard Bank because of its Jewish partners." Since 1941, the SBC, for all intents and purposes, had been a clearinghouse for the Reichsbank's dollar holdings.

Secretary of the U.S. Treasury Henry Morgenthau noted in his diary that suspected management of German dollar holdings in the United States fell on Credit Suisse in Zurich. Morgenthau, therefore, had the Swiss American Corporation, a Credit Suisse subsidiary, placed under surveillance. The services the major Swiss banks performed for the Germans during the war were an important reason why Swiss assets were blocked in the United States. Marco Durrer, who had read the Morgenthau diaries in Washington, reported on them in his 1984 study on Swiss-American financial relations.

A fundamental lesson of the early history of the Eurodollar is this: freezing assets doesn't do much good. In fact, it hurt the United States more than it helped. For one thing, the Americans could no longer observe global cash flows, thus losing an important news source. Moreover, their policy helped to give birth to a new currency that has become an integral part of the global monetary system and over which the United States does not exercise notable influence.

Concern over blocked accounts, however, was not the only trigger behind creation of the Eurodollar market. The British pound crisis in 1955–57 was also a contributor. In its wake, Whitehall barred British banks from financing non-U.K. trade in sterling and generally limited refinancing of trade credits in pounds. British banks, therefore, had to look around for a new currency with which to finance international trade; otherwise, they risked losing a traditional business.

At the same time, the era of dollar shortages was coming to a close. The large U.S. trade surpluses began to disappear, and from 1957 on, British banks were building up dollar balances for their foreign trade business, after having received the permission by the British Treasury — as always, staffed with excellent people — in an era of exchange controls.

By the time the members of the European Economic Community (EEC — the future European Union) abandoned their exchange restrictions in December 1958 and introduced full convertibility, a European market for dollar deposits and credits was already in existence — most European states had amassed large dollar reserves. Statistics issued by the Bank for International Settlements (BIS) in

Basel show how quickly that market grew. In 1963, short-term foreign currency deposits in the commercial banks of the European Union (EU), Sweden, Switzerland, Great Britain, and Japan amounted to a converted $12.4 billion ($9.3 billion were U.S. dollars). By 1970, deposits had risen to a converted $63.4 billion (with $53 billion actually U.S. dollars). In 1985, that total had reached $1.5 trillion.

The bond market's development was similar. The cumulative volume of issued bonds crossed the billion-dollar mark for the first time in 1967, with $527 million on the accounts of U.S. enterprises. After the limitation put on foreign credits in January 1968, U.S. companies' Eurodollar bond issues grew fourfold that year to $1.963 billion. By 1971, the total was $3.28 billion and in 1972, $5.5 billion. By the end of 2001, it had topped out at $4.607 trillion.

The Eurodollar market owes its tumultuous growth to the United States. The Interest Equalization Tax (IET), introduced in 1963, drove foreign debtors from the American capital markets. In 1962, John F. Kennedy and his secretary of the Treasury, Douglas Dillon, had openly encouraged Europeans to raise capital on their own markets. Dillon accepted that this could ruin the domestic banks' profitable foreign bond business. But his primary concern was the balance of payments deficit. The IET for foreign shares was 15 percent: 2.75 percent for short-term bonds of less than three years duration, and 15 percent for long-term bonds. Such overall conditions were sure to keep foreign debtors away from the U.S. market.

In 1965, Lyndon Johnson introduced the Voluntary Foreign Credit Restraint Program (VFCR), as an addition to IET, in order to dam the capital outflow via credits. The program remained voluntary, didn't do much, and was replaced in January 1968 by a quota regulation, the Foreign Direct Investment Regulations, for foreign investments. A newly created Office of Foreign Direct Investments within the Treasury oversaw the quotas. But these regulations only affected banks domiciled in the United States. The result: American banks began to found foreign subsidiaries, which could operate on the Euromarket free of national regulations like Regulation D that was established to diminish the dollar outflows.

The Euromarket knew neither the famous Regulation Q that barred American banks from paying interest on deposits up to thirty days nor the limit on interest paid on time deposits to sums under $100,000. Here, the Euromarket provided better conditions for investors, and American banks helped themselves in order to satisfy domestic capital demand. The Federal Reserve tried to blunt the outflow through the imposition of a 10 percent reserve requirement for imported credits, but by that time most of the capital had already been imported. All in all, it was a great example for well-meant but poorly thought-out interferences in the market, which, at the end of the day, only benefited London as a financial center and the British Treasury instead of the national tax authorities.

Eurobonds were popular because they were issued as bearer debentures and the interest was free of withholding taxes. The typical small investor in Eurobonds was the fiscally overcharged Belgian dentist with an account in Luxembourg. However, the overwhelming portion of Eurobonds — in the early years up to 80 percent — ended up in Swiss investment accounts.

The U.N. pension fund was among the first to take a close look at Eurodollar issues. In the early sixties, this fund had massive investment needs. It was the time of decolonization. An endless number of new countries were admitted to the world organization and sent new permanent personnel, selected according to a fixed quota system, to New York. The London broker Julius Strauss of Strauss, Turnbull & Co. became the "court purveyor" of the UN pension fund. Other large institutional players were the open bond funds of the Swiss banks.

One should not forget just how the flourishing Eurobond market collapsed in Italy. In order to support the lira's exchange rate, and to dam the capital outflow, the Banca d'Italia, on July 1, 1973, imposed an interest-free deposit requirement of 50 percent on all foreign securities.

Siegmund Warburg in London was first with the idea of issuing a dollar-denominated euro issue. Siegmund had grown up on the Uhlenfels estate in the Swabian mountain pastures, kept his Swabian accent in English his whole life, learned the banking business with Max Warburg in Hamburg and N. M. Rothschild in London, and emigrated to the British capital in 1934. Once there, at age thirty-one, he opened, with the support of some of the best names in the financial establishment, his own house, which he called New Trading. In it, he continued the tradition of innovative issues Carl Fuerstenberg (of the Berliner Handelsgesellschaft) had launched in Germany. After Julius Baer became established in London, I got to know the impassioned bookworm — like so many in his family a great intellect — as a pleasant and clever man. His face down to his sharp nose and his hypochondria tendencies reminded me very much of my father. Warburg, who died in 1982, was a close friend of my brother, Thomas.

On July 17, 1963, Warburg placed a $15 million bond issue bearing 5.5 percent interest for Autostrade (a motorway holding) in Italy with a guarantee given by state-owned Istituto per la Ricostruzione Industriale (IRI). Swiss banks bought into the issue heavily. In those days, $15 million was a huge sum.

The Autostrade issue has historical importance — no matter if it really was the very first offshore issue or not — because it brought the business with European customers back to Europe. Until the introduction of the Interest Equalization Tax, international borrowers procured funds from the American capital market. It was always an American bank that took the lead (for example, Lehman Brothers, who were heavily engaged in that business). Besides, most American investment banks only had a vague idea about foreign bond issues, and the domestic co-issuers didn't have customers for the product. Buyers were Europeans. Looking back, it was a very strange construction. American issuers and co-issuers earned commissions and fees for the bonds, which in fact were designed by Europeans for Europeans. But European banks were poorly rewarded for bringing in customers. At best they were invited into the selling groups and had to make do with a commission of 0.5 percent while American co-issuers pocketed at least 1 percent.

The business migrated. However, Warburg, White Weld, Kidder Peabody, Dillon Read, and the Deutsche Bank, which was very active in dollar issues, left clearing and settlement of the Eurodollar bonds to the New York banks. Settlement presented no difficulties as long as trading volumes remained within manageable limits. "L'intendance suivra" (Logistics will follow), Charles de Gaulle used to say about such secondary problems. Several years passed before the introduction of euro clearing.

In the beginning, trade in Eurodollar bonds was, compared to today, pretty archaic. In the secondary trading, every morning the teletype would spit out yard-long lists of trading houses and the bond issues they offered. Julius Baer was a large customer at all of them, especially after 1970, when we began to build up Baerbond, our first fund and one of the first in Europe. Every buy-and-sell order triggered long teletypes noting receipt and delivery instructions for each security.

Instructions for the custodian bank came in the mail or on telex, and New York banks only delivered if instructions and fulfillment were identical to the letter. Back then, New York banks had very little personnel qualified to handle international securities. This led to an accumulation in refused deliveries, which, in New York, were dubbed "DKs." The clearing centers didn't bother reporting that they had refused to carry out our instructions, so that in Zurich we assumed, as did all the other banks, that everything was okay.

The dynamic growth of the Eurobond market deepened this chaos and led to a clearing crisis, which, in 1968, began to take on frightening dimensions. Brown Brothers Harriman was the clearing agent for Julius Baer. Every player on the Euromarket had his or her own New York correspondent bank as a custodian address for Eurodollar issues; before the introduction of electronic data processing, all banks were under enormous pressure to work through the large increase in the volume of orders.

Stanley Ross, who grew up in the Eurobond business with Kidder Peabody — later he would enter Eurobond history with Ross & Partner through introduction of the gray market by publishing the early market rates of the primary trade via Reuters — finally flew to New York in order to search for his securities at his custodian:

> I found a fat individual in a short-sleeved shirt with open collar and chewing gum in his mouth. . . . It took a while before he came back with a thick, shabby three-ring folder that he slammed on the table. I found all my telexes carefully cut into strips for every entry and exit instruction. When I opened the folder, bits of paper flew out, every one of them highly important documents. One or two minutes later, a comforting arm was draped over my shoulder and a deep voice said, "Don't let it get to you, Stanley. I've been here for six weeks and turned a $7 million debit into a $21 million credit."

The comforting arm belonged to Wolfgang Kron of the Deutsche Bank in Frankfurt. Those were enormous sums at a time when $25,000 was the normal bond trade volume. It was not at all unusual for Swiss banks, which back then accounted for 90 percent of the market's purchasing power, to see their bonds, payable on the value date — only twelve to eighteen months, even two years later — without receiving a due date coupon.

Julius Baer was among them. Our stock market director, Peter "Pedro" Hangartner, noted the arrears as well as the payment differences. Warning signals came from Brown Brothers Harriman as well. An implosion threatened. In 1968, therefore, we sent Albert Merz to New York in order to get a firsthand look at Brown Brothers Harriman's situation. We had discovered at least two hundred differences, relatively harmless compared to Merrill Lynch, which wrote off $20 million with an eye on the chaos in the Eurobond deposits.

Merz had recently completed an internship at Brown Brothers Harriman and knew the house. One of the advantages of a small bank is the simple criteria for using personnel. Pedro Hangartner, my cousins, and I decided quite simply that "Merz has experience in New York. Let him solve the problem." At the time, he had worked for us for fourteen years. Merz grabbed two people who spent six months around the clock going through every trade with Brown Brothers Harriman and Baer Securities in New York. If the bank had bought, let us say, $200,000, nominal for a client, and done so in five or six separate purchases with the correspondingly different delivery dates in order to obtain the best price in each instance, the transactions could become quite intricate. Obtaining physical possession of the securities and redeeming the coupons, therefore, took intensive work.

With one eye on the creation of Euroclear, the first international clearing society on the Euromarket, Merz restructured our portfolio securities account at Brown Brothers Harriman into domestic bonds (American issues for which Brown Brothers Harriman has remained our settlement house to this day) and Eurobonds (which were then all delivered to Euroclear). If one of the banks with whom we worked at the time had failed, we would have faced serious problems. As it was, the settlement chaos *only* resulted in losses on interest. Our customer accounts were credited with the coupons, but we had neither securities nor coupons in our possession. That was untenable. One time, Merz protested so vigorously that the frightened U.S. bank simply sent us a check for several hundred thousand dollars.

Several houses did not survive the back office crisis and had to merge; for example, McDonnell & Co., Hentz & Co., and Hayden Stone, honorable names, all of which were absorbed into Sandy Weill's empire. Weill's professional beginnings reached into securities administration, and he was the first to invest in electronic securities administration.

Morgan Guaranty Trust's creation of the Euroclear system in December 1968 came just in time to prevent the collapse of the secondary market, and it is a good example for capitalism's ability to reorganize itself. It solved all the settlement problems. Euroclear began with fifty subscribers. In 1985 it had fifteen hundred, and today more than two thousand. The only weakness in the system was that it belonged to only one bank. Four years later that was remedied. A total of 118 banks and financial service providers subscribed to the twenty thousand shares, and, in the underwriting prospectus, Morgan Guaranty committed to not holding more shares than the other largest shareholder. Julius Baer subscribed to 2 percent.

The practical advantages were much more important. Before the advent of electronics, every morning Euroclear sent a long telex with all settled and unsettled trades. This kind of reporting had not existed before. With electronic data processing, services were dramatically expanded, and today everything is automatic. At the same time, CEDEL (Centrale de livraison de valeurs mobilières), a parallel organization founded a little later, provided competition and market dynamics (CEDEL is now named Clearstream).

An integral part of the Eurobond market's history is the foundation of the Association of International Bond Dealers (AIBD), which for all practical purposes coincided with the Euroclear launch. The association did yeoman work in organizing the market, setting up its rules and regulations, and, not least, through training new recruits. Pedro Hangartner lent his knowledge about Euro convertible bonds to the enterprise and gave lectures at workshops in Montreux.

Our London subsidiary, Julius Baer International Ltd., was represented in the underwriting syndicate with hundreds of issues. Our annual report for 1975 shows that we were co-issuers that year of 129 Eurobond issues. In 1976, the number had climbed to 229 and, in 1977, had reached 247.

But the Eurobond market was not spared its own crises. The overnight collapse of the Penn-Central was especially painful for us. The bank had recommended the stock on the assumption that the enterprise was too large to fail. Our customers were anything but pleased when in 1970 the shares in their accounts were suddenly worthless. As Penn-Central's actual lead bank, Goldman Sachs was pursued by indignant plaintiffs and obliged to pay substantial damages. These, as Lisa Endlich, a former Goldman Sachs vice president, noted in her history of the company, devoured a sizable portion of the partners' capital.

Chrysler bondholders also lived through dramatic times, watching their bonds slump to 30 percent at times. And the conviction of junk bond king Michael Milken did not help the mood of the market.

An episode all its own was our project to launch the first Multi-Currency Bond Fund for American clients through our U.S. subsidiary, Baer Securities. Today such a fund would be commonplace, but in December 1978 our prospectus provoked a strongly worded letter from Paul Volcker, then president of the Federal Reserve Bank of New York, to my cousin Nicolas. The tenor of the letter was that what we planned was unpatriotic. At the time, the dollar was once again suffering from galloping consumption. Naturally, none of us was eager to provoke Volcker's wrath.

The Euromarket did not collapse, when, in January 1974, the United States lifted capital controls and restrictions; on the contrary, it profited from the fact that American banks and investors now had unencumbered access. Arbitrage was the name of the game. It was only a qualified accident that two banks collapsed that year, the Franklin National Bank and the Cologne-based Herstatt bank, and that the secondary banking crisis started (see page 250). Introduction in the early seventies of freely convertible exchange rates — following Richard Nixon's decision to lift the dollar's gold convertibility — brought new risks to the foreign exchange markets, which existing internal regulations and controls could no longer handle. So long as fixed exchange rates existed, it was not so important to avoid large open positions. Rates moved within a narrow range, and central bank intervention stabilized the markets. Suddenly these supports were gone.

The Iran crisis also brought great unrest. It was to date the last time the United States used blocked accounts, freezing all Iranian assets in American banks and obligating their foreign subsidiaries to do the same. It didn't help that the Vietnam War film *Apocalypse Now* appeared about the same time. Stupidly, the Carter administration, already plagued by so much bad luck, had overlooked the fact that Iran was also a large debtor nation. Iran was forced to stop its interest payments, credits became doubtful, and the banks tried to compensate through the frozen assets they held. The situation became so confusing that in January 1981, the United States offered to make a deal.

As a result, it became clear that the Euromarket was not as well protected against unilateral action as had been thought. Arab investors, therefore, preferred Arab banks and thus supported their expansion. One more time the U.S. policy of blocking assets only damaged itself.

And what about Switzerland? That the Euromarket passed by Switzerland, except for its banks, is only one of many missed chances. The financial center in Switzerland, unlike Luxembourg or London, never found far-sighted supporters in politics and administration, aside from the introduction of the tighter bank secrecy act on March 1, 1935. But at the time, the country was caught in a severe economic crisis, which forced it to act.

As a financial center, Switzerland continues to lose in importance. The executive, the legislature, and the bureaucracy have little sense for international developments and their larger context. Little Luxembourg, in contrast, managed the structural change from steel industry to banking center very well (and managed to keep one hand in developing commercial uses for satellites). Nobody, moreover, can claim not to have received sufficient warning.

This failure weighs more heavily since Switzerland could have had excellent chances. In the early seventies, the dollar deposits of the large Swiss banks were surely higher than Swiss franc deposits. Swiss banks were always one of the most important players on the Euromarket. But withholding taxes and issue fees crippled Switzerland's Euro business.

22

BERENBERG-GOSSLER (1968–88)

Sauerkraut and sausage

My ties to Hamburg began back in New York. My mother was a friend of the Warburgs, who had homes in New York as well as Hamburg, beginning in 1894, after Felix Warburg married the daughter of Jakob Schiff, who, as Salomon Loeb's son-in-law, became a partner at Kuhn, Loeb & Co. In 1902, Felix Warburg's older brother Paul married Nina Loeb, whom he had met at his brother's wedding. He then became a partner at Kuhn, Loeb & Co., helped found the Federal Reserve, and became vice president of the Board of Governors. A third brother, Max Warburg, led the bank in Hamburg and, in 1919, was one of the eminent personalities in the German delegation to the peace conference in Versailles.

Max Warburg, in the twenties a member of the Reichsbank's general council, emigrated to the United States in 1938. His daughter Lola married the industrialist Rudolf Hahn, whose brother Kurt Hahn founded the Salem Boarding School in Germany and then Gordonstoun in the United Kingdom. In Salem he educated Prince Philip, and in Gordonstoun, Philip and his son, Prince Charles. It is worth noting that Lola Warburg, for whom her friendship with Prince Philip meant a great deal, was at times very close to Chaim

Weizmann. Max Warburg's son Eric hired our nanny Emma Schmidt after he married Dorothea Thorsch on Valentine's Day in 1946. Emma raised Eric's first-born son, Max, on the Warburg estate in New Rochelle. Today, Max is head of the M. M. Warburg and Co. Bank in Hamburg.

Eric Warburg knew many languages and led an extraordinary life. In the spring of 1918, at age eighteen, he entered the Fourth Guard Artillery Regiment in Potsdam. At Christmas that year, his battery cannonaded mutinous sailors from the Berlin palace, and he fought against the Spartakists before learning the banking business — first in 1920 in London with N. M. Rothschild and then in 1923 in the United States with Kuhn, Loeb & Co. When he arrived in New York, the Immigration and Naturalization Service (INS) accidentally stamped a residence permit into his passport, which helped him enormously when he returned in 1938 as a refugee from the Nazis — he had no problem obtaining U.S. citizenship.

After Pearl Harbor, Eric reported to the U.S. Army and in the summer of 1942 graduated from officer training school in Florida, together with twelve hundred other ninety-day wonders. As he was getting ready to receive his graduation certificate, Warner Marshall, a cousin of U.S. Chief of Staff George Marshall, whispered in his ear to slam his heels together Prussian-style, which he did. This drew the irksome question of where he learned to do that. "The Guard Field Artillery Regiment 4 in Potsdam!" he exclaimed.

On May 6, 1945, in Augsburg, Eric experienced his personal "grande finale" of the thousand-year Reich. He interrogated Hermann Goering, who had Aryanized the Warburg bank in Hamburg in 1938. (Goering had been in charge of the Third Reich's five-year economic plan.) The interrogation lasted for twenty hours. As fate will have it, I also knew the second interrogator — Ernst Englaender (my wife's boss at Interba before our marriage). At the end, the corpulent "Reichsmarschall" — as Eric addressed him after he realized how important that title was for Goering (since it separated him from a common marshal) — balked at entering the transport plane that was to take him back to Luxembourg because it was too small for his own feelings of self-worth. Eric finally said, "Herr Reichsmarschall, we will vouch for your safety."

To his wife's horror and that of his other relatives, Eric was drawn back to Hamburg very early on. An invitation to his house in 1948 could be bizarre. I was once present at a dinner with two German generals. It all seemed an impoverished feudalism. Hamburg was badly destroyed during the war, and back then everything seemed very provisional. I had traveled to Hamburg for the reopening festivities of the Berenberg-Gossler bank. Until his death in 1990, Eric always gave a dinner for me when I was in Hamburg, and so long as I was on the board of Berenberg-Gossler, I regularly visited the city.

The bank house Joh. Berenberg, Gossler & Co. has a long history extending back to the end of the sixteenth century. The Berenberg family hailed from the Bergisches Land in today's North Rhine Westphalia and had immigrated to Antwerp during the Reformation. In the course of the Counter-Reformation, they were forced to leave the Spanish Low Countries and finally settled in Hamburg in 1585. Like the Brown Brothers, the Berenbergs first entered the textile trade. Toward the end of the seventeenth century, they moved into finance. By the nineteenth century, they were totally focused on the banking business. During the Third Reich, Cornelius Baron von Berenberg-Gosler, who in 1939 freed Fritz Warburg — one of Eric's uncles — from the clutches of the Gestapo, withdrew from the active banking business into a pure holding. He came back into banking on June 21, 1948, the day the new currency, the D-mark instead of the Reichsmark, was introduced.

I came to Berenberg-Gossler through Heinz "Heio" Lessing, born in Trier in 1909 as the son of a woman from Trier and a Prussian officer. According to his daughter-in-law, Lessing's father lived in a more feudal style than the fortune that Lessing's grandfather had amassed through a train engine factory in Russia allowed. He invested his last funds in a sizable estate not far from Meersburg on Lake Constance and sent his son off to the nearby Salem school.

Lessing's talents did not remain hidden. Since he wanted to become a banker, Lola Hahn-Warburg used her good standing with her brother Max. So in 1928 the young South German arrived to begin his apprenticeship at the Hamburg bank, M. M. Warburg & Co. Bank. Warburg, supported the promising young man's career by sending him to an internship in New York, where he remained from 1931 to 1934. Lessing knew well how important a step that had been. In a letter he wrote to me in 1985, he remembered "how difficult but important such a stay is for one's training. Fifty-four years ago — and thanks to the personal intervention of my teacher Max Warburg — I came to the International Acceptance Bank Inc. in New York. The Bank of Manhattan took over the bank a little later, and after the Second World War it merged with Chase. Back then you could only take 10 marks across the German frontier. As a student employee I earned $25 a week and I had to make do because money transfers out of Germany were not permitted. I earned my crossing by working as a deck mate on a small 3,800-ton tanker, a pretty rough trip without cargo, only a little ballast."

Lessing's third training period was as commercial director with the organizing committee of the Olympic games in Berlin, where he met Leni Riefenstahl, the famous photographer and purported man-eater. During the Second World War, Lessing served as an officer in the Wehrmacht. Warmed by his horse, which he slept alongside in the Russian winter at Stalingrad, he wangled leave in order to get his mother out of jail. She had been imprisoned because of her Jewish ancestry. He traveled to the responsible military headquarters in Mulhouse (Alsace), and after his mother was back on the estate, he returned to Stalingrad.

After the war, the Americans gave Lessing, "captain in the

reserves," a political clean bill of health, meaning he was free of Nazi taint. That made him a much-courted man. Not surprisingly, given Germany's wartime destruction, he opted for the Alsen Portland-Cement factory in Hamburg, whose owners were out of the question for a leadership position because of their political pasts. As Alsen's general manager, he knew the Schmidheinys — the Swiss cement dynasty — very well, and that's how our paths crossed.

Heinz Lessing gave my wife and me a taste for summer sailing tours in the Aegean. Twice we cruised with four to six other friends of our host on the *Isafan*, the Alsen flagship, through the Greek Mediterranean. Too much of a good thing, however, were the sauerkraut and sausages we were supposed to devour for lunch when the temperature on the water hit 113 degrees F. Our hostess knew no mercy — only in her memoirs would she later write about her "malice" — but neither did her passengers. As soon as Monzi Lessing turned around, sauerkraut and sausage were thrown overboard.

In subsequent years, we chartered a yacht two or three times and got to know the enormous difference between a German and a Greek captain. The Greek had no maps and trusted his memory, while his German colleague held a small staff meeting every time we sailed. In 1967, we returned just before the outbreak of the Six-Day War. The boat brought us to the Athens airport at 5 a.m., where we noticed that something wasn't right, without having any clear idea of what it might be. The puzzle was solved when we arrived in Zurich. The Israeli army under the leadership of its chief of staff, Itzhak Rabin, had begun fighting on all fronts.

Lessing alone was responsible for my accepting a seat on the Berenberg-Gossler board despite our friendly ties to many other German banks and our family friendship with the Warburgs. Lessing said good-bye to the cement business in 1959 in order to become general manager of the Joh. Berenberg, Gossler & Co. bank house. In 1961 he became a general partner.

At least four times a year, beginning in 1968, I flew at 7:20 a.m.

with Swissair to a board meeting in Hamburg that began at 10 a.m. in their postwar building on the Jungfernstieg. Even though the Berenberg did not change its name to "Baerenberg" after my coming on board, I always liked flying to Hamburg. Heinrich Berenberg-Gossler, who chaired the meetings, was what you might call a character — a large, powerful man, very well-regarded and, as president of the Anglo-German club, very impressive.

On the board, I encountered the impact of longer-term contracts for the first time. The management of the bank had profit-sharing contracts that ensured a more than adequate income when business was slow, but during phases of dynamic growth could quickly balloon into huge sums that irritated many, especially since the head of the much larger Norddeutsche Landesbank (a state-owned bank in Northern Germany), who was a board member, earned far less. Representatives of the other two investors on the board agreed that management made too much money. Today's excesses cannot easily be compared with the problems of those days (the seventies), since tax-avoiding options were as little known as the "incentives" offered down below. High bonus payments came from small earnings during slack times. Times change, a few successful acquisitions are made, and bonuses skyrocket. There is only one surefire way to handle this problem: don't sign long-term contracts.

Important partners of the Berenberg-Gossler bank house, with 25 percent each, were, in addition to the Norddeutsche Landesbank, the Bank of Montreal, and the Philadelphia National Bank. (Today, besides the Landesbank, the Belgium Compagnie Du Bois Sauvage is an important partner.) Looking back, I think that my votes on the board were cast in the interest of the investors. Personally, the contacts to the Bank of Montreal and the Philadelphia National brought me new connections in the United States. But I was also lucky that the bank never got into trouble. Management always acted prudently.

The Berenberg family and their partners were more than

excellent business friends. They were extremely charming hosts who gave me new insights into Hamburg and its mentality. I felt close to them and very much enjoyed the atmosphere. The days ended with a formal dinner at the Anglo-American Club on the Alster River, where ladies are only allowed in at night. These evenings — with ladies — were de rigueur and had the pleasant side effect of making one quickly forget the serious business discussions of the day.

I met many new people, who often became friends, through Berenberg-Gossler and my visits to Hamburg. I encountered the pianist Justus Frantz here, for example. From the board, in addition to the charming Ernst Wolf Mommsen, a descendant of the historian and the hereditary Prince zu Fuerstenberg, I remember Professor Dr. Friedrich Thomée, the Volkswagen CFO. He persuaded me, an inveterate owner of American cars, to buy an Audi. He drove a prototype, a four-door Audi Quattro that was never mass-produced because it was too fast — which didn't prevent him from saying that this was a car I had to have.

After an unhappy snow and slide experience in the Engadin, I really did buy an Audi. Convertibles were not being made then (or not yet again), so I settled on a sedan. But because the four rings — symbol of the Auto Union — conjured up memories and smells of the two-stroke predecessors, which ran under the label DKW, I ordered a car without the decorative rings. But it had a radio. Very important. On the first drive with my family, I heard the somber news that Roberto Calvi, the head of the Banco Ambrosiano, had been found hanging under the Blackfriars Bridge in London. That had consequences for our own bank (see page 293).

23

ALPBACH

The ABCs of banking (1965–80)

What had begun in 1945 under the sober name of International University Weeks was, at first, a meeting of knowledge-hungry war veterans from academia. Postwar hardships, where spiritual needs trumped bodily requirements, and Simon Moser, a philosophy professor at Innsbruck University, had dictated the meeting place, a remote Alpine village in the Tyrol. Nor should the unofficial patronage of the French occupation forces, which were open to all intellectual exchange and other cultural matters, be underestimated. (Austria was under four-power occupation from 1945 to 1955, and Tyrol was part of the French zone.) In the other zones of occupation, no such uncontrolled meetings held so soon after the war would have been possible.

With Innsbruck badly damaged and food strictly rationed, where could the initiators go? They found Alpbach, in whose cemetery the Nobel Prize-winning physicist Erwin Schroedinger would be buried sixteen years later, in 1961. Whenever I was in Alpbach, I always made a pilgrimage to the grave of this family friend.

Arthur Koestler gave the alpine village and its European Forum (its name after 1949) literary immortality in his book *The Call*

Girls. The subject matter lay at his feet, so to speak; he only had to pick up on it. Koestler, the idol of my American school years, had a house in Alpbach and thus could in all comfort observe the doings of the academic world during its summer exodus.

With his disclaimer that all his characters were fictitious, Koestler protected himself against any legal problems that might arise from his description of an international academic circle whose members knew each other well from other seminars and thought about improving the world in this rural idyll. Among them was a lady professor who at night climbs into bed with the strapping chauffeur, "whose tanned torso was uncovered." The novelist described what happened afterwards: "A moment later he was overcome by the indelible experience of being buried in an avalanche on the Schlafberghang."

I would like to emphasize at this point that my wife always accompanied me to Alpbach. She only objected when I had invited a boring Swiss speaker. "The man has no humor," she would say, and threaten not to come again in case of repetition.

The first gathering of Swiss sat around the campfire in short pants in the late forties and practiced thinking about world renewal. That was before my time. With growing prosperity, the European Forum became noticeably more urbane but without any real luxury. We were all lodged in modest guesthouses and hotels.

The early morning sports program that began at 8 a.m. under the motto "Relaxed and fresh into the day" remains with me as a residue of the founding years. I admit freely that I preferred to focus on breakfast at the friendly café rather than listen to the whistles of the gym instructor, which is how I came into conversation with Karl Otto Poehl. He too did not think much of early morning exercise and preferred to begin the day with fresh rolls rather than lengthy jogs. Epicureans often like each other, and so we became friends. Later, his career boomed. In 1970, the trained journalist switched from the executive suite of the Association of German

Banks to the ministry of economics and a year later into the ministry of finance, where he rose to a state secretary's chair (the top official in the German ministerial hierarchy). In 1977, he became vice president of the German central bank, the Bundesbank, and from 1980 to 1991 he was its president. A splendid example for Paul Henri Spaak's dictum: "You never know where journalism will lead you, after you leave it." He crowned his career with a move to the splendid private bank in Cologne, Sal. Oppenheim Jr. & Cie. We were honored when he came to the centenary of our bank in 1990.

Georg Zimmer-Lehmann led the banking seminar at the European Forum. He was a director of the Oesterreichische Kreditanstalt (at that time the country's most prestigious bank) and a talented organizer with excellent connections. In the Austrian prewar period, he had met leading politicians like Chancellors Kurt von Schuschnigg and Engelbert Dollfuss, and later, of course, all the statesmen of the alpine republic: Chancellors Julius Raab and Leopold Figl, President Adolf Schaerf, Finance Minister Reinhard Kamitz, and two socialist chancellors, Bruno Kreisky and Franz Vranitzky. His influence on the Alpbach Forum goes back to 1949; in 1976 he became its secretary general, a post he held for the next eighteen years. With his energetic commitment, this gifted networker turned Alpbach into a late summer meeting place for the world of finance, which the American ambassador in Vienna attended as a matter of course. If you failed to register for the forum, he would call at once and insist in the friendliest fashion that you attend. Of course, such attention is flattering, and I therefore came more often than I would have wished. In the end I was given a badge of honor in the form of a pin.

Once, Hermann Josef Abs, the chairman of the Deutsche Bank, entered the hall and saw the name plates prepared for the forum on the table — Hermann Josef Abs, Hans Baer, Friedrich Wilhelm Christians (Deutsche Bank) — and said spontaneously to my wife, "Ah, the ABCs of banking."

Abs was a fascinating gentleman. If some complain that he was not a man of the resistance in the Third Reich — a most unlikely position for anyone in our business — they should not forget his contributions to Germany's reconstruction. He supervised the reconstruction of the Deutsche Bank after the allies had pulled it apart. He was chief of the Kreditanstalt fuer Wiederaufbau (KFW), founded in 1948 for the reconstruction of Germany. He led the German delegation to the London debt negotiations in 1952, where he negotiated the tolerable debt agreement that reestablished Germany's creditworthiness. He was the man with the many seats on supervisory boards and the great capital reorganizer of the Federal Republic. His powers became too much even for the conservative Christian Democrats to whom he was bound by faith, status, and origins. Abs was born in Bonn, deeply Catholic, and, according to his own confession, "always first a Christian and then a German."

The law limiting acquisition of supervisory board seats entered Germany's legislative history under the name Lex Abs. Abs' comment was, "Of all the measures ever taken to protect my health, this was surely the most decisive. Now I don't have to work so hard." The Hamburg news magazine *Der Spiegel* once devoted a cover story to him with the headline "ABSolutismus," and he himself once cracked a joke in answer to a question of how he spelled his name: "A like Abs, B like Abs, S like Abs." But despite all that, he remained a modest gentleman with a crafty charm, who only stood out thanks to his elegant suits and a very old leather briefcase, which he hoped would last to the end of his days.

During his lifetime, a joke made the rounds that after his death a higher authority asked him to change heaven into a joint stock company. He presented his draft to St. Peter, who was delighted but had only one reservation: "You cannot make God *only* the deputy chairman of the board."

Alpbach offered far more opportunities for discussion and the exchange of ideas than one could expect from forums and congresses (because the modest accommodations didn't inspire you to leave the party early). The international financial situation at the beginning of the seventies and the worrying development of the dollar offered enough grist for conversations. That way I learned firsthand what my colleagues were thinking about.

I met Friedrich Wilhelm Christians, a great collector of Russian twentieth-century art, at Alpbach, as I did his Deutsche Bank colleague Wilfried Guth, a very intelligent man, and Franz Ulrich, who died early. Juergen Ponto, the chief of the Dresdner Bank, remains unforgettable. He was shot and killed on July 30, 1977, by German Red Army Faction terrorists, actually by the sister of his godchild. He was a good-looking man who my wife valued highly and who was married to the pianist Ignes von Huelsen. At a World Bank meeting in Manila in 1976, Ponto provided a moving dinner speech — traditionally the major banks host the event — about the debt crisis in the third world: "There may be no space for them in our balance sheets but hopefully in our hearts."

It was as depressing to bury him as it was Alfred Herrhausen in 1989. He too was an Alpbach acquaintance. We had met in the vacation home of the publisher Fritz Molden, a social pillar of the Alpine village. Terrorists had blown up Herrhausen's armored limousine. At the funeral, a hundred riot police were on hand while Grenzschutz (the national police forces) tanks surrounded the church and controlled admission. All in all, it was not the kind of cortege one might wish for the last rites. Herrhausen was not inclined to hide his brilliance or his superior position. A good-looking man, he was proudly aware that with the Deutsche Bank, he led Europe's most important bank, at least at that time.

Five years later, I flew to another funeral in Frankfurt. Hermann Josef Abs had died at an old age and was ushered out of this world with a solemn requiem mass. My attendance at the funeral — usually "la seule reunion mondaine à laquelle on peut se rendre sans invitation" (the only social occasion one can attend without an invitation), as Edmund Rothschild put it, but in Hermann's case you did need an invitation — led a colleague to remark on the flight back, "I would not have expected you at this funeral!"

During the funeral, James Wolfensohn sat next to me on the church bench and, for a former Royal Australian Air Force officer, looked nervously at his watch. Between the Graduale and the Al-leluia, he left with the words, "I have to catch the plane to Wash-ington. My appointment as president of the World Bank will be announced tonight."

I could only congratulate him but had to ask myself if he would be happy in that job. It was no accident that Jim Wolfen-sohn and I sat next to one another in the pew. We had known each other forever. Like me he was a cellist — but also a great fencer — and was friends with the Schmidheiny family. Wolfensohn's career at Schroders Ltd. in London and at J. Henry Schroder Banking Cor-poration in New York was meteoric, but he never won the top job. Given his Jewish ancestry, he was told he could never expect to be-come CEO. Thereupon he switched to Salomon Brothers, whose unofficial motto of the house was "Dress British, Think Yiddish," and he can take credit for becoming the financial savior of Chrysler Corporation. At their low point, Chrysler bonds were traded at un-der 30 percent.

Of all the speakers I brought with me to Alpbach, I liked going with my friend Fritz Leutwiler the best. He sat in the back of the car and wrote his speech on his knees while I steered the car through the Alpine passes. Amazingly, he didn't lurch from side to side; the convertible was too small for that. It would never have occurred to Leutwiler or me to arrive in a helicopter or in a chauffeur-driven limousine.

Alpbach's original charm was its compactness, something it has lost today with twenty-five hundred participants. That is a deci-sive disadvantage, just like in Davos, which cancels the possibility of informal acquaintanceship at the breakfast table of a small alpine café. Friendly connections can only be built if people have not advanced too far up the career ladder. In the final analysis, such events live on from bringing together just the right mixture of those who have already arrived with those who show great promise, something Georg Zimmer-Lehmann did extremely well.

I had met Fritz Leutwiler during the first Banking Summer School held under Alfred Schaefer's direction at the Buergenstock in 1959. The theme of the meeting was the Financing of Technical Progress. Leutwiler was three years older than I and had worked at the National Bank since 1952. After completing his university studies and his thesis, he spent four years as a journalist and secretary of an association for a sound currency but had never worked in the private sector, except for six months of training at the SBC in London. On the Buergenstock and in subsequent years, we used to stroll together a lot in the evenings.

His abilities were never concealed; my cousins and I would have liked to have him as partner in our bank. When I explored the idea, he was a mid-level manager at the National Bank and basically liked the prospect. Our silent agreement was, "If I am not promoted the next time, I'll join you." Leutwiler was up for promotion four times, and he was promoted four times. That was the end of an almost twenty-year-long flirt. Not even his decision to float the franc without asking his vacationing boss could stop his career, which says a lot for his boss and predecessor Edwin Stopper, who also tended to lack proper respect for authority. However, Otmar Emminger, president of the Bundesbank from 1977 to 1979, wrote in his memoirs, *D-Mark, Dollar and Currency Crisis*, that the story that Stopper had not been consulted was not true. He had been in telephone contact about the floating and had approved Leutwiler's intention. Leutwiler himself would later recount how simple the closing of the foreign exchange market on January 23, 1973, had been. He feared that further support of the dollar would lead to the National Bank facing a flood of $500 million ten minutes after the market opened. He had told Finance Minister Nello Celio that was the reason why he would prefer not to open the foreign exchange market. Celio's succinct answer was, "So, don't open it."

It was Leutwiler too who during our evening strolls developed the idea that one outside partner was not sufficient; we needed a second, which is how Ernst Bieri appeared on our radar screen.

Leutwiler was a multitalented man, very smart, art-loving, funny, and at times quite biting. "The great thing about having worked as a central banker is that you get your telephone calls returned," he used to say. His comment during the 1983 crisis was, "I may have to save the banks but certainly not the bankers." As treasurer of the Kunsthaus Art Museum, he once faced the task of drawing up a balance sheet for a weak year. His dry comment was, "You have to have been part of at least one insolvency." About the qualities the head of the central bank needs, he said it wouldn't hurt to have taken acting lessons; selling the policies of the National Bank well was at least as important as the policies themselves. Asked by a journalist during the 1979 dollar crisis how he felt personally, given so difficult a situation facing the National Bank, he replied, "President of the National Bank and well-being are two irreconcilable concepts."

When he became president of the National Bank in 1974, he gave its sober headquarters on Zurich's Boersenstrasse a civilized ambiance. Instead of the mirror-smooth linoleum floors, on which you could slip just looking at them, he had rugs laid down. Pictures were hung on the walls and sculptures put in the rooms.

Leutwiler was also president of the foundation that, since the death of Hulda Zumsteg, managed the Kronenhalle restaurant, with its remarkable art collection in the spirit of its late owner. Today, it is the only museum with its own kitchen and an excellent wine cellar.

Paul Volcker's later decision to join the Committee of Eminent Persons to research the dormant accounts in Swiss banks was, in the end, Leutwiler's achievement. Volcker's condition was, "In Switzerland, I don't do anything without my friend Fritz Leutwiler."

An anecdotal reminiscence is connected to the annual Overseas Bankers Dinner in London's Guildhall, to which I was invited in my capacity as president of a foreign merchant bank. Fritz Leutwiler, who spoke excellent English and was a brilliant public speaker, delivered the keynote address. He was introduced by Prince Charles. The world doesn't know how funny the Prince of Wales can be. He has great charm, which I experienced many times later on. The Overseas Bankers Dinner, with the governor of the Bank of England presiding, is a black-tie affair. The president of the National Bank wore a tuxedo, of course, but had the misfortune of losing a button in the taxi. So he had to speak with an open tuxedo. I will always remember the torn-off button.

24

WORLD BANK

Brothels don't serve fried eggs

Our SR-100 flight from Zurich to New York landed so late at night that we missed the connecting flight to Washington. The last plane had left sometime before. We were on our way to the annual meeting of the World Bank and the International Monetary Fund (IMF). Swissair personnel put Paul Jolles, head of the Swiss office of foreign trade, Otmar Emminger, vice president of the German Central Bank, Edwin Stopper, president of the Swiss National Bank, Franz Aschinger, business editor of the *Neue Zuercher Zeitung*, and my wife and me on a bus and lodged us — I'm not kidding — in a brothel. The girls in the lobby were quite unmistakable. We drank champagne with supper and, being dead tired after the long flight, fell into bed. The next morning, my wife awoke with a healthy appetite and looked forward to a couple of crisp fried eggs.

"But you can't get eggs here for breakfast," I said fatigued.

"Well, if you say so. I don't know my way around here," she replied, somewhat intimidated.

We packed our clothes in our suitcase, opened the door, and found Franz Aschinger, who had come out of his room at the same time, licking the corners of his mouth. "So what did you eat?" I asked.

"I ordered a couple of fried eggs for breakfast."

Aschinger liked to live in high style and always wore white dinner jackets for even the most mundane of occasions, which kept his popularity among his colleagues at the *Neue Zuercher Zeitung* within bounds. But he was a great billboard for the renowned newspaper, which he had joined in 1946. He had excellent contacts and was a close friend of the well-informed Otmar Emminger. What Aschinger wrote was widely read and well-received. In his columns, he always urged Swiss entry into the IMF, which took place with some delay, unfortunately too late for the talented economist, who would have liked to become the IMF's resident director, a job for which he was highly qualified. So in 1968 he went to the Swiss Bank Corporation (SBC) as an economic counselor and, until his retirement in 1975, also taught at the University of St. Gall.

The joint meetings of the World Bank and the IMF were indispensable and a focal point of my annual travel program. Most of the time I flew together with Fritz Leutwiler and Paul Jolles, a very smart man. As mentioned earlier, the annual meetings take place in Washington, D.C., and then every three years in a country to which the World Bank and the IMF want to give added prestige and status (a tradition that continues today), such as the Philippines, Brazil, and Kenya.

I always took part in these meetings because I had made it a rule to know all the leading people in my industry and to invite them to Zurich. The journey and the side programs were good opportunities for making new friends. The World Bank meeting in Nairobi, for example, didn't unfold without the obligatory safari.

Participation at World Bank meetings mandates an invitation, and for reasons of self-esteem, you receive a name tag with the colors for a "special guest." Otherwise, it isn't worth the trouble of coming to be categorized as a "visitor."

I was invited simply because I knew all the World Bank presidents, and if necessary, I didn't shy from applying a little muscle.

The first time I flew to a World Bank meeting in Washington, D.C., Robert S. McNamara, President Johnson's secretary of defense during the Vietnam War, was president. McNamara had four predecessors. Founding president and owner of the *Washington Post*, Eugene Meyer, held the office for only six months. John McCloy quit after two years to become high commissioner in Germany. Eugene Black, McCloy's successor, came, like McCloy, from the Chase Manhattan Bank, and his period in office, thirteen and a half years, remains a record. John Wood, finally, was chairman of First Boston.

Of these four, I had the best contacts with Eugene Black, whom I had met first when he was president of Chase Manhattan. Among McNamara's successors, I was closest to Lewis Preston, elected in 1991, easily recognizable as a New England patrician. He had been head of Morgan Guaranty in London. Unfortunately, he became very ill and died surprisingly early. So James Wolfensohn inherited the great task of leading the World Bank.

Some five thousand bankers visit the general meetings of the IMF and World Bank, which take place every year in October. Unlike the still relatively frugal Alpbach, the World Bank meeting is excessively luxurious. Antoine Jeancourt-Galignani, owner of the Galignani bookstore on the Rue de Rivoli, at the time head of the Banque Indosuez, describes the meetings in his memoirs as a jolly trade fair with a round of meetings and cocktails. When he took part for the first time in 1981, the French bankers were still shocked by François Mitterrand's election as president of France and the expected wave of nationalizations. I always found the display of wealth excessive. Even during the worst world financial crisis in the early eighties, caviar rained down onto the plates of third world representatives while champagne poured into their goblets. The major American banks were usually the sponsors.

At these feasts, many participants knew no restraint. Very unsympathetic. Of course, it was also impossible to get a decent hotel room during the conference. Rooms were assigned according to office and function. Central bank governors of African states were automatically ranked higher in World Bank protocol than bankers, just as at the Prussian court lieutenants ranked higher than professors. To boot, there was always an endless number of wives and family members. Naturally, these people did not fly in on commercial airliners but on huge state-owned jets.

25

SECONDARY BANKING CRISIS (1967–74)

Like at the court of a medieval king

If ever a prize were awarded for the most elegant crisis management, the trophy would surely go to the Bank of England for the way it made the secondary banking crisis pass by almost unnoticed. These events did not enter the literature of finance until many years later.

Given the ownership situation of Julius Baer International Ltd., founded in London on March 29, 1969, the crisis did not pass us by unnoticed. In order to explain, I have to go back to 1967, when the United Dominions Trust approached us with the idea of founding a joint enterprise under the name UDT International Finanz AG. We were the minority partners and handled the business in-house. For a while, the second minority stockholder with a 15 percent share was the Norwegian Norinvest, a group of the leading Scandinavian banks. UDT International focused on financing export risk-insured businesses.

Our success led us to building up Julius Baer International Ltd. under mirror-image reversed ownership. We held 51 percent of Julius Baer International Ltd. in London and the International Finance & Services Ltd., a wholly owned subsidiary of the United Dominions Trust Ltd. (UDT), the remaining 49 percent. From day one we did an excellent business, thanks to our partner and its owner, Barclays Bank, who helped us with new issues and the Euromarket. In Zurich, however, there was opposition. The first deal we did in London was bank acceptances for Japanese houses, which brought in an extra 0.25 percent. When Willy Himmelsbach heard about it, he shot into my office and enraged, cried out, "I can do that kind of business too." (Japanese banks had still a bad credit reputation in the sixties.)

UDT was a well-established financial institution whose status as a bank was put in doubt in 1967 by a failed garage owner named Kirkwood. He challenged the right of access to a collateral, with the argument that UDT was a finance house group but not a bank or a credit institute under the definition of the Moneylenders Act. British banking law was very rudimentary at the time.

The famous Lord Denning decided the case. He determined that the law did not define the term "bank" and that UDT did not meet several criteria of a bank. On the other hand, Lord Denning held that four of the five major English banks considered UDT a bank, and that it was a maxim of English law to respect common practice. That decided the case. In order to avoid future doubts, the government quickly approved the Companies Act. Section 123 permitted certification of banks, so long as they did not reflect on the Schedule VIII status of clearing banks. This created a new kind of bank with lower status and, as a rule, with less financial strength.

Like many other secondary banks, the UDT concentrated on — let's call it for what it is — installment credits. Furthermore, there was industrial financing as well as mortgage credits and a strong overseas business through export financing. Thanks to our UDT partnership, we came, virtually overnight, into a profitable South African business as well, because, given the political circumstances, Julius Baer International was the right business partner for UDT's offshoot in Johannesburg. UDT's majority stockholder, Barclays Bank, introduced us to South Africa. Our business relations were limited to South Africans of English ancestry. On my business trips, I did not fail to see that South Africans discriminated against their colored population much more than the Americans. A curfew imposed on blacks was a new experience. Thus our chauffeur could not return to his family at night but had to stay in a stuffy little room in the hotel cellar, during the hottest time of the year. On the other hand, our relations with our business friends were always pleasant, intellectually stimulating, and socially very appealing. I admit that despite apartheid, we tried to acquire UDT Johannesburg for Julius Baer. Our conversations with Christian Lodweyk Stals, then senior deputy governor of the South African Reserve Bank in Pretoria and later governor of the central bank, were very fruitful but in the end a failure. In the late sixties in Switzerland, few objected to cultivation of business ties with the apartheid regime or to investment in South Africa. Today that is quite different. "High treason is a question of time," as Talleyrand liked to say.

In 1972, Barclays sold most of its UDT shares to Prudential Insurance, the U.K.'s largest insurance company, which then held a 26.5 percent share. Eagle Insurance bought another 10 percent of UDT. Looking back, one has to admit without envy that Barclays' management had a good nose and the sale at the right moment saved it a lot of grief later on.

Growing affluence was responsible for the establishment in the late fifties of a number of secondary or fringe banks, as they were often called. They developed in tandem with increasing demand for credit fueled through the newly discovered installment credit. In 1955, the British Treasury fired the starting gun for formation of secondary banks when it told local and regional authorities to no longer expect covering their financial needs exclusively with government loans. This created a new market for debt issues whose actors offered industrial investors more interesting conditions than did the established deposit banks like Westminster, Midland, Barclays, or Lloyds Bank. In effect, a secondary market was created, from which the term "secondary" was derived. It was introduced in order to distinguish them from deposit and clearing banks.

The roaring growth of the Euromarket and the Bank of England's open door policy, which brought joy to every reputable foreign bank in London, fueled the boom among newcomers as much as deregulation did. The competition and credit control act adopted in the fall of 1971 reduced the required minimum liquidity for deposit banks from 28 percent to 12.5 percent for all banks. At the same time, it ended the deposit banks' interest rate cartel and the legal limit on interest payments. The possibility that one day interest rates on loans would rise above 10 percent in order to throttle demand was, in 1971, beyond anyone's imagination. At the time, the discount rate was stuck at 5 percent.

Only two years later, however, the rapid rise in interest rates triggered the secondary banking crisis. In addition to the historically high interest rates in the wake of the oil crisis — prices increased fourfold in the winter of 1973–74 and rose up to $100 a barrel — and the accompanying inflation (12.6 percent in 1974), the crisis had a second reason: thanks to cuts in government spending and tax increases, the real estate market, already badly damaged by high interest rates, collapsed. You would have to cite the aggressive business policy of the secondary banks as a structural reason as well. Within a few months, houses spoiled by cheap short-term money were in trouble.

Slater Walker is a textbook example for how quickly the situation worsened. In May 1972, White Weld (it was later taken over by Credit Suisse as one of the first of many acquisitions) put on the market a $20 million Slater Walker International convertible bond issue paying 5.25 percent interest, maturing in 1987. The issue was oversubscribed. Less than two years later, the Bank of England had to save Slater Walker, and Jim Slater was forced to retire. The charismatic newcomer had £130 million in long-term credits and £225 million in short-term credits outstanding with assets of only £85 million ($220 million). That sealed his fate.

Slater Walker was a classic example in more ways than one. Jim Slater surrounded himself with younger managers he had re-cruited from other houses who were dependent on him. Nor was his autocratic leadership style unique. Auditors from the Board of Trade, in their report on the company's bankruptcy, described the climate in the supervisory board of the London and County Securities, which I discuss in greater detail later on, as "like at the court of a medieval king."

Slater Walker's "leadership cadre" was lured with higher salaries and preferential shares. They could buy shares with a down payment of 2 or 3 percent and had several years' time to pay off the rest. (Compared to today's option excesses, a childish and harmless way of improving compensation almost tax-free.) It was a solid business so long as stock prices rose, but the crisis brought a sobering awakening. In order to avoid the laborious payment for worthless shares, Slater Walker introduced the stop-loss scheme for the securities.

The prominent names from public life that the secondary banks used as decorations were equally typical. Slater's billboard, Peter Walker, was a conservative MP who became a cabinet minister in Edward Heath's government.

The banks had only themselves and their generous loan polices to blame for the far-reaching consequences of the real estate collapse. During the 1971–73 boom, some financial institutions gave mortgage credits of 75 to 80 percent of the estimated value and, in addition, liked to participate with "a slice of the action," so that their commitment could at times rise to 90 to 100 percent. Or as the Bank of England summed up the situation: the boom "encouraged the fringe banks to extend their position in property lending, particularly at the speculative end of the market." Without the necessary margins, the banks lacked all protection when, in 1974, property values collapsed. The drama was repeated twenty-five years later in Switzerland, a sign of the regrettably short memory in our business. The major and cantonal banks were harshly punished for their negligence.

The immediate trigger for the crisis was the news, published on November 26, 1973, that Donald Bardsley, elected to the supervisory board of the London and County Securities not five months before, had resigned. The experienced merchant banker had fought against booking commissions received on long-term credits as one-time income. Instead, he wanted to distribute earnings over the term of the loan. The board, however, had rejected any changes in accounting practices. Otherwise, it would no longer be able to hide the house's difficulties. As the Board of Trade auditors would determine, the bulk of semi-annual profits as of September 30, 1973, of £1.9 million (before taxes) came from the sale of securities and properties, but these earnings rightly should not have been listed in the regular accounting statement. A quick aside: the world's astonished reaction to the Enron story only shows how short its collective memory is. These things are not that new. In the end, it is always the bookkeeping. At the most, what is new is the readiness to accept as coin of the realm what the PR department puts out.

After Bardsley's resignation was made public, confidence collapsed at once. At the urging of the Bank of England, the First National Finance Inc. had to absorb the London and County Securities. The new board's special audit discovered all kinds of irregularities. The house finally collapsed in March 1975 with a loss of more than £50 million ($130 million), a huge sum for the time. One director went to jail, two others got away with fines.

I only discovered the historic origins of the London and County Securities from Walter Eberstadt. Like most London merchant banks, the house had German roots. His father had founded it under the name of G. Eberstadt & Co. — the 40 percent of the

"Co." was divided between Charles Warburg and Henry Blunden. Both wanted to continue the enterprise after Georg Eberstadt's death in 1963. Walter Eberstadt agreed so long as his parents' stake was acquired and the name of the bank was changed. Warburg and Blunden then brought in Gerald Caplan. Walter Eberstadt described what happened next:

> I took one look, was appalled, but felt I could not go on being an obstacle. If they wanted Caplan, so be it, provided he bought Mother's shares and the firm was renamed. First Caplan quibbled. He'd eventually name the firm London and Country Securities, but he wanted to keep the Eberstadt name, at least in parentheses, for the first two years. Fortunately we remained adamant. At first I felt foolish and a little envious. Caplan took the firm public, the share price multiplied manifold, but the business soon got into trouble. . . . Caplan escaped criminal prosecution by fleeing to Florida. The episode was a reminder that one irreplaceable asset is one's name.

The "lifeboat idea" for salvage of the damaged bank ripened during the crisis marathon at the Bank of England on December 19, 1973, under the direction of the newly installed governor, Gordon Richardson — a session triggered by the endangered Cedar Holding, which was heavily engaged in the mortgage market. If in the wake of the crisis of confidence, it was reasoned, investors withdrew their deposits from secondary banks and moved their funds into the large clearing banks, it would be only natural that the clearing banks use this money to help the secondary banks, which would thus win time to recover.

The collapse of the Herstatt bank in Cologne on June 26, 1974, worsened the creeping crisis of confidence. All lines of credit dried up. The capital needs of secondary banks leapt from £53 million to £443 million in the second quarter and up to £994 million ($2.57 billion) as of the end of September.

Given UDT's shaky basis — with £1.225 billion in assets, it was the largest financial house with the status of a bank and as of midyear in 1974 clearly in difficulties — the clearing banks thought it appropriate to signal the limits of their lifeboat engagement. Together with the Bank of England they set the limit at £1.2 billion — 40 percent of the capital reserves of all English and Scottish clearing banks — of which UDT alone at times required £500 million. At the peak of the crisis, in March 1975, the lifeboat engagement had grown to a total of £1.285 billion ($3.64 billion).

As part of the lifeboat concept, the shareholders agreed to inject new capital into endangered banks. The governor of the Bank of England, for example, expected Prudential and Eagle Star to invest new capital in UDT, which they did with an unsecured convertible bond issue of £30 million.

In November 1974, Leonard Mather took over the UDT leadership. He came from Midland, had a reputation as an energetic manager, and lived up to it by immediately plunging into the books and revaluing the credit portfolio, including mortgage loans. With the necessary provisions and write-offs, he came up with a loss of £54.8 million. Given these losses, the equity base shrank critically. As a result, the Bank of England called and invited — if not demanded — that we take over UDT's share in Julius Baer International Ltd. We followed this "invitation."

UDT did recover, albeit slowly, and was able to reduce its lifeboat borrowing from £500 million to £100 million in 1980 but did not succeed in building up enough capital to survive, so that finally Trustee Savings Banks (TSB), later merged as TSB-Lloyds, took it over in 1981.

On January 29, 1975, Julius Baer Holding became the sole owner of Julius Baer International in London; at the same time, it sold its share in UDT Internationale Finanz AG in Zurich. At the

time, the merchant bank in London was bigger than the parent
bank in Zurich and earned very handsome profits despite the per-
ilous times. But given the uncertain perspectives, it obviously made
sense to reduce the business.

The takeover necessitated an inventory. Since the auditors
wanted to include even the ashtrays, I permitted myself, in an attack of incautious irony, to suggest that they stop being so stupid;
otherwise, they would have to descend into the cellars and count
the wine bottles. They promptly marched into the cellar and that
cost us another £20,000. Roy Bridge was not only an able executive
director, but he also knew his way around the Grands Crus and had
invested heavily in them.

Bridge had made his career with the Bank of England — as
head of the foreign exchange section he was a globally well-known
personality, on the best of terms with the international world of
central bank governors — and after his retirement on January 1,
1970, came to us as executive director. That someone from the
Bank of England would join us caused general surprise. We were
able to win him because he was "terribly pro Swiss" and knew my
cousin Peter very well. For us a real stroke of luck. As long as he was
with us — he died in September 1978 — I never traveled to a
World Bank meeting or to an international conference without
him. Brian Bennett succeeded him on our board; he had been
Bridge's successor at the Bank of England. One of Bridge's ironclad
habits was a visit every evening to the Overseas Bankers Club for a
gin and tonic. "After ten minutes at the bar, I always know what is
going on in the financial markets," I recall him saying.

Soon after his arrival, I received a very unpleasant phone call.
It was early in the afternoon. Would I please come to the governor
of the Bank of England the next morning at nine? What had happened was that an "agent provocateur," I can't explain it any other
way, had come in at lunch — when the counters are not fully
staffed and the cashiers who are on the job are not always in good

form — to ask if the Bank Julius Baer could carry out a repayment in cash for him in England, something that is strictly forbidden. The cashier told him, "We're sorry but that is strictly forbidden." Unfortunately, he added, "but the bank next door will be happy to do it for you." That was a very serious offense, and I was given a very harsh reprimand. Happily, that was the only unpleasant incident. For the rest, I turned up at the Bank of England for many years with the annual financial statement under my arm "to discuss the figures." The head of the discount office — I well remember James Keogh — took a cursory look and handed it back to me with "Okay, we go for lunch." That was a sign of distinction. If something wasn't right, we did not go to lunch. There was no socializing when there was trouble. The Swiss Banking Commission in Bern doesn't do it any differently.

The Bank of England likes to put chosen top personnel in positions that will do the bank the most good, unembarrassed to admit that it needs to know what is going on with us. One effect of this sophisticated headhunting was to avoid having retired top managers live off their pensions, which is how Brian Bennet came to us as a board member.

On our own, we had found Sir Frank Figgures and made him a member of our board. Sir Frank was a diplomat and Charles Mueller's predecessor as director general of the European Free Trade Area (EFTA) in Geneva. He liked Switzerland a great deal and was a charming man.

Arthur Wetherell, who died in 2007 at age ninety-seven, succeeded Henri Jacquet, our first managing director, who came from a merchant bank. Wetherell had started his banking career in July 1927 at Martins Bank in Liverpool, a city still reeling from the economic crisis that followed the First World War. In 1939, he came to London's Lombard Street — in the credit business for the raw materials trade. In 1942, he joined the Royal Air Force and was assigned as an officer to the 123rd Wing of the Second Tactical Air

Force. Shot down not far from Hanover, he became a prisoner of war. After his release from the RAF in May 1946, he continued his career at Martins Bank. He was named chief overseas manager as well as a member of the governing board in 1961. After Barclays took over Martins in November 1969, he was faced with the question of whether he wanted to retire at age sixty. Instead, he came with us.

In 1974, Donald Bardsley followed Wetherell. Bardsley had triggered the secondary banking crisis when he quit the board of the London and County Bank. Bardsley, a very sober man, had been director general of Martins Bank and had a network of excellent contacts. He remained our general manager until Julius Baer International Ltd. gave up its independent status on January 1, 1982, and was changed into a subsidiary (branch office). From then on, Bardsley was president of our bank's advisory board.

Undoubtedly, 1974 was the most dramatic year of my life as a banker. On top of the secondary banking crisis, we had the spectacular collapse of Cologne's Herstatt Bank and the months-long agony of the Franklin National Bank in New York. Headquartered in Long Island, Franklin National was one of the twenty largest banks in the United States and had entered interbank dealings in the early sixties. In 1969, it set up a first branch outside the United States. In July 1972, the Sicilian tax lawyer and financier Michele Sindona took control of the bank through acquisition of 21.6 percent of the holding — without having any concrete idea of the bank's quality. The virtual monopoly the bank had enjoyed on Long Island had protected it for a long time, but its credit portfolio was poor and it depended on short-term credits to finance long-term obligations to an unhealthy degree. During the 1974 banking crisis, Franklin was close to collapse.

Given Franklin's importance in the United States and its connections to the international banking system — Franklin financed its activities to a large degree on the Euromarket and, in hopes of speculative earnings, was a very active foreign exchange player — the American regulatory authorities decided on new measures in order to avoid an international crisis. As it would turn out later, the regulatory authorities were not up to date in Sindona's case either. They had forgotten to declare his subsidiaries "Fasco AG" and "Fasco International" as bank holdings. Thus Sindona could pump money from Franklin into his Fasco subsidiaries without fearing intervention under the Federal Reserve Act.

Franklin National engaged heavily in the foreign exchange markets in order to bolster meager earnings from its core business, egged on by Michele Sindona, whose Italian institutions had made a great deal of money in this sector. From 1972 to 1974, daily turnover at the house ranged as high as $3.7 billion. The New York Federal Reserve paid no attention to this, but the other banks did. In November 1973, two top managers at Morgan Guaranty Trust told the president of the New York Federal Reserve that they were concerned about the size of these daily trades. This unusual step was triggered by the Deutsche Bank's unwillingness to handle clearing for Franklin National, by Commerzbank's decision to no longer do any business with Franklin, and by the growing number of questions that were being asked about the institution's creditworthiness.

Morgan Guaranty and other banks no longer concluded futures contracts or spot contracts with Franklin National. As the Morgan managers explained, refusal to do any foreign exchange business with Franklin National could lead to the banks closing Franklin National's access to their Eurodollar lines and perhaps even their federal funds. Franklin's London branch worked with 1.2 billion Eurodollars, and it would be impossible to absorb this sum on the American market. The insolvency of the U.S. National Bank in October 1973 — it was taken over by Crocker National Bank — had already sensitized European banks. Crocker National tried to ignore commitments made in connection with National Bank letters of credit (as Ambrosiano tried to do later with IOR, the Vatican Bank), and the

Federal Deposit Insurance Corporation (FDIC) refused to pay at first, much to the chagrin of overseas banks who then backed off doing business with U.S. banks.

Representatives of the New York Federal Reserve agreed that the situation was potentially explosive and that further clarification was necessary. In the end, Franklin's management succeeded in calming Fed concerns, but the New York central bank set up a Franklin crisis staff that carefully observed its performance report on a weekly basis and prepared for the possibility that Franklin might need a "discount window advance."

On May 8, 1974, Franklin had to draw on $100 million in Federal Reserve funds. But the accumulated foreign exchange losses were many times larger. On the weekend of May 10–12, the Federal Reserve and Franklin National discussed the problem. On May 11, Richard Debs, the first vice president of the New York Federal Reserve Bank, informed the Bank of England and all the other larger central banks of the tremendous losses, and Franklin embarked on the long road through a managed crisis that ended on October 8 with a declaration of bankruptcy and the subsequent sale at auction.

The house's undoing proved to be excessive short-term debt, which, in the wake of the oil crisis and the high rate of inflation, became massively more expensive. Most of them were certificates of deposit (CDs) with a term of less than 90 days and federal funds. Franklin National's savings deposits fell from 83.5 percent in 1964 to 51.6 percent in 1974, and its equity capital dropped from 8.1 percent in 1964 to 4 percent in 1973. The downward spiral was speeded through a decision in 1973 to bet on lower interest rates and to continue short-term exposure in the expectation of receiving more favorable conditions for long-term obligations. This at a time when interest rates for short-term instruments like federal funds had risen from 11.9 percent to 21.3 percent in operative costs. Bad debtors and large foreign exchange losses due to unauthorized contacts and insufficient controls added to the bank's woes.

Realizing the dangers facing the international banking system, the Federal Reserve pumped $1.77 billion into Franklin National in order to avoid an uncontrollable collapse. Franklin National had $2 billion on its foreign exchange books, while Herstatt had "only" $200 million. It is worth adding that in October 1974, Michele Sindona had moved to New York's Hotel Pierre, after the Italian judiciary had issued an arrest warrant for him, where he had a lovely view of Central Park. Later he was arrested and sentenced and subsequently murdered in jail.

The crisis awareness of American central bank managers was quite different from that of their colleagues in Frankfurt. In September 1974, Richard Debs pointed out that a collapse would ruin confidence in the foreign exchange market, would diminish the reputation of U.S. banks, and in a worst-case scenario could lead to a general banking crisis and to an economic crisis. Interbank business had suffered greatly through the abrupt closing of the Herstatt bank and the refusal of the German Bundesbank to take over the international obligations in the foreign exchange trade.

Part of the prudent handling of the Franklin National Bank — in my memory clearly the best managed banking crisis of my life — was the invitation on May 13 of leading Swiss bankers to a dinner at the American Embassy in Berne. Ambassador Shelby Collum Davis, an insurance expert by profession, had, as a financial pro, a perfection understanding of the situation. In the ambassador's presence, a representative of the Federal Reserve told us that the Americans would assume Franklin National's foreign exchange business and respect all contracts. With that, the crisis was over and we could drive home safely — it was an instructive experience in banking and the counter-example to the attitude of the German Bundesbank in the Herstatt case. It adopted the simple position that supporting houses that had not followed the rules was not the central bank's job, and it cared not a whit for the consequences.

Shelby Collum Davis, a stocky man who never forgot a name

and knew the first names of every member of the Baer family, spent a long time as ambassador in Berne. He knew Switzerland very well, since he had studied in Geneva and had met his wife there. Switzerland became his hobby and his profession. He had specialized early on in Swiss insurers like Swiss Re, Winterthur, Bâloise, and Zurich, and had traded these securities before he became ambassador. After his mission was over, he often came back to Switzerland to ski. He preferred the Engadin and stayed at the Suvretta House. There I saw that he was always master of his fate — even outside of office hours. Skiing down a valley, an avalanche thundered down behind him and his wife, and we feared for the worst. Quite suddenly, Shelby and Catherine crawled out of the snow and greeted us calmly and happily.

26

HERSTATT (1974)

If you know the names of the players,
the game is over

I never slept as badly in my whole life as I did during the banking crisis after the Herstatt Bank shut down on June 26, 1974. I got the news in London in the offices of a correspondent bank. I had intended to meet with our colleagues there and talk about routine business.

The problem wasn't so much our position with Herstatt. Willy Himmelsbach, our chief dealer, had sensed the risks early. Back then, the heads of the banks' foreign exchange divisions still talked to each other. The world was smaller and the phone was state of the art. After Himmelsbach had learned in the spring of 1973 from several colleagues about the huge turnovers his colleague Daniel Dattel at Herstatt was making, with other banks as well, he reacted at once and cancelled options and futures trading limits, very much to the annoyance of the Cologne bankers. Within a year, our bank reduced the risk in dealing with Herstatt from several million to a few hundred thousand Swiss francs. In the end, we could even settle those contracts and come up with a small net gain.

Like the Federal Reserve in New York in the case of Franklin National, the German federal banking supervisory office had received clear indications from the market about the disturbing risks with which Herstatt was operating, but had not bothered to react, even though early in 1974 two banks, the Westdeutsche Landesbank and the Hessische Landesbank, had lost heavily in foreign exchange trading.

For us and for many others, the drama began after Herstatt was shut down at 3:30 p.m., a time when German banks usually closed their offices. American and British banks, however, had not closed yet, meaning that important foreign exchange dealings had only been half-settled, that is, the D-marks were paid and the dollars were left open. A number of first-rate houses had to fear heavy losses, among them Morgan Guaranty and Seattle First National. Hill Samuel, for example, a renowned London house, faced a loss of DM 55 million or £9 million ($23.4 million). Only after the courts arranged preferential treatment for foreign creditors (something the law surely did not provide) did the British bank recover a part of its money and could limit its losses to £1.2 million.

The Herstatt closure, which clearly had not been thought through, unleashed a quake in the international banking system unheard of since the early thirties. Market confidence in the Clearing House Interbank Payments System (CHIPS), an electronic dollar transfer system headquartered in New York, was severely shaken. The international credit system threatened to collapse. Dollar settlements from antecedent foreign exchange transactions could no longer be carried out, even though D-mark transfers to Herstatt had already taken place. Andrew Brimmer, the former governor of the Federal Reserve whom I knew from IMF meetings in Washington, D.C. as a highly intelligent and very charming man, determined that at least a dozen banks had sold D-marks to Herstatt on June 24. Delivery of dollars was due on June 26. On that day, the selling banks instructed their correspondent banks in Germany to debit their D-mark accounts and to transfer the outstanding sums to the German regional central bank to the credit of Herstatt. At the same time, the selling banks expected to receive dollars from their London or New York clearinghouse. When Herstatt closed down at 3:30 p.m., foreign exchange trade was still active in New York. In the meantime, the German regional central bank had credited the sums to Herstatt, but the bank was shut down before the Herstatt dollars could be credited to the foreign banks.

The clearing weakness was not effectively ended until the fall of 2002 with the launch of the CLS bank — an acronym for "continuous linked settlement." The CLS bank credits the money to both sides at the same time. Given a market volume of $2 billion per day as well as the collapses of Drexel Burnham Lambert, Barings and Long Term Capital Management (LTCM), it was high time for introduction of such a clearing center.

With the uncontrolled closing of the Herstatt bank, everything threatened to collapse. Foreign exchange trading fell worldwide to a minimal volume, until a few days later the twelve largest New York trading banks, who together controlled the Clearing House Interbank Payments System (CHIPS), agreed to introduce a contingency clause which permitted banks to call back payments up to a day after feeding the funds into the system. The banks recognized that even the spot business was not without risks, and traders only did business with the most reputable houses. Small and mid-size banks had great difficulties working with foreign exchange, and even then could only do so with payment of risk premiums.

Even after introduction of the contingency clause, the market remained very nervous and the traded volume remained extremely small, not least because the Franklin National crisis had not been put behind us. The German Bundesbank ignored the Federal Reserve's suggestion made in July to create a special fund in order to settle Herstatt's debts to international banks, debts that resulted from the interruption of the payments stream. It was not much consolation for the affected banks that the Herstatt affair's threat to the world economy was less than that posed by Franklin National. Herstatt's risk in foreign exchange dealings was $200 million; Franklin National carried $2 billion on its foreign exchange books. But it would have served the general interest had the Bundesbank supported Herstatt and led it into controlled bankruptcy, especially since more than enough means were available to do so.

Banks now became much more cautious in their foreign exchange dealings, which suited the purpose of the Bundesbank, for it considered the exchange rate futures trade, after exchange controls were lifted, a depraved form of speculation rather than a sensible practice of currency price formation. But as Michael Stuermer so accurately wrote in his history of the Sal. Oppenheim bank, the Herstatt closing "threatened the reputation of the entire German credit system. A wave of international mistrust hit even the largest banks, and especially private bankers."

Subsequently, the Euromarket experienced a flight of deposits from the smaller banks. Interest rates jumped, and the quotation for Eurodollar bonds sank, an added problem for secondary banks, which had accepted short-term money and invested it into long-term bonds. Concerted action by the central banks helped prevent the crisis from escalating. Thanks to Gordon Richardson's initiative — as head of the Bank of England he had collected extensive experience in dealing with crises of confidence in just a few months — the Standing Committee on Banking Regulations and Supervisory Practices of the group of Ten, also known as the Cooke Committee, was formed in the autumn of 1974.

After June 26, the credit windows on the Euromarket closed for us as well. Only the then five major Swiss banks (today there are only two) continued to trust us, as did a few friends abroad, among them the Deutsche Bank. Among the three great banking crises I experienced, the Herstatt bankruptcy was the most serious for us, even though we did not suffer any direct losses.

An enduring memorial for Herstatt's downfall is the deposit guaranty fund in Germany, which private banks — in this case not public — created at the instigation of the German federal banking supervisory office and to which all private banks contribute. It was tapped just recently in order to save investors in the failed Schmidt Bank from suffering heavy losses. By the way, in 1989 when we founded the Bank Julius Baer (Germany) AG in Frankfurt, a wholly owned subsidiary of the Baer Holding AG, the federal banking supervisory office insisted that the holding provide a guarantee for the obligation to perform for the benefit of the deposit guaranty fund.

I knew the banker Iwan Herstatt, who was an inch or two taller than I, as I did the whole Gerling family and the corporate group to whose empire the Herstatt bank belonged. Through Hans Gerling I also met the sculptor and architect Arno Breker (one of Hitler's preferred artists), who had designed Gerling's corporate headquarters in 1951. In addition, I also became acquainted with Hjalmar Schacht, long-time president of the Reichsbank. He too was an impressive gentleman. He sat down next to me and we talked about family firms for a long time. As much as I dislike saying this (Schacht was an old Nazi prosecuted in 1946 in Nuremberg), he was very nice. Rumor has it that his grandson lives in Kiel today, where he drives a taxi; he is said to have inherited his grandfather's distinctive face and narrative talent.

The Herstatt Bank had proved a lucrative investment for Gerling, and one he had built up with great determination over the years. Iwan Herstatt had been trained as a banker, although the family had pulled out of the independent banking business after the death of his grandfather. His father had been director of an insurance company. The dynamic son, full of the joys of life, proud of always carrying with him a stack of account-opening forms when he frequented one of his numerous soccer or philharmonic clubs, used the chance to make himself independent and to give the old name new life when, in 1955, after the death of the owner, the bank Hocker & Co. was up for sale.

Within twenty years Herstatt had turned the small bank with fifteen employees and total assets of DM 5 million into one of the largest German private banks with a staff of 850 and assets of more than DM 2 billion in his own resources. Gerling held 80 percent of the outstanding shares, having successively bought up the shares of the other partners (among them Emil Buehrle).

The successful bank stumbled because of insufficient controls over the relatively new foreign exchange division under Daniel Dattel, whose mistakes made him well-known. He had been spoiled by the dollar's fall over eighteen months from DM 4.20 to DM 1.80. When the dollar began an intermittent recovery, the counter-movement caught some people unaware. The positions it had adopted in futures transactions brought the house massive losses in a short time. As Herstatt wrote in his memoirs, he informed Gerling on June 15 that they had to count on a loss of DM 470 million to DM 520 million. Gerling declared at once:

> The bank must be held if only to avoid a backlash against the Gerling group. Since loss coverage had to be paid in cash . . . exhaustive deliberations were undertaken with the result that only a major bank could carry out the capital reorganization. Dr. Gerling should act as borrower, pledging his shares as collateral. . . . Then came the fateful 26th of June. . . . When I returned to the bank around 3 p.m., I still hoped to soon hear something positive about the capital reorganization negotiations. A short time later I received a call from an official at the bank supervision. He told me that unfortunately negotiations had failed and that therefore the

bank would have to be closed immediately. A directive ordering the closure was on the teletype. . . . I had barely put down the receiver when Mr. Weiler called on behalf of Dr. Gerling ordering the closure of the bank.

The Herstatts were a Protestant family. They came from Valenciennes in French Flanders, at that time part of the Spanish Netherlands. During the Counter-Reformation, the family was forced to leave their home since they were not ready to abjure their faith. Via Aix-la-Chapelle and the Dukedom of Juelich, they reached the arch-Catholic city of Cologne, where they received permission, as one of the few reformed families, to establish a factory and a trading house. The Herstatts were silk weavers, a capital-intensive business, and, realizing in the middle of the eighteenth century that they could not compete against the centers of the silk industry (Lyon, Valenciennes), moved to reduce the size of their business and to invest their working capital into banking. Their bank financed the young Alfred Krupp and other iron-making pioneers, the new chemical industry (fibers, colors), and the founding of insurance companies and railroads. After Johann David Herstatt's death in 1888, the bank was closed. His son was only nine months old. The family transferred the bank business to the Bank J. H. Stein. The capital was more than 5 million talers ($3.7 million gold dollars, roughly $180 million today).

As for the foreign exchange trade, which in the end broke the Herstatt Bank's neck, a comment by John Kenneth Galbraith is illuminating here: "If you know the names of the players, the game is over."

It should be mentioned that lower margins in the credit business after the lifting in 1972 of the credit interest agreement surely contributed to the bank's failure. The Reichsbank had introduced the agreement during the banking crisis of the early thirties in order to enable the survival of the smaller banks.

27

THE MUTUAL FUND BUSINESS
(1959–71)

Miniskirts promoted the fund business

My uncles were not interested when I wrote them in 1949 that Wall Street brokers were taking great interest in the market for investment funds and were building up a capacity to reach customers with investment capital in the $5,000 to $10,000 range. The argument for risk diversification made immediate sense to me. But my uncle Walter wrote back to me that the funds had been a "fad" before the stock market crash. And furthermore, he wrote:

> I can remember an article about it under the designation "the synthetic customer," which is true insofar as every brokerage firm added such a trust and speculated wildly for it with the inevitable result of heavy losses. This didn't prevent UBS, for example, from making a lot of money with their investment trusts, because stupid people who think banks know everything better than they do are willing to pay 5 to 7 percent for their cut. In my opinion, everybody can form his own investment trust, and if he

doesn't have enough money he had better not touch the shares but buy gilt-edged bonds instead.

So much for my sober uncle.

Encouraged by the general success of this investment instrument in the United States, where it had emerged in the twenties, my cousin Nicolas ignored my uncle's bias and, toward the end of the fifties, decided to take over sale and distribution of the Fidelity Funds in Switzerland. Later he added Eurunion. Back then Fidelity was already the largest vendor of funds worldwide. The real inventors of collective wealth management, however, are the much older Scottish Investment Trusts in Glasgow and Edinburgh — for example, the famous "Scottish Widows."

Union Bank of Switzerland (UBS) founded the first Swiss investment company, INTRAG, on December 7, 1938. Fritz Richner, my daughter-in-law Gabriele Baer-Richner's grandfather, was INTRAG's president. After INTRAG, Richner launched the AMCA Trust Fund, the first flexible trust in Switzerland. In the early sixties, Richner wanted to start an investment fund for women and had even discovered the right person to run it — Emilie Lieberherr. The future Zurich city councilwoman (executive) had raised the Fonda acting family's children in Hollywood as their governess, spoke fluent English, and after her return to Switzerland worked for Richner, who quickly spotted her general talent and her flair for banking. But a UBS majority did not favor the idea, and Lieberherr, who in all probability would have put her political talent at the disposal of the Radicals political party (the grand old party of Switzerland), wandered over to the socialists.

Basically, the funds business is very institutional. Wealth managers sell their customers a packaged market product very much the way a grocer sells Nescafe. That makes the wealth managers very one-sided. If you don't carry the right brands, your customers run away and that's the end of the business right there.

Lehman Brothers launched the first bank-owned funds. However, they did not name the fund after Lehman but after the address of the bank — "One-Williams-Street." If we had followed that lead, we would have had to call our fund "Bahnhofstrasse 36." Hidden behind this "distancing" is a marketing theory — a different name for an unsuccessful fund would not sully the name of the parent house. Carry this theory to its logical conclusion, and a father should give his children a different last name. In practice, hiding your name is not a good idea. Funds should be managed as successfully as possible, and those that do not perform well should be withdrawn from the market.

After we had sold the Fidelity fund for seven or eight years — mostly to customers in southern Europe — we decided that, given the sizable margins, we should develop our own funds. We were well acquainted with the legal perils of authorization procedures, thanks to our work for Fidelity, and we knew that we had the technical savoir faire to administer the funds ourselves. The legal framework was also clear — after the first federal law covering investment funds had gone into effect on February 1, 1967. (The first decree about foreign investment funds was issued on January 13, 1971.)

On March 1, 1970, Julius Baer founded its own first fund, the Baerbond, a pure bond fund. Our trade division, headed by my cousin Peter and with Pedro Hangartner as trading chief, was responsible for the fund's rapid development. Helmut Saurer organized our success. When we issued our first fund, its capital subscription amounted to 50 million Swiss francs. Today the Julius Baer and GAM investment funds manage 182 billion Swiss francs ($145 billion). Much of this growth is due to the internationalization of our fund business that Peter Spinnler began to develop in 1990. In 1992, we founded Julius Baer Investment Funds Services (JBIFS). It brought together our entire fund business and our cooperation with domestic and foreign banks. A number of German and Italian houses sell our funds today, and we again have business ties with

Fidelity. Within the framework of "best advice doctrine," we sell their funds to our customers just as we do UBS and Pictet fund shares. Fidelity places our funds on the American market, and UBS and Pictet offers them to their customers. At the same time, JBIFS manages the funds of other Swiss houses.

All told, thirty-eight hundred investment funds are accredited in Switzerland, and more than two thousand are foreign, mostly from Luxembourg. The unfavorable general framework for the funds — here too Switzerland has missed a chance — led the fund business to move to Luxembourg.

A scandal-ridden outsider who ended his days in the poor house helped the fund idea break through in Europe. Bernie Cornfeld's IOS (Investors Overseas Service) began selling mutual funds to American soldiers in Europe in 1956. One of the world's largest sales organizations developed from these modest beginnings. In 1969, Cornfeld had close to five thousand employees, a million customers in more than one hundred countries, and managed assets worth $2.5 billion. With $750 million in assets back then, the UBS subsidiary INTRAG remained far behind.

While houses like Lehman Brothers still pondered the names to be used for selling funds, Cornfeld, who liked to make fun of Swiss banks' asset management — "they move ten shares of Nestle from one account to another" — had known for a long time how to sell funds successfully: with celebrity endorsements and girls in miniskirts. "The skirts were at see level," Roy Bridge used to say. Geneva was full of pretty "mini-skirted wall-to-wall girls" in Bernie Cornfeld's service. He himself married Heidi Fleiss, who later ran a flourishing call girl ring in Hollywood.

No woman without a miniskirt ever got a job with him, and Cornfeld had no problem winning prominent names like former German Vice Chancellor and Federal Minister Erich Mende. The title of a book about Cornfeld was *Do You Sincerely Want to Be Rich?* And it was a question he asked of all prospective employees.

Intellectually, this wasn't very exciting, but looking back you can't deny that this genius salesman had a clear sense of distribution. Nor should we conceal his contribution to Geneva's cultural life. IOS generously helped finance the Orchestre de la Suisse Romande's international tours.

In the sixties — that is, before his publicly demonstrated obsession for girls in miniskirts — he once knocked on our door. He wanted to distribute his funds through Julius Baer. As Juergen Luethi, our later CEO, remembers it, the conversation lasted twenty minutes before we took him to the elevator. The door had hardly closed when Luethi and I spontaneously looked at each other and shook our heads. It proved to be a wise decision. It saved us many millions and protected our reputation.

But one should not forget that when, in February 1970, Cornfeld spoke as a guest at a New York bond conference and predicted that the IOS funds would manage $15 billion by 1975, everybody took him seriously. IOS was one of the largest Euromarket customers, and on many stock exchanges the steady purchase and sale of larger blocks of shares brought in fat commissions. But the fact that from the fall of 1968 to the spring of 1969 IOS had subscribed to $40 million worth of convertible bonds on the Euromarket, which defaulted, is something else.

When in September 1969 IOS holding went public, the issue price of $10 for 11 million shares slumped to $4. Walter Eberstadt, with Model Roland at the time, had refused to participate in the lucrative introduction of IOS shares and was promptly eliminated from the broker list. In a rescue operation that IOS turned down, N. M. Rothschild & Sons offered $1 per share. Two years later everything collapsed.

Bernie Cornfeld had always had certain regulatory difficulties, not only in Switzerland, and had therefore set up his headquarters in Ferney-Voltaire (in France), soon known as Bernie-Voltaire. The home of the enlightenment philosopher, who himself had made a fortune with the manufacture of watches, lies close to the Geneva border. Cornfeld's sales vehicle was the Fund of Funds. Once he was forbidden to use it and had to invest directly, it led him into marshes of illegality. The idea behind the Fund of Funds was anything but stupid. How did the regulators come to forbid it? But because Cornfield violated the ban, he ended up in prison. Today, umbrella funds are once again legal.

The IOS affair led to a complete stagnation of the funds' business for almost ten years. Only in the early eighties did demand revive noticeably. Today, future prospects for funds remain good, even in bad years. Funds cannot exclude the systematic risks of any market, but it reduces the individual risk of an investment. By looking at the rising savings rate (at least in Europe, though not in the United States) and at some of the bad stock market experiences, the future growth of this branch of investing can be estimated with some degree of certainty.

28

MEXICO (1955–82)

Sovereign countries don't go bankrupt

René Beyersdorf was not only a friend of our family and until the seventies our representative in New York, but he had a talent for business and, thanks to his mother tongue, good contacts in the well-organized French financial community in New York. As far as I can remember, during the war and postwar years, he and his Belgian colleagues liked to talk about Sofina, a Belgian company involved in building, financing, and running power plants and street-car construction firms. Today, Sofina is a financial holding company listed on the Brussels stock exchange.

Walter first met Beyersdorf in 1938 after Beyersdorf had founded the Beyersdorf-Terlinck bank in Brussels. My uncle could not have found a better man to manage Baer Custodian in New York than this small, very sympathetic and obliging gentleman who was moreover a true bon vivant. He spoke French with my mother and English with me. He went to the office every day, ran the business well, and maintained a familial contact with us all. He died in 1997 at the biblical age of ninety-five. His two children wrote a loving obituary in which they remembered their wild flight from Europe and their father's never-ending optimism.

It did not remain unnoticed in the family that Beyersdorf once received a check for $100,000 for his work in building up our Mexican promissory note business. Sitting in his garden, Werner remarked about the fee, "If anybody ever gets $100,000 in profit sharing from me again, I'll close the joint."

The business Beyersdorf built up for Julius Baer was the trade with Mexican promissory notes before it became a global phenomenon. He once described the practical difficulties this way: "A lunch at 12:30 means 12:29 for a Swiss, for a Mexican, however, 1:45 — approximately." The sophisticated bon vivant, whose major talent lay in handling people, overcame such problems as well.

Promissory notes served mostly for financing the commodity business. Pemex, for example, would buy pipes; Mexican authorities would install telephone switchboards or build harbors and airports. For lack of something better, these commodity businesses were financed by short-term bills of exchange for three, six, or nine months. Thanks to their high interest rates of 12 to 13 percent, they brought us very solid profits. We also worked with dollar promissory notes, but they earned a lower rate of return. We financed them with 4 percent notes. The rate of exchange for the peso remained very stable during the long reign of the Bretton-Woods system — at 12.49 to the dollar. Of course we bought the high rates of interest at a recognizable price. For us, these notes represented a steady war of nerves. We bought large amounts and trembled about our debtors' state of fiscal health.

We had been officially represented in Mexico since 1972, although Baer Mexicana S.A. had been founded for formal reasons on March 1, 1966. Our business developed so quickly that Julius Baer, despite its small size, was soon the largest lender among all European banks in Mexico and thus became market leader in the Mexican notes business. If Julius Baer decided that interest rates in line with market conditions should be 13 percent, then they paid 13 percent interest.

In the sixties, it could happen that I would telephone Beyersdorf late at night in Europe, say 10 p.m., and decide to buy a large amount of Mexican paper for the bank — "large" in terms of the times. For example, we were the first European bank that gave money to Pemex, the Mexican oil company. Generally the amounts were in the $500,000 range for three to six months at a rate of 4.5 (450 basis points) above the reference rate for first-rate debtors.

Later, Pemex would take our money out of a sense of loyalty even after it had become a giant — however, not at the comfortable conditions of the early years, but in a range of 0.125 "over."

In 1965, Juergen Luethi took over our Mexico business in Zurich. Julius Baer had investors who only bought peso-denominated papers at our bank. Luethi reported to Beyersdorf in New York as the new man charged with selling the notes. Whereupon Beyersdorf asked him whether he had ever been to Mexico. The then twenty-five-year-old admitted he had not. Shaken, Beyersdorf said, "How can you sell Mexican notes without knowing the country?" And then he sent the young man on a two-week vacation into the country of the Aztecs, with the company paying the bill, much to the envy of several of his Zurich colleagues.

Among my Mexican memories are the steelworks we financed. We proudly watched how the workers were trained, and we saw the first steel cast pass the hot rolling steel installation. Next we learned that all the workers disappeared after payday. After a month, they had received more money than ever before in their lives and decided not to come back again.

In light of the sizable risk in our own portfolio of several tens of millions of Swiss francs (and individual amounts among our customers), the bank remained vigilant in Mexico. Somewhere early in 1982, Luethi got a bad feeling and decided to reduce our exposure to a few million. Curtis Lowell, the representative of our bank in Mexico, was not overjoyed, because our move dried up his source of income.

Lowell came from Chicago, and his original name was Loewen-berg. Once, he demonstrated how it was in New York if you tried to reserve a restaurant table under his name. When he said he would like a table for Lowell, he was told they were "sold out." Whereupon he thundered into the receiver, "Colonel Lowell!" "Yes, sir!" And the table was reserved.

To that extent, he can claim that his military training as a tac-tical scout (U.S. Army Military Intelligence) and his deployment in France and Germany during the Second World War, paid off. Lowell was a friend of the family, especially since he married the woman who had been meant for me. June Edelstone went to college with my sister Marianne and was very attached to me until her path crossed with Lowell. He established himself in Mexico and led a successful ball-bearing business, which he liquidated because he wanted to come home. We were looking for someone who could take care of sales and marketing of our notes in Mexico after Ernesto Rosenthal retired. Lowell took over our representative of-fice in April 1972. The decision paid off for him in dynastic aspects as well. Curtis Jr., his son, who did an internship with us and thus learned German, lives in Zurich today and often meets me on the Bahnhofstrasse with his wife, Olivia. He is friends with my son and has his own asset management firm for South American clients.

Our representative office was always a hybrid. On the one hand, it looked after our commercial business with notes and was therefore a very official part of the local banking scene. On the other hand, it had to take care of our asset management customers. But they were uncomfortable with a commercial representative. So basically we damaged our asset management business with our com-mercial business.

In 1982, we lived through a profound crisis, not only in Mex-ico, and one that thoroughly refutes former Citibank CEO Walter Wriston's comment that "no sovereign government has ever de-faulted." As a student of history, he should have known that the past is loaded with insolvent sovereigns. After Mexico, other Latin American countries, with the exception of Colombia, collapsed, and subsequently so did the Philippines and a number of African states. The Anglo-Saxon banks were struck hardest, but German banks were hit as well, as they watched underdeveloped but highly populated and resource-rich countries go bankrupt. Neither the World Bank nor the International Monetary Fund (IMF) had foreseen the crisis. A panic was avoided thanks to the thoughtful and sovereign actions of the IMF's managing director, Jacques de Larosière, who orchestrated negotiations with the debtor nations and suggested to the markets that this was mainly a liquidity crisis. He did so with success.

Essentially, highly liquid credit markets had misled third world governments into taking on exorbitant debt. At the same time, these governments did not think about abolishing their investment barriers, because they feared that capital imports would forfeit their strongly socialist-inspired economic independence, nor were they ready to provide the necessary safety for investments.

29

Banco Ambrosiano/UBS Participation (1972–82)

You can't run the church on Hail Marys

St. Ambrose is Milan's patron saint, but the Banco Ambrosiano, which perished in infamy, did not carry his name in its title with blasphemous intent. Giuseppe Tovini, a lawyer from Brescia, founded the bank in 1896 after earlier having set up the Banca della Valcamonica and the Banca San Paolo di Brescia. Tovini wanted to create a Catholic counterbalance to the young nation's lay banks. The 150 Catholics who scraped together the million lira start-up capital gave the bank a statute with a *clausola di gradimento* (consent clause). Before the shareholders were recorded in the register, they had to show their baptismal certificates and character references from their local priests.

The Banco Ambrosiano was the house bank of Milan's aristocracy and of the Catholic establishment in Italy's financial capital. Franco Ratti di Desio, who led the house for many years, was a nephew of Pope Pius XI. The Montini family, of which Pope Paul VI was a member — he was cardinal archbishop of Milan before his election as pope — also had close ties to the Ambrosiano bank. Catholic institutions like the archbishopal seminary or the Milan cathedral's workshop were often among the shareholders. The guild held 180,000 shares, which at the last recorded price still amounted to £ 5 billion ($4.2 million).

The *clausola di gradimento* only disappeared with the stock's introduction on the primary exchange in May 1982. That was a month and a half before the Banca d'Italia liquidated Ambrosiano. Until then, the shares were traded on the *mercato ristretto* (the restricted market), which had less stringent publication requirements for balance sheets and shareholders. The bank didn't have to submit a consolidated balance sheet and only partially had to consolidate its foreign subsidiaries. This made it easier for Roberto Calvi — whose professional life was posthumously put on film in *I Banchieri Di Dio* (*God's Bankers*) — to engage in his maneuverings.

I'm sure I crossed paths with Roberto Calvi during World Bank meetings in Washington. He was a foster child of his predecessor, Carlo Alessandro Canesi. Calvi's tight-lipped character, his cold efficiency, and his stiff manners brought him the sobriquet "il Prussiano." The Prussian had made himself indispensable in Ambrosiano's expansion abroad. In the sixties, he acquired a majority stake in the Banca del Gottardo, located in Lugano, Switzerland, and then founded a holding in Luxembourg. Calvi became head of the bank in 1971 at age forty-five and attempted to turn the house into an Italian merchant bank. At any rate, his position in high finance developed to the point where he met Fiat boss Agnelli for a tête à tête. Agnelli's only comment, cited in Rupert Cromwell's book *God's Own Banker*, was, "How can you go through life if you can't see further than the tip of your nose?" Except for wartime anecdotes — both had served in the cavalry — they had nothing to say to each other.

Michele Sindona stood at the beginning of Calvi's decline. Sindona helped him obtain an option for the purchase of the very profitable Banca Cattolica del Veneto. In return, Calvi agreed to take over from the Sicilian financier an obscure holding company built around a leather tannery for $40 million. With the money Calvi paid Sindona — via an Ambrosiano subsidiary in Luxembourg — the latter secured control of Franklin National.

The Banca Cattolica was again put up for sale after the Vatican concluded that ownership of worldly goods in the form of participation in Italian industrial enterprises (for example, Lancia) was no longer timely for a spiritual institution. More important than further expansions — such as acquisition of the Credito Varese and the Toro Insurance Company — were the ties Calvi developed to the Istituto per le Opere di Religione (IOR). Pope Pius XII had founded the Vatican bank in 1942, and it proved the ideal offshore vehicle for a banker averse to all transparency ("a secret known by two people is no longer a secret"). The IOR never published an annual report, let alone a balance sheet. The five cardinals who made up the board of directors were never more than decoration. The absolute ruler was archbishop Paul Casimir Marcinkus, not a trained banker, but an energetic and pragmatic American of Lithuanian origin who lived according to the maxim "You can't run the church on Hail Marys." Marcinkus stood apart from the slightly built members of the curia thanks to his Irish guard size. For a time, he had been the pope's unofficial bodyguard, and Pope Paul VI, who appointed him in 1971, held him in especially high regard. The athletic clergyman doubtless had a few very worldly sides. He was a great golfer before the Lord (a member of the Aquasanta golf club) and talked knowledgeably with Calvi's children about waterskiing in the Bahamas.

Marcinkus' ambition was a cardinal's purple, which he hoped to obtain through profit-oriented management of the bank — the Vatican was always in need of funds. This ambition allowed Calvi to harness the IOR — through the inexperienced archbishop — for his businesses. If for no other reason, the ties to the IOR were important because of foreign exchange restrictions on Italian capital export, which did not apply to the Vatican. Marcinkus was a member of the board of the Ambrosiano subsidiary in Nassau renamed, in 1971, the Cisalpine Overseas Bank. But most important, the IOR was the de jure owner of finance societies domiciled mostly in Liechtenstein and Panama over which Calvi held far more than 15 percent of the Ambrosiano shares, and thus he effectively controlled these companies himself. Of course that was illegal, especially when the shareholders had not approved the acquisition and it was not published in the annual report. Of the $1.2 billion missing when Ambrosiano collapsed, Calvi had borrowed about $800 million for purchase of his own shares. He then smuggled the shares, at rising prices, through the books of his many subsidiaries before parking them in the finance companies, formally under IOR ownership, and then mortgaged them for the credits he received. Thus a company named Astolfine with the modest capital of $10,000 had, in the end, liabilities of $486 million at the Peruvian Ambrosiano subsidiary Banco Andino, secured with 2.1 million shares priced at $200, which, however, were quoted at $36. In a letter dated January 20, 1975, Marcinkus acknowledged in IOR's name the ownership and at the same time gave Ambrosiano limited commercial authority. If you want to put it in such a way, Calvi was the spiritual teacher of Enron's financial advisers. His trick was simply to control himself and not allow liabilities to show up in the balance sheet. To that extent, the Enron saga is really nothing new.

The seventies in general were bad times for Italy. They reached their absolute nadir in 1978 with the Red Brigades' murder of former prime minister Aldo Moro. At the time, only three institutions were still functioning: the Communist Party, the church, and the Banca d'Italia. The National Bank had kept a careful eye on Ambrosiano and reacted quickly to the information Michele Sindona — imprisoned in the United States and in his solitude disappointed in Roberto Calvi — had provided.

In April 1978, a dozen inspectors of the Vigilanza (the Italian name for the bank supervision authority), a quarter of the entire staff, were assigned to a special audit. It lasted six months. The inspectors threw a very suspicious eye on the affairs of the Banco Ambrosiano Luxembourg and the Cisalpine Overseas Nassau. It did not escape them that Nassau had received through the Banca del Gottardo $200 million while the other side of the ledger had 183 unspecified "fundings." They suspected that Zurich-based "Suprafin," which held 15 percent of the Ambrosiano shares, was behind it. In their five-hundred-page report, the officials noted that Ambrosiano was undercapitalized and organizationally inadequately structured. All power lay in Calvi's hands, and the board merely approved his decisions. The Vigilanza called the bookkeeping experts superficial and said they did not ask questions. All in all, a model we know well because of Enron.

The great difference back then was that Calvi's political influence was far greater than that of the Enron managers. Through his membership in the notorious secret Masonic Lodge P2 (Propaganda Due), he began, with the help of a compliant Roman district attorney's office, an intrigue against Mario Sarcinelli, the head of the Vigilanza. Sarcinelli was imprisoned for four weeks on remand on vague charges. Thus warned, the Banca d'Italia, then under the direction of future Italian president Carlo Azeglio Ciampi, opted for an indirect approach. That explains why the public learned almost nothing about the case beyond a brief note in the newsweekly *L'Espresso* that the district attorney's office in Milan was investigating. But the Italian financial world did not pay attention. Otherwise at the end of the debacle, ENI, the Italian national oil company, would not have been the largest single creditor with losses of $160 million.

The Guardia di Finanza launched the next attack. Calvi succeeded in at least partially neutralizing the investigation of his backroom machinations. However, in July 1980, his passport was confiscated. Thanks to P2 he was able to retrieve it in time for the

World Bank meeting in Washington, D.C. When, in March 1981, agents of the Guardia di Finanza searched the home of P2 boss Licio Gelli, they found whole dossiers full of receipts and money orders, including one for $800,000 payable to a Geneva account in favor of Ugo Zilletti, one of the highest officials in the public prosecutor's office. Apparently, this was the offering for the small favor of returning Calvi's passport. The magistrate was forced to resign on April 8, 1981.

It turned out that, through its ties to the lodge, Ambrosiano in effect owned the *Corriere della Sera*, one of the leading Italian newspapers. The Rizzoli family did not have the financial resources for the expensive takeover of the newspaper — it was the time before the great rationalization in the strongly unionized printing trade — and Ambrosiano was the only bank to help out Rizzoli. In the end, it cost the house L 300 billion. Rizzoli was a brother mason in P2. Suddenly Rizzoli held Ambrosiano shares in trust — with money the bank had given — and so again stabilized Calvi.

Prudently, Calvi also assured himself of the goodwill of all the political parties. Even the communists owed the Ambrosian Bank 11 billion lira directly and another 20 billion lire through their newspaper, *Paese Sera*.

Calvi's good luck was our misfortune. In February 1981, the Westminster bank put together a syndicate that provided Ambrosiano $50 million for five years. We lent our name to the syndicate. Due to great demand, the credit was increased to $75 million. As it turned out, Calvi was desperately dependent on this money for his banks in Liechtenstein and Panama in order to finance their indispensable capital increase following losses at the construction firm Genghini (a P2 connection) and at the Spanish Banco Occidentale. The contracts were signed on April 8, a month before the Banca d'Italia was able to persuade the government to issue more stringent controls over the banks' foreign capital participations. Starting in February, the energetic Beniamino Andreatta had been minister of the Treasury. The trained economist had read the Vigilanza report and had urged the IOR to end its ties to Calvi.

But in the same month, the Ambrosiano boss's ties to the P2 lodge became public. Gelli had disappeared in March 1981, after the Milan public prosecutors accidentally discovered his tracks: in Palermo, agents had interrogated an Italian-American surgeon involved in the drug trade who had visited Gelli in Arezzo. When they investigated, they found in the vault of his factory a complete P2 membership list that included two cabinet ministers, 50 generals and admirals, 24 journalists, 39 members of parliament, Angelo Rizzoli, and editors of the *Corriere della Sera*.

Violations of the foreign exchange rules came to light as did the illegal engagement with the *Corriere della Sera*. (Italian banks were not allowed participation outside their own business.) Calvi was arrested on May 20, 1981, in his capacity as chairman of the Ambrosiano subsidiary La Centrale, which had directly taken over the shares in Rizzoli, whereupon the Midland Bank stopped a planned credit for $25 million. It was to go to the Ambrosiano subsidiary Banco Andino in Lima. Other houses quietly did not renew their credits, and the Banca del Gottardo signaled that it was no longer ready to continue managing the hidden operations. Ambrosiano Services Luxembourg thereupon took over those operations. Calvi was sentenced to four years in jail and a fine of L 16 billion. He appealed and was freed, at least for the time being.

In July, Monsignore Pellegrino de Strobel, IOR's CFO, who seldom left the Vatican, traveled to the Banca del Gottardo in Lugano together with Filippo Leoni, the head of Ambrosiano's foreign department, to confirm what he suspected, namely that Manic SA and United Trading Corporation, two IOR spin-offs, had been badly misused. They owed $900 million to the Latin American Ambrosiano subsidiaries, debts secured with Ambrosiano shares. With them, IOR was not only the technical owner of the declared 1.6 percent but at least another 10.2 percent of the bank. On paper, he controlled the bank, but in practice Ambrosiano controlled itself.

The Banca d'Italia continued to investigate Ambrosiano. It demanded from its foreign subsidiaries a record of all amounts due, as well as a list of all stockholders with more than 10,000 shares, and, after Calvi's conviction, suspended Rizzoli's voting rights.

In this situation, Calvi saw his last salvation with IOR, which, in August, somewhat reluctantly issued the famous "letters of comfort." In these letters, IOR confirmed controlling the companies in Liechtenstein, Luxembourg, and Panama to whom Ambrosiano subsidiaries in Peru and Nicaragua, the Banco Andino and Ambrosiano Group Banco Commercial, had lent money. The text was laconic: "This is to confirm that we directly or indirectly control the following entities. . . . We also confirm our awareness of their indebtedness toward yourselves as of June 10, 1981, as per attached statement of accounts." With that, both houses calmed down, for the moment anyway.

But the signatures of the two letters were dependent on two conditions: publication would not involve any liabilities, and the whole affair was to be settled by June 1982. Accordingly, Calvi wrote IOR a letter with the complementary closing that, whatever might happen, IOR would not have to expect any "future damage or loss." The letter was written on Ambrosiano Nassau's letterhead.

Just how difficult it was to judge Ambrosiano's situation from the outside was demonstrated by the involvement of Olivetti owner Carlo de Benedetti in October 1981 when he bought a 2 percent share. Even Ciampi assumed that the bank was fundamentally sound, as the capital increase proved. Treasury Minister Beniamino Andreatta's comment about the flamboyant Olivetti owner's engagement in the bank was, "The ways of capitalism are strange."

De Benedetti was supposed to have taken over leadership of the house but was no match for the much smarter Calvi. After sixty-one days, he left and sold his shares at a handsome profit.

Once more Calvi had survived, but he could no longer prevent the stock exchange supervisors from introducing his stock on the primary market. After that, it was only a matter of time before the first list with the names of the major shareholders on it would begin to circulate. But already, on March 19, 1982, it came to a parliamentary inquiry in Rome, after de Benedetti had commented publicly about the $800 million loss at Banco Andino. In the wake of the bad press under which Ambrosiano now suffered, the Catholic small shareholders began to sell stock in April. In May, the shares fell 20 percent in one day.

On May 31, the Banca d'Italia sent the results of its clarifications to Calvi with the order to hand one copy of the report to each member of the board. Each board member had to confirm that he had received enough information to comply with his obligations. In addition, the Banca d'Italia demanded the protocol of the meeting. The content of the letter was that all told, $1.4 billion was missing at the Banco Andino, Ambrosiano Group Banco Commercial in Managua, and at Ambrosiano Overseas in Nassau; the money was lent to unnamed third parties.

The shocked and terrified board members began to imagine their future in jail, and Calvi went underground. On June 12, a Saturday, the evening news reported that he had disappeared.

On Thursday, June 17, the financial newspaper *Il Sole 24 Ore* published the whole text of the Banca d'Italia's May 31 missive. At the end of the day, the stock was down another 18 percent, meaning the price had been cut in half in the month and a half the stock had been on the major exchange. That same evening, stock exchange supervisors ordered the shares suspended, the Banca d'Italia assumed provisional leadership of Ambrosiano, and Calvi's personal secretary jumped out of a window. The next morning, a London street cleaner discovered the banker dangling on the north side of Blackfriars Bridge. During the morning, the Italian consulate general confirmed the identity of the dead man.

In the meantime, Calvi's successor at Ambrosiano discovered the "letters of comfort" and quickly traveled to the IOR in Rome, only to be confronted with Calvi's letter asking for letters of patronage and at the same time absolving IOR of all responsibility. But the Vatican Bank would not get away so easily, a fact that Antonio Occhiuto, a former deputy director general of the Banca d'Italia, made clear to Archbishop Marcinkus, pointing out that Calvi's letter to the IOR had been written on the Ambrosiano Nassau letterhead and that Marcinkus was a board member of that institution. Calvi's "counter-letter" only proved that the IOR had worked together with the Banco Ambrosiano in a financial fraud.

The IOR leadership refused to accept that argument, ultimately to its own detriment. It gave up the chance to save Ambrosiano with an infusion of $300 million. On July 13, Pope John Paul II put three Catholic financial experts — Philippe de Weck, the former president of the Union Bank of Switzerland (UBS), Joseph Brennan of the Emigrant Savings Bank in New York, and Carlo Cerutti of Italy's STET — in charge of clarifying who was responsible.

Meanwhile, the Ambrosiano subsidiaries in Nassau and Luxembourg collapsed. Shortly thereafter, the $75 million credit that Westminster had put together became "doubtful," meaning interest and redemption could no longer be paid. At a creditor meeting in London on July 28, 1982 (Juergen Luethi, our chief loan officer at the time, remembers TV crews setting up cameras outside the main entrance while the bankers entered the house through a side door), Giovanni Arduino, a provisional appointee, announced that claims on Ambrosiano Milan were protected through the Basel Concordat of the central banks concluded in 1975 in which the central banks pledged to take over foreign liabilities of banks on their own territories. But much to their dismay, the representatives of the foreign banks learned that the Banca d'Italia did not plan to take over the liabilities of foreign holdings. This was formally correct but a little sly and in practice penalized foreign lenders. They would have done better had the Banca d'Italia simply dropped the Banco Ambrosiano. Alarmed Luxembourg authorities thereupon demanded guarantees from all Italian banks for their subsidiaries in the Grand Duchy, and within forty-eight hours. The central banks, in turn, in 1983 renewed their concordat obligations.

On November 26, 1982, the Vatican's Secretary of State, Cardinal Casaroli, presented the recommendations of the three wise men to the college of cardinals. They did not admit to any legal obligations, but certainly to moral responsibility, and suggested paying $246 million. That was enough to cover the demands of the foreign banks vis-à-vis the foreign Ambrosiano subsidiaries.

How did Ambrosiano's collapse affect our bank? In his memoirs, my cousin Roger Baer wrote, "During my time in Bonn I decided in 1982 to cut my ties to the family bank, mainly because I was not sufficiently informed about the bank's course of business and I wanted to be financially independent, which, as a family shareholder was not easily possible."

What had really happened? Our annual family meeting took place on the weekend of June 18–20, 1982, on the Buergenstock. The most important item on our agenda was as usual the report about our course of business, which my cousin Nicolas, Roger's oldest brother, delivered. It was based on the best information available at the time. In late afternoon, I heard the news on the car radio that Roberto Calvi had been found dead.

Until then, we had not paid much attention to the uproar around the bank. At the time, Milan as a financial center was hard to survey. Moreover, our risk management was not all that sophisticated. As a result, the business relationships our group maintained with Ambrosiano and its numerous subsidiaries came to light, which we had not previously considered. Peter Baer, Pedro Hangartner, and Juergen Luethi sat down together on Sunday morning to discuss the situation. It took two days until we had a rough overview and a few days more until we were aware of all our engagements, including securities, at the widely ramified Ambrosiano group.

We had not reported this at our family meeting; there was no reason to do so. To that extent, Roger's reproach that he had not been adequately informed, raised weeks later, was justified.

In a memorandum of July 20, 1982, I gave an overview of the Julius Baer Group's interbank business. At the beginning of the eighties, we tended to differentiate between A banks and B banks. We had granted the A banks — at the time there were about 80 of them, all leading banks of a good country — lines of credit of £100 million with a maximum term of twelve months. The roughly 150 B banks, which all had to belong to the 500 largest banks in the world, had credit lines with us from 15 to 25 million Swiss francs with a maximum term of six months.

The Ambrosiano group had always belonged to our B banks with a credit line of £25 million, including the Banca del Gottardo. The Banco Ambrosiano, with nonconsolidated total assets of $13.4 billion, was Italy's eleventh largest bank and a member of the Inter-Alpha Group of Banks to which several good friends of our house belonged, all of them leading institutions in their home countries, among them the Berliner Handelsgesellschaft und Frankfurter Bank in Frankfurt, the CCF in Paris, and the Kredietbank in Brussels, which held 3 percent of Ambrosiano's capital. Management itself had to listen to not unjustified reproaches from the board as to why Ambrosiano had not been stricken from the list of accredited banks in view of the alarming news that had come out since the beginning of 1982.

The Banca d'Italia tried to put together a group of twenty-five Italian banks before July 13, 1982, which was to support the Ambrosiano group up to $2.5 billion. But on July 13 the Ambrosiano Holding itself requested a forced administration in Luxembourg. At the same time, the appointed commissioner announced plans to invite creditor banks to a meeting within fourteen days. Julius Baer's management decided, after detailed discussions, to inform family and board only after that meeting, which finally took place on July 29, since the loss risk could not really be assessed beforehand.

Had IOR not waited for so long but accepted its responsibility quickly, Ambrosiano could have been saved. Instead, it was first merged with the Banca Cattolica del Veneto into the Banco Ambrosiano Veneto, which then merged with Cariplo (Cassa di Risparmio delle Provincie Lombarde) and a number of smaller regional banks into the Banca Intesa. Since the merger with the Banca Commerciale Italiana, the bank operates under the name IntesaBCI. Banca Intesa announced in summer 2006 a merger with San Paolo-IMI to form a European powerhouse and is now called Intesa-San Paolo.

That the name of our house — as a result of our participation in the Westminster Bank's Ambrosiano credit — ended up in the newspapers was, of course, very unpleasant for us. At the beginning of the eighties, that was still the equivalent of a mortal sin. For my cousins Roger and Uhlrich Baer, it was a reason to give up their holdings. In fairness, Roger wrote that it was his idea to give up his responsibility as a family shareholder.

The phone rang twenty-four hours after the offer from UBS to acquire my cousins' shares was made. Nikolaus Senn, the head of UBS, was on the line. He said very clearly, "What you don't want, we won't do," and wanted to know our views about a UBS participating interest. We had no objections in principle. My brother, Thomas, and I negotiated a contract with UBS. That's how it came about that the major bank, as of November 30, 1982, joined the partnership contract as if it were a family member but with the added commitment as "partner of last resort." Should the family's share fall below 30 percent, the UBS would be obliged to take over the rest. Later, when a tranche of family shares were for sale, my cousins and I decided to test our ties — just as Allied forces sent their tanks to East Berlin once every year — and offer Robert Studer the shares. He needed no more than five minutes to say yes.

We always got along very well with UBS and its representatives Nikolaus Senn, Robert Studer, and Mathis Cabiallavetta. Internally, at first, we were not sure how the market would judge UBS's entry. We worried that we would no longer be seen as independent. As an experienced newspaperman, Ernst Bieri thought publication of the news would help us — it communicated the impression of additional security. And that's how it turned out. The creditworthiness of the Julius Baer bank was never again a subject for discussion.

The upshot of our "marriage" to UBS was that of a model marriage. But it was never consummated. Our bank could never build up a privileged relationship, for example, in UBS's underwriting business, where we generally were given a poor allotment of bonds to sell. On the other hand, the UBS was not represented on our board. We simply lived peacefully side by side.

After seventeen years, this excellent relationship was dissolved in the wake of the merger between UBS and SBC (the Swiss Bank Corporation). The annulment was mutually agreed upon. At its annual meeting in May 1999, the Julius Baer bank decided to take over the 11,600 registered shares. (As you will read later on, the recent purchase by Julius Baer of the UBS subsidiaries resulted in a renewed participation of UBS in Julius Baer.)

For UBS, this long-time investment was not a bad deal but was a model for a "private equity transaction" *avant la lettre*. One has to compliment this major bank on its keen sense for investing in family-dominated enterprises.

30

Business in Japan (1977–92)

Asleep on the desk

In order to distinguish Peter Hangartner from Peter Baer, Hangartner became known in the international trade as "Pedro" — perhaps an allusion to his curly long hair and his mustache, which he did not abandon until his silver hair became prominent. Pedro was a full-blooded Wall Street operator. He grew up in Uznach in eastern Switzerland, the youngest of nine siblings. He completed his bank training at a local savings and loan, went to Geneva to the Swiss Bank Corporation (SBC), then on to London to Vickers, da Costa & Co., and finally to New York to Model, Roland & Stone, an institution among securities traders on Wall Street. "Rolf Roland was the trader and Leo Model the intelligent one who did all the deals," was how Pedro summed up his teachers' division of labor. He worked for them for six years before they sent him to Paris in 1961 in order to take over the arbitrage business there and later set up a branch office in Zurich. But the idea of having to endure one more foreign broker brought together all Zurich banks. They threatened not to work with Model, Roland & Stone in the future if they established a Zurich branch.

Leo Model began his professional life in Frankfurt as a stock market trader. He then emigrated to the Netherlands and began working with Rolf Roland. After the German occupation in 1940, he managed to flee with the help of the Cologne banker Carl Deichman and establish himself together with two partners on Wall Street. In 1953, Walter Eberstadt moved from Lehman Brothers to Leo Model, where he was made a partner in 1959. Model's big idea was selling Americans on greatly undervalued European securities and Europeans on good American stock. In times of fat commissions, it's a great business.

In 1962, Peter Baer brought in Pedro as head of our stock trading division and as his number two. The two had first met during their London years. After Peter's internship in 1951, he worked for the Banque Worms in Paris and then for Singer & Friedlaender in London; Pedro was employed by Vickers, da Costa, a broker. Both did arbitrage. One day, on the telephone with Pedro, Peter complained about a deal. He noted that Pedro spoke with a pronounced Swiss accent, and vice versa, so they met for a drink. Both went to New York in 1955 — Peter to Burnham & Co. (later Drexel, Burnham, Lambert) and Pedro to Model Roland Stone. That's how the acquaintanceship ripened into friendship, which lasted until Peter's death on November 11, 1998.

At first, I wasn't comfortable with the idea of bringing an international high-caliber type into the house. Realizing that he was a superior international trader wasn't that easy to accept psychologically, at least for me. But the bank needed somebody like him.

When tombstones — the page-filling ads for new issues that list all the lead managers and all the other co-issuers in the syndicate — were still widely used, my wife regularly made a point of telling me when she didn't find the name Julius Baer. Whereupon I would call Pedro and ask, "Peeedroo? Why aren't we in the syndicate?" "I'll take part, if you give me the money," he would answer.

Julius Baer was a favored co-leader because of our stance high up on the alphabet. When it was no longer profitable, we dropped out of the co-lead position. Competition today has reached the point where you have to issue a billion dollars in order to make as much money as you used to make with 100 million dollars. When it still paid off, a glass of champagne was served at the management lunch as a gesture of recognition. It had no influence on the bonuses earned by the new issues department; it was only a question of prestige and sporting ambition.

Tombstones, which disappeared at the end of the eighties, were taken very seriously in the banking world. Salomon Brothers, for example, only took part in a new issue if the firm was named on the left shoulder of the ad. Appearing on the right side of the lead manager was not good enough. Causally connected to this culture was a pronounced hierarchy that differentiated between the lead manager, the co-lead manager (whose name could appear on the left shoulder), and the rest of the syndicate.

Until the early nineties, Japanese convertible bonds, which Julius Baer issued, were an important source of revenue. The reason we entered the flourishing business with Japanese convertible bonds goes back to Pedro's love of golf. He shared this passion with Dr. Seitaro "Seji" Kaga, the head of Nikko Securities in Zurich. The dean of the Japanese financial world in Zurich was a knowledgeable man and a charming gentleman. He had studied in Hamburg, established himself in Zurich in 1970, and had worked carefully to improve Swiss understanding of Japanese financial market instruments. When he arrived, Japan's financial world did not have the kind of reputation that opened many doors.

Seitaro Kaga worked hard to improve the reputation of his country in Zurich. He assiduously lectured and wrote studies about Japanese financial markets. The economic successes of his homeland helped him a lot. In 1974, he engineered the first loan in Swiss francs by a private Japanese company; in 1975, the first convertible bonds denominated in Swiss francs; and in 1978, the first yen bonds of a Swiss issuer on the Japanese market. Since these notes were all guaranteed by Japanese banks, their success was assured. Note that most of the borrowers were unknown in Europe. To their amazement, during a visit to Japan, my cousin Nicolas and Pedro discovered that these borrowers could not have had much of a reputation in Japan either. During a visit to Takara, a housing equipment company, they found a disappointingly small enterprise. The banks had provided the guarantee on orders of the Ministry of Finance. In finance, Japan is not a free country.

The boom in Japanese convertible bonds was triggered by the decline of the dollar in the mid-eighties. Within five years, the value of the American currency vis-à-vis the Swiss franc dropped by almost half and forced investors to look for alternatives.

The breakthrough in the business of issuing Japanese convertible bonds came for us halfway by accident. Through the 1977 Texon scandal, Credit Suisse was much too occupied with its own problems and for a time could not open entry to the Swiss franc market for Japanese borrowers. So Seitaro Kaga, as representative of Nikko Securities, had to look at alternatives for the planned convertible bond issue. Before Julius Baer could enter the field, however, our new issues department — with advice from Dr. Kaga, who, thanks to his Hamburg education, spoke better German than English, something that didn't help us very much, since we had to submit our documentation in English — worked for two weeks at fever pitch in order to deliver to the Japanese Ministry of Finance all the required numbers and documents about responsibility, size of the business, and business conduct.

The fact that Julius Baer was the first nonmajor bank qualified to issue Japanese loans and convertible bonds increased our standing in the banking world and gave us the opportunity to look out for our good friends as comanagers of desirable issues and to make sure they received a decent contingent of bonds to sell. In this way, Julius Baer came to reciprocal business deals.

Once on the Japanese market, we placed, by 1992, no fewer

than 27 issues with a volume of 1.2 billion Swiss francs. Moreover, our success with new issues persuaded us to launch the Convertible Bonds Fund.

We had begun in 1977 with Takara Standard, the Japanese housing equipment company, for whom we issued 35 million Swiss francs worth of convertible bonds bearing 5.125 percent interest with maturity of six years. In the next year, we handled three convertible bond issues, including one for Citizen Watch, much to the chagrin of the Swiss watch industry, which protested loudly against our giving money to a Japanese firm. But the Swiss National Bank overrode their objections.

Pedro conducted most of these negotiations with the support of Albert Merz and Leo Loretan. Among the many pleasant memories from those days: the prestige-conscious Japanese debtors were reliable contractual partners. They would stubbornly insist on favorable conditions and liked to bargain for an eighth of a percent, but there were never any unpleasant surprises with them as was so often the case with the Americans. Nor did they go bankrupt even if they were not always first-class. The mighty MITI (Ministry of International Trade and Industry) made sure of that.

My cousin Nicolas, in his capacity as president of the board of directors, presided over the festive luncheons. The photographer always made the first money — and not bad money at that. He had to deliver prints in time for dessert. Although we did not forego the passe-partouts, we remained thrifty enough to do without the gold-printed text, which some houses used to tickle the good mood of their clients. It was enough to present a watch. If the lunch was not given at the bank, it was held in a special room at a restaurant. In those years, the four or five black limousines parked outside banks during the lunch hour always waited for their Japanese passengers. Expenses did not matter.

Issues for which we worked with Nikko Securities as well as Nomura and Yamaichi were usually taken in at par. We had to have the money ready that day and already exchanged into dollars. But we could charge our customers a fair commission for our disbursement. We issued the bond at 105 percent and earned good money from proprietary trading. It was normal for the bonds to rise to 130 to 140 percent, but there were some that vaulted up to 300 and 400 percent. Given our cautious approach, we were usually ready to sell the bond at 120 percent.

Convertible bonds were a business that benefited everybody: the banks, the customers, and the borrowers. The idea that the bonds were issued in order to push shares of poor companies onto the stock market did not occur to us. There was reason behind the fact that in the eighties, hardly a week went by without a large Japanese convertible bond issue. Japanese high finance boosted prices on the exchange so that the bonds — usually just before their decline — could reliably be changed into shares. The next convertible bond issue hit the markets soon after. Only a very few borrowers were in a position to repay the loan. The money wasn't there. It was, as Pedro put it, a merry-go-round. In the end, Japanese shareholders paid the bill, just as at the end of the Internet and telecom euphoria, it was the shareholders who paid. In Tokyo, stock prices collapsed abruptly in 1989 after the index had briefly crossed the 40,000-point mark. Today it is still less than half its historic peak.

Even before the collapse, the business had moved from convertible bonds to warrant issues. With warrants in a long position, we often lost money. Since there was no exchange for warrants — today the financial world has moved forward in this sector — and the time difference made trade into a nighttime business, nobody could really control prices. Traders on both sides faced growing temptations. Significantly, Swiss local banks that nobody had ever heard of suddenly were in the business. Usually Zurich traders or their spouse or a cousin who wanted to engage their buccaneering instincts was behind it.

Given my habit of shortening my sleepless nights by surfing

through the TV programs, I usually knew Tokyo stock prices when I got to the office. It was obvious to me after the first price slump that the market was turning and it was high time to get out.

We therefore closed our office in Tokyo, which my cousin Nicolas had opened on November 7, 1987, with a large reception at the Hotel Okura attended by many well-known personalities, including Toyota president Dr. Shoichiro Toyoda. We closed the office without ceremony in 1992. Ever since, our office in Hong Kong has handled what Japanese business remains. My cousin Roger, Swiss ambassador in Tokyo from 1987 to 1993, was appalled when he learned of the closing.

Seitaro Kaga died a few years later, in February 1996. He had pancreatic cancer. I had the honor of writing an obituary for Japan's secret consul in Zurich in the *Neue Zuercher Zeitung*. Dr. Kaga had brought his homeland as close to me as is possible for a foreigner to come. The customs and practices of the Tokyo financial center took some getting used to for someone from the Occident. In my time, we had to grasp that a Japanese went to sleep when a European got up. The country suffered under a chronic lack of sleep. Even in the lobby of a luxury hotel, everybody except the waiters were asleep. People didn't sleep at home. No room. Living space in an average apartment in Tokyo is not generous. During the week, they often didn't bother going home because it was too far away. That's Japan. Instead, they went to a restaurant after office hours, drank too much, and went to sleep on their desks in their beehive offices, wrapped up in newspapers. In the Japanese ministry of finance, only the director general had his own office.

But our Japanese listeners (of our lectures) didn't sleep soundly. During a joint presentation, we unwisely gave contradictory prognoses for development of the dollar. One member of the audience noted the discrepancy. Which one was correct? he asked. I squirmed out of the dilemma with the excuse, "We practice democracy."

*

In March 1986, the erstwhile Barclays Bank (Suisse) S.A. was brought to our attention, because Barclays wanted to sell its 40 percent participation in the bank. The bank was originally formed in 1934 under the name Société Bancaire de Genève and was controlled by the well-known Zilkha family, a banking dynasty originating in Syria.

The family, active in the bank, were the Lawis, related to the Zilkhas. The Lawis (the controlling shareholders) were not in a position to acquire the remaining 40 percent then on the market. Only after we had acquired the minority position available from Barclays did the Swiss Banking Commission intervene to inform us that they would insist that we obtain 51 percent participation in order to maintain the charter of the Geneva bank. Thus we wound up with a controlling majority, because the banking commission so insisted. This led to situations that were not always easy, because the Lawis naturally continued to think of the institution as "their" bank. Interestingly enough, it was Fritz Leutwiler, the president of the Swiss National Bank, who encouraged our Geneva exponents to continue by stressing that a Swiss bank without a branch in Geneva was unthinkable.

A most encouraging factor played a big part in our decision from the beginning, namely the fact that the Lawis are close relatives of the family of Lord Kadoorie in Hong Kong, a place with which we had flirted for quite some time because of the developing China euphoria. The Kadoories, in turn, were not sure what their fate in a Chinese Hong Kong would be in the long run and welcomed a strong base in Switzerland as a standby. At that time, the Kadoories did not own only the famous Peninsula Hotel but also, more importantly, the public utility China Power and Light, which disposed of the only nuclear energy power station in the region. My cousin Nicolas maintained a friendly connection with Lord Kadoorie, who, among other things, was a lover of fast cars, even in his later years. Nicolas looked after the relationship with the Kadoorie family, which also had their origins in Syria.

Rudolf Bieri, the former finance secretary of the Swiss Federation, chaired the board of our new bank in Geneva for many years. Another excellent choice in the longer run was Charles Mueller, who is a retired Swiss diplomat formerly married to Marlise Mueller-Bruegger, a childhood friend of my late wife.

As we became more confident in our Hong Kong activities, we convinced the former representative of Swiss Re in that city to join the Baer organization upon his retirement. Rob Brouwer, a music lover and well-acquainted with the Hong Kong business establishment, allowed us to develop a fairly successful money management operation in Hong Kong. To have a good music friend on the scene was an immense help to me during my several tours of the Tonhalle Orchestra to the Far East.

31

SWISS AMERICAN CHAMBER OF COMMERCE (1973–78)

I won't ride in a Mercedes

I came to my first important honorary office thanks to a change in the bylaws of the American Chamber of Commerce. The presidential dignity of the American Chamber of Commerce was exclusively reserved for U.S. citizens, but in the beginning of the seventies, not many Americans showed up at the chamber in Zurich. So the American Chamber of Commerce obtained special permission from the parent organization, signed up under a new name, Swiss American Chamber of Commerce, and appointed me president. In theory and practice a nominating committee selects the president. Neither the predecessor nor the managing director of the chamber of commerce may belong to that committee.

It is the task of a chamber of commerce to represent the interests of its members. (Back then there were twelve hundred; today the number has doubled.) As a result, Walter Diggelmann, as managing director (until 2005), and I had to take a stand on a host of questions, including the tedious matter of work permits. With the youthful high spirits of his thirty-one years, Walter occasionally risked somewhat challenging letters, for example, to State Secretary Paul Jolles. Walter learned quickly that allowing me to cosign them did not damage his cause.

As president, I was much more engaged in the chamber's leadership activities than my successors ever were. Every two or three weeks we held meetings; otherwise we telephoned (about current affairs), and for the rest everybody did his or her own work. The office consumed a lot of time even if one didn't take part in every one of the between twenty and thirty luncheons a year.

These lunches developed by Walter were a profitable business for the chamber. Tickets cost SFr 100 ($80). The two hundred people who usually attended these meals came without culinary expectations but were more interested in what supportive influence the guests around the table of honor could have on their own careers. At the very least, these luncheons served to find another job for some of the participants.

Among my most enduring memories are the prominent speakers I mobilized for the annual general meeting, for one of the many lunches, or for some other occasions. We welcomed the NATO commander for Central Europe, American cabinet members, federal councilors (members of the Swiss cabinet), and ambassadors accredited to Switzerland, all of them noteworthy personalities who would warmly remember their reception in Zurich.

Walter staged the chamber's general meeting with great care at the Grand Hotel Dolder as a major social event that included speeches by the ambassadors from both countries. Some three hundred to four hundred people took part at this event where the greetings were followed by discussions of chamber business and, at the end, by the meal.

In June of 1974, John Kenneth Galbraith came from Gstaad and spoke "on the history of money and its possible lessons." That night, I hosted a dinner for him at my home, which Walter remembers so well, because upon leaving, Galbraith told him to "keep the dignity of your organization."

The next year, Federal Councilor Ernst Brugger (he held the economics portfolio in the Swiss cabinet) did us the honor. I was embarrassed rushing through association business in his presence. Who likes to bore a cabinet member with such minutia? But Brugger, who was used to such situations, exonerated me by saying, "My thanks for your introduction, Mr. Baer. One can learn democracy from you."

Paul Volcker, the head of the U.S. Federal Reserve and a friend since he was president of the New York Federal Reserve Bank, delivered the 1976 lecture.

Gianni Agnelli spread more glamour than the sober chief of the central bank. We ate with him at the bank before his lecture, after which we went down to the bank limousine parked outside, admittedly not a Fiat, but with the door open to usher him in. "I won't ride in a Mercedes," he said, and squeezed himself into the car of the Zurich Fiat agency. Afterward he explained that the paparazzi were just waiting to photograph him in a Mercedes. Thus, at the beginning of the seventies, a lesson about brand awareness and the power of pictures.

Countess Faber-Castell, by birth a Sprecher von Bernegg, gave me my second lesson in brand awareness. I was a member of the Faber Castell pencil company's board of directors, and we had scheduled a board session at our bank — with the customary note pads and sharpened pencils. The countess came, saw the pencils, discovered the rival name Caran d'Ache on them, and, outraged, swept out of the room. Although unintentional, we could not have given her a greater insult.

I don't remember exactly how I got to know the Aga Khan. We probably met for the first time in St. Moritz. His property was right next to the Suvretta House. Or perhaps I met him when I solicited him as a speaker. In any case, he agreed to talk to the chamber of commerce. As he would tell me later on, he had written his remarks while going over the Julier Pass on his way from St. Moritz. He came with the begum, a graceful, distinctive and simply ravishingly beautiful woman (from whom, all the same, he separated). During the meal, she sat next to Emilie Lieberherr, an outspoken Zurich city cabinet member, visually quite different and probably ideologically too, but the two women got along famously.

My acquaintance with the Aga Khan ripened into friendship, which led to our spending vacations in Sardinia, where we stayed at the Cala di Volpe, his hotel on the Costa Smeralda. The invitations were uncomplicated. What he served was simple, and none of the international snobs at the table objected. The only complication: no one was allowed to step onto his balcony. After all, a sniper could have been hiding in the bushes. At the beginning of the eighties, recollections of the Red Brigades were still fresh.

The launch of the *Yearbook of the Swiss American Chamber of Commerce,* which we developed from the annual report, was our idea. Today it is the indispensable Swiss-American handbook. Our motive at the time was that we should know what we are talking about and what we're doing, meaning collecting statistics and evaluating the main focus of Swiss-American trade relationships. In that sense, the yearbook was for me simply a leadership instrument. (Just as I insisted that the bank's different divisions prepare a report at year end about what they had done, so too these statistical reports served education, management, and planning equally.) Expenses were kept low because from the start we had issued the slogan that it was an honor to work with us. The major banks, the large insurance companies, and the National Bank generously made available their best people for the accounting of Swiss-American economic relations. We could never have paid them an appropriate fee. Walter assumed the burden of coordination. At the end, thanks to advertising, the chamber made a little money. In order to provide institutional order, we founded the Yearbook Editorial Board with the chief economists of major Swiss companies as members. Professor Bruno Gehrig, president of the Swiss Life board, served for a long time. At the time, he was still working for the UBS (Union Bank of Switzerland). This concentrated economic expertise was so valuable to me that I remained on the editorial board until the mid-eighties.

It was not by accident that we published the first edition of the yearbook in 1976 — we saw it as a contribution to the U.S. bicentennial. Thanks to my sabbatical in Oxford in 1975, I could even shine with an appropriate essay: "The Spirit of 1776," a shorter version of my rumination about the monetary beginnings of the United States.

Some time ago, Walter reminded me of a lasting contribution I had made. In September 1975, we were invited to a regional meeting of American chambers of commerce. While looking over an old annual report during a moment of boredom, I noticed that something wasn't right about the eagle in the American Chamber's signet. He looked to the left. Walter examined the bird and determined that all heraldic eagles look to the right, the American eagle just as much as the Aigle de l'Empereur (Napoleon's). From that moment on, even the eagle of the chamber looked to the right.

32

SABBATICAL AT OXFORD (1975)

They are so innocent, and we are so decadent

After twenty-four years at the bank and a year before my fiftieth birthday, I felt ripe for a change. In the business, we'd had a crisis every couple of years, but none of them prevented our continued growth or the fact that we were continuously better off. The transformation of the bank to a public company took place on January 1, 1975; my cousin Nicolas became president, and I decided the time had come to do something different.

I owe my intellectual and spiritual renewal at Oxford to my late brother-in-law, the physicist Joergen Olsen, and to my sister Marianne, his wife, both of whom had studied physics and earned their doctorates at Oxford. My sister was a student of Lord Cherwell — known as Frederick Lindemann before his elevation to the peerage, and Churchill's scientific adviser, not least because he could explain the most complicated relationships in simple terms. As a teetotaler and misogynous eccentric, however, he was quite different from the prime minister.

The Olsens knocked on the door of the economist Peter M. Oppenheimer, and the senior lecturer encouraged his college,

Christ Church at Oxford (the only one that does not call itself a college), to issue me an invitation to come as a visiting fellow.

What seems complicated was in fact quite simple and enriched me for three months with experiences I would not have wanted to miss. In thinking about a sabbatical, I had no clear idea at which institute or university I should spend my term of freedom. Where can you go when you run a bank?

Oxford opened a totally different world: sociable, rich in spirit and knowledge, far removed from money, and blessed with superior social qualities. The literature about Oxford is inexhaustible, from Evelyn Waugh's *Decline and Fall* and of course *Brideshead Revisited*, to Muriel Beadle's *These Ruins Are Inhabited* — and not to forget Harold Acton's immortal words at the sight of a junior eight crew on the Thames: "Oh dear, they are so innocent, and we are so decadent." But to experience Oxford itself, and through the sinecure of a visiting fellowship, is, as an experience, unbeatable.

I did, in fact, become an "inhabitant of a ruin." For the three months at Christ Church I lived in the guestroom of Tom's Tower. I had the tower and its one and a half rooms on the third floor to myself, and there was no telephone. Tradition demands that a factotum lock up the whole complex at 10 p.m. When invited out for dinner, I had to leave early if I wanted to sleep at home in the guestroom. Otherwise, I would have to find a night's lodging outside the campus walls.

The college expects visiting fellows to eat four times a week in the dining hall at the faculty's high table, by candlelight and in cap and gown. Once a week I traveled to London to take care of business. That was the proviso my two partners had demanded for letting me take a sabbatical.

Quite often evensong preceded dinner. A distinguished college like Christ Church maintains its own cathedral choir, much in the same way American universities maintain their athletes — which already intimates a fundamental spiritual difference. Besides, a beautiful voice can make a scholarship possible. For evensong, the interested faculty would gather for the cortege — or in more Christian terms, the processional — in the inner courtyard and march into church, listen to the choir, be moved to tears, and make their way, led by the dean, to dinner.

No longer used to wearing the robe, vanished on the continent long ago, these evenings in academic gowns gave me a lasting experience, even if I felt somewhat removed into the world of Dr. Faust. The robe is simply a uniform. It strengthens the collective identity and hides material differences.

Bachelors dominate among those members of the faculty who come to High Table — visually really a high table, since it is placed in an elevated position in the refectory, and thus is clearly separated from the students. Those who had families rarely attended more than once a week. The occidental custom of sacrificing all social life on the altar of the family claims a price. Oxford and Cambridge have retained a remnant of the old academic world because these universities were reformed relatively late. Celibacy for tenured fellowships was only scrapped in 1876. Guests are admitted to High Table on Thursdays, and the colleges compete among themselves for the most prominent personalities. That reaches all the way up to invitations in favor of the queen, who once honored Christ Church with her presence and caused a stir by her custom of dining while wearing elbow-length gloves. I made a contribution to this competition by inviting Sir Georg Solti and — in her own right as a TV personality — his wife, Valerie.

An honor student always says grace before dinner — in Latin, of course. And in his robe. His academic hat hangs on a hook in the waiting room during the meal.

Dinner at High Table is continued in the Common Room with port, dried apples, and open conversation. Port is designed to promote discussion. The colleges are renowned for their excellent stock of vintage ports. In general, the wine cellars are outstanding.

Wine stewards, drawn from the faculty, manage them very professionally, as I had occasion to learn during my time, which just happened to fall during a period of high Bordeaux prices. When I asked about the buying policy during this phase, I was given the wonderful answer, "Young man, we sold." You won't find such a large holding of so comprehensive a range of great years in clarets anywhere on the continent outside of France. It is, however, somewhat of an exaggeration to claim that Oxford and Cambridge's wine cellars abut each other. But their cellars are really huge.

Nor could I say anything negative about the quality of the kitchen. The scholars tend to ignore money, at least within certain limits, but not the good life. Bills for these evenings were modest. On my final bill, dinners for the semester amounted only to a few pounds. The college enjoys the privilege of not paying excise taxes.

Port, obligatory in England after every cultivated dinner, is drunk in this land of tradition and complicated rules only after the Loyal Toast to the queen, and is offered only after the prayer of thanksgiving. The toast is prosaically short: "The Queen." Everybody rises when the host says it. Should a toast be drunk to Switzerland, as it was during a dinner we gave for the Bank of England at Claridges, it is never "Switzerland" but "La Suisse." Everybody pours their own port and simply passes on the carafe. It is important to respect the clockwise tradition. The carafe always travels to the left. To grab it from your neighbor on your left, only because you are thirsty and too deeply engrossed in your conversation to apprehend the situation, is scorned. If you don't want to wait for the next round, you simply move your glass left and your neighbor will fill it.

The ceremony of the loving cup, where everybody drinks from the same vessel, is obligatory at all great dinners and, of course, at the Lord Mayor's dinner. Taking a swallow from the cup is the most harmless part of the ceremony, which allegedly goes back to the times of the Anglo-Saxon kings. Edward the Martyr was stabbed to death at the instigation of his stepmother when, at a dinner, he held a goblet with both hands and could not defend himself. Ever since, legend holds, no one drinks with both hands without being sure a companion covers one's back. Today, this memorable ritual symbolizes that no one at the table wishes evil toward someone else. The goblet filled with a dry wine wanders clockwise around the table, with the host drinking first. At very large dinners, two goblets are circulated simultaneously in order to save time, one moving clockwise, the other counterclockwise. Sometimes bets are made on which goblet will go the farthest. Since seating at the table is usually tight and not everybody is a Nureyev, the Loving Cup demands full concentration in order to avoid disaster. The ritual needs to be well-observed in order to perform everything correctly, especially since three persons are always involved.

What interest did Christ Church have in inviting someone like me? Simply in order to not lose contact with the real world of nonacademic life. At Oxford, nobody is interested in money, which is quite different from Harvard. While professors at Harvard frequent Wall Street with hectic activity and never have time for taking a walk, Oxford was unbeatable as a place of personal enrichment, because I would seldom again talk so casually to all kinds of people. One of the ironclad college rules demands that at lunch you sit down at the next empty chair. Your neighbor to the left can be a junior reader, while the one to the right a Nobel Prize winner. Hierarchy doesn't exist. Naturally, you talk to each other, and just as naturally you stroll of an afternoon deep in conversation through the famous University at Oxford Botanical Gardens or the wonderful parks.

On my first day at Oxford, I learned during my introduction — again very civilized — that you don't bring flowers to people of limited means who have invited you to dinner. You take a bottle of wine instead.

The only interruption of my idyll came from a board of directors' meeting I had not expected to attend. I justified my absence on my sabbatical. Board Vice President Maximilian Steiner wouldn't accept my excuse and leave me in my idyll but called me to Zurich. In any event, I briefly got to see my wife. Entry to the cradle of English scholarship was denied Ilse because of her sex. Ladies were not permitted to attend even official dinners. Only Valerie Solti was allowed to come when the college invited her husband. But the qualified journalist came in her own right as a BBC reporter and not as a wife. I am always urging this regulation onto Zurich's Baur au Lac Club, which periodically is faced with the question of accepting ladies but already suffers from a lack of space. Under the rule of "in her own right," the club could co-opt a female stock exchange chief or ambassador.

During my time at Oxford, Benazir Bhutto, the future prime minister of Pakistan, was a student. Her father, Ali Bhutto, a previous prime minister, had been a student at Christ Church. At his urging, Benazir became an enthusiastic member of the Oxford Union Debating Society, founded in 1823. The society is modeled on the House of Commons, and in addition to the debating halls (with gallery), it has its own restaurant, two libraries, and a billiard room. Britain's political elite regularly appear there. Student debaters dress correctly, down to the carnation in their buttonholes, and dine by candlelight before debating. They take acting lessons and prepare meticulously, including applying the right makeup, for their speeches. Benazir spoke about the constitutional removal of an elected president. She had the task of pleading for the impeachment of Richard Nixon. I wouldn't have missed that speech, which everybody from hairdresser to teacher could come and hear. My sister and my late brother-in-law, Jørgen Olsen, came. It proved a huge success — 345 of the 347 members of the Oxford Union voted for impeachment.

But the beautiful Benazir only became president of the Oxford Union on her second attempt, even though she was a member of the standing committee and treasurer. Her election, as a woman, surprised her father the most. But he knew Oxford. When he was asked if he would accept an honorary doctorate and replied that he would, his old college, Oxford, said no, and thus lived up to the old rule that Oxford does not award honorary degrees to statesmen and politicians.

Christ Church didn't expect anything academic from me that went beyond my intellectual powers to provide. I was available to students who really didn't know what to do with me. I frequented other institutions like Nuffield College and the Oxford Management Centre, and wrote, with a view to the 200th anniversary celebration of the American Declaration of Independence, a small treatise on the beginnings of the dollar, the development of the American banking system, and how the heavily indebted city of New York could raise money. I was prompted to do so by a pointed remark John Kenneth Galbraith had made in his book *Money:* "It is to the Dollar that for the moment the history of money ends."

The consumptive dollar of the mid-seventies was ripe for a historical examination. The fact that a currency, which disgruntled settlers had launched in reaction to restrictive British monetary policy, had undergone repeated chaotic phases can be explained through its history. The dollar originated in the flight from monetary discipline, and it has kept this birthmark until today. The study of the early history of the dollar against the contemporary (1975) background of the Tax Anticipation Notes to stave off New York's bankruptcy gave me an opportunity to consider the Aristotelian definition of usury and the farmers' aversion to interest paid on credit, which inspired the gentleman farmer Thomas Jefferson to fling hateful tirades against the "bank mongers." Then I followed the phases of inflation. The Civil War, as well as the First World War, led to noticeable currency depreciation; under Franklin Roosevelt, Washington deliberately practiced a monetary policy that put prosperity ahead of stability as a political goal.

Despite a cumulative budget deficit of $200 billion that the

Second World War brought with it, U.S. currency went through a stable phase until 1967. In 1968, however, the United States recorded a budget deficit of $25 billion for the first time and this trend continued through the seventies. Dollars again appeared on the much-disdained Euromarket and finally hollowed out the whole Breton Woods system.

The history of American banking, on the other hand, is a history of panics and bankruptcies, until the New Deal and the Glass-Steagall Act changed the banking structure. After the bank holiday in March 1933, only 12,000 of the 17,800 U.S. banks reopened their counters. The financial innovation of the colonial era, with its first attempt to issue paper money, found its continuation in the present when New York's city fathers issued so-called TAN's (tax anticipation notes), RANs (revenue anticipation notes to bridge delayed income), and BANs (bond anticipation notes) to reduce the dramatic short-term indebtedness of $6 billion. The refusal of the banks to bridge-finance New York's monetary needs did not help their reputations, badly damaged as they were through their reckless $11 billion engagement with the real estate investment trusts (REITs), which was only reduced many years later. My conclusion: the dollar had not reached its end, as John Kenneth Galbraith thought, but the importance of the dollar as center of the international monetary system started to diminish. In my short work written while I was at Oxford, titled *The Spirit of 1776: A View of American Monetary History,* I came to the conclusion of a monetary coexistence. Galbraith very kindly offered his assistance in revising the manuscript. Four years later, the monetary specialist and Harvard luminary brought me to his university as a visiting fellow.

33

THANKS TO GALBRAITH AT HARVARD (1978–79)

Leave me alone, I'm Swiss

John Kenneth Galbraith, who died in 2006, asked me to come to Harvard during the 1978–79 winter semester — to the Institute of International Affairs, located in a modern office building near Harvard Square. Later it moved to the new Center for Government and International Studies complex on Cambridge Street (between Quincy Street and Sumner Road). Looking back, I think he used me as a spy. Henry Kissinger founded the institute in 1958, and since 1998 it is known as the Weatherhead Center for International Affairs. The reason is typically American. Albert and Celia Weatherhead had donated $25 million to the institute. The income from the foundation is large enough to maintain more than one professor — an archetypical example of the importance of private financial support of the academic world.

Unlike at Oxford, Harvard visiting fellows have to find their own apartment and pay for it. As compensation, I could take my wife along. The apartment was across the street from a hospital with a very active emergency ward. Ambulances shot out of the garage at night with blue lights flashing and sirens howling.

That was not the only difference compared with the academic idyll of Oxford. In contrast to academic gowns, sneakers and sweatpants dominated at Harvard. I had my own office at the institute with a desk and telephone. I managed to avoid the waiting line for seminar registration by finding the nearest phone booth and registering by telephone, which allowed me to pass my first test. Allegedly, registration rituals are designed to not make life easier for students but to test their practical abilities.

The spacious campus with its sparsely ornamented brick baroque architecture definitely has its charms. Nightlife was not regulated. The presence of women didn't shock anybody. What I especially liked was Harvard's nonchalance: no security controls, free access for everybody, acceptance of beards and tieless shirts at lectures, no questions asked. You could sit down in a lecture at two in the afternoon with a sandwich and a glass of milk and nobody was irritated; nor was a neighbor with a familiar face annoyed, and many prominent faces sat in the lecture halls. It was like Auden's saying, "Private faces in public places are nicer and wiser than public faces in private places."

Intellectually, I felt less spoiled at Harvard than at Oxford. Private financing of the university system tends to focus the mind on making money. At Harvard, I found no one who had time to stroll with me along the Charles River, to watch scullers and oarsmen rowing in double sculls, coxed fours or an eight, and talk about God and the world. Scholars preferred founding their own study centers — Daniel Yergin, for example, with his Cambridge Energy Research Associates — and writing expert opinions for the oil industry. In addition to the money they earned, they collected practical experience.

During my time, Samuel Huntington was the institute's director. He's a classic representative of White Anglo-Saxon Protestantism, which explains his book *Clash of Civilizations*. Huntington lives in a lovely brownstone in Beacon Hill, across the river from Cambridge, not far from the center of old Boston. He is married to a charming woman, also a genial host, from Italy.

Nor did I suffer from any lack of variety, since I always encountered good friends at the institute. It deliberately promoted the presence of fellows from overseas in order to generate reliable friends for the United States among the ranks of global leadership. Europeans can only learn from this practice. I met Steven Stamas, the former president of the New York Philharmonic, Pierre Keller, my colleague at Lombard Odier (another Swiss private bank) and my successor as a visiting fellow, and Peter Sutherland, the long-term director of the General Agreement on Tariffs and Trade (GATT). They all belonged to the institute's executive committee.

The political climate during my sabbatical at Harvard was permissive, but there were no strong Left leanings. My wife was a little naïve in disregarding an antiapartheid protest against South Africa. Students had thrown a picket line around the library where she had an appointment. The strikers tried to stop her from entering the building, but she passed the picket line, simply saying, "Leave me alone, I'm Swiss."

I was expected to submit an analysis of my visit to the institute, addressed to Harvard president Derek Bok. Galbraith urged me to do more than just praise my experience. Naively, I risked some critical remarks about an outdated foreign policy in the containment and rollback style of the cold war, which was still in the grip of body counting. I was by no means alone in this. A number of the fellows decided to leave in the middle of the semester. They didn't support the cold war atmosphere. I remember an Australian pastor who freely admitted that he couldn't tolerate the political climate. In all fairness, I must admit that Samuel Huntington did not resent my frankness. We've stayed in touch.

Ilse and I were regular guests on Francis Avenue in John

Kenneth and Kitty Galbraith's large house. Once or twice a week we showed up for dinner. The Indian cuisine — the heritage of his time as ambassador in India and of a factotum he brought with him — was a marked counterpoint to the colonial style elegance of the premises.

34

FROM THE SWISS BANKING SCHOOL TO THE SFI (1986–2005)

Not enough crazies in Switzerland

I got to know Ernst Kilgus through music. In 1978, when I became treasurer of the Tonhalle Society (the corporate framework of the Zurich Symphony Orchestra), he had already spent six years on the society's board. I got along very well with the quiet observer who missed nothing and was totally disinterested in pushing himself toward the center of attention.

Kilgus' personal history has always impressed me. After the *Matura*, his graduation from high school, the future scholar worked for Credit Suisse in order to earn the money for his studies. At a young age and while he was still a teacher, Ernst was elected in 1962 as headmaster of the Zurich-Freudenberg high school. In 1968, the University of Zurich offered him a professorship for "financial and managerial accounting and financial doctrine." His predecessor of the long unoccupied chair was Karl Kaefer, the pope of Swiss accounting. As Kilgus told me later, the dean had introduced him into his new field with the succinct instruction, "You'll handle everything on the right side of the balance sheet."

Kilgus did just that for three semesters as a young professor busy with preparing his lectures and mastering the vagaries of his new job, which included the Swiss Federal Higher Professional School for Tax Experts, Trustees and Auditors.

In 1970, the faculty, which included legal scholars and economists like Hans Nef, Werner Kaegi, and Arthur Meier-Hayoz, had a new assignment for him: creation of a learning institute for banking. Kilgus was the only full professor who had ever seen the workings of a bank from the inside.

So on October 1, 1970, he moved into a five-room apartment together with one assistant and two filing cabinets and became founding professor for the Institute of Swiss Banking. Kilgus' historic achievement was the introduction of managerial accounting practices in Swiss banking. At the beginning of the seventies, banks were still unfamiliar with cost accounting and had great trouble defining their "products." Indeed, they thought that they didn't have any products. Given this background, distinguished bankers doubted whether the transfer of industrial cost accounting to the service sector made any sense.

Education, research, and expert judgments are the typical tasks facing any university institute. Kilgus added banking instruction and training, which made him a permanent guest at the training center of the UBS (Union Bank of Switzerland) on the Wolfsberg and the SBC (the Swiss Bank Corporation) in the Seepark Thun.

Kilgus summed up the results of this educational training in a commemorative publication in my honor with a comment that, over time, he could identify by the style of a banker's argumentation to which bank the banker belonged. Another insight persuaded him that Switzerland needed a banking school for further education of the workforce, especially for those banks that couldn't afford their own training centers. In 1986, he brought me the idea of a Swiss Banking School. For a long time already I had worried about the lack of schooling facilities for the next generation of bankers in Switzerland.

I was very aware from my own practical experience that we lacked facilities for continuing education. At Julius Baer, we helped ourselves by sending talented youngsters to the Harvard Business School for three months. Juergen Luethi was one of the first who registered at the business school. Admission was not based on academic credentials but on practical abilities and passage of an entrance exam in which the IQ and TOEFL (Test of English as a Foreign Language) judged the level of English proficiency. As I remember it, knowledge of language is more important than IQ. In the meantime, our house abandoned the idea of separating someone for a long period of time from wife and family. Not everybody considers a hundred days away from one's family as an honor and a unique opportunity to win some distance from one's everyday life. Today, two three-week compact courses are in style. And tuition at the Harvard Business School has reached a level that not even Swiss special institutes of learning have reached: $50,000.

I cannot claim that we only received applause for the idea of continuing banking education in Switzerland. As the driving force behind the banking school, we tried to include everybody, beginning with the Swiss Bankers Association (SBA), but they took so much time that we developed the alternative idea of a privately maintained foundation. The natural quintet was the Swiss Bank Corporation, the Credit Suisse, UBS, Julius Baer, and Vontobel. The large banks were not overly enthusiastic — understandable, since they had just built up their own training capacity — but they supported us nevertheless. Credit Suisse, when Rainer Gut ran it, gave sizable support to the Stern School of New York University and every year sent fifty to seventy trainees to New York City.

Kilgus wrote the training program and designed an education plan. In order to have some idea of what was going on in the

Anglo-Saxon countries, he spent three months in the spring of 1987 looking around the London School of Economics, visiting the Harvard Business School, and traveling to two other American banking schools, one in New York, the other in Seattle. In addition, he took a summer course at Instead, the international business school in Fontainebleau, where the tendency of the mostly Japanese students to kneel for hours on small pillows they had brought with them remained part of his anecdotal memory.

The foundation's board was constituted on June 2, 1987: Heinrich Steinman of UBS, Kurt Steuber as education chief of SBC, William Wirth for Credit Suisse, and Dr. Hans Vontobel for the Bank Vontobel. I occupied the Julius Baer seat. As our first president, we chose the very intellectual William Wirth. Raising the foundation's capital posed no problems for anyone. Every bank contributed SFr 50,000 ($33,000).

The first day of school began three months later, on September 21, 1987 — a considerable achievement for everyone involved and a great success for Kilgus, even if the regional banks did not at first use their assigned quotas. After four years and a lot of persuasion, they finally did send their people. Initially, they had thought further education was a waste.

All seats were taken from the first day on, even though the tuition was hardly modest. It amounted to SFr 5,000 ($3,300); today the fees are SFr 22,000 ($16,000). What banks got for their money was a first-rate faculty, with many proven experts at the disposal of students, as well as a few interesting American professors such as Kilgus' close friend Ingo Walter from New York University, who, when asked how he liked Zurich, gave the memorable answer, "I am afraid there are not enough crazies."

Education at the Swiss Banking School, which took place outside office hours, cost a lot less than sending somebody to Harvard for three months. Training took place in three blocks of time, each three weeks long, over a two-year period. The idea of three weeks came from the length of the military reserve training in Switzerland. If banks could do without their people for officer training courses, they could spare them for professional education as well. It's true, though, that three times two weeks also led to a satisfactory conclusion. The shorter time frame turned out to be the only change made since the launch of the banking school.

In the founding year, Kilgus invited the foundation's board members to teach the first block on a Saturday. No one dared turn down the invitation. But I had a hard time with my lecture about front running, known in the financial world as profiting from inside knowledge. Who likes to tell innocent young people about such immoral things? In fact, students were very interested and questioned me hard. I couldn't satisfy them with the trader's old argument of "I have to serve the market."

My intellectual contribution to the banking school was the Advanced Executive Program introduced in 1997. I had observed that even upper management needed a brush-up of knowledge from time to time. Kilgus wrote a program and teaching plan; he was really a born schoolmaster — and as such without illusions about the value of schooling in life. Admission to the advanced program comes at the earliest five years after completion of the three-part course. It lasts ten months, three days a weeks, from Thursday to Saturday.

But we didn't only make friends with the Swiss Banking School. The leaders of the Bankers Association, both employed today in the National Bank, were annoyed that we continued on our own instead of waiting for them. Looking back, it is clear that we really could have invented a kind of patronage to include them; the University of St. Gall was irked that the banking school had been set up in Zurich. Moreover, continuing banking education at the university level remained for the time being a purely Swiss-German matter. It took six years before we could set up a parallel course at the University of Geneva, thanks to our friends at Lombard Odier (now Lombard Odier Darier Hentsch).

*

With the redefinition of Switzerland as a financial center, the last two of the large Swiss banks, UBS (Union Bank of Switzerland) and Credit Suisse, no longer delegate anyone to the banking school. My son is now president of the Swiss Banking School and, with the recent creation of the Swiss Finance Institute (SFI), an all-Swiss institution is occupied with teaching and research as well as continuing education in finance. The banks and the Swiss National Science Foundation founded SFI in the fall of 2005. In addition to research, it will coordinate the educational activities and thus take over the school. The banks have jointly set up a fund of SFr 75 million ($58 million). Government and universities provided further funds. All in all, the SFI will generate SFr 200 million ($154 million) thanks to a triple-leverage mechanism. The banks have thereby made a substantial contribution to ensuring the institute's long-term sustainability. Its activities will be split into research and executive training. The ambition is to increase Switzerland's attractiveness for researchers, teachers, students, and participants in executive training programs. Over the medium term, the research stream aims to achieve a leading position in specific areas such as wealth management and risk management. Mainly, helping universities establish appropriate structures supporting research projects and developing a coordinated postgraduate program will promote research.

For internal training, in 1985 Julius Baer launched the JB College. My son had copied the idea from Salomon Brothers. Every year some twenty-five promising talents, handpicked out of the Baer system from all over the world, assemble for eight days in order to get to know each other, people from various disciplines, and of course meet the management committee.

35

Musical Reminiscences

Goldberg's shirt and my bicycle

The British crown prince deserves the sobriquet of a most charming host. I have already written that he is a brilliant public speaker. He is also very open-minded culturally, and I had occasion to experience his qualities as a host when he invited guests to Buckingham Palace for Georg Solti's eightieth birthday celebration. That was in 1992.

I was greatly surprised that Buckingham Palace had come up with such an intelligent seating arrangement — those around me were all acquaintances, among them the Oxford scholar Isiah Berlin and on my left the wife of Ronnie Grierson. Somebody had taken the trouble of researching the personal background of all the guests. I learned later that Lady Solti had helped. That evening she also took over the role of master of ceremonies. The Prince of Wales had thought up a surprise — the guests should make music for the man who had always made music for them. He said to Georg, "If you can't stand it, you can always go out for as long as it lasts."

One of my neighbors at the table was a blond, fine-figured woman with a large décolletage. Lady Weidenfeld. I allowed myself repeated glances at the lovely view. After a while, Lady Weidenfeld began to laugh and between pears and cheese asked: "Don't you remember who I am? I was Rubinstein's lady friend!"

Then I remembered. I recalled the many Sunday evenings with Arthur Rubinstein and his lady friend at the Dolder Grand Hotel. It was toward the end of the sixties, beginning of the seventies. But Rubinstein was more than a fascinating pianist and a bon vivant. He was a brilliant conversationalist who could enchant his friends late into the night with his stories. He knew no inhibitions.

When I got to know Rubinstein more intimately, he was already over eighty but still in enviably good form. He had no trouble sitting with us until three in the morning at the Dolder smoking his heavy cigars and then boarding a plane at 7 a.m. on the way to his next concert. I was puzzled why he still underwent such strenuous schedules. "Why do you do it?" I asked. "I need success," he replied. "It's like a drug."

Success remained true for a long time. When Rubinstein came into his dressing room after a concert, he looked as fresh as most pianists do before starting to play. His white tie was immaculate, no button was out of place, and no collar was moist. As such, he met the demands of the conductor and teacher Max Rudolf (the father of my friend Bill Rudolf) who opined, "You can recognize an amateur by his wilted collar after a concert."

Annabelle Whitestone, Lady Weidenfeld's name before she married the publisher George Weidenfeld — the two had wed in 1992 and at Solti's birthday party they were almost still on their honeymoon — had been Rubinstein's literary agent in Spain and had helped him with the writing of his second memoir. The legendary pianist had lived with the former convent student ever since, for the longest time at the Dolder in Zurich. The couple moved into an apartment in Geneva shortly before his death.

My personal ties to Rubinstein were further developed through Isaac Stern. In the course of his lifetime, Stern introduced me to innumerable contemporary musicians. Through Justin Thannhauser,

I had made contact with my mother's generation of musicians — to the Busches, to Rudolf Serkin, and to George Szell. Whenever Rudolf Serkin came to Zurich, he practiced at her home. The attraction of the house at the Bergstrasse was the large Bechstein piano (and Serkin was one of my mother's great flirts). Yefim Bronfman, originally Isaac Stern's accompanist and today a celebrated soloist, practiced at the Bergstrasse as well. Szell, a close friend of the violinist Edith Peinemann, had wanted to live in Zurich after his retirement from the Cleveland Orchestra and had even rented an apartment but never had the chance of moving in. He was a very unapproachable man, whom God had given little charm. "The U-Boat Captain dies" read the *New York Times* headline over his obituary.

Isaac Stern introduced me to the multitalented Leonard Bernstein — a great genius except for his table manners — and to other musicians of my generation, among them the late Eugene Istomin (a Serkin student) and Yo-Yo Ma.

Meeting these artists brought me more than musical fulfillment. For me it was life itself. Nothing has fascinated me so much as seeing Isaac Stern, Krzysztof Penderecki, and the conductor Moshe Atzmon lying on the floor together deep in the study of the violin concerto's score that was to be performed for the first time. That was in 1977 in Basel. Penderecki had written the violin concerto for the centennial of the Allgemeine Musikgesellschaft (the Basel music society).

I like artistic brilliance and glory best when they are coupled with human warmth and a sense for the simple joys of life. Stern would call me at night from some part of the world to tell me a joke. Georg Solti, on the other hand, remained distant. He was never affable. But in London he gave very stimulating dinner parties where I met noteworthy people, among them the Duke of Kent, former British Prime Minister Edward Heath, and Lord Dahrendorf.

Stern would surely have liked giving dinners but had no

chance, because his wife, a Lithuanian native and in everything the quintessentially thrifty housewife, kept house with a — to quote Friedrich Schiller — "modest weekly stipend."

Georg Solti and Isaac Stern are no longer alive, so it is natural that I should begin with Christoph von Dohnanyi in a review of my musician friends. Christoph spent many Sundays with us at home when he was a guest conductor at the opera or the Tonhalle concert hall. In Zurich, a weekend often lies between rehearsals and concerts. He liked being in Zurich together with his wife, Barbara Koller. On one evening, Zurich friends, the ophthalmologist Professor Christophe Huber and Aartje, his wife, shared the conversation with us — and with the filigree gentleman with the narrow, long face and mop of white hair. He was in great form that evening: informal, talkative, relaxed in the company of his admirers, decisive in his opinions, and, as a charming snob, joyfully ready at all times to set a provocative counterpoint to prevailing opinion. When he curtly dismissed the current fad for "original instruments" and catgut strings in place of today's steel strings as "professional," he gave a persuasive musicological reason: Mozart's epistolary documented his interest in the progress of instrumental technology. Everything was presented casually and gently in the beautiful — and today quite rare — German of Berlin's educated bourgeoisie. To that extent it is clear that with him a whole epoch is ending: the intellectual and sociological counterpoint to the Third Reich.

That same evening, Christoph told us about his father. During the war, Hans von Dohnanyi had been assigned to Admiral Canaris' counterintelligence service and was arrested in 1943. Christoph visited him at the Moabit prison and in the Oranienburg concentration camp, where the SS officers called his mother "dear lady" and in other ways showed their civilized side. Christoph described the night bombings in Berlin and his memories of the war as a pleasant alternative to the monotonous daily routine.

I also owe Christoph the bon mot that a conductor was a kind of animal tamer and an orchestra a pack of dogs in need of training. His prescription: he did not stop the orchestra during rehearsals but let them play.

I met Lorin Maazel, Dohnanyi's predecessor as chief of the Cleveland Orchestra, back in the fifties. That was in Lucerne. Once again Isaac Stern brought us together. Like Herbert von Karajan and Christoph von Dohnanyi, Lorin has a slight figure. Born in Paris-Neuilly, he had been a wunderkind. And he knew his worth. In Pittsburgh, one of his first posts, the orchestra's president and patron handed him his checkbook. Lorin was invited to write in his own emolument, which he did promptly: $1 million, in the fifties an unheard-of sum.

I'd like to have hired Lorin for the Tonhalle Orchestra and wanted to negotiate with him. But he didn't bother himself with material things. "Talk to my attorney." The attorney's ideas, however, were too absurd for Zurich's limited means. So Lorin went to Vienna.

Several years ago, when Lorin married the actress Dietlinde Turban, we celebrated his reentry into married life at Cap Ferrat near Antibes. The last time I saw him was in March 2003 when he conducted his "Ring without Words" with the Bavarian Radio Symphony Orchestra at the Tonhalle. His reply to a toast to his American homeland: "They're all gangsters. They stole the election."

The first musical friend of the Baer family was surely Szymon Goldberg, he too a wunderkind. In 1925, at sixteen, he became concertmaster of the Dresden Philharmonic. In 1929, the members of the Berlin Philharmonic elected him as their concertmaster. In 1934, Goldberg was kicked out of the Aryanized Berliners and toured Europe. When he came to Zurich, he lived either with my uncle Werner in the Spiegelhofstrasse or with us. At times, the shirt for his white tie and tails hung out to dry on a laundry line in our garden. Then we were strictly admonished to ride our bikes as far away from the shirt as possible.

The Second World War surprised Goldberg during a tour of Indonesia. The Japanese interned the violinist in Java in 1942. One day he was ordered to the camp commander. Goldberg thought that his last hour had really struck. But the commander had a different idea about his future. He wanted instruction in playing the violin and offered Goldberg better living conditions. And what did he do at the end of the war after four years of Japanese interment? He married a Japanese woman, an enchanting lady from a wealthy family who had studied in the United States with Rudolf Serkin. She died in 2007.

After the war, Goldberg went to the United States, became Serkin's close friend, taught at the Yale School of Music, and in 1955 founded the Netherlands Chamber Orchestra in Amsterdam, which he conducted for twenty-two years and finally turned over to David Zinman. For his final assignment, he assumed the leadership of the new Japan Philharmonic Orchestra in Tokyo in 1990.

Isaac Stern belonged to those musicians whom my artistically gifted mother had cast in bronze. Today his bust is displayed in Carnegie Hall. In 2002, it was lent to an exhibition in Indianapolis. The esteem was mutual. Stern never stopped in Zurich without coming by my mother's house for tea.

Stern wrote in his memoirs that we had first seen each other in 1948 in Lucerne. But I wasn't in Lucerne then; I was in New York. At the Zurich June festival in 1951 he played Sibelius' Violin Concerto with the Tonhalle Orchestra. Hans Rosbaud conducted. And I wasn't in Zurich at the time either. In actual fact, Stern called us one fair evening at home in the Freudenbergstrasse.

"Are you the famous Stern?" my wife asked surprised.

"Yes," he responded directly.

That must have been in 1955. Stern had gotten my phone number from the Leventritts and had called to announce his performance in Zurich and Lucerne. Thus began a friendship that I will always cherish.

My next memory is entwined with a concert in Nice. The following day, my wife and I brought Stern to the airport in my small convertible. Three policemen were waiting for the artist: "Are you Mr. Stern?"

"Yes."

"Then please give us the fee you earned last night!"

In the fifties, we still lived in a time of foreign exchange restrictions, and he was not allowed to take French money out of the country. So Ilse and I took it and we spent it on our vacation.

Through Isaac Stern I know that artists are the best experts on foreign exchange. He came back from Moscow once with a bundle of airline tickets six inches thick — all Aeroflot tickets, the fee for his concert. Clever.

Isaac's cello partner, Leonard Rose, whom Isaac described in his memoirs as a wonderful neurotic, once quite abruptly said to me during a dinner at my mother's house, "Hans, I need to talk to you," and pulled me into the next room. There he fished a bundle of lire notes out of his shoes — his fee for a concert in Italy. (The next day I gave him dollar bills in exchange.) That must have been in the early sixties.

The Istomin-Stern-Rose trio, frequent guests of my mother, had, after a modestly applauded debut at the Ravinia Festival in 1955, agreed to take a break, only to score a great success at the Israel Music Festival in 1961. As Marta Istomin remembers, the sequence of Istomin-Stern-Rose arose like this: pianist Eugene Istomin and violinist Isaac Stern were the youngest soloists at the first Casals Festival at Prades in 1950, where they enjoyed playing trios with the legendary cellist. This inspired the idea of Istomin and Stern forming their own trio, choosing Leonard Rose as cellist.

Isaac liked to eat as much as I do and appreciated informality at the table. He liked to eat at Zurich's Kronenhalle. And for him, the waiter would run out to the sausage stand on the Vorderen Sternen. Isaac wanted sausage from the grill, not from the pan, the way the Kronenhalle kitchen prepared it. He drank without excess but could empty a bottle of vodka, tastefully enriched with a lemon, in one evening without any problem, and without anyone noticing. In that sense, he was totally a Russian.

Isaac managed this lifestyle for a long time without it affecting his health. He tended to be too heavy even as a young man. I liked him much better that way than after his heart operation. Successively he underwent bypass surgery and received new heart valves.

He had suffered a heart attack in Zurich right after a concert. That had to have been in the mid-eighties. He couldn't come on stage to acknowledge the applause. I went into his dressing room and found him lying on the couch. We didn't even have a doctor on hand. Since then, the university hospital always sends one to the concert, who sits in a reserved seat in order to be immediately available in case a doctor is needed.

By nature, Isaac was a generous man. He gave everything he had. His art, his wit, his time. And he was immensely helpful. Once, he spontaneously grabbed the X-rays of my damaged neck vertebra, which was threatening slowly to paralyze my left hand, and consulted a New York specialist. (He in turn recommended a colleague in St. Gall.) I was deeply touched that Isaac, who himself was quite sick, simply took my file under his arm and brought it to New York. World-famous violinist seeks doctor for friend in Zurich.

A gregarious man, Isaac liked dealing with people, supported the young and in general new talent — I need only point to the documentary film *From Mao to Mozart* that received an Oscar — and committed his admitted love of power to a lofty purpose: the salvation of Carnegie Hall. That achievement alone makes him immortal.

On his sixtieth birthday, I gave Isaac a copy of the original score of Beethoven's Violin Concerto. He jumped on the score like a wild animal. "I'm looking for a particular passage. How did Beethoven write it?" My dumbfounded reply, "Have you never looked it up?" "No." So it was a great joy for me to give him pleasure with the copy, although he himself could easily have found one.

The whole world lay at Isaac Stern's feet. In the end, he wouldn't necessarily play where he could earn the highest fee, but he would play, for example, in Russia, where he had to fly with Aeroflot for a whole year in order to use up his money. Or he would play in Nantes, surely not the most prestigious venue in France. Yet the town had an old wooden theater with wonderful acoustics and an energetic doctor who guaranteed him a pleasant stay before and after the concert. It was no different in Zurich. Often his fee wouldn't cover his expenses, having spent a week at the Baur au Lac, practiced Penderecki, and — generous as he was — invited people to lunch and dinner. Nevertheless, he kept coming to Zurich because he had friends there.

No study about cultural governance ever mentions the importance of the human factor. As always in life, personal relationships and charm decide whether you can win someone over or not. Many people have money; charm is much less widespread and can never be replaced by money. Art needs personal appreciation, a heartwarming reception, and all the other stimuli that give wing to creativity.

The corner of 57th Street and 7th Avenue outside Carnegie Hall was named Isaac Stern Place on May 16, 2003, a sympathetic honor for a great artist who was also a great human being outside the world of music, not in the least because he liked to needle everything he found pompous.

After Isaac died, I saw the price genius demands. He had a family but no affinity for his children and was divorced at an advanced age. Success demands ambition and in the last analysis a high degree of egocentrism.

Isaac died as a result of his second heart valve operation. The weekend before the September 11, 2001, attacks and with one of the last Swissair flights, I visited him in the hospital after the operation. He was in the intensive care unit. Getting to his bedside was a steeplechase. In the corridors, I stumbled over the bicycles of the pizza couriers who in cap and short pants delivered the culinary alternatives to the inedible hospital fare. Isaac died on September 22, never knowing of the attack on the World Trade Center.

My friendship with Georg Solti rested on quite different foundations. Irma Schaichet had introduced us to the musician who had remained stranded in Zurich in 1939. Georg had a small job as a repetiteur in Lucerne when the war broke out and his father urged him in a telegram to remain in Switzerland. Given the employment ban for refugees, this wasn't quite so simple. Until the end of his life, Solti had never quite come to terms with those difficult times in Switzerland.

Georg was often a subject of Werner's letters to my mother. In 1944, he wrote that Georg had fallen overboard while sailing. In his letter of March 26, 1946, Werner went into greater detail:

> Now a few lines about the Solti case. Nelly [Baer] gave me the enclosed copy of a letter from the American consulate general and asked me to write to you if you would take care of the necessities and get your affidavit for Solti in addition to the needed sponsors. However, it is not a hundred percent sure that Solti will make use of the affidavit, but probably ninety-nine percent after Hungary apparently is out of the question for him and he has gathered only negative impressions from his recent trip through Germany — Munich and Stuttgart. Frankly, I cannot imagine that an artist would play for a public to which he has absolutely no connection and about whom he only knows that their "national comrades" had gassed and burned his own brothers and sisters.

On February 5, 1947, Werner reported to my mother:

Solti was here for three weeks with his wife (ex-Gitermann). They stayed with us for a week. He is terribly nice but she is an unpleasant goat. Solti accompanied two evenings of Lieder here and garnered fabulous reviews. In addition, he cut concert records with [the violinist Georg] Kulenkampff for England and all in all earned about SFr 1,000. On their journey to Munich, the couple stupidly tried to smuggle out SFr 500 and were caught. In order to avoid jail, they (or rather I) had to come up with another SFr 500, and at that they got away cheaply. But three weeks' worth of labor are gone. Solti was very spoiled here by his former opponents."

The great difference between Isaac Stern and Georg Solti is that Georg took himself very seriously and was deeply impressed by his own success. The gift of humor wasn't placed in his cradle. He reserved his collective energy for his music. He lived on a low flame when he wasn't standing on a podium. Once I drove him to the dentist. An acute and painful matter. The doctor wanted to give him an injection. "That's out of the question," Georg said. He did what he could to avoid doctors. He suffered from the pathological fear that an injection could damage his sensory abilities.

Georg was happiest in Chicago, even though he had to live in a hotel because of some anti-Semitic incident. With her uncomplicated nature, pleasant disposition, and readiness to give him a family life with the two daughters whenever he wanted one, his wife, Valerie, surely provided much needed support. As a matter of fact, she was an integral part of his success.

Georg had a hard time with Zurich and the Tonhalle Orchestra. For a long time, the resentment he took with him from his refugee days weighed more heavily than his friendship with us. Basically, our rapprochement only came about through the centenary

of the Julius Baer bank, even though he had conducted a guest performance during the 1978 Zurich festival.

My siblings and their families and my cousin Roger, together
with English friends, among them Lord Claus Moser, celebrated Valerie Solti's fiftieth birthday in August 1987 at the Suvretta House.
Director Mueller staged the feast with a *déjeneur sur l'herbe* —
(a bosky lunch) in the Maloja valley. There were red-and-white
checkered tablecloths at nine thousand feet, and a meal prepared by
a special kitchen brigade. At night in the bar, our conversation
jumped from her birthday to the bank's jubilee three years hence.
The obvious idea: Georg should conduct the jubilee concert. But
what should be played? My spontaneous suggestion: "Beethoven's
Ninth, for sure: 'Be embraced, you millions!'" However, none of us
in the Suvretta bar thought about the fact that Zurich didn't have a
professional choir or that the Berlin Wall would fall in 1989, with
the result that Beethoven's Ninth was played everywhere. My spontaneous suggestion drowned a little.

Georg flew in the more than a hundred-strong London Singers
for the concert. Without a professional choir, he would not have
conducted the symphony. It would turn out to be my most expensive witticism. When, somewhat taken aback by the expense, I allowed myself the jocular question if ninety singers wouldn't have
done as well, he became hopping mad and calculated that it would
have been more expensive to practice with a domestic choir for several weeks of intensive labor to make it concert-ready.

In London (Guild Hall on November 27) and in New York
(Metropolitan Museum on November 29), we made do with the
soloist Bettina Boller and a large chamber group from the Tonhalle
Orchestra, which played Haydn's Symphony No. 82, "The Bear,"
with Matthias Bamert conducting.

With the jubilee celebration, Georg's relationship to Zurich began
to relax. On January 25, 1996, he conducted the *Eroica,* and on July

12, 1997, for the opening of the Zurich Festival, Mahler's Fifth Symphony. It was his last concert ever.

George Solti died quite suddenly in the South of France. He was an intensive worker right to the end. Equally at home in England, in Switzerland, and in Italy, where he enjoyed going on vacation, he had decreed in his will that he was to be buried in Budapest. I'm not so sure he seriously meant to find his last resting place in a country where he had twice been unwelcome. But at the same time, he bequeathed the Liszt academy two grand pianos.

It cannot be claimed that the academy tried very hard to say a dignified good-bye to one of its greatest sons. Some two hundred mourners were squeezed into the conservatory's narrow cloister. The lovely Liszt Hall remained closed. Georg Solti is buried next to Béla Bartók, in a modest grave at the side of the ostentatious tomb of the composer.

36

ARTISTS I HAVE KNOWN (1935–2000)

A dead mouse in the red wine

My mother was a close friend with two fellow sculptors, Hildi Hess and Johanna Baenninger. Part of their ritual was a weekly drive to a restaurant. Leo, my mother's chauffeur and butler, drove them and became a permanent fixture. The only thing that ever changed was the car. For a time it was a Jaguar, unhappily a model that often lost a wheel. But we got off lightly. Leo was butler and guardian angel in one.

The habit of dining out crystallized from long afternoon teas on Bergstrasse, and I attended when it could be arranged. Sculptors, painters, writers, and other artists gathered at these tea hours, which were prolonged by a bottle of wine. Among my memories of life at Bergstrasse is the dead mouse in the red wine. She slipped out of a bottle and enlivened conversation dramatically.

Once it happened that the playwright Max Frisch and the painter Hermann Sigg left the restaurant at the same time. It didn't escape the artist that Frisch walked more and more slowly the closer they came to his car — until he stopped, embarrassed, in front of his Jaguar. Smiling, Sigg forgave him by pointing to his own automobile, not exactly modest.

It was at one of these prolonged teas that I first met Rudolf Bettschart and Daniel Keel, the two Diogenes publishers, both from Einsiedeln, the Catholic center of Switzerland, where they were born two hours and twenty minutes apart and had been friends since their school days. Hildi Hess introduced them to our family. At the time, she was Daniel Keel's "landlady, university and (girl) friend"; I owe this quote to Rudolf Bettschart. His brother married my sister.

Hess, the daughter of an oriental scholar, and a pupil and friend of Germaine Richier, with whom she corresponded with great polish in French, became in my eyes the embodiment of a gentle-woman: no beauty, but in voice and bearing most sympathetic. Her hometown of Zurich took little note of the artist to whom we owe a bronze bust of the playwright Friedrich Duerrenmatt, which in turn inspired the writer to a very vivid story of its creation. It can be found in a volume of his memoirs Diogenes published. Daniel Keel helped mitigate Hess' material needs in later life.

My mother and Hess had met through Germaine Richier, their common teacher. In 1938, Richier taught my mother to manage the hurdle that separates craft from art, after Alfons Magg, a student of the German sculptor Adolf von Hildebrand, taught her the funda-mentals of sculpting. In 1933, she had posed as a model for a por-trait and became so fascinated that she wanted to sculpt on her own. My mother's friendship with these artists bequeathed my sib-lings and me three substantial Germaine Richier works: *Cheval à six têtes*, *Crapaud*, and *Escrimeuse*.

Our connection to the artist, who during the war was married to Charles Otto Baenninger, survived our years in the United States and Germaine Richier's return to Paris in April 1946. Werner wrote to my mother in a letter dated April 30, 1946: "Unfortunately, Mrs. Baenninger has moved to Paris and that tears a sizable hole into the circle of our friends."

In New York, my mother had registered at Columbia University in Oronzio Maldarelli's class for stone working. What she created she exhibited, usually in group shows. In 1958, she was accepted into the society for Swiss female painters, sculptors, and artisans. On her seventy-fifth birthday in 1977, we published a catalogue of her sculptures.

Her best-known works are her portraits. She modeled Arthur Rubinstein (the bust can be seen in the guesthouse of the Israel Philharmonic Orchestra in Tel Aviv), Rudolf Serkin, Isaac Stern (today his bust stands in Carnegie Hall), George Szell (in Severance Hall, Cleveland), Hermann Weyl (at the Institute of Advanced Study in Princeton), and Pablo Casals. My mother never sold her work. "One doesn't sell self-made art, so as not to compete with others," she once said.

In our family, the feeling for music was innate, while Hans Mayenfisch awakened our interest in the visual arts. Over the course of many decades, the trusted partner became a family friend. When he was brought to his grave in January 1957, the painter Ernst Morgenthaler wondered in his graveside remarks how "someone who had lived happily removed from all art until his fortieth year would suddenly turn toward the intellectual world." Morgenthaler suspected that Mayenfisch's friend Oscar Reinhardt was behind this move.

But it's also possible that the scholar Emil Staiger had opened Mayenfisch's eyes, given that the banker had always been interested in literature. Staiger was a good friend, and through his wife well-connected in Zurich's textile industry where Mayenfisch had his roots, and, like him, was an impassioned hunter. The cordial influence the great scholar had shouldn't be underestimated. And it was probably Staiger's suggestion that prompted the University of Zurich to award Mayenfisch an honorary doctorate in recognition of the bequest of his art collection to Zurich's Kunsthaus art museum.

Mayenfisch's criteria for collecting art strongly influenced us and fashioned our buying habits for a long time. He purchased only Swiss art and limited himself to artists he knew personally. "One only buys art from artists one knows," he professed. It fitted his time and his conservative upper-crust world. Art served the national identity, and supporting artists was a patriotic duty. Fulfillment of this duty, moreover, added entertainment value to the sybarite's life. Mayenfisch was friendly with Charles Otto Baenninger, who cast his head in bronze and thus created an archetypical portrait of an industrialist; and he was friends with Paul Basilius Barth, Hermann Haller, Hermann Hubacher, and Ernst Morgenthaler, who painted his portrait during thirty sessions at his studio in Zurich Hoengg. The oversized picture showing him with a cigar in his right hand hangs in our bank as a loan from the Kunsthaus Zurich. Once a month, Mayenfisch hosted a dinner for the artists, which Oscar Reinhart enjoyed attending. The passionate host, who liked to present a crusty exterior — the product of a Prussian-influenced education that was fashionable in Zurich for a long time — ran a splendid house on the Hitzigweg, just below the Fifa building. Fifa has continued to grow and has recently completed a new headquarters building near the zoo to accommodate 350 employees.

For a long time, Mayenfisch remained a bachelor. He finally got married at the end of the 1930s when he was already at an advanced age. His mother hardly acknowledged his bride, who had worked in a perfume shop. Olga Mayenfisch proved that she had qualities of her own and that her late husband's spirit lived on inside her: she donated about SFr 8 million for the Kunsthaus' expansion in 1976. Alfred Schaefer, the chairman of UBS and the Kunsthaus, had given her the idea of donating the money.

Olga was, of course, guest of honor at the festive inauguration that ended with a dinner the city of Zurich gave at the von Muralt estate on the other side of Lake Zurich. After the speeches at the Kunsthaus, the hungry city council and the other festive guests hastened into a public bus — and who was left behind? The aged donor! She stood lost outside the Kunsthaus, where I accidentally discovered her and quickly took her with me.

Because he came late to collecting art, Mayenfisch escaped the education a gallery owner could have provided, as well as avoiding the danger of becoming an artistic snob, and thus saved a lot of money. His whole collection of three hundred works had not cost more than a million Swiss francs. He had already presented it to the Kunsthaus in 1929 — he was president of the purchasing committee — and had promised on that occasion to leave his future acquisitions to the museum. The Zurich Kunsthaus owes him thanks for the majority of its modern Swiss art collection. It is a testament to the man's greatness that he presented the collection without attaching any strings. The curators could freely decide about storage and possible future sales.

My parents, uncles, and aunts adopted the criteria they used in their own collecting from Mayenfisch, as well as the idea of forging ties of friendship with the artists. Werner and Nelly Baer, in addition to my mother, developed a weakness for sculpture and began to sculpt.

They used Mayenfisch's criteria to limit their own collections, meaning they concentrated on Zurich's "academy" artists. Few knew the painter Varlin, even though he was from Zurich, and it was Peter Baer who first bought a Max Gubler. Later, after visiting a certain gallery, I would buy Varlin's *Wall Street* as a lithograph. Still, Willy Guggenheim, Varlin's original name, was not completely ignored. The artist himself noted in retrospect in 1943, "I am renting a huge greenhouse in the Tuerler estate at Beethovenstrasse that cannot be heated in winter. Two famous art collectors in my studio: Dr. Mayenfisch and Mr. Baer. Living reclusively as I do, I am ignorant of Zurich's celebrities and confuse their names, call them Meyerbeer, Wolf or Fox. Again, nothing."

When I think about it, I come to the conclusion that in art we looked less for original or trailblazing work than we did for the social connections. Here, too, we followed the Mayenfisch example.

My uncle Werner and his wife, Nelly, thought differently about collecting, and emphasized the great European names, which, however, didn't prevent them from celebrating the Zurich artists and buying their paintings and sculptures. In the case of Hans Falk, Werner did not only give him a commission to paint the stock exchange but also made suggestions as to how the artist could become better known. Falk executed many versions of this painting. Falk, whose temperament was that of a jolly good fellow, became a friend of the family. We discovered that during his New York years, he lived with his girlfriend on the twentieth floor in a shuttered New York hotel on Times Square. Drug addicts hung out down in the lobby. It was the neighborhood in which he painted. Only later would he prefer Stromboli, one of the Aeolian Islands of Italy.

The other artist friend I made through Werner was Hermann Sigg. In 1952, Nelly had acquired several of his watercolors, products of time spent in Greece. René Wehrli, the director of the Kunsthaus, counseled her in selecting the works. With his expert knowledge of art history, he would prove an important adviser. Nelly was also friends with Hermann Haller and Karl Geiser. She had purchased a large Haller statue, and Karl Geiser painted her portrait.

Even though they could stand perplexed in front of the scrawny Giacometti figures, Werner and Nelly put together a collection of works by Rodin, Maillol, Bourdelle, Renoir, Picasso, Matisse, and Marini. That the works of Marino Marini are so richly represented is a result of the war. Married in 1938 to Mercedes Pedrazzini, a member of the Ticino family, he had lived in Milan, first taught at the Villa Reale in Monza, and, beginning in 1940, taught sculpture at the Academia Brera. In order to evade the air war, he moved to the Ticino in 1943 and got in touch with sculptors living in Zurich, like Fritz Wotruba, Germaine Richier, Haller,

Baenninger, and, for a short time, Giacometti. They in turn brought him together with Werner, who supported the artist, since Marino Marini (of Italian nationality) was officially forbidden to earn a living in Switzerland for fear of displacing a Swiss artist. Part of these acquisitions can be seen today in the Werner and Nelly Baer Hall in Zurich's Kunsthaus.

The high quality of their sculpture collection inspired the Bern Museum of Art and the Zurich Kunsthaus to mount an exhibition in 1959. And together with his brother Walter, Werner donated to the Kunsthaus Henry Moore's greater-than-life-sized sculpture of the *Reclining Figure*, which was exhibited only after his death. And just to demonstrate how circles close, Marino Marini and Henry Moore, who met at the 1948 Venice Biennial, became close friends. Today, Marini's work graces the Marino Marini Museum in San Pancrazio in Florence and a small museum in his native Pistoia. In addition, the Neue Pinakothek in Munich and the Civica Galleria d'Arte Moderna in Milan contain other important works of his.

A conversation with my artist friend Hermann Sigg reminded me once again how locally the art business was organized in the fifties but also how important intellectual and material support was for the artists themselves. As a painter from the canton of Zurich, Sigg could not exhibit his work in the Helmhaus because it was reserved for artists from the city of Zurich. Cantonal artists had to exhibit in Uster, Waedenswil, or other country communities. Those who wanted to exhibit needed an endorsement from the GSMBA (Gesellschaft Schweizer Maler, Bildhauer und Architekten) — the Swiss society of artists, sculptors, and architects jury.

Sigg's contact with our family came through Nelly and Werner, who met the young painter at one of the GSMBA's evening affairs in 1950 or 1951. These cheerful occasions usually took place in the Kunsthaus cellar. The artists donated contributions in kind for the raffle, and my uncle belonged to those who diligently bought tickets. In 1947, the Zurich chapter of the GSMBA, in recognition of

Werner's artistic abilities, had accepted him as a sculptor candidate and in 1948 as an active member, and probably the only banker ever accorded that honor. In 1949, Werner became treasurer and a member of the board. He occupied that office until he died on February 2, 1960. Later, his son, my cousin Peter, was the association's treasurer.

Among the artists who found their way into our circle of acquaintances through Hans Mayenfisch, I was closest to Ernst Morgenthaler. The house in which he lived on the Limmattalstrasse in Zurich Hoengg still stands. I often visited this enchanting man in his studio. He painted both of my children.

Sasha Morgenthaler, his wife, was a talented artisan. Thanks to her high-priced dolls, her name today is better known than his. She handcrafted every doll, sewed every jumper and blouse, collected hair, and, if possible, cobbled the shoes, and needed a lot of money to buy her materials. She sold very little. The Sasha dolls were much too expensive for use as children's toys. At the time, they caused real drama in the Morgenthaler household. The artist complained about his wife's passion, which used up all his money. Today, the dolls are worth more to collectors than his paintings.

Among the painters I am closest to today is Hermann Sigg. The farmer's son, born in 1924, is the last of our painter friends. He executed a portrait of my aunt Marie-Blanche Baer, Walter's wife, after he had first painted Werner and Nelly's dining room, which also housed their sculpture collection. The architect Konrad Furrer had turned three rooms into a dining room, and Sigg was faced with the task of creating a background for the sculptures, which didn't show up well against the bare walls. The artist decided upon very small sections in order to create a spatial climate that made the sculptures seem larger. Sadly, a new owner had the house torn down.

Walter Sautter was another painter and a family friend. He had served in the field artillery and was a good rider. In 1925, his father had written the musical comedy *The Sixtieth Birthday*, which the composer Paul Burkhard, a grammar school friend of Sautter's, had turned into the musical *Oh! My Pa-Pa,* whose success assured the Sautter family of revenues that still flow today and provided the painter with the foundation for a good life, to which he contributed portraits. He painted my uncle Walter, was very entertaining, and lived in Zumikon, where I would often visit him and his wife.

Rudolf Zender exemplified the cliché that artists can only be creative living in poverty. The painter was married to a woman from a wealthy family in Winterthur but lived for six to nine months every year in a small Montparnasse attic after discovering that Swiss comfort could not be reconciled with his work. He was, however, as Hermann Sigg remembers, "a good salesman."

Anyone who ever dives into the art world remains imprisoned forever. Art is as important to our lives as our daily bread. A Marino Marini painting is among my early acquisitions. Ilse and I visited him in 1954 in Milan on our return from our honeymoon — resulting in my acquiring a painting with my last 5,000 Swiss francs, and trembling that I had spent so much money on a work of art. Marini was so touched by my interest that he wanted to give me the painting. But his wife, Marina, thwarted the generous gesture.

My friend Isaac Stern had a similar experience when he visited Marc Chagall at his house in the South of France and brought his latest recording with him. The artist was delighted, painted a cover for the record, and wanted to give the picture to Stern, but Chagall's wife, Valentine, appeared quickly and put in her veto. Artists look for a muse but generally live with a partner who looks after their interests.

Gallery owners, like antique book dealers, live off educating their public. They awaken their interest, develop their ability to differentiate, sharpen their sense of quality, and tickle their desire and drive for ownership. Otherwise, they won't do any business. Gallery proprietors also appeal to the social needs of their audience and live off their faith in the ennoblement through art. With increasing age, the idea of immortality through collecting becomes a (silent) argument.

My own career as a collector — insofar as I can be called that — began very traditionally. Justin Thannhauser introduced me to Picasso's graphics, and my connection to Swiss artists developed naturally through my family. On my way to the office I always passed my uncle Walter cast in bronze: concentrated, with crinkled nasal roots, a small, spiritual head signaling heightened sentimentality but also a mild melancholy. Charles Otto Baenninger had modeled him in 1944. At that time, Baenninger stood at the peak of his creativity. He had modeled Oscar Reinhart (1946), Cuno Amiet (1937), Hans Mayenfisch (1942), Emil Buehrle (1957), and Charles Ramuz (1946). Oscar Reinhart, with the strong face of a German industrialist, and Hans Mayenfisch, with his marked dueling scar, the hanging eyelids, and the well-nourished face of a Swiss gentleman, are very representative works. The bust that the sculptor, born in Zurich in 1897, had chiseled of his wife Germaine Richier (the two had met in the studio of the sculptor Emile-Antoine Bourdelle, who died in 1929) resembles in its monumentality more a portrait from the age of Constantine. Then Baenninger was still strongly under the influence of his teacher Bourdelle. Over the years, he found his way to Roman classicism. His best-known work is *Die Schreitende* (*The Strider*) on the Utoquai in Zurich (1942–46).

I also knew Hermann Hubacher (1885–1976) very well. He too was a friend of the family. Son of an engraver, he graduated from the arts and crafts division of the technical college in Biel and shared his studio on the Zollikerstrasse with a wall painter in Zurich. Steeped in a strong sense of humanism, Hubacher made those whose portraits he painted and whose busts he sculpted into saints, including Augusto Giacometti. In our family, he was closest to Werner and Nelly who, during the war, had stored their collection in Hubacher's studio in Faulensee on Lake Thun. Of an opening in October 1945, Werner wrote to my mother:

The Hubacher opening, which took place on the Saturday before your departure (from Paris to New York), was a great event. At the beginning, however, the stage direction did not work all that well. Dr. Franz Meyer, who wanted to greet Hubacher in his opening remarks, had to determine in the middle of a sentence that Hubacher wasn't in the room. Instead of quick-wittedly stopping his talk or cracking a joke, he continued dead seriously with his speech, which was personally directed at Hubacher, until, several minutes later, he appeared in the hall, which of course triggered great laughter and applause. Afterwards, Giacometti, as a friend, made a charming speech.

Hermann Haller, born in 1880, won international recognition. His studio in the Hoeschgasse in Zurich Seefeld, where the younger generation of sculptors around Marino Marini, Fritz Wotruba, and Germaine Richier would meet, still stands. Haller came from Berne, had studied architecture in Stuttgart, switched to painting, studied with Franz von Stuck in Munich — together with Paul Klee — and in 1905, during a visit to Rome and under the influence of Etruscan art in the Villa Giulia, found his way to sculpture. The Berlin gallery owner Paul Cassirer — married to the actress Tilla Durieux — devoted a show to the young Haller's work in 1909. In the twenties, Haller was among the best-known sculptors in Germany. Justin Thannhauser too showed his work in his Berlin gallery. His *Jeunes Filles* introduced a new style that in many ways made him a precursor of Giacometti. But the sculptor always remained conventional enough to be beloved and successful. He and Cuno Amiet represented Switzerland at the Biennale in Venice in 1934.

Among my second collection, which combines Swiss and American artists, Hermann Sigg has a place, as does Silvio Mattioli. Mattioli was the only iron-working sculptor who forged his "synthetic material" in a smithy. His ancestors were all blacksmiths.

Born in 1929, he did his apprenticeship in Winterthur with a stone-mason, set up a studio in Zurich in 1953, and since 1968 has lived on a farm. He forged the Bank Julius Baer's iron gate.

Raphael (Raffi) Benazzi, born in Rapperswil in 1933, is a compact roly-poly who is close to me if for no other reason than he lived and worked in New York. He had spent a year in San Francisco before he settled along the Hudson in 1976, which is where I made his acquaintance. My son was a close friend of his. Raffi works wood, iron, and other metals into simple forms. In New York's harbor he discovered old oak wood trunks that had been used to build piers and which, over years of being in the water, had become as hard as stone. He sawed them into compact discs of identical size. A polished disc rests on a pedestal at eye level in my doorway. When I walk by it at home, or by other "time orbs" at the bank, I have the concentrated shape of a century before me.

A cylinder with small holes punched into it towers out of the green in my garden. Rene Vonaesch, a man from the middle generation, cut it out of simple construction steel, shaped and welded it: a heap of rust — the rust protects against further corrosion. Why I like rust so much is not hard to understand. It reflects my bias toward the past.

The Bank Julius Baer's collection focuses on contemporary Swiss art and consciously supports the next generation of artists. It remains to be seen if the collection has staying power. Among the objects exhibited at the 2001 Helmhaus show, one or two paintings surely have a chance of escaping the warehouse. Whether it still makes sense today to conceive a collection in national terms is something the present management of the bank should think over seriously.

The value of the spectacular Tinguely lamps, which for a long time hung in the Café Muenz near St. Augustine's Church, is beyond much doubt. The Café Muenz belongs to the bank's new building, and my cousin Peter Baer had the idea of hanging these lamps — if you will, applied arts in the tradition of a Tiffany or a Diego Giacometti — in a café that had not yet been built.

Peter and Tinguely met by accident. My flying enthusiast cousin was readying his plane for a trip to Geneva when Jean Tinguely turned up. He had missed his plane and was desperately looking for alternative transport. "I urgently have to go to Geneva," he exclaimed. In his quiet way, Peter looked at the sloppily dressed fellow, didn't really know who the other man might be — Tinguely looked like a clochard — but didn't find him dangerous, and said, "Well then, I'll fly you to Geneva."

Peter only learned who his passenger was after they were in the air. They began to talk, and Tinguely at once told him about his lamp sculptures. They were very powerful and crazy and could only be seen in his studio, a shed near Fribourg. Instinctively, Peter thought that they could be something for the Café Muenz.

At our next Thursday lunch, he told Nicolas and me about it. Of course we were taken in by the idea, especially since the room was high enough (and still is) for large, cantilevered lamps.

When the outer shell of the building was ready, Tinguely appeared in the Bahnhofstrasse, looked at the construction, and said yes. The man from Fribourg with his striking walrus mustache, who liked to work in one-piece overalls, was very generous. We had agreed on fourteen lamps, but in the end he installed twenty because he had such a good time doing it. Originally, he wanted to make the café into a nightclub, which is why Tinguely painted the ceiling black and tinted the windowpanes. Tinguely had only screwed colored bulbs — no white ones — into the fixtures. It was part of his artistic style and personal preference.

Irene Ackermann has particularly vivid memories of working with Tinguely. She managed Peter Baer's office and helped the artist with her usual great flair. As she soon discovered, he had very set ideas and was hard to push into doing something he didn't want to do. The café was finished in July 1983, and Tinguely insisted that

Irene pay him in cash. As she remembers it, he took the money to a carpet store in order to purchase a nomad rug. He was convinced that his motorbike would look very good on it. He had to demonstrate the rug at once, so he stopped his car in the middle of the Bahnhofstrasse, opened the trunk, rolled out the carpet, and ran like a madman around the newly acquired piece, patently ignoring the streetcar conductors who rang storm bells around him.

Tinguely's lamps had a sequel: Naoharu Nomura, president of N. Nomura & Co. Ltd. Kyoto, and for us an important partner during the flowering of our business in Japanese convertible bonds, came by to see my cousin Nicolas back in 1986, discovered the Café Muenz, was enchanted by the lamps, and let us know that he too wanted something similar.

It turned out that Nomura was about to establish a café at his Kyoto headquarters. So we talked about it to Peter Baer who contacted Tinguely through his secretary. It took months before they were able to reach the artist. In the spring of 1986, he was very ill. But by summer he was better and agreed, on the condition that Irene Ackermann would take over the organizational tasks involved. So he began to collect new scrap iron and deconstructed lawn mowers. He bought toys by the dozen and looked for animal skulls that could become part of his lamps in Kyoto. By the end of December he had filled three large containers with what he had found, and the bank chartered the freight area of a plane for Tinguely's materials. In mid-January 1987, Irene flew to Kyoto with his assistant and began preparing for the installation, together with a Japanese electrician.

Tinguely arrived a week later. Once he got going he must have worked at a feverish pace. He marched up and down the café like a lion, and in addition to his scrap metal collection, quite unexpectedly conjured up out of his containers chocolate and drinkables, like champagne, whiskey, and cognac, which the Japanese liked very much. After two or three days, Nomura showed up at the construction site, totally confused in view of the chaos, and confessed, "I'm a little shocked."

That must have been exactly the reaction Tinguely wanted. With a nightclub just as he had imagined it within reach, he could not be stopped. He wanted to hang large black mirrors on the walls. So his assistants went out and found twelve black mirrors in Kyoto. Inspired by the mirrors, he set about creating tables for the club, but he had not brought enough material with him. So he put his whole team in a car and drove down to the harbor and grabbed whatever any wrecked ships might yield. After a week of intensive labor, the nightclub was fully furnished and Tinguely himself was delighted by the café's black interior, which, in the evening, really was a "night club." Nomura too was satisfied — and relieved.

Privately, I have now reached my third collection, whose emphasis is on American abstract expressionism. Among the artists on my walls: Adolph Gottlieb from the expressionist group The Ten, the ninety-year-old Conrad Marca-Relli from the first generation of expressionists and a trailblazer for collage technique, and Robert Motherwell, about the same age, who died in 1991 and to whom I owe this wicked phrase: "The public history of modern art is the story of conventional people not knowing what they are dealing with."

Three California artists make up a small group within my collection: Sam Francis, Peter Plagens, and Viola Frey. Plagens began as a curator, and in 1975 he wrote the catalogue for a San Francisco exhibition before he made his name as an artist. I discovered Plagens and Frey through the New York gallery owner Nancy Hoffmann. Talking to her is always a pleasure. Serge Poliakoff belongs to the abstract painters. In his youth he earned a living playing the guitar in Parisian brothels. He only discovered abstraction in 1937 after meeting Wassily Kandinsky. After the war, Poliakoff became a leading representative of the Ecole de Paris. Italo Valenti, born in Milan in 1912, belongs to the same generation in my collection as Motherwell — Valenti too is an abstract painter.

Lynn Chadwick, who came from textile design to art (his first sculpture was made of aluminum and balsa, for which he received the sculpture prize at the twenty-eighth Venice Biennale in 1956), and Ben Nicholson (1894–1982), who shuttled between the abstract and the figurative — but always remained true to unexcitable and harmonic colors — are the two Britons.

I have a bronze relief of Ossip Zadkine that I bought at an exhibition. The gallery owner Frank Lloyd (Marlborough Fine Arts) made me aware of Fritz Wotruba. Oscar Wigglis' sculpture was the bank's gift upon my retirement. Born in 1927 in Solothurn, he is probably better known in France and Germany than in Switzerland. After graduating from high school, he completed a mechanic's apprenticeship at the Von Roll Steelworks, studied architecture at the ETH, and settled in Paris in 1951, where he has had a studio in Montrouge since 1956. Without his expertise in steel presses and cutting machines, his work would surely not have been possible.

My new orientation toward the abstract expressionists was a result of the time I spent in New York and of my interest in Picasso. In memory of those days, a vase stands on my mantelpiece, decorated on one side with a very revealing female figure. During my wife's lifetime, I always had to place the vase in such a fashion that the details could not be seen.

Another approach to present-day international art came with the expansion of our bank to London. Frank Lloyd gave my cousin Nicolas and me a private seminar, which included a sentence that has stayed with me for life: "A picture does not hang on a wall, a picture is the wall." Lloyd's business reputation may not have been totally untroubled. First there was the story about Francis Bacon and then the Rothko scandal, which earned him $9.3 million in fines. The dealer, who died in 1998, was born in Vienna in 1911 as Frank Levai of Hungarian-Romanian ancestry, and had a partner named Hansi Fischer, whose preeminent artistic virtuosity was only exceeded by Lloyd's business acumen. Together with Walter Eberstadt (later in his life, Lazard Frères' partner), the two of them served during the war in the engineer corps, which the British liked to staff with war-willing refugees. Fischer suffered in the service and hated stuffing bags with sawdust, at times the major occupation of this unit. In Eberstadt's memoir, however, Lloyd's role in the 220 Company was that of "an invaluable procurer of supplementary rations. Each morning he bought up the entire output of 'Bath' penny buns from a nearby bakery. He sold them to us for two pence, a profit margin even Marlborough would later find satisfactory. He never once touched a saw or shovel."

I could follow Lloyd's strategy from up close. He sponsored Rothko by giving a prominent art museum one of his pictures. If the gift was accepted, he could list the prominent exhibit venue in every Rothko catalogue. Then came the second step: he offered a museum a Rothko for nothing but with the proviso that it buy a second painting. In effect, he offered two pictures at half-price each and most contemporary art curators cooperated enthusiastically.

Through Frank Lloyd I also discovered Robert Motherwell and Jules Olitski, born in 1922, whose four-meter-long *Silk Spray* hung in my office for a long time. In the nineties, inspired by the wonderful sunrises and sunsets at his New Hampshire country house, Olitski loved to paint landscapes. I'm still sorry that I don't own a picture by Mark Rothko (1903–70). I had met him in New York, but was too conservative to expose myself to his creations. Admittedly, it doesn't take much courage to buy recognized art. All you need is money.

A collector lives from the guidance a gallery owner provides. For example, Nancy Hoffmann in New York told me in December 1996 without embarrassment, "I have an exhibition of Peter Plagens' work; you have to buy a picture," which is how I came to hang a gray Peter Plagens in my office.

I also obtained an urn, which the Californian Viola Frey had formed and painted, from Nancy Hoffmann. She had described the amphora on the phone. Without Nancy I would own one important piece less. The rich chromo painting gladdens the heart. Having to look exclusively at Plagens and Olitski paintings could cause depression.

It is noteworthy and perhaps inexplicable that with all our artistic friendships, there was no painter or sculptor of international renown to be found. That may be for several reasons. One of them is surely that Switzerland, being a wealthy country, didn't produce a large number of world-class artists overall. In the lineup of Nobel Prizes, we look considerably better.

A good interlude was my short get-together with Marc Chagall in the famous Restaurant Kronenhalle. Chagall was on his way to the United States to receive an honorary doctorate. When I questioned him as to which university, his answer was short and to the point: "Plusieurs" (Up to you).

37

Tonhalle (1977–91)

When music is the food of love

It should have been a forewarning for me that no famous musician ever lived in Zurich, with the exception of Erich Leinsdorf. Violinist Pinchas Zuckerman, for example, wanted to settle in Switzerland. That must have been about twenty-five years ago. We had not been friends for long. He sat on a couch in my home while several logs crackled in the fireplace. I thought his idea of moving to Zurich was legitimate and couldn't imagine that Zuckerman would have any problems. A violinist of his stature could only be enrichment for our city. I asked him to give me a few of his records, and I handed them on to the attorney who was to request a residence permit for him.

One or two weeks later, a uniformed official of the police strode into my office and said, "Unfortunately, I have to tell you that Mr. Zuckerman cannot reside in Zurich."

"Why not?"

"He is not famous enough."

"How did you come to that conclusion?"

"We asked around."

During the cold war, David Oistrakh was not allowed to perform in Zurich. The Cantonal Alien Police refused to give a working permit to "the emissary of communism" for two concerts at the Tonhalle. Without a work permit for a concert, no musician domiciled outside Switzerland can pick up a musical instrument on a Zurich stage. (Concertgoers have little idea of the bureaucratic costs that precede a foreign orchestra's appearance in Switzerland. Even the orchestra's manager needs a temporary labor permit.)

The hostility of the authorities toward the arts outraged the pianist Sviataslov Richter so much that he decided never to play in Zurich again. And he has kept his word. But at least he played in Berne, where the authorities were not as obstinate. When Richter announced an evening at the Grand Casino, all of art-interested Zurich — including my mother — boarded the train to Berne so as not to miss the event. It was a cold winter night. Afterward, the press featured articles about the propriety of listening to a *horribile dictu* — communist artist.

The presidency of the Tonhalle Society was not a vigorously pursued goal in my life but an accidentally acquired honorary post, which in addition to all kinds of burdens also brought me some glory. To report to the governor of Hong Kong, across a giant dining hall, the arrival of a renowned symphony orchestra is truly a great honor and was one of those unique experiences the Tonhalle Orchestra made possible for me.

The impulse came from the then future mayor of the city, Thomas Wagner, whose parents I already knew. His father, Professor Dr. Hans Wagner, was an ophthalmologist with an international reputation, a very charming man, and as a great music lover one of the pillars of the Tonhalle Society. Thomas had degrees in medicine and law, was ambitious and promising, and, at the time, a young city councilman. He had been a member of the Tonhalle Society's board since 1970. He became president in 1975 at a comparatively young age, after Hanno Hebling, the features editor of the *Neue Zuercher Zeitung*, had thrown in the towel.

Even though its means were limited, the orchestra had

achieved a great deal after the Second World War — at first under Hans Rosbaud, in whose house we were often guests, and following him, Rudolf Kempe, with the charming and talented Charles Dutoit as backup. Dutoit achieved world fame as head of the Orchestre Symphonique de Montreal.

Klara Haskil and Otto Klemperer belonged to the unforgettable personalities of Zurich's concert life. When they appeared on stage together, word was that patrons went to see which one would die on stage first. Both of them were already very advanced in age, and Klemperer had suffered from a stroke. Klemperer could be pretty unabashed. His question after an underwhelming Paul Hindemith lecture is legendary: "Maestro, where are the toilets around here?" I had a somewhat different experience. Waiters on duty during Thé Dansant (Tea Dance) at the Baur au Lac regularly cried on my shoulder. They had to earn their tips by procuring young girls for the conductor. He was notorious for bringing young violinists in for couch casting.

The name of the Tonhalle Orchestra is inextricably linked to Volkmar Andreae. The conductor had decided Zurich's musical life from 1906 to 1949 and is a permanent part of my childhood memories. All told, Andreae conducted more than 1,150 concerts and performed 800 different works from over 200 composers. He personally knew many important composers of his day and had a precise idea of their intentions — from Béla Bartók to Arnold Schoenberg and Richard Strauss. Andreae spent a great deal of care in developing modern music, which had come to Zurich with the advent of Wagner, Bruckner, and Brahms.

Hans Rosbaud also fostered the musical avant-garde. His was a universal intellect, grounded in classical and modern philology as well as mathematics and the natural sciences. However, until 1957, Rosbaud remained the second man at the Tonhalle. Back in 1949, the Tonhalle board had chosen Erich Schmid as Andreae's successor. He had been conductor of a choir in rural Switzerland and in 1957 switched to the Radio Beromuenster Studio Orchestra.

Participation in the social life of artists appearing at the Tonhalle had become an early habit, thanks to my friendship with Isaac Stern, Leonard Rose, Rudolf Serkin, and other soloists. In practice, that meant a late postconcert supper with conversation about God and the world and then falling into bed early in the morning with a full stomach and the uncomfortable thought of getting out of the sheets at six. I have never been sorry for having done it and can only cite de Gaulle: "Meeting for a meal and talking together is a good habit." For me, the high point of an evening at a concert was the visit to the artist's dressing room and getting together for dinner afterward. The social rounds at the Conti, in the Kronenhalle, or the Baur au Lac Club with conductors, soloists, friends, and other inspiring company intensified art and life and occasionally spiced it with telling incidents. Zubin Mehta would spend half an hour on the phone before he would come down to eat. On the trip from the airport to the hotel, I once watched Leonard Bernstein chew three cigarettes and swallow the tobacco.

What is best after a concert? The grilled sausage on the Bellevue Platz. For me that's not a joke. Experiencing the human side of artists was always most moving. The geniuses on stage opened up their human side with their stories, anecdotes, fears, and needs. I have always found these evenings, which my wife fearlessly shared with me, a great enrichment — including the simple but hospitable reception at the home of bachelors Christoph Eschenbach and Justus Frantz on nearby Kroenleinstrasse 40. A few mismatched glasses, some bread and cheese, and whatever else turned up in the refrigerator, and Eschenbach would play Chopin until one or two in the morning. Unforgettable. Including the darkened room and the lighted candles. For me, Christoph Eschenbach remains unsurpassed in Zurich, at least in terms of musical fulfillment these so human neighborhood meetings afforded. Because we were neighbors, we often took extended walks on Sunday mornings.

I well remember Eschenbach's foster mother, the archetype of the piano teacher with grey hair — a charming lady, whom he would often bring to lunch on Sunday. His real parents — the mother an opera singer, the father a professor of musicology in Breslau — had died during the war.

In practice, however, I did not worship Apollo but Hermes. I didn't begin my Tonhalle career as a friend of the muses but as a city delegate. Of course, no one is elected president straightaway; you have to prove yourself first on the board and on the committee, the board's operative body. Thomas Wagner, not yet the mayor, was looking for a treasurer after he was elected president of the Tonhalle. I moved up to the treasurer's job in May 1977 but was not properly elected to it — with charter and entry into the commercial register — until the autumn of 1978.

The Tonhalle Society is a complicated organization whose charm is readily apparent only to lovers of legal folklore. It is based on the donor contract concluded in 1937 between the city of Zurich and the Tonhalle Society, which created the Congress Hall Foundation: the society contributed the land and the city of Zurich the necessary subsidies for the music. For that reason, "representatives of the city of Zurich" make up the board's majority. Basically, the Tonhalle Society is a cultural institution of the city in the form of a nonprofit, tax-free association. It may be worth noting that structurally it looks back on the same history as the Zurich Opera House and the Kunsthaus. The enthusiastic founders could no longer bear the financial burden and, with bankruptcy threatening, called in the city. It jumped in and allowed the associations and foundations to hold on to the house — but then the complications began. In any event, it would have been smarter if the city had taken over all the assets. Instead, Zurich prolonged structural circumstances that at best have folkloric charm. And that includes the

unsuitable legal foundation for the legitimate theater whose administrative board can do nothing in critical situations but pull on the
emergency brake — to the extent that they have no assets or are
not ready to sacrifice those they do own.

Our willingness to accept such circumstances is a weakness. If
we don't want to risk sinking into total cultural insignificance, we
will have to modernize our organizations. In the process, the redis-
covery of good manners should be an essential part of modernization. The way Zurich treats donors is witness to a remarkable
indifference. Olga Mayenfisch, who gave millions for the Kunsthaus
expansion, was left standing on the sidewalk. And who was absent
at ceremonies marking the donation of an important collection of
seventy Old Dutch masters that the Koetser Gallery had bequeathed
to the Kunsthaus? The mayor himself. The legacy was worth SFr 30
million ($22 million). And those are only two examples of a lack of
interest.

It didn't take much effort to dig into the Tonhalle Society's
problems. After Samuel Hirschi, the society's secretary, retired, the
accounting became badly confused. His successor was not up to the
challenge of sorting out the issues. Thanks to Ernst Kilgus (about
whom I've spoken previously), the balance sheet became readable
again. Kilgus discovered all kinds of irregularities and restructured
the accounting practices. In turn, I brought in KPMG (formerly
Fides) as auditors in order to restructure the balance sheet, set up a
modern accounting plan, and thus found the means, without much
friction, for financing artistic endeavors. It was my first sponsoring
in order to make a more modern handling of Tonhalle monies possible. It was not the only one. I had to make an expert opinion
available in order to sensibly invest pension funds and other assets
that would not be required immediately. Otherwise, the finance administration could not be persuaded to lift its rules that such monies
be given to the city as loans at fixed rates of interest.

The society's complicated structure, with its oversized board of thirty people and the endless committees, burdened the president with all its responsibility, at least in the eyes of the public, while in reality decisions were being made by the various panels for whom raising the artistic level was only one of several — and by no means the most important — motives. Nor were all the board members enthusiastic supporters of the musical arts. Richard Baechi, as newly installed director of the Tonhalle, had secretly imagined the "inner" board as a society of nineteen engaged, musically interested upholders of culture, eager to learn what was going on at the Ton-halle, and inspired by serving the muses. The disappointing reality was that it was a mentally passive group, whose attitudes could reach all the way to total disinterest. They awoke from their leth-argy only when political interests had to be protected. Then they took sides. Ernst Kilgus reminded me about one board member, an occasionally aggressive train engineer, who would become furious about the fees paid to conductors and soloists. But for all the labor union undertones, we always succeeded in dampening emotions. Publicizing fees only remained a threat.

Even the board members themselves found that their large number was not a viable situation. During my time in office, their number was reduced to ten, not least because co-opting qualified people for so large a panel is not at all easy.

I was elected president on June 26, 1982. The criteria used in choos-ing a president have remained hidden. Thomas Wagner had been a city councilor, and his predecessor — or rather his predecessor's predecessor — Willy Hardmeier, who was elected for the first time in 1947, had been director of the Raemibuehl high school. The long-time Tonhalle director Richard Baechi gave him an excellent report card. Kilgus too remembers with great respect his authoritar-ian or strict leadership style — depending on your point of view. I remember Willy Hardmeier from my uncle Walter's invitations after a concert, where he was a regular guest — which gave my cousins Uhlrich and Roger, who had been Raemibuehl students, an opportunity to show off their social skills.

My criteria for a successor were clear: beyond a genuine interest in music, he or she must be ready to take the honorary office seriously, have time for social obligations, and have money or access to money. Peter Stueber's election was the perfect choice and a stroke of good luck.

Money is indispensable for great art and for producing contemporary works, essential for any endeavor that hopes to be taken seriously. If we had based our budget on full houses, we would have had a crisis every time Christoph Eschenbach put Charles Ives or Arnold Schoenberg's *A Survivor from Warsaw* on the program — with the predictable result that our audience would have spent a comfortable evening at home in front of the TV.

I don't find that audience response so hard to understand. Even after sixty years of regularly attending concerts, I don't appreciate the avant-garde on my first try. When I once admitted my musical limits to Eschenbach, he replied somewhat uncomprehendingly, "But you collect modern painters."

Yes, but in the case of modern art, I take a brief look at a piece, step away, and see it again. Modern music, on the other hand, I listen to once and am a bit overtaxed. That is the fate of avant-garde music: it is performed once, only reaches the listener acoustically, and already its fate is sealed.

Music certainly suffers under the grind of our daily rhythm. I never went home before a concert to change my clothes but would come to the bank in the morning already dressed in a blue suit for the evening. You could tell by the clothes people wore just who was going to a concert that night. It didn't help that Eschenbach's concerts went on past eleven o'clock, which virtually forced me to eat beforehand. A full stomach does nothing to stimulate your concentration — one reason why, during my term of office, we began concerts earlier. It goes without saying that afterward we would also sup with the artists.

My wife rejected out of hand Eschenbach's efforts to win her over to a greater understanding of the avant-garde when she said, "I'm tired at night and do not wish to receive a musical education. I go to a concert to enjoy myself, not to be irritated." So much for the practical limits of receiving new impulses.

At the same time, we needed to make up lost income. My arrangement with the artistic director called for having a program of the artistic avant-garde at the next June festival followed by an evening of Justus Frantz, whose star power we hoped would bring the money into the box office, which Alban Berg did not.

Ever since the establishment of the Schleswig-Holstein festival, Frantz' and Eschenbach's ability to attract a large public has been beyond doubt. It was an ingenious inspiration, for example, to record Mozart's Concerto KV 242 for three pianos together with German Chancellor Helmut Schmidt. In the fall of 1983, when the three of them played the concerto with the Tonhalle Orchestra (for a TV production this time), Helmut Schmidt told me that Frantz and Eschenbach had half-kidnapped him for the recording in London. True, he had voluntarily boarded a military plane, ready to play along for a good cause, without, however, having any idea of how far that would take him. He really didn't know where he was going or what he was in for.

There are other technical means to solve the income problems connected to the fostering of modern music. The concert world doesn't have to end with Gustav Mahler and Richard Strauss. In planning programs, we emphasized the links to financial reality. We knew very well that a performance of Hector Berlioz' *Grande Messe des Morts* with its prescribed two orchestras and three choirs — the Tonhalle Orchestra, the Orchestre National du Capitole de Toulouse, the Vienna Singverein, and the Czech Philharmonic Choir, all under conductor Michel Plasson — would cost far more than we could take in even in a covered stadium. So after extensive discussion, we decided to take the risk and calculated the costs closely. Isn't it marvelous to make art possible rather than to prevent it?

Keeping statements of accounts within subsidy limits is only a secondary virtue, but nevertheless essential in making viable any artistic enterprise worthy of the name. Growth rates in subscription sales and filled concert halls are not a goal but a prerequisite for taking risks, knowing full well they will not earn any applause from mass audiences. "The Composer and His Public" series, to which composers were invited to introduce themselves and to comment on their works, was one such effort. All are hopeless exercises in a city where even Arthur Honegger and Frank Martin are difficult to win over the audience.

The board met regularly four or five times a year. Professor Kurt von Fischer, Hindemith's successor to the chair for musicology at the University of Zurich, brought the full authority of his personality to every program discussion. These conferences were not simple. According to my own understanding of the situation, programming remained the domain of the artistic director and of the business manager. If I heard that Isaac Stern, Pinchas Zuckerman, Lorin Maazel, or Itzhak Perlman were available, I conveyed the information. Other suggestions came from Guido von Castelberg. He had been a board member for decades, was very musical, educated, on the best of terms with the musical world, and — unlike most other board members — wasn't shy about walking into the artists' dressing rooms and talking to them. That didn't stop the worldly gentleman, whom I had known since our common kindergarten days, from making my life very difficult. I found Daniel Bodmer's cooperation, on the other hand, very constructive. He left behind a complete collection of all Tonhalle programs.

The seven-member executive committee came together every two weeks. We met at the bank in the morning at eight and continued until noon. Potential differences were usually dissipated during the meal. Dr. Wilhelm Knecht, Walter Kull, and Dr. Dieter Sprecher represented the City of Zurich on the committee, and Dr. Sylvia Staub the Zurich Canton. From the Tonhalle Society, Jules Orsinger as treasurer and Cedric Guhl completed the panel.

Orsinger, a gentleman in every sense of the word, ran the asset management division of the Swiss Bank Corporation (SBC). His ability to reach back into SBC's infrastructure when, for example, we needed a larger conference room for our board only made him more valuable.

The musical arts are similar to waging war. You need money, and more money, for it. When I became a member of the board of the Tonhalle Society, Carnegie Hall seemed a successful example of how to finance such an institution. My silent goal was a Tonhalle of European rank, with an orchestra that would increase Zurich's prestige and attractiveness. Intuitively, I sided with the great Anglo-Saxon musical life that I had watched since my time in New York and about which, thanks to Isaac Stern, I was always well-informed.

My ideas were not universally well-received. The board was afraid of becoming dependent on private donations and, in meager times, facing the end. Thomas Wagner — who agreed with my aims — thought support of culture was a public trust. The majority of the board shared his opinion. Nevertheless, Wagner succeeded during his eight years in office to increase the Tonhalle Society's membership from four hundred to fourteen hundred. For that alone, he deserved a facsimile copy of Brahms' Fourth Symphony, which the Tonhalle Society thanked him with upon his departure. But it is another matter that the service we provided to members exceeded the annual dues they paid.

It was indicative for the innocent circumstances of the times that the city did not tie its subsidies of SFr 7 million to any clear performance mandate. In practice, we never had a problem obtaining a supplemental credit from the head of the city's finance department. But once Tonhalle and the opera were no longer under the aegis of the finance office, but directly under the mayor's control, that golden age ended abruptly.

As newly elected mayor, Thomas Wagner had the obvious idea of concentrating cultural affairs under his aegis. The city council in 1983–84 agreed to place the musical institutions along with the legitimate theater and the Kunsthaus Museum under the mayor's care. In practice, however, the money for cultural affairs depended on the city council's goodwill, especially since the total amount, now gathered under one department, had become more visible. Wagner enjoyed only limited support outside his own party, and the city council let him know it through the budget it approved (and didn't approve). Tonhalle and the Opera House were clearly better off under the wings of the finance department. Who wants to attack an institution from which one hopes to obtain money?

So we were under pressure to find new sources of revenue. I therefore invited Sir Claus Moser to our annual general meeting on January 31, 1986. The chairman of the Royal Opera House Covent Garden, chief statistician of the British government, vice chairman and board member of N. M. Rothschild & Sons (where he lost the last money he had, as he jokingly said), warden of Wadham College, a man who had befriended countless musicians, married to a Swiss from Arosa, held a lecture — admittedly a very exhaustive one — with this question as its title: "Who Should Pay for the Arts?"

Unfortunately, Guido von Castelberg cut off any discussion about Moser's lecture. The brilliant jurist, who had a reputation for not liking people much, found the exposition boring and irrelevant to Zurich. I'm not sure he was right.

Several years later, I found that before a guest performance in Zurich, my friend Lorin Maazel limited himself to a short introduction and told the orchestra to go home instead of rehearsing intensively. "Why are you doing that?" I asked.

"I will get much more goodwill from the musicians for the concert tonight if I let them go home and drink tea," he replied.

Christoph von Dohnanyi made a pointed comment: "In Zurich, rehearsals stop where they begin elsewhere." Naively, I told this anecdote to the music critic Mario Gerteis, who promptly published it in the *Tages-Anzeiger*. Two days later I found a registered letter from the orchestra's union leadership on my desk. I had violated the peace provision of the labor contract. Truth offends. I admit that the letter caught me unaware, since I got along well with the musicians and had a number of friends among them. They recommended that I not take the letter too seriously.

The strongest resistance to private financing came from the two orchestra representatives on the board, whose clout had grown substantially after the reduction in the number of board members. They shuddered to think that they would draw their salary without governmental guarantee, and they suffered under the idea of having to live with some uncertainty during times of economic downturn — a great fallacy from my point of view. Only government could afford to scrap the (national) Radio Beromuenster Symphony Orchestra without further ado. Under private sponsorship, that would have been unimaginable.

On the other hand, subsidies had not covered the salaries of musicians for some time. In no way was government a reliable partner for life. At the time, however, the orchestra saw it differently. The musicians compared themselves to secondary school teachers (extremely well-paid in Switzerland and especially in Zurich), aimed for maintenance parity, and expected the same security. They disavowed the idea that some material pressure furthered creativity.

Today that phase has long been overcome, and all those involved welcome a broader revenue base. Over the last ten years, total revenues have grown by 35 percent, while city subsidies rose at a below-average rate of 19 percent. The very fact that income from subscriptions and ticket sales could only be boosted by 14 percent in the same time frame, and that membership contributions actually declined in absolute terms, indicates how right it was to look for additional donors.

Nor could the board do much with my ideas for private support of the arts, since it believed that help for the muses was a public duty and therefore private engagement unnecessary, given the tax bill that fluttered into each citizen's home. It did offer help in founding an arts support association but vehemently opposed a supporters' club on the grounds that it would be too elitist. So in 1984 we came up with an association of patrons. And some in all seriousness proposed annual dues of SFr 100. We finally agreed on SFr 600. Today individual dues are SFr 1,400. Companies pay SFr 10,000. In the meantime, the patrons' association contributes just about a million Swiss francs to the Tonhalle's budget. The income from member dues, on the other hand, has been declining, down from SFr 410,000 ten years ago to SFr 300,000 today ($230,000).

Originally, the new funds were to have been used for extra concert cycles, fees for well-known conductors, and special events outside the ordinary budget. But once the orchestra was divided into two bodies, it amounted to a direct financial alimentation for the musicians.

The intensive engagement with financing culture — 5.2 percent of total city outlays — inspired examination of the general economic background and the importance of culture as an attraction of the city. It was also an opportunity to show the trades, who generally furrowed their brows at the word "culture," fearing waste of public monies, how much they actually profited from the muses. For that reason, the Julius Baer foundation financed a study published in 1985 on *The Economic Importance of Zurich's Cultural Institutions* (the opera, Tonhalle, Kunsthaus, legitimate theater). The result of the investigation Daniel Bischof put together (I too worked at it and with great pleasure, down to distributing questionnaires), thanks to the modest subsidies of at the time about SFr 80 million, some SFr 200 million flowed into the local economy. Today these numbers would be somewhat larger without any substantial change in the relationship. We wanted to use the study to enlighten members of the city council and other politicians on the economic interconnections and at the same time motivate the business community to do more for Zurich's cultural life and to do it out of enlightened self-interest. The study is still in demand today and has found many imitators — imitation being, as the French like to say, the sincerest form of flattery. Thus Salzburg, for example, published an investigation about the economic importance of art.

Over and over we were reminded — disagreeably — when guest concerts were scheduled that the Tonhalle is relatively small (as is the opera in Zurich) and that income from ticket sales is limited. Orchestras demand a fixed sum, independent of the size of the concert hall. For example, in 1984, Georg Solti was supposed to perform in Geneva with the Chicago Symphony Orchestra during a European tour. When the famed Victoria Hall burned down on September 16, he desperately started looking for an alternative venue and called me in the evening to see if he could come to Zurich. In the end, the performance couldn't take place because even in a sold-out house, we would be $30,000 short. I had to admit, "We can't do it. It's too expensive." At the time, we hadn't come up with the idea of having a corporation jump in, arrange for a lovely evening, use Solti's appearance for client relations, and to put itself into a favorable light. That concept took time to build, and I can only thank the Julius Baer bank for favoring the Tonhalle in its own PR work. Today, sponsoring is a budget anchor. In the 2002 season, the Tonhalle could book SFr 1.9 million from private sources.

Over the last twenty years, readiness to look for private support has greatly improved. Of course, good answers to the question of public or private financing that will hold forever don't exist. But in their early days, museums, theaters, and operas were almost always private initiatives or enjoyed private subsidies. Without private donors or legacies, museums could never have survived.

The long overdue separation of the Tonhalle and Theater Orchestra — its official name — into a Tonhalle and Opera Orchestra proved much easier than feared. With 168 official positions, it was one of the largest orchestras in the world, but not large enough. The orchestra of the German opera on the Rhine with houses in Duesseldorf and Duisburg had 250 musicians. For its double mission, the Tonhalle and Theater Orchestra was simply too small, especially since demands on both are very high. The opera performs every night and twice on weekends. Artistic standards were bound to suffer. You can't rehearse Monteverdi in the afternoon and perform the opera *Tosca* at night without consequences. Moreover, no conductor of international renown except Christoph Eschenbach cultivated chamber concerts or bothered playing Haydn symphonies with small ensembles. They all wanted orchestras with a large number of musicians in order to make a greater impression on the public — one explanation for always having Mahler, Bruckner, or Shostakovich on the program.

In order to make up for the missing musicians, the orchestra's management would hire up to thirty-two "extras," a solution that is artistically inadequate because the extras change often and therefore don't make any contribution to an orchestra's uniform sound. That realization took hold slowly; on the other hand, there wasn't enough money to hire new full-time musicians. Right at the beginning of my term of office, Thomas Wagner, as new mayor, struck the drum loudly and ordered a 3.5 percent down-the-line budget cut.

If we really wanted to reach our goal of catapulting the Tonhalle Orchestra into the major leagues of European orchestras, the separation into two bodies and the subsequent increase in the number of musicians of both ensembles was unavoidable. Opera and concert orchestras have two different repertories.

If ever in my life I have accomplished a heroic deed, it was this separation of the orchestra, to which (in addition to the prospect of opening the renovated opera house) Nikolaus Harnoncourt gave the last impetus with his Monteverdi cycle. He gathered together his own players for the work, which badly strained the resources of what was called the "blue formation." This formation was recruited from musicians who usually played at the opera house and generally were not available for the rest of the repertory. The concert orchestra unofficially was named the "red formation." On Sunday afternoons a mixed group known as the "purple formation" was on duty at the opera house. The concert formation of the Tonhalle was always dependent on reinforcements from the opera formation.

Seen purely as a personnel question, the division of the orchestra into two bodies was to some extent preordained: some musicians preferred playing on the stage, others in the pit. Almost all of them opted on their own for their traditional formations. It was, therefore, relatively simple to divide the 168 musicians. At a meeting on December 8, 1983, the Tonhalle Society decided to abrogate the contract with the Theater AG (the opera) as of the end of the 1983–84 season. After the city council, at its meeting on January 16, 1985, had agreed, some 90 musicians moved to the opera at the beginning of the 1985–86 season and another 80 remained at the Tonhalle. The daily performances at the opera mandated a larger orchestra. Subsequently, Alexander Pereira, the head of the Zurich opera, was able to enlarge his orchestra to bring it back up to par, thanks to his large budget, where the addition of a few more musicians was hardly noticed.

We didn't quite dare do that at the Tonhalle. We were able to add three musicians by juggling the budget but were still eleven short; and even then we would have been under the international norm for a concert orchestra — 102 musicians. Today, twenty years later, we have at least gotten that far in Zurich.

Back then we had to fight for every new job. Not the least of our difficulties arose from having to divide the subsidies. How much money went to the opera? What was left for the Tonhalle? We discussed this through many nights, and not always objectively, among the three of us, since the subsidy provider was part of the triangle. For me, it was very important that this difficult orchestra separation, even though some of it was arranged in advance, take place without resentment and without endangering the good relationship between the Opera House and the Tonhalle.

I got along extremely well with Christoph Eschenbach — Richard Baechi and Thomas Wagner had brought him to Zurich with a two-year contract that was prolonged for another year to the end of the 1985–86 concert season — but the press, probably under the influence of the orchestra, built up an aversion toward him. The sometimes terrifying polemics against the artistic director of the Tonhalle mounted among the musicians. They had already toppled Gerd Albrecht with the claim that "he was a destroyer of occidental culture who was not even capable of striking a beat in three-quarter time."

Richard Baechi, who had early on recognized Eschenbach's talent as a conductor, retrospectively thought that when Eschenbach came to the Tonhalle, he had musical and artistic status but little experience as a conductor. The orchestra valued the conductor very much as a chamber musician and as an empathetic pianist but refused him total recognition in memory of Rudolf Kempe's luster.

Kempe was a serene personality and an internationally renowned maestro. Eschenbach, on the other hand, was a young man who still had to prove himself. He had to show that he was not only an outstanding pianist but a man to be taken seriously on the podium. Other countries and the foreign press appreciated his importance and his significance. His interpretations of Mozart's piano concertos, which he conducted from his instrument, made all of his listeners happy. But Zurich treated him with increasing disdain, something his great success with the public did not change.

The local press, however, began firing at him immediately and made his life as difficult as they could. Quite simply, the media bullied Christoph Eschenbach. The press, as I remember so well, used

Jessye Norman's performance of Mahler's *Das Lied von der Erde* to accuse him of misplaced tempos. In fact, the conductor had held several intensive artistic conversations with the singer on just that point. The critic, undoubtedly with underdeveloped information, simply wrote about "willful slowdown of tempos." By the way, Jessye Norman is an especially charming person, who wrote me a personal note of thanks that evening.

Andres Briner, music editor of the *Neue Zuercher Zeitung* and one of my mother's regular guests at tea, launched the harshest attack. The musicologist and Hindemith student opened his assault in October 1982 with the ambivalent remark: "This skepticism is limited to Eschenbach's not very great prospects of ever mastering orchestral techniques and not on his general abilities as a musical interpreter."

After that he systematically intensified his criticism. On February 1, 1983, he concluded a review of a performance of Bruckner's "Romantic" symphony with the words: "As a pianist he can master such problems analogously. Facing the Tonhalle Orchestra on that evening, however, it seemed as if all his deep knowledge was bogged down during the artistic transfer from the conducting musician to those playing the music."

We read that devastating review while sitting with Eschenbach in the Roten Gatter on the Limmatquai, as I remember it, a semi-intellectual nighttime tavern, when Justus Frantz walked in and said, "What the NZZ is doing to poor Christoph is outrageous. The newspaper should be sued."

Eschenbach himself suffered greatly under these personally destructive reviews and understood the consequences: "I can't afford these reviews in the world's best newspaper." Once Frantz got going, he didn't spare me: "If you were any good as president, you'd sue the NZZ tomorrow."

Subsequently, the lawyers gathered in my office after the concerts and examined the reviews for any possible libel. As a matter of principle, we let it go with an angry reply but had to stand by as matters became even worse.

At the final concert of the 1983 June festival, the *Neue Zuercher Zeitung* editor wrote:

> It has not happened since Volkmar Andreae's tenure and certainly not since the foundation of the Tonhalle Society that the orchestra has before it a chief conductor who is an excellent musician but does not have enough experience in the symphonic sphere, and, moreover, one who, because he has not yet mastered the complexities of the music, is almost always overtaxed. The musicians ... have actively helped Christoph Eschenbach become a conductor, and they will have to continue doing so in the future.

Whereupon I wrote to Fred Luchsinger, the editor-in-chief of the *Neue Zuercher Zeitung,* asking — with all the understanding in the world for critical judgment — whether such personally lacerating remarks were appropriate for someone who had won international recognition as a pianist and conductor. By return mail, Luchsinger wrote back that the comments were certainly tough but not personally wounding, and that he would take care not to interfere in a music critic's business.

After the October 25, 1983, subscription concert (which included Alban Berg's Chamber Concerto for piano and violin with 13 wind instruments 8), Andres Briner served up a strongly poisoned compliment: "Obviously Berg's aims are very clear to the conductor Eschenbach. Unfortunately he is someone whose head and hand, thinking and execution are not often in sync, but this time they formed an entity."

That was enough to persuade Hans Escher, one of the pillars of the Zurich establishment, director general of the Credit Suisse, a major *Neue Zuercher Zeitung* shareholder, and auditor of the Tonhalle Society to intervene with Fred Luchsinger in writing a letter. The two of us delivered the letter in person. Hans Escher wrote, "Such slanderous remarks cannot possibly be derived from the concerts themselves and therefore must be the discharge of the critic's almost pathological aversion against the chief conductor. In full recognition of editorial freedom they seem to me to cross the lines of good taste against a conductor of recognized international stature."

After that, it was quiet, and Eschenbach left.

The hostility of Zurich's critics survived Eschenbach's move to Houston — Mario Gerteis accused him of "Prussian drill" and "bombastic effect" after he left — surely catching fire because of the unconventional personality structure of the conductor who today travels between Hamburg, Paris, and the United States. The committed bachelor and great aesthete collects Cy Twombly, is an outstanding C. G. Jung scholar, has a lively interest in the psychology of the visual arts, and at least in Zurich intensively favored modern music. I found him a very challenging human being and can only repeat that his nightly seminars with or without Justus Frantz belong to my most intense musical memories. It remains to be noted that since his departure, nobody in Zurich conducts an orchestra from a piano, except for Rudolf Buchbinder. Geza Anda had introduced that tradition along the Limmat.

As a conductor, Eschenbach has thoroughly refuted Gerteis' doubts: chief of the Houston Symphony Orchestra from 1988 to 1999, he is today the leader of the NDR Symphony Orchestra, artistic director of the Schleswig-Holstein Music Festival, Directeur musical de l'Orchestre de Paris, and chief of the Philadelphia Orchestra. He ignores Zurich and the Tonhalle in his resume. It is one way to take revenge.

✳

We were looking for a successor even before the Tonhalle Society elected me president. It was my idea to simplify the procedure and to consult Isaac Stern in Antibes rather than put together a search committee. Thomas Wagner had no objections. I picked up the then still-practicing ophthalmologist from the hospital for the flight to Nice and had to wait for a long while because Thomas was still in the operating room.

In Antibes, Isaac lived at Du-Cap-Eden-Roc, or to be more specific, down in the Eden Roc, with its excellent restaurant whose culinary qualities the epicurean Thomas Wagner knew how to value. In the summer heat, the splendid house on the Cote d'Azur was just the right place for a lively discussion. My secret wish was to get Christoph von Dohnanyi or Lorin Maazel. During the course of our conversation, however, Isaac said, "I would prescribe Zinman for Zurich." Isaac's recommendation was less influenced by the fact that Isaac and Zinman were both under contract with the ICM talent agency than they were the common friends and acquaintances that Zinman and I have in the music world.

Zinman's choice began another epic flirt like the one I'd had with Fritz Leutwiler. But this time I came out as a winner in the end. I visited Zinman, who as successor of our old family friend Szymon Goldberg, had conducted the Netherlands Chamber Orchestra in Amsterdam from 1964 to 1977 and the Rotterdam Philharmonic from 1979 to 1989. He knew the musical life in Berlin and London, enjoyed Europe, and showed some basic interest. But he had just agreed to take over the Rochester Philharmonic Orchestra, and he didn't want to take on more than one post as chief conductor.

All right. We could wait. But at the end of his engagement in Rochester, he told us that he would now go to Baltimore. Under his leadership, which he assumed in 1985, the Baltimore Symphony Orchestra became a major institution and Zinman extended his contract, but in January 1987 he did give a guest concert in the Tonhalle.

After Wolfgang Sawallisch had used his wife to block our efforts to get hold of him — "I don't know if you realize that my husband is the uncrowned king of Munich" — we engaged Hiroshi Wakasugi. Wakasugi had led the renowned WDR Radio Symphony Orchestra before he took over the Tonhalle Orchestra for four years beginning in 1987. The conductor and the Tonhalle Orchestra had gotten to know each other in 1984 during a Swiss tour for the Migros grocery chain. In addition to Wakasugi, we also had a second permanent conductor working for a time — the charming Michel Plasson who, however, was too firmly anchored in the Latin hemisphere for Zurich's German-inspired music world. At the end of 1989, we again had to switch gears quickly. So we hired Claus Peter Flor as permanent guest conductor and Wakasugi's successor.

In the winter of 1990, shortly before I broke my hip skiing — a painful reminder that Jews belong in cafés! — I received a completely unexpected call from the ICM agency in London: "Mr. Zinman would now like to come to Switzerland." I had hoped to sign the contract while I was still in the hospital, but the final version was signed by my successor, Peter Stueber. Peter had to negotiate with the hard-boiled attorneys. Zinman kept Baltimore but he took Zurich as his second post. His new argument was that thanks to Swissair, Zurich was so close to Baltimore that he could combine the two jobs as chief conductor.

Introduced to Zurich by Peter Stueber in 1995, Zinman seems to have liked what he found. When he gave up Baltimore in 1998, he accepted a job as artistic director of the Aspen Music Festival as a second position next to Zurich. When Zinman first raised his conductor's baton in Zurich, almost fifteen years had passed since Isaac Stern had brought his name into consideration. But today everything is in good order. The city of Zurich's decision in the autumn of 2002 to honor Zinman's achievement with the Kunstpreis (art prize) was long overdue. Two years earlier, France had made the conductor a Chevalier de l'Ordre des Arts et des Lettres.

Professional praise for the Tonhalle began earlier. In a conversation with Alfred Zimmerlin, Georg Solti commented on the Tonhalle Orchestra's development:

> The Tonhalle Orchestra has moved into the class of good European orchestras. Three or four orchestras in Europe are really of the very first class: Berlin, Vienna, Concertgebouw, and perhaps the London Symphony. And there are five or six in America. But then there are about ten other orchestras who come close, and the Tonhalle is surely among them. The sequence is irrelevant. I only want to document that the orchestra has improved. Above all, it has become younger. That happened between 1978 and 1990. You could talk of a renaissance.

38

THE CHILLED PIANO (1982–88)

You're all so nice so I'll let you all in

Ambassadors of culture are always received with open arms. In my capacity as a banker, though, such pleasant experiences are rare. From the outset, a businessperson is not perceived as a distinguished figure, especially not in the Far East, but the president of a symphony orchestra definitely is. There aren't too many who preside over a hundred artists.

In my life, I've seen that music can open doors and make hospitality possible even without a symphony orchestra in tow. But a large orchestra, of course, acts like an open sesame to quite splendid residences. It happened occasionally that some of their owners overstretched their means. In Hong Kong we knew a prominent ship owner and member of the Sulzer Board, with a marvelous art collection, who gave a huge party for the Tonhalle Orchestra. When we went to Hong Kong again several years later, we knew that he'd not been spared from the global shipping crisis, and we wondered before we got there what our reception would be like. It turned out to be as splendid as our first visit. The only difference was that the art collection was all labeled "Property of Chase Manhattan Bank." As Hjalmar Schacht once told me, "A large debtor is a strong debtor."

I liked the large and small tours of the Tonhalle Orchestra the best when my wife accompanied me. The first tour, to China in February of 1982, was the longest as well as the most exciting and inspiring. It lasted for three weeks and took us from Hong Kong — where we had gone for the Hong Kong Arts Festival — to Beijing and Shanghai. Ferdinand Leitner and Christoph Eschenbach took turns on the podium. Smetana, Bruckner, Mozart, Haydn, Beethoven, Schumann, and Saint-Saëns dominated the program. But great Swiss composers of the twentieth century like Heinrich Sutermeister, Conrad Beck, Frank Martin, and Klaus Hubert were also represented — a small concession to the Swiss endowment of national culture, the Pro Helvetia Foundation, which had tied massive financial support of the tour with the duty to perform Swiss music. It was an honorable thought, but putting that music across to the public is only possible at the expense of popular success. Yet we faced no controls of any kind. The foundation did not expect billings, journals, or even a travel report, which, given the amount of money involved, astonished me.

Nor did Hedwig Bruengger, the Swiss cultural attaché, and a very engaging personality, object when at the requests of our Shanghai hosts we repeated Camille Saint-Saëns' A-Minor Concerto instead of Heinrich Sutermeister's Cello Concerto.

Our soloists were violinist Miriam Fried, cellist Esther Nyffenegger, flautist Guenther Rumpel, clarinetist Hans Rudolf Stadler, and trombone player Joseph Klingelhoffer. All told, we were 146: 96 musicians and 50 others, one of whom, Cedric Dumont, the founder of the Beromuenster Radio Orchestra, became a friend. He was a tall, very well-educated man with sparkling eyes who had grown up in Hamburg. Europe owes him the "Eurovision Melody," for which he receives royalties every time it's played. Well-read gourmets would know his culinary dictionary, whose 870 pages discuss 12,000 gastronomic concepts from Aachen liverwurst to Zurich veal. It is the Swiss answer to the Larousse Gastronomique.

We embarked on our journey out of curiosity and in search of a small adventure. The Cultural Revolution was still fresh in our memories. The Berne string quartet had played in China in 1979, and Isaac Stern traveled to China the same year. With the documentary film *From Mao to Mozart*, the violinist had morphed into a movie star. Tonhalle director Richard Baechi decided it was time for a China tour and knocked on their door. The generous invitation for the orchestra to perform at the 10th Hong Kong Arts Festival increased our interest, and China issued the invitation, albeit an oral one. Our hosts deliberately avoided a written invitation or a tour contract. The travel and customs formalities were in theory so difficult that they signaled — not without finesse — that a "friendship invitation" did not need written form. Today every board of directors would break out in a sweat if it were to face such a situation. But all things considered, it worked well. A contract wouldn't have helped us with the chilled and out-of-tune piano we found in Beijing.

From our impressions of *From Mao to Mozart*, we all thought beforehand that the tour would be a memorable one. (Isaac Stern had had the idea for the film quite spontaneously while he was sitting on the plane. It made the documentary's producer rich.) The Swiss TV station DRS wanted to send a camera team to cover the Tonhalle tour. However, the orchestra demanded a fee of SFr 10,000, which the TV station was not prepared to pay. The orchestra would have to make do without visual media coverage. I then offered to pay the SFr 10,000 myself, but that too was unacceptable to DRS. So a historic Zurich opportunity was wasted. At the press conference after our return, reporters were more interested in that episode than they were in the tour itself.

In preparing for our appearance in Hong Kong, I took lessons in protocol from Donald C. Bardsley, the head of Julius Baer International in London. The huge reserve officer with the friendly eyes behind massive horn-rimmed spectacles — he had advanced to major during the Second World War and was wounded in Burma — knew questions of procedure well and prepared me for the governor's reception with the slightly sadistic zeal of a drill sergeant.

Chris Patton, then governor of Hong Kong and later the European Union commissioner for foreign relations, appeared at this festive occasion resplendent in a uniform cut in the imperial tradition of the nineteenth century that culminated in a two-cornered hat (to be carried under the right arm in enclosed rooms). I reported to him — from one end of the hall to the other — the arrival of the orchestra. Without a microphone. That was a matter of honor! But not so simple in the huge dining hall.

My standard line during the speeches I delivered during the tour was that the orchestra had taken me along to deliver the speeches. In fact, that was the truth. It was of course a joy to present the orchestra and delegation, especially since Zurich's most important representatives, Mayor Dr. Sigmund Widmer, and his predecessor, Dr. Emil Landolt, were among the members.

In China, I had to submit my speeches twenty-four hours in advance or at the very latest, in the morning, including those I was to ad lib. Officially, this was so the interpreters could prepare themselves; in reality it was so our hosts knew what to expect. In any event, I could repeat to myself a maxim from the historian Hermann Heimpel: "The best improvised speeches are still prepared speeches." I even had to make a speech in the Great Hall of the People in Beijing. Mayor Sigi Widmer was scheduled to speak, but he got delayed en route and informed me in time so that I could prepare my remarks. For me, the great switch in speaking to a Chinese audience was the pause I had to put in after every second sentence so that the interpreter could take over.

In Beijing, we lived in the children's tract of the Swiss Embassy and had three rooms at our disposal, which meant I could polish my speeches at night without interruption. In Shanghai, our hosts assigned my wife and me a huge suite. It wasn't a suite but a virtual excess of rooms. As a banker who paid his own way, I had never come close to living in such splendor. But as guest of a socialist state, I got to know a new world and the distance that separates the hierarchy from the people.

Upon arriving in Shanghai, we had made ourselves comfortable in a bus at the airport but had not gone a hundred meters before we were stopped. A Chinese official approached and asked for the "chief." It turned out that he didn't mean the conductor, he meant me. He had been instructed to pick me out of the bus and put me in a huge black limousine with drawn curtains. The limousine looked like a twenty-year-old Chevrolet and was probably a Russian Zil. I had no choice but to agree and, embarrassed as I was, get into the black monster. Otherwise the bus with the orchestra in it wouldn't have proceeded. At least I was allowed to take my wife with me.

The five concerts the Tonhalle Orchestra gave at the city hall allowed me to refresh my contacts with the sizable Swiss colony in Hong Kong, to make new friends, to visit our offices in the crown colony, and to cultivate contacts during dinner invitations. When dining, an orchestra — all sensitive artists — is a good medium for creating an inspired atmosphere, which everyone from the consul general to the local business magnates and representatives of the large Swiss trading houses enjoy, and where everyone goes home elated.

For me, this major tour was also a marvelous opportunity to get to know the musicians better and not to have to address them so formally. After the ten days we spent in Hong Kong, there were many occasions to do just that during the next ten days in the Central Kingdom.

For as long as Hong Kong was still under British sovereignty, entry into China was strictly controlled. We traveled from the crown colony in a new, very well-cared-for train to Guangzhou with four tons of baggage, got off, and walked through a large metal door. Good-looking officers with whom my wife flirted welcomed us. Naturally, the border patrol had been informed about our arrival, and the commanding officers greeted us with great charm by saying, "You're all so nice so I'll let you all in."

The uncomplicated border and customs controls dazzled us. Deeply impressed by this VIP reception, we climbed into the waiting busses and drove to the hotel. A large reception committee met us there. Of course, we hadn't been in our lodgings for more than ten minutes before the police arrived and unceremoniously collected our passports.

As fate would have it, spending the night in Guangzhou coincided with the Chinese New Year. It was freezing cold in the room. We rolled around in our beds and wondered about the quality and safety of Chinese fireworks. They exploded so loudly that they could easily be heard through the closed windows. When we looked out the windows the next morning, the puzzle was solved. No windowpanes. They'd been broken some time ago and nobody had bothered to replace them. Perhaps they had no money for the glazier. In any event, intact windows clearly didn't belong to the priorities of the Chinese leadership. Quite a contrast to eating and drinking.

I recalled that the Chinese ambassador in Berne kept a kitchen brigade of eight people and thus assured himself of an outstanding culinary position in the nation's capital. After our return to Switzerland, his Excellency Li Yun-Tchouan gave us at least three thank-you dinners at his residence. I've had to make worse sacrifices in my life, since I am fond of Chinese cooking.

What I also liked on the China tour was the seating plan at dinners — it called for twelve people at one table — and the fact that nobody could sit down voluntarily at an empty table. Unless a table is fully occupied, food wouldn't be served. The rule was also good for social contact with the orchestra. Thus the delegation, the travel companions, and the musicians could not be separated, even the musicians among themselves. Food was served on what Americans call a Lazy Susan placed in the middle of the table.

To add to my experience from Oxford, I learned a new drinking ritual in China: gambai. You lift your liquor glass — nothing but the sharp Mao Tai is served — with your right hand and hold the bottom with your left. Then the liquor is downed. Why the left hand under the glass? So I can't do anything stupid with the other. It's similar to the ritual male embrace in South America, the *abrazo*. It allows you to feel if the other man is carrying a revolver. You embrace and tap the upper lung in order to determine discretely if a weapon is hidden there.

It was a part of the Chinese hospitality to fly us in a special plane, a new Boeing 747, from Guangzhou to Beijing, where Christoph Eschenbach joined us. Newly engaged at the Tonhalle, he replaced Ferdinand Leitner on the podium, and in a concert on February 11 conducted Beethoven's Second Piano Concerto from the piano. The appearance in the Red Pagoda, the largest concert hall in China (two thousand seats) was an exclusive event. Before the Tonhalle Orchestra's appearance, only two other western orchestras had performed there — the Boston Symphony under Seiji Ozawa and the Berlin Philharmonic under Herbert von Karajan.

For us, the guest appearance was especially memorable because the organizers had left the piano overnight in the unheated hall where the temperature dipped to minus 15 degrees Celsius. The piano was horribly out of tune, and some strings refused to emit a single sound when the hammer struck — because the piano was so chilled. In such a situation, most pianists would have given up. But Eschenbach had the guts to play the Beethoven concerto untroubled to the end and then not complain. For that he deserves great credit.

Our other soloists — Miriam Fried, Esther Nyffenegger, and Joseph Klingelhoffer — were much better off. Violin, cello, and trombone can fit into an artist's baggage.

The audience in China fascinated us because many of them endured such physical hardship in order to attend a concert. Those who bought tickets in advance had to pedal their bikes for two hours to get to the box office and then pedal two hours back, and after that spend the same amount of time at the concert itself. Under some circumstances, that could add up to eight hours on a bicycle for a two-hour concert.

Tickets were sold for one remingbi. That amount corresponded to half a day's pay, as our press representative discovered. Cloakrooms didn't exist. The audience sat in the concert hall in their thick quilted jackets. This paid off because of the underheated hall. Exemplary for energy conservation and the environment.

Thrift determined clothing. Most men and women still wore jackets that buttoned all the way up, with sewed-on breast pockets and folding collars in the style of prewar uniforms. Social status was determined by the quality and custom tailoring of the cloth.

At one festive dinner I met a Chinese in a dark blue business suit. I asked him how he had obtained it and if he was not afraid of being tabbed an individualist and a cosmopolitan.

"I've just come back from Paris where I bought this suit and now I want to see what happens when I wear it," he explained.

No doubt, the country was opening up. But supervision remained. We traveled with the strict recommendation from the embassy not to visit anyone privately. Such visits don't do anybody any good, since everybody will be under suspicion of espionage, we were told. That was hard on the musicians who wanted to get in touch with their Chinese colleagues to talk about music.

By the same token, hotels were closed to the local population. In fact, hotels were extraterrestrial zones and out of bounds for Chinese citizens. Only our visit to the Shanghai Conservatory gave us a chance to exchange experiences, scores, strings, and notes for the oboe, bows, and other sound aids.

The excellent interpreters were well-organized and at the same time helped keep us under supervision, as we learned to our amusement. On our last evening in Shanghai, my wife didn't particularly want to listen to Bruckner's Sixth Symphony again, or the Flute Concerto No. 1 by Mozart. Instead, she felt like taking friends to the circus. But together we only had one interpreter and "spy" whom I had not told that I would again be going to the concert. I was late but made my way to my seat, but who got the neighboring seat? My spy! "Good evening, Mr. Baer," he said.

The encyclopedic memory of the translators amazed us over and over. They would have passed every Swiss citizenship test with distinction. They probably knew more than the examining experts. Minister of Culture Huang Zhen left a deep impression, not because of his huge ears but because he had invited us to a state dinner in the hall of the Peoples Congress, stayed until well past midnight, and showed up for the official breakfast at the hotel the next morning at seven — with a picture he had painted and a poem he had written for the Tonhalle. The picture was on the left of the scroll he gave us and the panegyric on the right. After we had stuttered our thanks, we asked, dumbfounded, "When did you do this?"

"During the night," he replied.

It is unthinkable to expect such creative achievement from the leaders of our own cultural bureaucracy in the West. The last European minister of culture of such stature was André Malraux, and — *horribile dictu* — the German Democratic Republic's Johannes Becher.

The only blunder we made in the diversion of shared invitations was a dinner in Beijing that started at 10 p.m. Only about half the guests we expected showed up. The reason: mid-level bureaucrats only had access to a car until ten o'clock. Cabinet and subcabinet members had round-the-clock use of an official automobile with a chauffeur.

Any remembrances of this memorable tour would be incomplete without reference to a suitcase full of remingbi that our hosts delivered with the instructions that the money be distributed among the orchestra, the conductor, and me, because the musicians had played so well. The fact that my hosts thought of me showed that Chinese intelligence didn't function all that perfectly. I passed the money on to the orchestra management. All they could buy with the nonconvertible banknotes were sweaters and travel memorabilia.

The China tour was not the only one during my term of office but certainly the most exotic. During a tour of the Far East to Taiwan, Hong Kong, and Japan two years later, it was not the chilled piano that brought us trouble but an overheated pianist. Alexis Weissenberg collapsed in the middle of Brahms' Piano Concerto No. 1 in D minor. Once again Christoph Eschenbach saved us. He took over, and the listeners in the Bunka Haikan gave him an enthusiastic ovation.

In Japan I got to know Dieter Chenaux-Repond, another very sympathetic ambassador. What made him even more likable was the pleasure he took in dining. He became a frequent guest of ours in Zurich. Japanese sponsors had made the appearance of the Tonhalle Orchestra in the land of the rising sun possible. All this at the urging of their enterprising ambassador. They came up with half a million Swiss francs. The Tonhalle is an established orchestra in the Far Eastern island empire, and the subsidy is quite normal. Only the Vienna and Berlin Philharmonic are able to cover the expenses of such a tour from ticket sales.

Among my memories of that Japan tour were Tokyo's sky-high prices. For a farewell party with the orchestra and guests, I would have had to spend $25,000 to $30,000. And that was a bit too much.

✳

The Tonhalle's 1988 South American tour on the occasion of the fiftieth anniversary of the Swiss Chamber of Commerce was another high point. It had been inspired by an inquiry from the Mozarteum Argentino. Unlike Chinese, I am familiar enough with Spanish that I could risk giving the first part of my speech in the famous Teatro Colon in the native language. A Spanish teacher at our bank helped prepare me so well that I could respond to the requirement of courtesy and "do as the Romans do" without embarrassing myself.

In his memoirs, Isaac Stern remembers his first concert in Buenos Aires and how delighted he was with the mighty hall with its twenty-four hundred seats, to which a thousand standees are added. The Teatro Colon has the same U-form as do European opera houses but has much more generous proportions. The distance between the rows in the orchestra are so wide that no one needs to pull in legs when a neighbor wants to pass by. The acoustics amazed Isaac, which he described as "sheer beauty." In that hall you can hear a pin drop. The warm, rich resonance and wonderful clarity assure the Teatro Colon of top billing on touring wish lists for the foreseeable future.

Hiroshi Wakasugi conducted in Buenos Aires, a fact that has remained in my memory because he flew with his wife but put her in tourist class while he sat in first class. *Il faut diviser les risques* (One has to divide the risks). Still, during stopovers, he selflessly went to visit her.

I remember visiting Hiroshi Wakasugi at his home in Cologne, together with Richard Baechi. At one point the bell rang, and his wife came in and casually said hi. In fact, she had just returned from Tokyo. The two had not seen each other for two months.

In Buenos Aires, where we were spoiled by lavish invitations to haciendas and took over a whole restaurant for our dinners, we developed friendly ties to Karl Fritschi, the Swiss ambassador there.

But his colleague posted to Brazil remained in Brasilia instead of attending the concerts in Rio de Janeiro and Sao Paulo. He said he didn't have enough money to make the trip. So he missed a good opportunity to invite people and cultivate connections. My only concert tour to South America remains as a splendid recollection of my Tonhalle days.

39

The Organ War (1984–88)

Farewell from the organ for a nun's chapel

The bitter conflict over the Tonhalle's organ bothered me a great deal. The dispute had sectarian traits and at times became downright unpleasant. As freshly elected president of the Kongresshaus foundation, Claudia Depuoz was appalled to find a pile of embittered petitions regarding this matter on her desk. As I would later learn from Urs Frauchiger, a leading musical scientist in Switzerland, religious wars and intrigues are perfectly normal circumstances with regard to any organ acquisition. Organists may play pious songs but that doesn't mean they always act in pious fashion. Seen musically, they are loners and therefore can only be integrated socially on a limited basis. In addition, there are the battles between French and German schools about the makeup of an organ.

The old Tonhalle organ dated from 1872. Friedrich Hegar, the long-time Tonhalle music director, had envisioned it for the very first Tonhalle. With its thirty-four pipes, the instrument, owned by the mixed choir, moved into the "new" Tonhalle in 1895. In 1927, the instrument was expanded to fifty-two pipes and at the same time equipped with pneumatic machinery. In a third stage it was expanded once again — at the same time as the Kongresshaus construction in 1938 — to seventy-six pipes. An electric console and a mobile keyboard were added. Marcel Dupré gave the inaugural concert. The Parisian organist entered local music lore as the "Zurich organ maker."

The Tonhalle organ was usually played for choir concerts. Organ concerts were rare. The organ last underwent a general overhaul in 1951. It was no secret that the organ didn't function properly. A panicked Hanno Helbling, cultural editor of the *Neue Zuercher Zeitung*, had already demanded action to be taken, otherwise the organ threatened to declare its musical independence and to hold forth uncontrolled. With the Kongresshaus under reconstruction, the question arose what should be done with the organ: rebuild it or buy a new one?

If the Kongresshaus had been rebuilt without the unexpected extra costs, the organ would once again have been reconditioned. An extra SFr 160,000 were in the budget. But with the rebuilding fiasco and the formation of the Tonhalle operating company, whose function was to manage the facility, the situation changed. The Zurich organists wanted a general overhaul at a cost of SFr 300,000. Such funds were not readily available, and the question arose whether an organ that had already been expanded and revised three times would really sound any better after a fourth overhaul. In addition, during the 1938 expansion of the organ, its casing — the "prospect," in the terminology of organ builders — had been pushed forward a meter and a half onto the orchestra podium, much to the dismay of the musicians.

When former Migros CEO Pierre Arnold took over the leadership of the operating company in August 1984, he quickly came to the conclusion that another renovation of the organ didn't make much sense. His friend Alfred Gerber supported his conclusion.

Gerber was an engineer graduate and a militia officer — a good-looking man whose stature could not be overlooked: tall, powerfully built, and mostly blond in his earlier years, then white-haired, with black spectacles on his nose. In addition to his passions for physical pleasures and new cars, the music lover knew his way around the world of music. He had excellent connections all the way up to Herbert von Karajan, and as a generous patron was an important supporter of Zurich's musical life. The multitalented music enthusiast maintained an especially close friendship with the renowned Parisian organist and organ theoretician Jean Guillou. Alfred Gerber also belonged to the Tonhalle Society's donor association; he was its vice president. We couldn't have found a more suitable personality for the procurement of a new organ than this worldly engineer, with his extensive professional experience gathered at the Oerlikon Buehrle Corporation and his heavily padded wallet. His measures were as circumspect as they were competent, and his evaluation was not based solely on Jean Guillou's advice, as malicious tongues claimed.

Given Pierre Arnold's unbridled zest for action, the acquisition couldn't come soon enough. The resistance he met with inspired him to move even faster. He raised money quickly. The Goehner AG provided SFr 600,000, but only for a new organ, and saw the donation as a compensation for the foul-up of the reconstruction of the Kongresshaus Foundation's willingness to forego any recourse claims. He also quickly received pledges for another SFr 600,000. As head of the operating company charged with the reconstruction, he saw himself as the one authorized to take action.

On the board of the Tonhalle Society, Cedric Guhl handled the dossier. The careful clarification of the interests of everyone involved took much time and energy. In the summer of 1986 the situation looked like this:

- The mixed choir, as owner of the old organ, wanted a new one and desired a vote to that effect from the Tonhalle board.
- The board of the Kongresshaus Foundation, as

owner of the building, pushed for a quick decision.

- The orchestra wanted the new organ moved back to the wall, not the least for ergonomic reasons.
- Inquiries with five organ builders in Switzerland and abroad showed that most of them favored a new instrument over renovation.

From our point of view, therefore, the path had been cleared for a new organ. We left clarification of other questions to a committee of experts that included two organists, the president of the Zurich Music Commission, two gentlemen from the federal materials testing institute who specialized in questions of internal acoustics, the head of the cantonal monuments and preservations office, and the architect responsible for construction of the organ prospect. This group developed the basic premises the board could use for its decision.

On July 4, 1985, the operating company presented the concept for a new organ, drafted by the German Kleuker/Steinmeyer syndicate, to the board. It approved the project with some reservations, since the large sums involved triggered controversy — even though it was clear that Pierre Arnold and Alfred Gerber would come up with the needed money. But that was something the board didn't understand.

In any event, the very fact that we were able to win approval for reducing the size of the organ, thus allowing us to set it back by 1.25 meters and freeing up needed stage space for large orchestras, was already a success. Moreover, this gave Pierre Arnold a free hand to sign a provisional contract with the organ builders' syndicate. Not everyone was happy with that decision, since the group was located in the Federal Republic of Germany — Kleuker in Bielefeld and Steinmeyer in Oettingen. The board again left the organ's style and disposition to the experts. The technical discussions that ranged from four-foot trumpets, reed pipes, flue stops, violae d'amore, quints, and bass to horizontal reeds, keyboards, and pedals would have far overtaxed the board. After the fact, I remember my delight about the concept of "Spanish trumpets" (horizontally bounded pipes). Unfortunately, the monument and preservation official thought its horizontal positioning so "Spanish" that he banished it behind the organ prospect.

We delegated the disposition of the organ to Alfred Gerber. Under his leadership, the following men met in Paris on November 24, 1985: Jean-Louis Coignet, organ expert for the city of Paris; Jean Guillou, Titulaire des Grandes Orgues de St. Sulpice; Daniel Roth, he too a "Titulaire" at St. Sulpice; Klemens Schnorr, professor of organ music at the State Music College in Munich (Staatliche Musikhochschule) and organ expert for the archdiocese of Munich-Freising; the intonators of the organ builders Detlef Kleuker and G. F. Steinmeyer; as well as Mr. Furtwaengler, the director for pipe building for the organ construction company.

The commission agreed on the conception and execution of the organ: it should give the Tonhalle a large instrument able to do justice to the entire organ literature rather than to any one-sided musical direction. At the same time, the new instrument was to reflect its own individual style. Some models were the modern concert organs that in years past had been installed in the United States and Japan, in Munich, Frankfurt, and at the Gewandhaus in Leipzig.

It was not a disadvantage to the planned acquisition, which had some reservations attached, that Coignet and Schnorr, who had not known each other beforehand, visited Zurich independently and closely examined the old organ. Poor condition and weak acoustics aside, Coignet, who had great respect for the workmanship that had gone into the instrument, reached the conclusion that the pipes had been laid too closely together. He found that it must have been conceived for a "nun's chapel."

Schnorr's verdict was no different. The Munich expert pointed out that the weak tone and lack of functional reliability as well as the missing casing (no covering, no back wall) would make renovation futile and acquisition of a new organ mandatory. His conclusion was that it was unfit as a solo instrument. In subsequent discussions, Schnorr took the trouble to dispassionately rebut the objections of his opponents.

As a methodically trained engineer, Gerber had made sure that Coignet and Schnorr looked at the organ independently of one another. The expert opinion and the subsequent acquisition were carried out with engineering precision. For his part, Cederic Guhl had asked Professor Raeto Tschupp, the canton Zurich's music expert, for an opinion. In his letter, he cited concrete examples as to why the instrument could not meet today's musical requirements. If the Tonhalle wanted to perform Janacek's M'sa Glagolskaja, Hermann Suter's Le Laudi, Rossini's Petite Messe Solennelle, Saint-Saëns' Third Symphony, or Guenther Bialas' Introitus-Exodus, purchase of a new organ was unavoidable. Professor Tschupp doubted, furthermore, that a renovation would be successful. The organ had already been enlarged twice without the desired results. Why? Because the 1927 expansion had destroyed the unity between the organ prospect and the organ works and left them divided into two parts. Another renovation would not remove that source of trouble.

Why the project provoked such bitter, and often public, opposition — it lasted far beyond the instrument's inauguration — remains a mystery. It's possible that not involving more local experts was a tactical error. Certainly many people resented Jean Guillou. The inauguration review in the Neue Zuercher Zeitung suggests that not everybody approved of the Tonhalle's ambition to have the new instrument raise its public image. But some simply had an emotional attachment to the old organ as a familiar piece of the Tonhalle's interior decor.

The Tonhalle's general meeting on January 28, 1986, erupted into harsh polemics against Gerber's organ project. Subsequently, I tried to defuse the situation by suggesting an audio test. The Tonhalle board and other interested parties flew to Brussels to listen to a Jean Guillou organ concert. We underwent a second such "listening test" in the church of Notre Dames de Grâce in Paris, and at the end of August 1986 we flew there to hear it.

Not all of Zurich had conspired against the great organist. At least Hans Erismann was an unhampered admirer of his art and defended it without reservation. Practitioners of church music, however, showed no understanding.

What finally brought some movement into the stalled situation was the news that asbestos dust had been found on the old organ. Pierre Arnold ordered the organ's immediate dismantling, with special emphasis placed on doing so without any accumulation of dust. To what extent this asbestos alarm was a false alarm, as a bitter opponent contended, while at the same time denying that Arnold and Gerber had any competency in the acquisition, is beyond my knowledge.

After the unanimous vote of the Tonhalle board in July 1986, another uproar occurred during the general meeting of the Tonhalle in January 1987. It seemed as if the new organ threatened the downfall of all music. Until the bitter end, opponents would not believe that the organ's supporters were also respected experts.

The hopes I articulated in my speech at the inauguration of the new organ on January 11, 1988 — that the sound of the new instrument would pacify forever the troubled world of our organ — were not fulfilled. It remains a fact, however, that Gerber, Arnold, and not least Guhl, as co-coordinator and moderator of the decision-making process, had made a valuable contribution to Zurich's cultural life. But the bitter aftertaste of a subjective and often wounding discussion remains. Little thanks was heard for the donation of the organ to the general public and for Pierre Arnold's prudent fundraising, nor for the enormous commitment of Gerber, who, I can only repeat, made a substantial material contribution to the organ.

Even if today the new organ is not played very often — it would be worth noting just how many organ concerts are performed outside churches — practical hurdles should bear some of the blame, for example, lack of hall availability during the season when one concert follows another. Also, the organ's technical complexity must be considered. It is equipped with two consoles, can be used mechanically and electronically, and, on top of all that, can be programmed. Organists have to practice rigorously before they can play it. The remaining obstacle: the operating company demands rent for rehearsal time.

Today, even well-meaning voices say the organ is too loud. But it was meant to be louder than the old organ that was destined for a "nun's chapel." I can't decide if it is too loud. Jean Guillou and Alfred Gerber were more than satisfied with the work they did. In addition to holding master classes with the organ, Guillou gave several concerts and cut records of organ recitals playing the instrument. I can only invite everyone to obtain the recordings of Guillou concerts in the Tonhalle and to form their own opinions.

The old organ was taken apart piece by piece and carefully stored before it was reinstalled in Zurich's Neumuenster Church. This is not to insinuate that the Neumuenster Church is, to use Jean-Louis Coignet's phrase, a "nun's chapel."

40

Festival Weeks (1987–99)

Radetzky in a cloud of sound

Historically, the Tonhalle Festival Weeks were founded because musicians only had seasonal contracts. They expired every year in May. Thanks to the festival, they could add a month to their engagements. The great conductors, usually only available in the summer, assured the public's interest. At the conclusion and high point of the season, the greats like Sir John Barbirolli, Karl Boehm, Josef Krips, Wolfgang Sawallisch, Carl Schurich, Erich Leinsdorf, and Bernhard Haitink swung the baton in the Tonhalle. In 1951, when Isaac Stern first played the June Festival Weeks, Herbert von Karajan arrived with the Vienna Symphony; Hans Rosbaud, Eugene Ormandy, and Rafael Kubelik conducted the Tonhalle Orchestra. The June festivals, therefore, were the climax of the season. Today in the age of jet-setting conductors, the Tonhalle spoils its customers during the season with great names. Not many other possibilities were left to hype the June weeks.

The idea to turn these June festivals into a city event drawing in the Kunsthaus and the opera came from Thomas Wagner. Supported by his active department of culture, he gave the festivals specific themes. Wagner's first June Festival Weeks, held in 1986, had the motto of "Music from England." The incentive was the exhibit in Zurich of the Fitzwilliam collection.

In 1987, the festival was devoted to the French Romantics, with a major Delacroix exhibit in the Kunsthaus as top billing and pièce de résistance. Musically a great deal was offered. In addition to Berlioz's *Grande Messe des Morts* for double orchestra and three choirs in the indoor stadium, the Tonhalle Orchestra under Erich Leinsdorf played as a special curiosity *Harold in Italy* (intellectually an interesting connection to the previous year's program).

For the rest, I remember the vanilla ice cream with warm perfumed cherries for the finale of the opening dinner. It was a difficult exercise for the pastry chef, given almost a thousand people, who instead of a stiff festive meal would surely have preferred to eat a piece of Cervelat, Switzerland's favorite sausage, between two slices of bread. I certainly would have been happier had things been simpler.

Full of good intentions, Thomas Wagner enveloped the lower basin of the lake in a "cloud of sound." Ten floating loudspeaker stations (with a total output of 100,000 watts) broadcast Berlioz's *Symphonie Phantastique* from the Tonhalle with Hiroshi Wakasugi conducting. It cost SFr 150,000 ($100,000) — not cheap, but good promotion for classical music.

The audience crowded the shore of the bay and the honored guests cruised on a ship through the cloud of sound. At some point it started to drizzle, which was just the beginning of a less than festive atmosphere. Political radicals used the cloud of sound for an appeal to free the king of Swiss jail breakers, Walter Stuerm. Just before that, Johann Strauss the Elder's *Radetzky March* faded in, which didn't do anything to uplift the musical experience of that black and rainy night. In any event, wind, waves, the ship, and the turmoil around François Mitterrand, who was invited to inaugurate the festival, overwhelmed the music. The entire happening embarrassed the organizers, especially since they had been warned but had proclaimed with great conviction that disturbances would be impossible.

Looking back, the unwanted intervention was truly essential to balancing out the evening — and to fully giving it the character of a memorable event. I now see the intervention as a real counterpoint and therefore, viewed in emotional terms, the ultimate climax of the evening, which otherwise would have been a touch too solemn.

Some invectives about his right-wing friends in Vichy, France, were tossed at François Mitterrand after his death. But for all that, we should not forget his ties to Switzerland. They allowed him to accept such ceremonial duties as the Inauguration officielle du Festival International de Zurich and to open the June festival. His brilliant dinner speech at the Dolder overtaxed me somewhat, just as Jean-Pascal Delamuraz's speeches, for me, always came down to feeling like an exam. With all the affection I have for French culture, without which large parts of Switzerland would remain incomprehensible, intellectual subtleties and allusions elude me, due to lack of practice.

Because in the dense program small delays accumulated, and since the speeches had lasted longer than planned, the gathering rushed to the ship without waiting for dessert (it was donated to a children's home). But that did not end the rush for our star guest. Our budget did not allow France's president to spend the night in Zurich. It would simply have been too expensive. Instead, the police, blue lights flashing, drove him to the airport so that he would not become a victim of the ban on nighttime flying.

On this occasion I also learned that in accordance with diplomatic regulations, Zurich couldn't greet a foreign head of state; that is left for Berne. Nor was it a *visite présidentielle*, which is why the president was received in Zurich by the French ambassador to Switzerland, the chief of protocol at the foreign office, as well as cantonal and city scribes. Federal Councilor Pierre Aubert, the

Swiss foreign minister at the time, was allowed to meet Mitterrand at the Muraltengut estate. That set off a dispute about costs. As I remember it, the Foreign Office finally agreed to pay for the cigars — surely the biggest item on the dinner bill.

It was all a bit much. The artistic aspect had been pushed too far in the background by the festival, at least for the taste of the music-loving public. With all due respect for French romanticism, the indoor stadium, cloud of sound, and shipboard tour were perhaps not exactly what a festival public had dreamed about.

After the 1988 festival, which, on the occasion of the fiftieth anniversary of the theater society, was held under the theme "Escape to Zurich" (many prominent German actors found refuge from Hitler in the Zurich theater), we experienced another musical high point: "Russian and Soviet Culture" as a theme brought the Leningrad (today St. Petersburg) Symphony, the Kirov Opera, and the Bolshoi Ballet to the Limmat. Even though in the end Gorbachev did not come, it remained a successful festival. It was one more musical climax.

The last years of the old festival, in part, steered far away from music. The theme in 1990 was "The Hundredth Anniversary of Gottfried Keller's death"; in 1991, "James Joyce and John Cage," in honor of the fiftieth anniversary of the writer, who is buried in Zurich; in 1992, "Brazil," on the occasion of the discovery of America five hundred years ago; and in 1993, "Magic Japan."

It doesn't take much imagination to realize that the old June Festival Weeks would die one day from their exaggerated perfection. To start planning with the Kunsthaus instead of the opera, which always has the highest costs and the longest lead time, was certainly a mistake.

It is only logical that the festival would be reborn in simpler form thanks to Alexander Pereira. Pereira, undoubtedly an important catalyst for Zurich's musical life, went back to the old pre-Wagner festivals, which, after all, could look back on a century-long tradition.

So in 1997 we launched the Zurich Festival without any communal participation and at the same time more modestly — Tonhalle, Opera, and the theater agreed (or not, as the case may be) to pick something appropriate out of their repertories, and, given the means available, make performances possible in interesting places. We got to the point with that concept, so that by 2002, when I retired as chairman from the festival committee and handed the baton to Peter Weibel — the chartered accountant and former CEO of Pricewaterhouse Switzerland who has joined the board of Credit Suisse — we managed to squeeze out a small profit for the first time. The Shostakovich series found an unexpectedly large audience.

41

ANTI-SEMITISM (1943-2002)

Nothing learned and nothing forgotten

In 1983, when Georg Solti told me that he would conduct the *Ring* at Bayreuth I asked him, in all seriousness, how as a Jew he could go to Bayreuth to conduct Wagner, the vehement anti-Semite. Solti's reply was short and to the point: "You don't understand anything about music." That could be, but I hadn't asked him about music. It irritated me that a star conductor would pay the Nazi Bayreuth, of all places, the honor of his appearance, a place where Adolf Hitler had flirted with Winifred Wagner. Didn't he feel embarrassed? In 1945, when he had gone to Munich, he could still cite the mitigating circumstance that he had taken advantage of a unique chance, as a beginner, to succeed Clemens Krauss and to launch a great career. And now?

As the child of a secular home I cannot claim to have developed a strong Jewish identity. My father led a rigorous scientific life. His ethical ideal was humanism. We didn't celebrate Jewish holidays at home. Our parents put up a large tree at Christmas and we celebrated Christian holidays.

So how does somebody become a Jew? Surely only through education and circumstances. Georg Solti's Jewish roots, for example, were irrelevant. He was a secular spirit who lived for his reputation and had no ties to Israel. All in all, Solti didn't see himself as a Jew, but more as a Hungarian, and he asked to be buried in Budapest.

Isaac Stern's Jewish roots, on the other hand, were an important part of his identity. He came from an enlightened home of Russian provenance and found entrance to Judaism through his wife. For Vera Stern, a native of Lithuania, the terrors she had suffered during the Second World War and her experience of having found a homeland in Israel formed her strong Jewish identity. "American Jews are more Jewish than European Jews," a friend of mine once remarked.

Cardinal Jean-Marie Lustiger, the archbishop emeritus of Paris, is another example of circumstance and education. A child of Jewish parents he grew up under the care of the Catholic Church. But baptism is not a reliable contributor of identity. One of my sister's grandsons was outraged that his parents had him baptized.

I experienced the reality of social anti-Semitism firsthand in the United States. A child from a Jewish home had no chance of being accepted at certain universities; moreover, vacation hotels that didn't want to accept Jewish guests sent their correspondence on stationery with the preprinted words "Church around the corner."

Social organizations shielded themselves just as much. In New York, the Metropolitan Club on Fifth Avenue, whose creation was J. P. Morgan's answer to the Union Club blackballing one of his friends, did not accept Jewish members until New York's financial crisis in the mid-seventies. The University Club, founded in 1865 and located on the corner of Fifth Avenue and 54th Street, was no different, although I often had lunch there — fortunately they didn't demand a certificate of baptism for a table. Neither did the New York Athletic Club, so rich in tradition and used for so many purposes.

The Jewish answer to the Union Club, founded in 1836 and correspondingly exclusive, was the Harmonie Club, launched in 1852 across the street from the Sherry Netherland. Until the end of the Second World War, it was the exclusive preserve of "our crowd," that is, the city's leading German-Jewish families like the Kuhns, Loebs, Lehmans, Goldmans, Warburgs, Sachses, and Schiffs. It only opened up and accepted other ethnic groups after the war. Before 1945, a Sanford Weill with his Polish-Jewish roots wouldn't have had a chance. Weill liked to frequent the Harmonie Club, even though it had the disadvantage of a kosher cuisine. (Discovery of the gastronomic qualities of the Four Seasons redeemed the Citigroup chief from this culinary Diaspora.)

The feudal Century Country Club, where I learned how to play tennis, is the answer to the anti-Semitic country clubs like Piping Rock on Long Island or the Westchester Country Club, where my son was a guest one summer. Since all clubs badly need money these days, club anti-Semitism is in sharp decline. Social pressure has also helped.

In the banking world, anti-Semitism is a privilege of commercial banks. It is only a slight exaggeration to claim that someone with a Jewish background won't advance far beyond chief runner in a merchant bank. Sandy Weill is the best example. The retired Citigroup chief applied for a job at more than thirty firms before Bear Stearns graciously hired him as a messenger delivering paperwork and stock certificates between brokerages. He won his Citigroup position through a series of clever mergers.

At investment banks, however, anti-Semitism is not an issue. Most houses have Jewish roots. I need only cite Paribas (the Bischoffheim-Bamberger family), Kuhn-Loeb, Warburg, Lazard Frères, or Salomon Brothers. Merrill Lynch, Harriman-Ripley, First Boston, Dillon Read, and Morgan Stanley are noteworthy exceptions. The first Jewish partners were accepted only in the sixties. Today, many offspring of Jewish homes work in those institutions, and it is no different at JP Morgan. On the other hand, the Jewish investment banks began accepting non-Jewish partners in the twenties. They would eat lunch together but never dinner.

James Wolfensohn's career at J. Henry Schroder in London is a classic example. He saw no chance of becoming chairman. It should be of some solace to him that today J. Henry Schroder is but a shadow of its former greatness, while he, as a Salomon partner in New York, caused a sensation with the Chrysler rescue and crowned his career with the presidency of the World Bank.

Switzerland practices a more subcutaneous anti-Semitism. My dentist asked me quite innocently, "In which guild are you?" (Guilds, derived from medieval corporations, play an important role in Zurich's social life.) He had no idea that Zurichers from Jewish homes are not welcome in the guilds. It's true, though, that the Baer families are members of the Golf and Country Club Zumikon.

During the dormant accounts affair, the Constaffel Society, one of Zurich's leading guilds, invited me to speak at the dinner held to celebrate the Sechselaeuten festival. Normally I would never have accepted that invitation. However, in view of the debate about the dormant accounts, I agreed but declined to march in the parade. I am reluctant putting myself on show — with flowers in the bargain.

The head of Constaffel who issued the invitation obviously had given the problem some thought, but his successor, who took office before I was to deliver my remarks, suffered the agonies of the damned at the idea that I might speak on the subject that had prompted his predecessor to ask me, and insisted that I agree to say nothing about the dormant accounts. So I talked about Worms on the Rhine, my mother's hometown, and the guilds. They are the two connecting links between Worms and Zurich.

Swiss naturalization practices were often flagrant. That the trustees at the Swiss Federal Institute of Technology (ETH) called Wolfgang Pauli, the Nobel Prize-winning physicist, an "unassimilated Eastern Jew" and twice refused him naturalization was as unnecessary as the repeated refusal to naturalize the musicians Alexander and Irma Schaichet.

The borders between anti-Semitism and social demarcation are very fluid. Chaim Weizmann, for example, liked to emphasize the distance between him and those who couldn't follow the sequence of a dinner menu or were otherwise socially challenged. Surely that didn't make him into a Jewish "anti-Semite" but simply stamped him as a product of the upper classes, which in England — to follow Nancy Mitford's dictum — divides into "U and non-U."

In Switzerland too, German Jews, including those from Alsace, walled themselves off from the Eastern Jews. Ever since Hannah Arendt pointed to the coresponsibility of Jewish councils in Nazi deportations in her book *Eichmann in Jerusalem*, we know that this distancing is not a Swiss specialty. Today, most of this is history, but the thought of the apathy and indifference of Jewish (and Christian) Swiss leaves a bitter aftertaste. One example: in 1938, Sidney Dreifuss, the leader of a Jewish refugee organization in St. Gall, helped with what many Swiss still see as the scandalous dismissal of Captain Paul Grueninger, commander of the St. Gall border crossing station, who let three thousand Jews enter Switzerland after the Swiss closed the Austrian frontier in August 1938. Grueninger was arrested, jailed, and died in poverty before he was rehabilitated in the midnineties. The letter of thanks the Jewish leader, Dr. Sali Mayer, wrote to the Swiss government for its exemplary attitude during the war is just as bad. On the other side of that ledger stand the powerful words the editor-in-chief of the *Basler Nachrichten* spoke in the National Assembly in 1942: "Our lifeboat is not overcrowded, it isn't even full. And so long as it is not full, we should accept those for whom we have room. Otherwise we sin against ourselves."

Swiss Jews could surely have done more, but they didn't want to. However, this lack of sympathy went far beyond Switzerland. Nobody in my own environment on the East Coast of the United States cared very much about what happened to the Jews. Supreme Court Justice Felix Frankfurter's reaction to the first reports of mass murders was significant. He refused to acknowledge them.

People helped as much as they could. My uncles in Switzerland went out on a limb to help refugees. Werner wrote a memorandum in which he pointed to the cold and insensitive practice of the National Bank of Switzerland in exchanging American contributions to help refugees at a lower exchange rate. From April 1942 to November 1943, the National Bank refused to exchange dollars that Jewish organizations sent to Swiss refugee aid organizations at any rate of exchange.

Werner — who was never very rooted in his Jewish identity and never visited Palestine but helped out of a purely humanitarian impulse — wrote in a memorandum:

> Substantial sums are being raised in the United States to help refugees living in Switzerland. If these sums are credited to the accounts of the Swiss aid committees, they cannot be used, since Swiss banks are forced to pay the credit in blocked dollars. The current way out is for American organizations to buy so-called free Swiss francs and then pay them to the Swiss organizations as free Swiss francs. Doing so, however, results in the loss of about 25 percent right now. But depending on the fluctuation in the free franc rate of exchange the losses could be substantially higher. The money raised in the United States to help these refugees, therefore, cannot be freely used, i.e., it is reduced by a quarter to a third due to exchange rate losses. But there are other reasons to post the credit in free dollars. The number of refugees is so large that their support has an impact on the total provisioning of the country. And since the whole supply situation is very tight, every extra burden counts double. Normally, Switzerland is dependent to a great extent on supplies from abroad, especially from overseas. These imports are now even more difficult since they need permission from the allies. More-

over, exporters demand payment in gold or convertible foreign currency. . . . Payment in free dollars would mean a moderate improvement in the Swiss supply situation.

The Swiss National Bank's decision in 1997 to contribute $75 million to a special Holocaust fund as a "humanitarian gesture" made because "the management of the SNB during the Second World War didn't counter the German Reichsbank critically enough" came pretty late. And the National Bank has retained the 25 percent it pocketed during the war instead of assigning the money to some charitable fund. A professor in Basel, Jacques Picard, discovered that the American Joint Distribution Committee transferred $3 million between 1939 and 1944 (and that after the 25 percent discount).

All in all, it's difficult to differentiate among the leading representatives of the National Bank during the war between legalistically concealed Germanophilia, anti-Semitism, and sheer greed. The Washington conference in 1946 rewarded the Swiss government with a hefty bill.

The learning impact cannot have been all that great. In its *Report on Dormant Accounts of Victims of Nazi Persecution in Swiss Banks*, the Volcker Commission generously concluded that "no evidence of . . . concerted efforts to divert the funds . . . to improper purposes" was found. But what the auditors discovered in individual cases was embarrassing enough.

When it came to thank the pro-Swiss Paul Volcker, who did all the work without pay, the idea was floated that the Swiss cabinet would give a dinner in his honor at the Lohn, the county seat of the government. But the then head of the Swiss foreign office, Bundesrat (Federal Counselor) Professor Dr. Joseph Deiss, managed to say, "All right, but not with the Jewish representatives." The dinner did not take place, and nobody was thanked, although the report was published without the much-feared minority opinion. To which one can only quote Talleyrand's comment about the Bourbon restoration after Napoleon's fall: "Ils n'ont rien appris ne rienoublié" (They have forgotten nothing and learned nothing).

I should note that after the publication of my memoirs in Switzerland, Federal Counselor Deiss phoned me at once to clarify that his remarks, whose accuracy he did not question, were not based on any anti-Semitic motives.

42

Dormant Accounts (1995–2002)

Fit and proper

The history of the dormant accounts is so complicated that I would like to begin this chapter with a general discussion of the background.

With the introduction of the 1935 Bank Act, Switzerland gave the discretionary duties of the banks toward their customers a legal anchor. This banking law obliged employees, in a stricter interpretation of professional secrecy, to maintain absolute discretion about the clients and imposed criminal sanctions on those who violated the law. Ever since then, account holders have been safe from the clutches of German, French, Italian, and other tax authorities who have tried since the 1920s to obtain information about the assets their taxpayers kept in Switzerland. The first were the French tax collectors after they had observed the exodus of French capital in 1925 to escape a threatened tax levy by the center-left coalition under Prime Minister Edouard Herriot.

After introduction of the Bank Act, the especially brutal German authorities, to the extent that they had knowledge or clues, often extorted the return of deposits to the Third Reich. According to estimates, some $50 million flowed back into Germany until 1945.

In 1945, deposits relevant to the balance sheet (accounts without securities) of foreign customers in Switzerland amounted to $300 million. The value of portfolios, and assets stored in vaults, amounted to an estimated $5 billion. How much of this money belonged to Jewish families is impossible to determine, because the banks — at least for reasons of discretionary protection — registered very few identity clues and surely did not record the religious persuasion of account holders.

The finance historian Helen Junz has discovered that, in 1934, Jewish families in Germany disposed of $1.6 billion in liquid assets, a sizable amount of which they were able to transfer to immigration countries. She estimated the liquid assets of Jewish families in Poland, Austria, Hungary, France, and the Netherlands at $1.3 billion. For Poles, Austrians, Hungarians, and the French, Switzerland was the country of choice for bringing wealth to a safe haven. The Dutch tended to prefer the United States.

After the war and the murder of 3.6 million Jews who had lived in Germany, France, Poland, Hungary, and the Netherlands, the legal situation remained unchanged. Directives for dealing with the accounts of the murdered and the missing didn't exist. Some bankers took the initiative in searching for account holders or their heirs. In some cases, heirs made representations of their own, but only in the rarest cases could they provide a valid will.

In 1947, the Swiss Bankers Association (SBA) issued a first invitation to report the assets of presumed Nazi victims without heirs, but the appeal didn't find much resonance. Only a few banks responded. A sum of $120,000 was found. At the same time, however, the Swiss refugee help organization, Schweizerische Fluechtlingshilfe, estimated that dormant assets in Switzerland amounted to $10 million to $12 million.

In a financial agreement with Poland reached on June 25, 1949, Switzerland agreed to transfer the dormant assets of Polish citizens in Switzerland to the Polish National Bank. In 1950, the

Swiss made the same deal with Hungary. A corresponding agreement with Romania was signed on August 3, 1951. In determining the amount of these assets, the government relied on data the banks provided. No legal reporting requirement was enacted.

On September 20, 1962, however, Parliament passed a reporting resolution. It required banks and other asset managers to list accounts whose owners had not made themselves known since May 9, 1945 (the day of Germany's unconditional surrender) and about whom one knew or assumed that they had become "victims of racist, religious, or political persecution." This very precise, but not very factual, limitation prevented inclusion of all accounts held by Nazi victims. At the same time, heirs had to come forward themselves. Banks and asset managers did not go looking for heirs, in deference to the Bank Secrecy Act. To the extent that they lived in the communist-governed countries of Eastern Europe, this practice undoubtedly was justified.

On the other hand, this very restrictive information policy led to friction. With the revitalization of the World Jewish Congress (WJC) after the election of Edgar Bronfman as president and the appointment of Israel Singer as secretary-general, the descendants of Nazi victims found up until then no support in their search for assets still in Switzerland.

In 1993, the WJC acquired documentation — through the London journalist Lawrence Lever — regarding the situation (it was written by Jacques Picard) and complained to the Swiss Bankers Association (SBA). At the same time, the WJC launched a media campaign.

The WJC and the SBA agreed on the formation of the Volcker Commission — which triggered sweeping changes in bank policies — and submitted its final report in December 1999.

Independently, a class action suit was filed in New York in 1996 against the major Swiss banks. On August 12, 1998, the plaintiffs and the defendants (Credit Suisse and UBS) reached a settlement for the payment of $1.25 billion to satisfy all claims. On July 26, 2000, Edward Korman, chief justice of the U.S. District Court for the Eastern District of New York, approved the settlement, and in a decision issued on December 8 appointed Paul Volcker and Michael Bradfield as "special masters" for the "claims resolution process for deposited assets." In that capacity the two men organized the work of the Claims Resolution Tribunal (CRT) for Dormant Accounts in Switzerland, which Judge Korman had set up. In 2001 and 2005, the CRT published the names of possible holders of accounts in Switzerland and examined all submitted claims. In all, twelve thousand people responded by reporting their claims to the CRT. By September 2005, some $269 million was paid to 1,993 persons.

On December 13, 1996, the Swiss Parliament created an Independent Commission of Experts under the leadership of Professor François Bergier to examine Swiss relations with Hitler Germany. In 2001 it submitted its findings in eighteen thick volumes and issued a final report in March 2002. So much for the background.

History caught up with me at an advanced age. My election to the board of the SBA in the autumn of 1990 and the assignment to the executive committee in 1991 were, given my age, in no way a matter of course. But I liked the idea. The executive committee has a certain prestige. You are invited to consult with the Federal Council (the Swiss Executive Branch) as well as with the Swiss National Bank.

The committee handles the business of the association and meets every three months in the morning in Zurich. The meetings of the board, from which committee members are chosen, take place semiannually in Berne in the meeting rooms of the Grande Société. My first major experience on the committee was the drama caused by the SLT-Thun (the Thun Savings & Loan). The somewhat annoyed large banks, given the Thun Savings & Loan's aggressive credit policy, had decided to set a warning example and let the heavily indebted bank collapse.

I felt quite uncomfortable about the idea of sending a bank into bankruptcy out of the blue, and I still claim today that nobody really thought this decision through and what the consequences might be. The clusters of outraged customers outside the bank branches who wanted their money back made for unexpected photographs from Switzerland, which the foreign press published with glee. And the employees, whose salaries were paid into a savings and loan account, lost at least a month's pay. At that, the debt distress was not so great that nobody could have helped out. The next day, on the other hand, nobody could draw a check from any savings and loan. The recipient didn't bother to differentiate between, let us say, the Bumpliz S&L or the Thun S&L. Nobody had foreseen such consequences.

Much more dramatic was the matter of the dormant accounts. Despite my almost fifty years of professional experience, I was no better prepared and no more informed about the details than my sometimes much younger colleagues. I frankly admit to having stumbled into the whole thing and to emerge, much to the shock of my family, as a conscious Jew.

As a practitioner, I had never thought very much about possible heirs to these accounts. I had never regarded these dormant accounts — that's all they ever were for the Swiss bankers — as a separate category. A report that the Bank Julius Baer issued in March 1964 about the "investigations according to the federal resolution of December 20, 1962, about assets in Switzerland of racially, religiously or politically persecuted foreigners or stateless persons" stated:

After the Second World War credit balances that have shown no activity over a period of years were transferred to an "heirless assets" account whose balance was credited in January 1963 to a "collective account of diverse creditors." Numerous assets had already been placed in this collective account, which had been put together in the late fifties from accounts without turnover. . . . At the time of the survey in accordance with the cited federal resolution (March 1964), the "collective account of diverse creditors" had about 300 items with a total value of approximately $17,000. Only a very few of these individual items corresponded to the assumption made in the federal resolution; the Swiss Justice Department's reporting office was notified of only 27 cases in the amount of 36,851.75 Swiss francs ($8,774.05). A statistical study issued by the Swiss reporting office published in the press shows that in all of Switzerland only 961 cases worth 9.47 million Swiss francs ($2.254 million) were reported. . . . In the course of this research all heirless portfolios and closed safes were controlled.

That was the situation in our bank. For 270 accounts with a total value of about SFr 40,000, some SFr 150 ($36) per account, the federal resolution didn't specify any reason for delivery to Berne. We had to leave them in-house. Our archive policy changed with Ernst Bieri's arrival, because he was a fabulous organizer. I had insisted that documents from the war years be stored. Bieri routinely destroyed everything that no longer had to be stored, but he did it in such a way that everything could be traced. The bank had set up the collective account so that no fees would have to be paid. In 1982, the entire sum was transferred into the bank's own account but remained clearly documented so that a legal heir could receive the money at any time. The Volcker Commission's auditors paid tribute to what we had done.

The Zurich Cantonal Bank had found a clever solution for its dormant accounts. They offset the accounts as soon as they had remained inactive for a set period of time and transferred the money to charitable institutions in the canton, and they did so, well aware of the risk that they would have to pay out once again should a justified claimant appear. The bank also published this practice in its annual report.

The very fact that the average amounts in the accounts we had were so small for a bank of our size is a sign that the account owners had cleared out all the funds except for a small part. And because my uncles knew most of their customers personally, they also knew whether the Nazi authorities had forced a payment order, and, therefore, they could use technical methods to stop the transactions. I confess with a certain amount of guilt that I never thought much about the problems of account fees and annual account entries.

The idea that heirs and claims existed and that we were obligated to look for them lay, for the longest time after the Second World War, outside anyone's imagination. I can only go back to my experience with the International Refugee Organization (IRO) truck in Kreuzlingen, which had been dispatched on orders of the IRO without even the least thought wasted on possible heirs in Australia or Poland, and further, I can point to the indifference with which my social surroundings on the East Coast of the United States reacted to the annihilation of the Jewish people in Europe. During the war years my generation had never heard of the Holocaust. This "New Testament" concept only found its way into historiography via Hollywood (the Israelis talk of the Shoah). The *Holocaust* miniseries and *Schindler's List* are the two films that helped make the Holocaust a well-known term.

Germany's postwar reconstruction society with its forceful drive for normalcy and for a sane world — depicted in films about forest rangers and the Austrian Empress Elisabeth — was basically no different from the Swiss or the American society. Nobody was interested in the past. Even the victims were absorbed in living and rebuilding. David Ben-Gurion accepted the reparations (the German term *"Wiedergutmachung"* is even worse) he negotiated with Konrad Adenauer under just such conditions. It wasn't a subject anyone discussed in the fifties. I didn't ask Isaac Stern's wife, Vera, about her wartime experiences until a relatively short time ago. It had never occurred to me to ask her earlier. The awareness of the monstrosity of industrially organized annihilation of human beings didn't come until the end of the seventies — with the concentration camp series *Holocaust* starring the lovely Meryl Streep and all those well-nourished inmates. Lack of authentic detail may be irritating, but the impact remained enormous. It seems it is up to Hollywood to write the history in our age of a TV-addicted mass society.

And I had to learn more about my own trade. The first impulse came from a front page story in the *Wall Street Journal* of June 22, 1995, where I found the name "Julius Baer & Co., Bahnhofstrasse, Zurich" in the first paragraph.

It happened during a three-day meeting in a house that Harvard University owned in Aix-les-Bains in France, not far from Geneva. I had picked up the paper out of boredom and because it was the only one available. The *Journal* wrote that the daughters of a Mrs. Moses Blum, deceased in 1987, had stumbled over the address in their mother's last will and testament. They should inform the bank in case of her death. The daughters concluded that their father had transferred money from Germany into a Swiss bank before he had been interned in the Dachau concentration camp in 1938. The story continued: "The family's search for that money quickly came to a rude end, however, here in Zurich. After first demanding a fee of SFr 100 ($76) for the administrative work, the Julius Baer Bank wrote back icily that the bank had no comment. Neither Mr. nor Mrs. Blum appeared to have been clients during the previous ten years, the letter said. 'Under Swiss law, banks are obliged to keep their records for a period of ten years only,' it added, 'and therefore our search cannot go any further.'"

Everyone at the meeting read the story and asked me about it. Numbed after reading it, I grabbed the telephone, dialed the bank's legal division, and asked to see the documents immediately upon my return. "I just happen to have them on my desk," I was told. It turned out that Mr. and Mrs. Blum had indeed opened an account at our house, but hadn't done so until 1954, and the widow had closed the account in 1972. The daughter had inquired about it in 1987 and 1988 and had been given the above-cited information. It really was not about an account that had been opened before the war and that had rested dormant since 1945. When Peter Gumbel, the *Journal* reporter, visited me at the bank on July 6, I documented all the facts of the case in great detail, and on July 10 he published an expanded explanation.

Two things bothered me while reading the *Wall Street Journal* story: first, that a fee had been charged for the search (the SFr 100 was a negligible amount as I would learn later), and second, that the official answer was that the incident had happened more than ten years prior and therefore the bank had no comment. If nothing could be said, for reasons of the Bank Secrecy Act, decency would have demanded pointing to the restrictive information policy instead of demanding a search fee.

Confrontation with a case the bank could clear up without provoking embarrassment had one disadvantage: I missed its inherent explosive power. Nor did I follow the discussions Israel Singer held with the SBA on August 15, 1995. In 1994, the secretary-general of the WJS had read Paul Erdman's historic reconstruction *The Swiss Account* and had begun to research the fate of Holocaust victims' deposits in Switzerland. I never asked him if the story in the *Wall Street Journal* had inspired him, but I could well imagine that it had.

Singer traveled to Berne and, if I remember correctly, the weekly *Weltwoche* reported that he and his entourage were intercepted at the Hotel Bellevue and told they couldn't meet in the SBA offices because that would violate bank secrecy. SBA secretary-general Jean-Paul Chapuis repeatedly cited this as a reason — a grotesque claim.

What was at stake during those discussions? Israel Singer and

his companions from the European Jewish Congress wished for —
as did Rolf Bloch in his capacity as president of the Swiss Federation
of Jewish Communities (SIG) — an all-inclusive settlement that
would take care of all potential claims. The SBA preferred individual solutions. What weighed more heavily, however, was this: representatives of the SBA did not take seriously Singer's insinuation
that lack of cooperation would force them to use the same methods
they applied in the case of Austrian president Kurt Waldheim.
Thomas Maissen, the Swiss professor of history at the University of
Heidelberg, pointed this out in his book *Remembrance Denied.*

Singer followed up that first round of talks with a visit on September 14, 1995, when he flew with Edgar Bronfman, the president
of the WJC, and a sizable delegation to Berne on Bronfman's private jet. Before the reception in the Cercle privé de la Grande Société, the SBA's grail, they had met with Swiss president Kaspar
Villiger, a meeting that Michael Kohn, former president of the SIG,
had hastily arranged (no easy task, since the president's aides didn't
know who Bronfman was and demanded a résumé) and arrived
quite late. At first the president did not want to receive one of the
members of Bronfman's delegation, the grandiloquent Avraham
Burg. Thereupon Burg threatened to raise hell before the assembled
media, and Michael Kohn advised Kaspar Villiger not to force the
issue.

I would doubt that Georg Krayer, the SBA president, was well
advised under the circumstances to hold fast to his dramaturgy, and
in the Salon des Jeux he read a ten-minute welcoming address that
was studded with technical details and to which we had to listen
standing up instead of sitting down at table right away. But most
likely it was not a good idea — given the delegation's delayed arrival and their scheduled 2 p.m. departure — to lay out the SBA
position with everybody standing up and hungry instead of having
them seated. Under these circumstances, even the kosher meal did
not save the meeting.

Looking back, neither the faded charm of the Grand Société nor Bronfman's misspelled name card ("Bronfmann" with two *N*s) provoked the antagonism, nor even the stiff greeting ritual, but it was the fact that the SBA did not understand Bronfman and the WJC. The WJC didn't want to discuss numbers but instead a process of verification. John Authers and Richard Wolffe summarized the results in their book *The Victim's Fortune: Inside the Epic Battle over the Debts of the Holocaust*: "By the time Singer, Bronfman, and their colleagues . . . thought they had agreed on a way forward, the bankers would continue their investigation of dormant accounts under conditions of total secrecy. A joint committee, including Israel Singer, would hire auditors and examine the process. Neither side was to discuss the findings in public until they were complete."

Here was the crux of the whole story. The representatives of the World Jewish Congress and of the Jewish Agency, puzzled by the unsuccessful efforts of survivors to find their deposits in Switzerland, no longer trusted the bankers. Through a London-based freelance journalist, in October 1992 they had ordered an expert opinion from the contemporary historian Jacques Picard that for the first time documented the legal framework and the common bank practices in use since the end of the war.

As Picard remembers it, the issue first went to the ETH's Swiss archives of contemporary history, which, in turn, recommended him. At some point, the WJC showed up, intending to buy the documentation. It had already paid the remuneration. Picard, however, was busy elsewhere, had no exaggerated sense of the value of his work, which he wished to qualify as a preliminary study, deposited ten copies in ten public archives, and returned the money.

The WJC knew, therefore, that the SBA had vehemently opposed the notification clause in the 1962 federal law "about assets in Switzerland belonging to racially, religiously, or politically persecuted foreigners or stateless persons" and had prevailed. Read the expert opinion — I had it translated into German in 1996 — and it becomes clear why the SBA had a credibility problem. It simply hid behind the Bank Secrecy Act and had never wanted to permit legally binding notification of assets. Yet it should have been struck by the fact that dormant accounts in 1947, 1949, and 1956 all totaled under a million Swiss francs ($250,000), while the registered assets in 1963 had reached SFr 9.5 million ($2.3 million). Georg Krayer's words of greeting in the Grande Société — surely prepared by the SBA's secretary general — did not deviate one inch from the attitude followed since 1949, something the well-briefed representatives of the WLC could hardly have missed.

Georg Krayer sensed that the Grande Société meeting had not gone well, especially given the somewhat chaotic end. The mob of reporters outside the door clamored for comment. For my part, I exchanged a few words with Israel Singer, who added at the end, "Come and see me in New York." For me, that was the key to what happened next.

Since Krayer was fully occupied with managing the Basel-based Sarasin bank, I suggested — supported by former Swiss ambassador to Washington, the late Edouard Brunner — that he find a lead lawyer to carry some of the burden. In the early sixties, the Federation of the Swiss Watch Industry — since 1954 confronted with antitrust accusations of involvement with organized crime — named Abe Fortas (who helped Lyndon Johnson legally seal his 1948 Senate election and whom LBJ appointed to the Supreme Court) as its lead lawyer. But Krayer could not warm up to the idea because it would have meant for him — and for his secretariat, which exercised great influence — a loss of power, and certainly a loss of face. With hindsight, this was probably the decisive mistake that blocked resolving the whole affair quickly and with manageable costs. So instead of strong leadership, we experienced an unending chain of errors, publicity disasters, and other PR fiascoes.

Finally, stinginess should not be underestimated as a motive.

The SBA's legal representative in the United States was an attorney with the distinguished Washington law firm of Wilmer, Cutler & Pickering who was, however, not a partner. I still find it incomprehensible that the SBA would allow itself to be represented by a non-partner only to save a few Swiss francs. The suggestion to appoint a lead lawyer is as well documented as the discussion in the SBA committee about account search fees. I tried to explain that very few Holocaust survivors or heirs of the victims had ever seen a SFr 100 banknote. My colleagues argued against my position with frightening lack of feeling. The Union Bank of Switzerland's (UBS's) Robert Studer and other representatives of the large banks vehemently demanded a search fee of at least SFr 1,000 ($760). Their argument: if we didn't ask for at least SFr 1,000, we would receive too many applications. In some cases, as much as SFr 5,000 ($3,800) was demanded. With the exception of the SBA's secretary-general, Jean-Paul Chapuis, and his deputy, Heinrich Schneider, who urged that relatives and heirs of Nazi victims needn't pay for such searches, everybody wanted to adhere to normal business practices. Should someone not know the name of the bank, fees would multiply on a per bank basis — thus UBS charged SFr 250 for a named business address, 900 for all branches in the canton Zurich, and 2,000 ($1,520) for a Swiss-wide search. And the question arose: Where should we begin?

During a TV interview, I had the idea of using the banks' ombudsman as a central clearinghouse. But unhappily, Hanspeter Haeni, the ombudsman, made the headlines because the search forms he used asked for an applicant's Christian name (the British version) instead of the American "first name." In his defense, it should be noted that the form had passed the inspection of Jewish circles without challenge and that the terminology had not provoked a collective uproar among the non-Christian minority in Britain. But in our case, the waves of indignation ran high. Once more, no antenna for the nuance.

During his repeated trips to Switzerland during the second half of 1995, Singer had the impression that the SBA didn't take him seriously — he wasn't even allowed to enter their offices — and never considered a joint panel to conduct a comprehensive examination; in other words, they never thought about any concerted action. The WJC secretary-general persuaded Bronfman to arrange a meeting with Senator Alfonso D'Amato, the chairman of the U.S. Senate Banking Committee. D'Amato wasn't Bronfman's natural ally, but the senator had a large Jewish constituency in New York and immediately sensed the explosive power of the issue; Singer succeeded in removing Bronfman's aesthetic objections. In this early phase, both were fair enough to await the outcome of the SBA's investigation.

I cannot stress enough that the WJC was not out to expose Switzerland on the pillory but was only interested in clearing up the question of the dormant accounts through a provable method. Therefore, Singer must have thought it a gross violation of trust that the SBA unilaterally announced the results of their inquiry at its semiannual press conference at the Savoy in Zurich on February 7, 1996, and that it was done in such desultory fashion. Thus Singer learned from the morning news that 775 accounts worth SFr 38.7 million ($33 million) had been found.

I was surprised and angered by the news. It was an affront even to SBA's executive committee. Moreover, I felt intuitively that this maneuver would not work out well. The representatives of the SBA could not claim political naiveté or the self-immunizing effect of having "meant well," since, at the same time, they had published results of a public opinion survey they had commissioned showing they had the support of the Swiss people. And they imagined that was enough to save them.

To believe that a public opinion poll would satisfy a man like Singer, a haughty millionaire like Bronfman, and the SJA was, to cite Talleyrand, "pire qu'un crime, une faute" (worse than a crime, a mistake). "You can't deal with a billionaire" is an experience I share with James D. Robinson. (He reached this conclusion in dealing with the murdered Lebanese billionaire Edmond Safra, who, for a time, was his vice president at Amexco.) It is difficult to understand how anybody faced with this track record could assume the casual admission that almost SFr 40 million ($34 million), having been found, was enough to protect them, and, for the rest, categorically block any cooperation or permit examination of the relevant documents.

It was as if the discussions in the Grande Société had never taken place. The large banks simply continued the political line they had developed in the fifties in a half conspiracy to downplay the whole thing and dismiss irksome questions with legalistic tricks. These decisions were made by the legal divisions of the large banks and by the SBA secretariat, a much lower level than top management, which had no idea of what game was being played, not then, and not since 1947. The amounts were simply too small. The lawyers, on the other hand, never went beyond a limited legal perspective.

Singer saw his suspicions confirmed, issued a sharply worded statement in Bronfman's name, and set his machine in motion. Senator D'Amato scheduled hearings for April 23, 1996, and Elan Steinberg, Singer's colleague in the WJC, supplied the media with material about Switzerland's financial relations with Germany during the Second World War. For American readers, who generally didn't know much about this chapter of contemporary history, most of the information was new and the impact was devastating.

Promptly, a dumbfounded Swiss ambassador in Washington, Carlo Jagmetti, asked me what was going on. My counter-question, "Don't you know Jacques Picard's expert opinion?" "No," he answered. "Then I'll send you a copy," I said.

For the time being, sending the report ended my active role in this drama. The upcoming annual general meeting of the bank in

May 1996 would complete my professional responsibilities. I was already focused on my farewell seminar at New York University. In connection with my retirement, the board of Julius Baer was sponsoring a four-day financial seminar at NYU's Stern School.

But Kurt Hauri, the president of the Swiss Federal Banking Commission, had a different idea about my immediate future. In February 1996, after a meeting of the SBA board, he invited me to come by his office. He was worried that it had taken outside pressure to find the 775 dormant accounts and the SFr 38.7 million ($33 million). From the bank commission's point of view, the suddenly emerged accounts posed a fundamental question of what was "fit and proper" — in other words a guarantee of impeccable management. Obviously, the banks had not operated in a fit and proper manner to date; otherwise, they couldn't suddenly have found the SFr 38.7 million. More embarrassing was the fact that this sum was a multiple of the 9.47 million established in 1963 and could therefore only increase the suspicion that even the 38.7 million was not the last word.

For the banking commissioner, the audit of the dormant accounts was evidence to be used in judging the satisfactory management according to article 3, paragraph 2, letter (c) of the banking law. In my testimony on April 26, 1996, at the D'Amato hearing, I was able to point to just that. Strangely enough, the question of "fit and proper" would later disappear in the general confusion, even though it was the concept that had persuaded us to take the D'Amato hearings seriously — perhaps because of the cantonal banks, which, thanks to a special law, were until recently exempt from the audit requirement. (But many of the dormant accounts turned up precisely in those banks.)

So much for the general part of the story. Trying to straighten out the details and to represent the Swiss banks at the D'Amato hearings would prove more difficult. In February 1996, I first called

Ernest Japhet, the long-time chairman of Bank Leumi le-Israel, and asked him how to stop the anti-Swiss campaign. At the time, Japhet was already living in New York. In Israel, he, like all the heads of major banks, had been condemned for illegal support of share prices. Japhet told me only one man could stop the anti-Swiss campaign: Curtis Hoxter.

Hoxter, who was born in Frankfurt and had emigrated in time, runs a PR agency on Lexington Avenue. I knew his name. He had repeatedly tried to offer his services to our bank. More importantly, he had Israel Singer's confidence, since during the Waldheim affair he had been the informal contact between Austrian chancellor Franz Vranitzky, Singer, and the WJA.

As I was planning my trip for the seminar at the Stern School in March 1996, I determined that I would have two free days before flying with Delta to Nice/Gassin. So I called Georg Krayer and asked him if I could do something for him, perhaps talk to Singer. The chief of the SBA said spontaneously, "A good idea. Do it. I still haven't received an answer to my letter."

The SBA had realized its colossal error. On March 18, 1996, it had faxed Bronfman an explanatory letter apologizing and asking for an early meeting with Krayer in order to reestablish mutual trust for future cooperation. It was not a great success, since the letter was written in German. I had offered to write the note and deliver it personally, but the SBA had insisted on doing it themselves. Bronfman allegedly tossed the fax into a wastepaper basket since he wasn't able to understand the language of Goethe.

Encouraged by Krayer, I arranged a meeting with Singer through Hoxter. The three of us (Singer, Hoxter, and me) met for afternoon tea at the Omni Berkshire Hotel. The atmosphere was pleasurable, and the only thing Singer said about the letter, which had clearly made the rounds (before being tossed), was, "I wouldn't have answered it either." It took me two evenings with Singer, the brainy lawyer-rabbi, to hammer out the fundamentals of how we would proceed, which we laid out in a memorandum. I received strong support from Heinrich Schneider, the SBA deputy secretary-general, who always faxed me back immediately.

What had we put down on paper in New York? We needed an independent commission made up of leading personalities, with the SBA nominating one half and the World Jewish Restitution Organization the other half. This committee would hire auditing firms to carry out the examination and, to the extent necessary, bring in other outside experts. The auditing firms would develop their own methodologies in order to identify the accounts of the Holocaust victims, and the commission would make sure that the auditing firms and the bank auditors would examine the banks in line with the agreed-upon procedures.

In conclusion, the commission would draft a report and publish its findings. These ideas were sketched out in a memorandum dated April 9, 1996, and were the beginnings of the later Volcker Commission, which, some people in Zurich would claim, was the only substantial thing I'd ever done in my life.

Unlike the ombudsman of the banks or the two representatives of the SBA, I always got along well with Singer. Not a trace of arrogance; on the contrary, a very winning and understanding personality. He would just as soon have reached an agreement based on that memorandum but had to consider the interests of the freshly mobilized Senator D'Amato and that militant blusterer in his own ranks, Avraham Burg. He handled the details very cleverly, insisting that the memorandum be kept secret. "Otherwise Senator D'Amato will cancel the hearings," he said. I had nothing against the D'Amato hearings. Internationally it was the best platform for the banks to reestablish the issue's correct proportions — that is if one had agreed to appear before a foreign panel at all.

Israel Singer is a short man with gray hair who holds a political science degree and is an ordained rabbi. He was born of Austrian parents, grew up in Brooklyn, and is married to a Bernese woman named Evelyne. At the time, he was about fifty years old and had made his money in the construction business, a rough trade. Before his election as secretary-general of the WJC, he had been a professor. He had made his reputation through the campaign he waged against Austrian President and former UN Secretary-General Kurt Waldheim. Verbal, worldly, always ready to exchange jokes, even if I called him at midnight, he wears well-tailored suits and combines Jewish observance with professional savoir faire and savoir vivre — except for the kosher Pepsi-Cola he drinks with all his meals. In New York we often ate in a kosher Chinese restaurant. Once, I arrived early and would have liked to order, but the cook didn't dare go near the stove until Singer had koshered the kitchen.

The project of an independent commission gave me some protection against Senator D'Amato's bank hearings scheduled for April 26, 1996. Daniel K. Mayer, the son-in-law of my late friend Herb Silverman and a senior partner in the law firm of Wilmer, Cutler & Pickering, which represented the SBA before the Senate Committee on Banking, Housing and Urban Affairs, handled the preparations. I had to tell the SBA in no uncertain terms that if need be, I would pay for the lawyer myself but would refuse to appear with the SBA's lawyer. That could be seen as snobbism on my part, but there are limits to saving money. In such situations, it is reassuring to have a heavyweight on your side — one who is also good-looking and in full control of the situation.

On the evening before the hearings, we submitted in writing a hundred-page-long answer to the questions we were given in mid-March. In my testimony, I condensed the answer to a single reply to this question: What did the SBA intend to do to clarify the dormant accounts? On the evening before the hearings, we all stayed at the Four Seasons Hotel in Washington. I would have liked to talk to Bronfman, but he had scheduled a meeting at the White House to make sure of the president's support. Instead, I discovered Curtis Hoxter in the bar and asked him about Singer's whereabouts. Hoxter went to look for him and came back with the news that Singer couldn't afford to be seen with me; otherwise Senator D'Amato would become suspicious and cancel the hearings. Singer's goal was clear: he wanted to persuade the public that agreement was the result of the hearing and not of any Swiss initiative. However, once the hearing was behind us, we all ate lunch together at the Four Seasons.

I didn't feel too comfortable at the hearings. The gallery was full, but the rostrum on which the committee sat was pretty empty with only D'Amato and California Senator Barbara Boxer and their assistants and lawyers present. Of course I missed what the TV cameras captured. For the most part, I talked to Senator D'Amato, who clearly was not anxious to grill me and regularly pushed aside the notes his assistants put before him. Occasionally, Barbara Boxer intervened, but since her questions concerned Sweden and I didn't realize at first that she had confused Sweden with Switzerland, I lost my train of thought.

Stuart Eizenstat spoke before I did, and so did the now famous Greta Beer, whose mother had tried without success to discover the accounts of her late husband in Switzerland. At the end of my testimony, I invited Greta Beer to come to Switzerland as my personal guest in order to help her put things in order. I got the idea while greeting her. We shook hands and, out of pure friendship, I added my left hand to cover her right. The spontaneous invitation shook the otherwise very loquacious senator, who called me "a very incisive person." He summed up the gesture the way it had been meant, "as an important gesture of goodwill."

Jean-Paul Chapuis and Heinrich Schneider, the two executive heads of the SBA, had accompanied me to Washington as chaperons. But during the two-day preparatory drill for the hearing conducted by the attorneys of Wilmer, Cutler & Pickering, it turned out that both of them had only a very rudimentary knowledge of Shakespeare's language. That didn't make our labors any easier.

On the other hand, and much more important, the large banks signaled their support. I did not want to testify only on behalf of the SBA, but wished to have the major banks behind me. At six in the morning (Washington time), before the hearing, I held a conference call with Robert Studer (Union Bank of Switzerland), Georges Streichenberg (Swiss Bank Corporation), and Robert Jeker (Credit Suisse). The atmosphere was pleasant. The tenor of the conversation ran to "plein pouvoir" (full powers for me): "We agree with everything. Whatever you decide to do is okay with us." After the hearings, they all thanked me very charmingly. The first to do so was Streichenberg, who called me at once after the hearings were over.

Looking back, I doubt that before I left for Washington the SBA had informed me fully about the substance of the issue. Only much later did I learn about the circular letter of the SBA and about the decision the banks' lawyers had reached in 1954, which was to not make public any information about cases that went back more than ten years. Nor did I know that the major banks had transferred some of the dormant accounts to subsidiaries, which were not required by law to register them. My lawyers too believed that I had not been fully informed. They advised strongly against having Paul Chapuis and Heinrich Schneider march into the hall with me, lest they too would be forced to testify if D'Amato saw them. Schneider could not be convinced. He came anyway and afterwards held a press conference in Swiss-German, even though we had all urged him not to do so, lest he provoke the U.S. press.

Senator D'Amato did not want to let Greta Beer travel to Switzerland without his lawyer. That wasn't exactly according to my taste. "Usually my guests don't come with their lawyer," I told him. We finally agreed on a neutral attorney, Willy Korte, an expert on stolen art and a very amusing gentleman who had found the cathedral treasure of Quedlinburg, which had been carried to Texas via army mail. Korte told great stories. Greta flew to Zurich in May 1996. I accompanied her to see Ombudsman Hanspeter Haeni and gave a lunch for her at my home. Her offensive remarks about "the colored who are ruining New York," however, spoiled my appetite.

Dr. Benno Degrandi, our bank's lawyer, talked to her at some length in the library before lunch, found out that her father had held a diplomatic passport, and, as an experienced military judge, Degrandi became suspicious. The father, Siegfried Deligdisch, had died a natural death during the war in a Budapest hospital, and his brother had taken over the family's knitted goods factory. Greta and her brother had emigrated to Italy after the war via Vienna. Finally, it turned out that her father's brother appeared to have control of the account that had never been found and that she had long feuded with her uncle. Later, Singer told Degrandi — more or less to underline his concern — that they could have come up with much better cases.

But again the major gaffe came from the Swiss side, which demonstrated no perception of the situation and committed one faux pas after another. The ombudsman, for example, sent the finding directly to Greta, although I had urgently asked that Trudi Zuercher inform her personally. Trudi was an employee of our New York branch who had already met Greta, had prepared her visit to Zurich, and accompanied her to Switzerland. The ombudsman did his best, at least from his point of view, and sent her a handwritten letter. But he did not pay attention to the included printed form with the name under investigation on it. Somebody from the secretariat had confused the names, so Greta Beer had received a search form in the name of "Eugen Stern." One more avoidable error.

On the day before the hearing, I sat in the garden of the Swiss Embassy in Washington with Federal Councilor Kaspar Villiger, the Swiss finance minister at the time. He had arrived for the spring meeting of the World Bank, and we talked about the fact that Americans didn't really grasp the concept of dormant accounts because they had adopted a medieval precept from their British colonial masters, the so-called Escheatment Law — that is, property reverts to the state if there are no legal heirs or the heirs don't claim in time. (To be more specific, unclaimed property reverts to the state after a specified period of time, for example, three years in California.) My suggestion to the finance minister who was in constant need of cash: "Adopt such a law and all your budget worries are over."

But clearly the memorandum of understanding on which I worked with Israel Singer had priority. It was essential that a representative of a major bank was a cosigner. I made that point of view my own and sold it to the banks by pointing to their large stake in American investment banking and the large percentage of Jewish personnel in New York. They had to be interested in a quick settlement if they didn't want to jeopardize the business they had only just built up. So literally at the last minute Joseph Ackermann flew to New York. The current head of Deutsche Bank was, in 1996, a managing director of Credit Suisse. I got to know my colleague — a casual acquaintance even though our offices in Zurich were only a hundred meters apart — as a very pleasant personality.

The memorandum of understanding was signed on May 2, 1996, in Bronfman's New York office in the Seagram Building (which he had to give up after Jean-Marie Messier's Vivendi resignation, just as he had to abandon the castle in France and his art collection, auctioned off in the spring of 2003) by Georg Krayer, Joseph Ackermann, and myself for the SBA. In addition to Bronfman and Singer, Avraham Burg and Zvi Barak signed for the World Jewish Organization and the WJC. Barak was a member of the Bank Leumi le-Israel board, an economist by training, and a fighter pilot. But he completely lacked the aura and the charm of a classic ace fighter in the style of a Captain Peter Townsend.

I had hoped to avoid flying to the United States twice in two weeks, but circumstances didn't leave me much choice. So one morning, Ackermann, Krayer, and I climbed aboard the Concorde in Paris for the signing in New York. On top of everything else, the plane landed three hours late, so that for the first and only time in my life, I rattled into town aboard a helicopter. Afterward, all the cosigners except for Bronfman, who pretended to have another engagement, ate lunch at the Four Seasons. Then I went to sleep for two hours at the St. Regis — Georg Krayer took the other bed — and at night we climbed back on the Swissair evening plane to Zurich.

In signing the memorandum, we had already begun to think about what the audits could cost. Afterward, it turned out that not one of us had any idea of the amount of work the project would require. Ackermann, as an executive of a large bank and the most cognizant with such questions, thought in terms of $150,000. At the end, the cost was more than a billion Swiss francs ($800 million), a sum the Julius Baer research department correctly predicted a short time later.

In addition to the SFr 300 million ($240 million) for the auditors, we had to add the internal bank costs — between SFr 500 million and SFr 800 million ($400 million and $640 million) — and other expenses. That was a terrible shock and stood in modest relation to the sums we found, which were disproportionately smaller. Krayer and I knew what audits cost in our own houses. But that an experienced CEO of a major bank had no idea of the audit costs for a large bank meant that we really didn't know what we had signed.

Then again, it remains doubtful if this knowledge would have helped us much in this highly politicized matter. At the time, we thought that total costs, including the accounts to be delivered to the heirs, would be in the neighborhood of SFr 10 million to SFr 15 million. Not the most favorable starting point from which to steer toward a compensation agreement that would have made the audit unnecessary. Personally, I compared the audit costs to a Wassermann test, which in my day was still mandatory in Switzerland if one wished to get married. Nobody, after all, leaves his bride alone at the altar only because he doesn't want to pay for the test.

Unlike the Wassermann test, however, Barak insisted pretty neurotically that we dispense with Swiss auditors. Instead, the auditing firms would have to resort to forensically qualified Anglo-Saxon accounting experts who as a rule didn't speak German or French, and certainly couldn't read the German script, still widely used in the German-speaking part of Switzerland by the end of the war, and who had to familiarize themselves with the material — with the banks paying the bills. The demand that only forensically qualified auditors be used provoked some bankers' anger, and they threatened not to allow the auditors on their premises. There was one advantage: their evidence would weigh more heavily. On the other hand, we would not be able to benefit from the "super tariff" of 30 percent to 40 percent, which our own auditors charged, but instead had to use outside firms, whose personnel demanded the highest fees while their bosses happily flew from Australia or New Zealand to meetings in New York. However, the *Neue Zuercher Zeitung's* report that an Australian accountant had taken a taxi from Geneva, where he had landed in late evening, to Zurich was a nonstory. The Hotel des Bergues would have charged more for a night's stay.

It was the largest auditing project the world had ever seen. Some 650 certified accountants (out of the 250,000 who work in houses with global operations) were mobilized from the United States, the United Kingdom, Australia, and New Zealand to wade their way through bank archives under the co-coordinating aegis of Peter Weibel, the Swiss head of Pricewaterhouse. If we had given the commission a managing director, which we had not done for cost reasons, we would in the end have saved a lot of money.

To give some sense of proportion, here are the results for the Bank Julius Baer. After the audit, twelve accounts were finally reported — two of them still current. (They had not been paid out after 1962 because they didn't correspond to the criteria laid out in the federal law.) The auditing costs for those twelve accounts with a total value of SFr 12,000 ($9,600) amounted to SFr 3 million ($2.4 million). In addition to the so-called team leader, a Briton, and his deputy, also a Briton, two Swiss helpers busied themselves with the dossiers of a bank, which in the time under question had twenty-five employees. They marched through our house for four months, making slow progress. But most of the expenses came from the endless conferences and meetings the leadership of Deloitte & Touche, the contracted firm, held with Michael Bradfield (Paul Volcker's deputy) in London and New York. That the auditors were paid at an hourly rate to learn how a Swiss bank operates outraged many of our own employees.

Nor do I want to hide one almost anecdotal experience. When we filtered out dormant accounts at our Geneva sister bank, the Société Bancaire Julius Baer, we found one that had been heavily padded. Through a Geneva law firm, which used a Parisian advocate, our legal department established contact with the rightful heir. The lady was not pleased. Yes, yes, she knew all about that, but at the moment she was not interested and to please leave things as they were. Obviously, tax reasons inspired the lady to prefer this inherited account "dormant."

Back to forming the commission. Who should be chairman? Both sides had compiled long lists of candidates. Together we thought seriously about former Canadian Prime Minister Brian Mulroney. We were a little afraid of naming an American, since experience had taught us that an expensive bureaucratic substructure would inevitably be involved.

But finally we asked the man I had thought about on May 2 during the taxi ride to JFK with Krayer and Ackermann: Paul Volcker. As Alan Greenspan's predecessor as chairman of the Federal

Reserve Board, he was doubtless the "eminent person" we needed. In order to get him, we were willing to tolerate his cheap cigars. The foul-smelling stogies are not a matter of personal spitefulness but an expression of a frugal lifestyle. Paul Volcker was hardly interested in money, but he had a sick wife to attend to. Professionally, he had first made a career in the bond department of the Chase Manhattan Bank, was therefore an interest rate expert, and as such *papabile* for the presidency of the New York Federal Reserve. I had met him in that capacity at a World Bank meeting.

At first, Volcker had little interest in our offer. He found the differences between the two positions too great. The banks were thinking of a total compensation sum in the $5 million range, the Jewish side demanded $50 billion. Moreover, he thought it unlikely that the banks would allow themselves to be fully examined. That was one concern we could remove. The Swiss Federal Banking Commission (SFBC) could order an extraordinary audit at any time under the motto of "assuring impeccable business practices."

We have to thank Fritz Leutwiler for Volcker's final agreement to serve. During our first phone conversation, Volcker had made it clear that "in Switzerland I don't do anything without first asking my friend Fritz Leutwiler." The long-time president of the National Bank, already failing in his health, persuaded him that it was his duty. The integrity of the Swiss banking system was at stake.

The Swiss members of the Independent Committee of Eminent Persons (ICEP), as it was called, were nominated quickly: the political science professor Curt Gasteyger, the certified public accountant Dr. Peter Mengiardi, former CEO of Atag Ernst & Young (who also had no clear idea of the costs facing the banks), and Klaus Jacobi, the late former state secretary in the Swiss foreign office, and as such its top diplomat. He grew up in the town of Bienne as the child of a manufacturer of upright pianos, was married to a friend of my wife, and, as it turned out, proved to be a tough defender of bank interests. (Jacobi died quite suddenly in September 2004.)

We had also nominated Professor Alain Hirsch, a legal scholar, who threw in the towel after the second session, appalled both at the rude style of the Israelis on the committee, and by their extreme demands. We replaced him with the Basel professor of constitutional law, Rene Rhinow. An excellent man. As an experienced parliamentarian, he almost never showed up for meetings.

Bronfman, Burg, Barak, and Singer needed a lot longer for their nominations, a result of elections in Israel where Benjamin Netanyahu unexpectedly defeated Shimon Peres. Suddenly, Ronald Lauder was enthroned; he had financed Netanyahu's election campaign. (Today Ronald Lauder, the former ambassador to Vienna and patron of the arts, is the president of the WJC as the successor to Edgar Bronfman.) In addition, Reuben Beraja, the former president of the Banco Mayo Coop Buenos Aires (which went bankrupt in 1999), and Avraham Burg were to represent the WJC, the Jewish Agency, and the World Jewish Restitution Organization.

I was not foreseen as a member of the committee and had no ambition to become one. But shortly before presenting the ICEP, with Paul Volcker as chairman and Reuben Beraja, Avraham Burg, Curt Gasteyger, Alain Hirsch, Klaus Jacobi, and Ronald S. Lauder (who flew to meetings as rarely as possible, even though he had his own private jet and usually arrived toward the end of the meeting, explaining that his plane had been out of order) as members, we determined that the work could not be completed as speedily without alternate members. So Singer and Barak (whom Singer once called a bull in a china shop, with good reason) were named as alternates on one side and Peider Mengiardi and myself on the other. Mengiardi, a pleasant man whose contributions were very helpful, moved up to permanent membership after Professor Alain Hirsch retired. Professor Rene Rhinow now became an alternate. The idea was to make Singer and me responsible for managing the group's daily affairs.

Back in 1988, Bronfman had received the German Democratic Republic's highest civilian decoration from Erich Honecker himself, the "Great Star of People's Friendship." Did he value counter-point by wanting to hold the first meeting of the Independent Com-mittee at his Chateau de Mery-sur-Oise in the Ile de France? I wondered. I felt like Georges Pompidou. "On n'a pas de château quand on fait de la politique" (*You don't have a castle if you're in pol-itics*). A castle was not the right framework for me. If this were the case, I would have to decline. Instead, we met on August 15, 1996, in New York.

The meeting drove us to the brink of exhaustion. Bronfman on one side and Krayer on the other repeatedly had to intervene in or-der to prevent escalation of the discussion. Bronfman's historic achievement is his disciplining influence. Barak, round as a barrel, highly impulsive and extremely rude, his unpressed shirt often hanging out of his trousers, allowed no one to finish talking but at the same time pretended most credibly to be in danger of suffering from apoplexy. Burg's rudeness did not lag far behind him. Once he demanded that Peider Mengiardi come up with six gold teeth pulled from a woman's mouth in Auschwitz after Mengiardi had dared to criticize his attack on Switzerland's federal president, Pascal Dela-muraz. Both in dress and manner, the two differed markedly from the quiet Reuben Beraja in his graceful pinstriped suits and elegant shirts. A stylish personality. It is really a great pity that he later had to defend himself against embezzlement charges in Argentina.

When Barak ("I was elected by the Israeli people") and Burg raved about nothing in particular in order to grind us down — at times the pattern of a tie could be an affront — I seriously feared, intermittently, that I was not up to the situation. During these mo-ments, Klaus Jacobi, steeled in countless negotiations, helped to stabilize me: "Just wait, sooner or later they'll calm down." And that was exactly what happened. After the second meeting, things slowly became more civilized. I learned quite a bit from this experi-enced diplomat.

The only one who matched Bronfman's self-confidence was

Paul Volcker. Neither of them was used to accepting anyone else's authority. Volcker would fly in at seven in the morning, open the session at eight, and in the afternoon get back on the plane for New York. Nobody could match his composure. When he didn't sleep, he doodled in his notebook. He could afford to do that because he had silently brought his secretary-general, the attorney Michael Bradfield, with him.

With Bradfield we felt like the bridegroom whose bride has neglected to tell him that she is bringing a child into the marriage. We had worked out an excellent and very detailed employment contract with Volcker, and in his "terms of reference" he didn't mention Bradfield at all. (The contract is still in my files.) Later he would comment that having smuggled Bradfield in was "the one smart thing I did."

It turned out that Bradfield, a partner in the Washington law firm of Jones, Day, Reavis & Pogue, had been Volcker's top aide for the last twenty years. He had accompanied him all the way from the treasury department to the top of the Fed. The more than SFr 5 million ($3.1 million) that showed up in the ICEP's account examination report under the item "other professional services" might have been used to cover his own substantial "expenses."

Still trapped by the notion that we had no money and couldn't afford to run up expenses, Volcker irritated us at the beginning with his estimate that "operating costs" would probably amount to $20 million. He was so amused by our irritated reaction that he told Ambassador Jagmetti about it. We really had no idea about the charges we were facing. Volcker proceeded with god-like authority, acting according to the motto that "if you want the truth, you have to pay for it." The individual banks paid for the audits. The SBA assumed general costs, including digitalization of the Yad Vashem list of Holocaust victims, which exhausted the association's reserves that had been built up over a hundred years.

Bradfield, a very energetic and endlessly hard-working man,

equipped with a good knowledge of the banking system's possible weaknesses, became the driving force behind the investigation. That in the midst of his labors doctors found an advanced case of glandular cancer, which they treated with heavy doses of chemotherapy, did not break his working zeal to any notable extent.

When I learned about his illness, I felt, in the tradition of an Alfred Schaefer, that we would have to dispense with his services. If someone is not in command of their full intellectual and physical capabilities, they cannot perform in a demanding office. I was sorry, but from where I sat, there was no other choice but to replace him.

To my mild surprise, the SBA wanted no part of that decision. The Swiss side of the committee also found that this was simply not done. Obviously, the gentlemen *already* knew each other too well to make uncomfortable decisions in the service of the cause.

This is what happened. Bradfield, encouraged during evening-long telephone conversations and examined by leading Swiss doctors, became, during the course of his illness, extremely anti-Swiss. Talking to me, he hit a false note at times. On one occasion he blurted out with a rebuking, "Oh, you Swiss." To which I had to reply, "Out of mere intonation, I can't accept that."

Even worse, the sick attorney dug more deeply into the dossiers, constantly increased the search criteria for the auditors, and expanded the framework of the investigation. The differences in the instructions given auditors — and published in the appendix to the Volcker report — on November 19, 1996, and on January 30, 1998, provide a striking example. The 1998 instructions under which the auditors finally went to work had expanded the mandate to the "closed accounts."

In the weeks that followed, Bradfield made these "closed accounts" his pet project, and the auditors became very nervous about his constantly changing framework. The investigation of the dormant accounts had brought to light all kinds of improprieties, including single cases of crass embezzlement. But no specific discriminatory intent lay behind those improprieties. As Volcker noted maliciously, Swiss banks treated all foreign account holders badly.

The sums these large audits found were by no means insignificant: SFr 72.3 million ($52.5 million), among them 543 accounts totaling SFr 65.2 million ($47.25 million). Ranked according to nationality, some SFr 23.02 million ($16.7 million) belonged to 875 French addresses.

After "only" SFr 72.3 million ($52.5 million) had been found, Bradfield changed direction and put the auditors to work on the closed accounts, as the January 1998 instructions required. The auditors found that until 1945, Swiss banks held a total of about 6.85 million accounts; some 4.1 million were verifiable, leaving a gap of 2.75 million accounts where no verifiable link to victims of Nazi persecution can ever be established. Of the 4.1 million accounts, 1.065 million had Swiss owners, while another 787,000 were savings accounts, leaving 2.25 million potential foreign accounts. The definition was deliberately construed to put as many accounts as possible under the category of potential foreign accounts. It was enough for even a well-known Swiss name to appear without a complete address to keep it out of the domestic accounts category.

A methodical blur was added by the fact that an account was not necessarily hidden behind the 2.25 million name-linked bank movements. It could simply have been clearing a check or some other activity with the bank. Among the 54,000 "victim accounts" that were found, a total of 26,000 fell into the category of "unknown account types," meaning they could neither be assigned to demand deposits nor savings passbooks, bank safes, security accounts, or "other accounts."

The auditors compared the names of the 2.25 million account holders with the names of the murdered, which had been collected from Yad Vashem, Poland, and other East European countries. Bradfield attached great importance to making sure that the digitized search did not fail because of variants in the names or spelling inconsistencies. His efforts required higher expenditures and were ridiculed in some places but in the end were justified. All it took was for a typist to put one wrong letter in a name and it would have disappeared in any match based on letter identity.

Any such automatic collation only provided a first indication, as the match with the names of prominent Nazis, which was also carried out, demonstrated. This match signaled 1,934 hits, but as the Independent Commission of Experts (Bergier Commission) determined, "Nearly all of the discovered 'matches' were based on randomly identical names," and therefore did not point to any "culprit accounts."

In matching the 2.25 million "foreign account holders" with the 5.5 million names of victims as well as the claimants the ombudsman had recorded, the auditors registered 280,000 hits in the sense of random-name identity. From this quota, in turn, they filtered out all those who could not be identical (significant differences in age, different middle names, deportation or death before an account was opened, the academic title of children). They came up with a total of 3,252 names. But 76,000 account holders had to be added although their names were not on any victims' list. Why? Their circumstances allowed a clear-cut assignment, for example, the way an account had been opened or the address (concentration camp) or an internal bank memorandum that the holder had died in a concentration camp.

The auditors then examined these 353,000 accounts to see if the owners were Swiss or foreigners, if after 1945 the account was active or not, what the account was worth, and the "final disposition," that is, if it was still open, had been paid out, or closed for a variety of reasons — fees charged, payment to Nazi authorities or for unknown causes.

Finally, the auditors isolated 36,000 accounts "closed, unknown by whom," and which possibly had borne the name of a victim of Nazi violence. (Out of this amount, as indicated above, 26,000 were part of the "unknown account type" category, meaning that they may not have been accounts at all.) Some 23,000 accounts were published on the Internet, after clearing them with the Swiss Federal Banking Commission.

The value of these accounts totaled SFr 35.7 million ($25.9 million). According to a wealth formula especially developed for the Volcker Commission by the interest rate guru Henry Kaufman, that sum would be worth SFr 411 million ($310 million) today. And that makes the proportions look quite different.

If you add the 36,000 accounts "closed, unknown by whom" and use an average base deposit of SFr 10,000, the billion-franc mark is crossed quickly, at least to the extent that the 23,000 accounts are considered, which were burdened for so long with closing and administrative charges that in the end nothing was left. The auditors dug up several very embarrassing cases, including more than 400 accounts that were illegally delivered to the Nazi authorities because of mismanagement or otherwise.

Paul Volcker traveled around the world telling one particular story. An au pair worked in Switzerland for a summer and received a few hundred francs in wages. She left the money in her account, believing she would come again next year. The bank liquidated the account after nine months, charging closing costs.

In another case, a dormant account in a private bank that had SFr 65,850 ($4,950) in 1990 was reduced to SFr 557 ($417) at the end of 1994. In 1997 it was promptly reported with this meager balance. Without the audit, the correct value would never have been determined any more than the unprofessional practice of burdening accounts with fees and other expenses (including the search fees that ranged from SFr 50 to SFr 3,000 and were debited to the account) until nothing was left.

But the auditors were denied the opportunity to examine closed accounts because the banks had plundered them. They, and all of us, came too late to the conclusion that the real scandal was not the dormant assets but the closed accounts. The cantonal banks, whose great political weight an outsider like Volcker could not assess, had pressured the Swiss Federal Banking Commission to set a last deadline for the auditors to complete their work and in doing so had bought the idea that in the end, the whole truth would not come out. As a result, the cantonal banks — unlike all the other banks — were not required to publish accounts that "probably" should have been assigned to a Holocaust victim. Bradfield had differentiated the results of the matches into two categories: "probable" and "possible."

Over time an unpleasant quarrel erupted between Volcker, needled by Bradfield, and Kurt Hauri, the president of the Swiss Federal Banking Commission. In April 2000, after publication of his commission report, Volcker wrote a letter to a New York judge, Edward Korman, in which he recommended delaying payment of moneys from the $1.25 billion settlement in order to pressure the banks.

In retrospect, the committee had to concede one major weakness. The work lasted much too long. It did not publish a 217-page report until December 1999, which included an investigation into the stream of refugee capital. At that time, the agreement reached with the collective plaintiffs on August 12, 1998, was almost a year-and-a-half old, and only a very few were still interested in the results. After the agreement, Volcker, rather insulted, had wanted to leave the commission but, thanks to our ardent pleas, remained on board. But he took vengeance of sorts by not even considering simplifying the investigation. On the contrary, he made sure it was made more severe.

We have only ourselves to blame that it took so long. We started at too leisurely a pace, took too long to constitute the committee, and wasted too much time with matters of little import and petty quarrels such as the qualifications of the auditors. Then we lost another year before the auditors went to work. The auditing firms feared lawsuits and wanted to insure themselves against such a risk. At some point, the problem landed on my desk, and I found a solution with Nikolaj Beck, a versatile man who worked at Swiss Re and is today is one of its senior managers. The lawyers also demanded that the International Committee of Eminent Persons, for reasons of limited liability, be constituted as an association. Otherwise, Ronald Lauder, for example, risked becoming a victim of class action specialists.

Belatedly, I think it was a disadvantage that we knew each other too well. The committee worked hard; it met every quarter, fifteen times in all. In Zurich, we met in one of the airport's conference rooms; in New York, we saw each other in Volcker's office at the Banker's Trust on Park Avenue. These meetings, often attended by the CEOs of the auditing firms, usually lasted until 3 p.m. Then each one of us jumped on a plane home. I remember the food with some horror. Kosher sandwiches. They didn't improve by being served in heaping amounts. The Swiss delegates made sure they at least had the opportunity the night before to have a decent dinner and feel human. We all mingled very informally. Nobody wanted to expose himself. Finally, I was very disillusioned by a telephone conversation that lasted for several hours during which we negotiated to the point of exhaustion about the final version of the report. Michael Bradfield worked the same tricks as Ernst Bieri once did in our own house. He submitted the report so late that major changes were no longer possible. I had suspected something like that and had wanted to see something beforehand, but Bradfield did what Volcker wanted and never thought about allowing any large-scale discussion.

Volcker was not interested in any censure or general reckoning with the banks. Zvi Barak was not far from the truth with his suspicion that an American chairman believed he was the committee. And that's how it was. With Bradfield as his instrument, Volcker had made sure he would get what he wanted. In the end, the committee was only an empty show. Since in my whole life my authority had never been challenged, I wasn't used to being treated so nonchalantly. I had prepared a few things I wished to have included and to set a few decisive accents in the report about the practiced improprieties. But telephone conferences are terribly strenuous. You never know exactly who is talking and when you can speak up to say something. Finally, I was simply too tired to continue resisting.

In the course of the investigation, my target acquisition had shifted. Our charge had been to settle the affair, but my attitude changed in the face of what I discovered. But Volcker never thought there could be any other assignment than to take the matter off the table. Accordingly, Bradfield's report was a whitewash for the banks: no deliberate misdeeds had been committed. And the committee agreed. An unacceptable procedure.

It is true that nobody had organized any great plunder. It was a Swiss variation — unorganized theft. Many examples can be cited regarding the misuse of accounts. We Swiss were only saved by the fact that no methodology was recognizable, as was the case with a German insurance company that had reserved blocks of numbers for their Jewish customers who were to be robbed.

Nevertheless, we could all be satisfied with the results. For a long time I worried that no report at all would be issued. In that case, we would have spent a billion without producing any result. Another possibility frightened me: a minority report that would have devalued the majority opinion.

I give high marks to the Jewish side that things went as well as they did. One reason — in addition to the friendly climate within the committee — may be that Singer was busily trying to commit German companies to compensation payments of 10 billion D-marks ($2.5 billion), while the Swiss framework had already been set by the $1.25 billion agreement. In any event, the politics of the WJC hadn't changed since the meeting in the Grande Société. Singer wasn't interested in putting the banks in the pillory, and there was never a "Jewish conspiracy to take over the world's leading financial centers," as Robert Holzach told *The New Yorker's* European correspondent, Jane Kramer.

As far as I know, Holzach never denied the summary of that conversation published in *The New Yorker* of April 28, 1997:

> One old banker here told me to think of Swiss anti-Semitism this way: "It's not a dormant account," he said. "It's a dormant feeling." He thought that maybe it had to do with "the old times, when the cattle dealers were mainly Jews." He told me, "No one likes cattle dealers," and with that he pretty much summed up the rest of his conversation. Robert Holzach, at UBS, wanted to reassure me that with one possible exception there were no Jews "at the top" in any of the three great public banks. He said that the banking scandal was really a war. It had to do with a Jewish conspiracy to take over the world's "prestige financial markets," something he told me is already happening in New York, London, and "even Frankfurt."

Immediately after the conversation with the long-time chief executive of the UBS, Jane Kramer sat crying in my office: "I have never experienced anything like it in my entire life," she wept, and asked what she should do. "Nothing," I advised her. Nevertheless, I was aghast that a talented banker would resort to such a diatribe, especially with a Jewish journalist. But friends that Holzach and I had in common from the Thurgau (themselves from a Jewish house) told me, "Calm down. This was nothing more than good old Swiss-Prussian military anti-Semitism."

Holzach's gaffe did not make waves, given the endless blunders and thoughtlessness the Swiss committed and which aroused the sympathy of the Germans who were much more experienced in those things. I can only repeat: there was never a Jewish conspiracy. We simply became victims of our own smugness. We had not done our homework. Too many of us, it turned out, were unable to meet the demands that the situation imposed. In their entire professional life, the Swiss bankers had only known normal business practices. They failed to meet their first test and fled into fantasies of war and conspiracy, which, on top of everything else, reached a broader public. Rainer Gut's popularity did not increase when, given the class action suit, he took charge — he and Georges Blum of the Swiss Bank Corporation had the best overview of the situation — and settled the dormant account issue with enough money. I wasn't too happy about it either, although back in 1996 an informant had told me that we wouldn't get away with less than $1 billion.

The uncertainties of the American judicial system are foreign to us. Experienced attorneys almost always tell their clients to settle. In Switzerland, though, where only a handful of attorneys have any understanding of the American legal system, the whole thing smelled of blackmail. To some extent, the American lawyers and their class action suits rained on Volcker's parade. Given the huge exposure of the major Swiss banks in the United States, they had no other choice but to reach a quick settlement. Credit Suisse's Jewish managers under the spiritual leadership of Louise Firestone, the head of the legal department, pleaded vehemently for an agreement. If she had left during those boom years, Credit Suisse New York could have buried its investment banking ambitions. Significantly, the CEOs of the major banks didn't worry about shareholder comments but only about public opinion and the *Neue Zuercher Zeitung,* which smelled a confession of guilt. Under the slogan "rough justice," the only thing that mattered was the return to a normal agenda as quickly as possible. Credit Suisse CEO Rainer Gut admitted as much publicly.

This $1.25 billion should be seen against the background of the $1.4 billion settlement that Wall Street investment banks (including a Swiss house) paid in 2003 for the rosy stock analyst comments, which took in so many investors. The banks pay, nobody speaks badly about anybody else, and life goes on. Americans will never understand the bitterness left behind in Switzerland. And we will only be the victims of our own attitude.

On the other hand, the Swiss never understood the Anglo-Saxon formalism during the audit when tiny sums like SFr 5.25 were written down, while the Swiss had long since answered the question about such disproportionate relations between effort and result. Loyalty to regulations is not a militia's strength. It works out often enough, but this time it went awry.

I can only repeat that the banks did well with the Volcker report. The SBA, for example, was not audited, and certainly not forensically, and that remains an omission. Furthermore, the fact that in the cauldron of the cold war, dormant accounts belonging to Poles were paid out to repatriated Swiss crassly contradicts legal doctrine designed to protect individual property. Nor did the report mention the agreement the legal staffs of the major banks had reached in 1954 to refuse information about matters that went back more than ten years. Members of the Bergier Commission for the study of Swiss activities during the Second World War found the relevant documents. When Bradfield learned about them, he interpreted this agreement as proof of a "criminal conspiracy."

For me, there's no doubt that a good part of Switzerland fell apart. I could not have imagined discovering such improprieties. But not even in my own family did I find only approval. One of them, a fervent patriot, who had served in the armed forces during the Second World War, ignored the results of the Bergier Commission, consistent with the motto: "We have not done anything wrong, and everything else is just slander." Writing thick books about the connections of American companies to Nazi Germany doesn't help either. Switzerland surely will not get a franc in restitution. But this reaction from the historian Walther Hofer, a retired professor at the University of Berne, whom I respect very much — he came from Bienne and was a friend of my wife — again demonstrates a fundamental misunderstanding. The aim was never to discredit Switzerland. The presentation of warmed-over stories was a means of cracking open the hedgehog position of bank secrecy and finally moving beyond a long drawn-out tale. Countering that others had also sinned is negative benchmarking and leads nowhere.

Back to the work of the committee. Already in 1997, when the large daily papers in Switzerland began to publish long lists with the names of dormant account owners (among them, embarrassingly, names of French aristocracy, whose addresses could have been found by looking in the Paris telephone directory, in case no one had a Bottin on hand), the committee had founded a Claims Resolution Tribunal (CRT). Its task: examine all claims raised. The tribunal approved 1,281 applications and rejected 5,415.

In the spring of 2001, Volcker and Bradfield, named as "special masters" by Judge Korman, published a list of names compiled on the basis of the audit that contained more than 20,000 probable and possible account owners. Among the names were Albert Einstein and Sigmund Freud. In December 2005, Sigmund Freud's grandson, Anton Walter Freud, was awarded $168,000. The award was posthumous. Anton Walter Freud had died in 2004 at age 83. A limit of six months was set for disposition of claims. Claims were made on only every fourth account, but then, on average, four claims per account. Altogether, 32,000 laid claim to the "deposited assets" and only 5,000 of them focused on the 21,000 published accounts. The whole claims process based on individual restitution proved extremely difficult.

*

Judge Edward Korman set aside $800 million out of the $1.25 billion to settle individual claims. By and large those millions were not redeemed. In November of 2001, the judge authorized the first twenty-four payments to survivors. Another thirty-five received their money in January 2002. All told, $10 million were paid out, some $3 million to a survivor in Australia. Greta Beer received $100,000 "for her efforts." Surely years will pass before all the claims are settled, provided the current pace is continued. In the spring of 2002, some 11,000 applications had not been settled, and in the spring of 2004 some $600 million were waiting to be paid out. More up-to-date figures are not available. CRT, the Claims Resolution Tribunal, refuses to issue any further information, perhaps at Michael Bradfield's behest.

The generous criteria used in accepting claims angered the Swiss press. It criticized the failure of experienced jurists in Zurich to examine the claims. Instead, horror of horrors, Americans had done so. The media's criticism showed how little the public understood Volcker's approach and how little the Swiss themselves had learned. They still split every penny and would in case of doubt prefer excluding a claimant, while Volcker would include doubtful cases. Everybody would be served best by taking the issue off the table as soon as possible. (The Federal Court of Appeals should have removed the last obstacles when in September 2005 it upheld Judge Korman's decision to allow a substantial part of the money — $67.5 million — to go to Nazi victims in the lands of the former Soviet Union.)

Instead, when Volcker visited Zurich in the spring of 2002, a reporter for the daily *Tages-Anzeiger* rushed up to me with the argument that much too much had been paid. I told her to stop insulting poor Rainer Gut. His success in negotiating this settlement will doubtless remain his historic achievement.

Gut may console himself for not having been the only victim of petty attacks. Jean François Bergier earned little public respect for his great achievement. Today, no one is surprised that the Swiss government thanked the scholar in sparse terms — a lukewarm letter drafted by a low-level chancellery official — especially those who remember how the government wanted to honor Paul Volcker's commitment (only "without the Jews").

Federal Councilor Joseph Deiss, the Swiss foreign minister, missed the boat in two ways: the dinner we thought to give in Lohn, the government's country guesthouse, in Volcker's honor was due just as much to Singer, who over and over again moderated the discussion and blunted the sharpest invectives against Switzerland.

In the end, Israel Singer seems to be the last victim of his undeniable successes. Edgar Bronfman decided to dismiss his general secretary in 2007, only a few weeks before he retired as president of the World Jewish Congress.

It can be handled differently, as I saw in Vienna on July 27, 2002, when the German ambassador gave a dinner for Curtis Hoxter's eightieth birthday and celebrated the jubilee with a charming speech titled "International Understanding." In the year 2003, the German president awarded Curtis Hoxter the "Great Federal Service Cross." A great gesture. But how did he accept it? "I must confess that my first wife would not have allowed me to accept it," he admitted.

My American friends honored me as much as they could in order to set a public counterpoint to the WJC campaign. Lehigh, my alma mater, founded the Global Council, elected me as chairman of the board, a year later awarded me an honorary doctorate, and published a flattering portrait in the campus journal. In the United States, the press generally took more note of my mediating activities than in Switzerland — down to the cover story in the 1998 New Year's Day business section of the *New York Times* headlined: "A human face for Swiss banks." I was pictured with my brother, the president of the board, and my son.

What concerns me the most is that Switzerland has learned

nothing from the whole affair. For me, that was decisive in having the subject of the dormant accounts worked up by the contemporary historian Thomas Maissen. I can only hope that the study, published in the spring of 2005 by the *Neue Zuercher Zeitung's* publishing house under the title *Verweigerte Erinnerung* (*Reminiscences Denied*), will be taken seriously so that we will not have any repetition of a visit an anti-American student paid me. He wanted to write his thesis about the dormant accounts without having read the Bergier report, because it was too long, but he claimed that the banks had been taken for a ride.

Perhaps that student was simply not "fit and proper."

43

Quo Vadis?

Metamorphosis of success

In 2006, assets managed in Switzerland amounted to $4 trillion. In the meantime, they have probably grown by another 3 percent to 4 percent. Those are impressive figures. Take them at face value, and the crisis years would seem to have been overcome. The business has begun to grow again. So is Switzerland well-positioned in international asset management? And do these business trends accommodate our traditional strengths as private bankers?

A look at the $3,200 billion ($3.2 trillion) in the Japanese post office's savings accounts and life insurance business shows that the size of the $4 trillion held in Switzerland is not overly impressive. True, classic private banking methods cannot reach deposits in the Japanese post office, but that does not reduce their importance — unless one is satisfied with saying, as the fox does in the fable, "The grapes are too sour." Worldwide, in the meantime, liquid assets have crossed the threshold of $97.9 trillion. Swiss institutions, therefore, manage no more than 3.5 percent of all assets.

If one searches further, one finds that no more than 85,000 persons worldwide command assets of $30 million or more. The patronage of this highly desirable clientele, which grows at an annual rate of 6 percent to 9 percent (that is, 5,000 to 7,500 people), is courted around the world. A conservative estimate would make 350 specialized banks and wealth managers in the world candidates for high-level asset management. On average, therefore, each house would have no more than roughly 250 such customers. That these people usually bring their own financial adviser to any discussions, who bargain hard about the conditions, does not take anything away from their attractiveness for the private banking sector.

The next lower level — millionaires worth between $4 million and $30 million — is made up of approximately 750,000 people. The majority of millionaires (all in all about 8.7 million individuals) own assets in the $1 million to $4 million range. According to the latest *Cap Gemini World Wealth Report*, High Net-Worth Individuals (HNWIs) hold $33.3 trillion in assets. Together with savers (individuals with $100,000 upward), they hold $65 trillion. This figure, as the *Boston Consulting Global Wealth Report* points out, accounts for the bulk of worldwide assets of $97.9 trillion.

A look at the geographic distribution reveals that most millionaires (2.9 million) live in the United States. Their annual growth rate is 10 percent.

From the Swiss perspective, it is noteworthy that only 7.5 percent of global assets ($6.6 trillion) are managed offshore — that is, not in their home country — and that half of them are in Europe.

And that too is only an infinitesimal part of the total business. The steady shift in the direction of institutional assets (insurance companies, pension funds) is clear. According to expert estimates, they now hold 55 percent of all professionally managed wealth. Add the $19 trillion invested in mutual funds, and the emphasis shifts even further in the direction of institutional investors. The occasionally heard objection that funds are not part of institutional investing, because they are operated for small investors, is simply not valid.

First of all, more and more pension funds and insurers invest in funds. Large customers, it is true, can acquire fund shares under different conditions than others, but the only consequence for providers is that growing volume reduces margins and condemns them to dynamic growth if they hope to increase earnings. For the most part, they draw on bank services at institutional conditions.

Even markets with a traditionally strong individual customer base, such as Switzerland, cannot avoid the trend toward institutional business. In the year 2000, the institutional and the private sectors were equally large, with 45 percent each. The latest figures show that institutions accounted for 59 percent, while privates were at 31 percent. In the last five years, institutionally managed funds added $1.126 trillion, while private investments were almost stagnant. Circumstances in Italy, which also has a large individual customer base, showed a similar trend. In France, in turn, more than half the private assets are bound collectively — and the tendency is a constantly rising one. In Germany, institutions boosted their share from 30 percent in 1991 to 44 percent in the year 2005. Insurance companies alone (without provisions for pension liabilities) managed only 19 percent of private assets in 1991 but 26 percent by the end of 2005. The share of the mutual funds went from 4.2 percent in 1991 to 12.1 percent in 2005. "The investment structure of private households has undergone a lasting shift over the last ten years" is the Bundesbank's comment on that development.

Here is an example from the house of Julius Baer. The loss of assets upon the sale of the private banking unit in New York was more than compensated for after only six months, thanks to the institutional business done with Julius Baer funds.

Generally, the dynamics of the fund business are highly visible. Fund assets managed in Europe have risen 32 percent since the year 2001 (until December 2005). Total assets in Switzerland, however, rose 31 percent in the same time, driven by the dynamics of the institutional investments. Those are figures worth thinking about, especially because the potential in this business is so self-evident.

Japan, for example, holds no more than 10 percent of liquid assets in stocks or fund shares. But Europe offers as much potential. While per capita, fund assets in the United States amount to $27,000, they are only $12,500 in Italy, $10,000 in the United Kingdom, and $7,200 in Germany.

The ability of life insurers to push ahead that far has tax reasons. They can influence lawmakers much more easily than private bankers. But the fund industry is also working to exploit politically the uncertain demographic prospects and the latent social security crisis in order to boost savings placed in funds. Given the harsh competition — worldwide there are more than 6,000 fund providers — and their high professionalism, global wealth management depends on three key elements: performance, brand formation, and distribution. In all three categories, Swiss money managers are sorely challenged, even if they only want to maintain global market share in liquid assets.

The former HSBC chief Alan Bond remarked that banks face two fundamental challenges: demographics and IT. Ten percent of HSBC employees (20,000 persons) today work in emerging markets; 35 percent of bank software is being developed in India. Growth is shifting to countries with great population density and large upside potential. It has not escaped the HSBC head's notice that only 25 percent of Mexicans have a bank account.

Today, Switzerland has reached the point where it is willing to admit having lost a chance in Eastern Europe. The president of Credit Suisse's board of directors admitted as much in an interview given on the occasion of the bank's 150th birthday. Will the same sins of omission be repeated in Latin America? And what will happen to the home market? In the long run, can we persuade sophisticated investors to hold a bank account in Switzerland if only for risk diversification purposes? And what about the Swiss franc? Since the seventies, the Swiss franc has risen steadily. Since 2005, however, it's on a weakening trend, most notably against the euro. We can't exclude the fact that the Swiss franc might lose its famous safe haven status, at least partly.

In Asia, Swiss banks are seriously courting the favors of local billionaires. The CEO of UBS proudly announced that UBS manages the fortunes of 50 percent of Asia's billionaires, while Credit Suisse probably looks after about a third of them.

In Europe, on the other hand, major banks — after a largely failed attempt in the eighties — are definitely overcoming their national limitations. Unicredito's takeover of the German HVB bank shows that as clearly as does BNP-Paribas' acquisition of the Banca Nazionale del Lavoro. Nor are they neglecting emerging markets. Today Unicredito is market leader in most of the Eastern European countries. The entry of a European bank — admittedly with ties to India that reach back to the nineteenth century and its own "asset management new markets" — into the Sundaram asset management firm demonstrates the opportunities in the onshore business just as much as the general expansionist impulse and global competition does. Elsewhere, emerging markets have long been recognized as an acquisition territory for wealth management.

In addition to globalization, which offers to the asset management business encouraging prospects but which always poses the question of the suitable strategic starting point, the unavoidable reduction in margins — triggered by harsher competition (and the tendency toward institutionally managed wealth) — will force a dramatic modernization of the banking business. The sale of Italian Unicredito's securities custody business, bundled into "2S Banca" with a volume of $500 billion, to the Société Générale — which now moves up to be the third largest custodian in Europe with a volume of more than $2 trillion — is a typical example of the rapid industrialization of the banking landscape through specialization, increased volume, concentration of effort, and the dismantling of vertical integration. This process has only begun. The regulatory requirements imposed by Basel II, and the Swiss banking commission's flood of new rules, will only speed it up in Switzerland. It is already clear that Swiss private banks are trying to boost their assets under management through cooperation. Lombard Odier Darier Hentsch services the customers of the Swiss Valiant Group, composed of many small institutions, and Vontobel, a private bank, handles the private customer business of the Raiffeisen Group, historically the bank of the small farmers and the rural population. The cooperation models are not totally identical, but the direction is the same: concentration on portfolio management, on the one hand, and distribution, on the other, is a win-win situation for both.

As long as the Swiss money managers realize that performance, brand building, and distribution remain the mainstays of the core business — globally — the future will remain promising.

Genealogy of the Baer Family

This concise narrative of the Baer family genealogy deals with the direct lines of ancestors and descendents of Hans J. Baer as well as those collateral relatives who were involved in the Bank Julius Baer. The biographical sketches of the individuals are almost entirely taken from *A Family and Its Bank* published by Bank Julius Baer in 1990. Where pertinent, information has been updated.

Ancestors of Hans J. Baer

John "Doe" Baer
Issachar Baer (ca 1690)
Issachar Berle Baer (ca 1720–1785)
Issachar Lehmann Baer (1760–1812)
Berle Lehmann Baer (1790–1848)
Josef Lehmann Baer (1816–1891)
Isaac (as of 1897: Julius) Baer (1857–1922)
Richard Josef Baer (1892–1940)

Descendents of Hans J. Baer

Monique Baer (b. 1955)
Raymond Julius Baer (b. 1959)
Julian Julius Baer (b. 1992)
Jamie Vincent Baer (b. 1994)
Timothy Jeremy Baer (b. 1997)
Jean Shari Baer (b. 2000)

Prominent Members of the Baer Family Involved in the Bank Julius Baer

Isaac/Julius Baer (1857–1922)
Walter Jacob Baer (1895–1970)
Werner Baer (1899–1975)
Ellen Baer/Weyl (1902–1998)
Hans Julius Baer (b. 1927)
Nicolas Julius Baer (b. 1924)
Peter Julius Baer (1930–1998)
Rudolf Erik Baer (b. 1938)
Thomas August Baer (b. 1937)
Raymond Julius Baer (b. 1959)

Biographical Sketches

John "Doe" Baer — The first name of one of my ancestors to be found in documents is that of Dob, the Hebrew transcription of Baer (a bear), and a synonym for the biblical name of Issachar.

Issachar Baer (ca 1690) — Issachar, son of John "Doe" Baer, lived in the Palatinate town of Heidelsheim, where he earned a living as a trader of hides and as a sideline gave small loans to artisans, for the Elector had granted a number of Heidelsheim Jews the right to lend money at interest. Issachar had a son, Issachar Berle.

Issachar Berle Baer (ca 1720–1785) — Issachar Berle went on to follow in his father's footsteps as a hide trader and moneylender. He had eight children.

Issachar Lehmann Baer (1760–1812) — Issachar Lehmann was the fourth son of Issachar Berle. He legalized the surname Baer, and it became the official family name. In 1788, Issachar Lehmann married Mamal Maier. They had a son, Berle Lehmann.

BERLE LEHMANN BAER (1790–1848) — Berle Lehmann took over the hide trading business from his father, Issachar Lehmann, as well as continuing his father's pursuit as a moneylender. He had a son, Josef, with his wife, Babette.

JOSEF LEHMANN BAER (1816–1891) — Josef Lehmann developed his father's hide trading business into a prosperous concern that became widely known throughout southern Baden. At the same time, he continued the moneylending tradition. During spring and autumn, many traders from Ulm, Augsburg, and other towns in the east used to pass through Heidelsheim on their way to the big trade fairs in Speyer and Frankfurt. Josef married Rosina Therese Dreyfuss. They had four children: Bernhard, Emile, Isaac, and Aaron.

ISAAC (JULIUS) BAER (1857–1922) — Isaac was Josef and Rosina's third child. In 1897, he and his brother Aaron changed their first names: Aaron became Albert, and Isaac called himself Julius. Isaac attended the Jewish school in Heidelsheim and began to work in his father's business at an early age. He found the moneylending aspect much more interesting than hide trading and eventually made the lending and exchanging of money his main profession. Isaac (Julius) married Marie Ulrich in 1891, and they had three sons: Richard Josef, Walter Jacob, and Werner. In 1883, Isaac (Julius) joined the August Gerstle Bank in Augsburg (Germany), where he began his training. He was twenty-six years old. In 1886, he joined the banking and bureau de change business of Samuel Dukas & Co. as partner and co-owner and remained there for eleven years. At the end of 1896, Isaac (Julius) left Dukas & Co. in Basel and moved with his family to Zurich. Between 1917 and 1922, he was deputy chairman of the Zurich Stock Exchange Association. Throughout his life, Julius Baer pursued a great many cultural and charitable activities. He was cofounder of the Zurich Theater Association, of which he was a board member for many years, and was also a

founder member of numerous other Zurich institutions and associations.

RICHARD JOSEF BAER (1892–1940) — Richard was Julius Baer's first
son. He became a limited partner in his father's bank, but his avid
interest in mathematics and physics led him on another path. In
1917, he started working at the Institute of Physics at Zurich University, where he qualified as a lecturer in 1922, and became a professor at the same university in 1928. Richard Baer was an active
sponsor and patron of the Relief Organization for German Scientists Abroad. He was also one of the cofounders of the Scholarship
Fund for Jewish Students in Switzerland. In 1922, he married Ellen
Lohnstein, and they had four children: Marianne, Hans Julius,
Ruth Irene, and Thomas August.

ELLEN BAER/WEYL (1902–1998) — Ellen devoted her life to music
and sculpture. She played the piano and violin and sculpted. Her
work is predominately busts and figures but also contains female
nude studies in plaster, clay, and bronze and is distinguished by its
musical feeling for rhythm and complex movements. Despite her
husband Richard's untimely death, Ellen was determined to carry
out his plans and thus emigrated to the United States, arriving with
her children in New York on May 30, 1941. In America, she
learned how to work in stone by attending a class given by the Italian sculptor Oronzio Maldarelli at Columbia University. Her lasting
friendships with Bruno Walter, Isaac Stern, Adolf Busch, Georg
Szell, Arthur Rubenstein, Georg Solti, and Rudolf Serkin date from
this period.

WALTER JACOB BAER (1895–1970) — Walter joined the bank in
1913 at age eighteen. As was the custom at that time, he was to
work his way up through the company, beginning with sticking on
postage stamps and running errands. One year later, the First World
War broke out and Walter entered the cavalry. In 1917, the young

officer was granted a period of foreign leave, and he used the opportunity to continue his banking education at the Deutsche Bank in Berlin. His stay in Berlin proved to be particularly fruitful. With most of the male bank employees away on military service, he gained valuable insight into the banking business. The war had come to an end when Walter left the Deutsche Bank and returned to his father's business. Walter's interests extended far beyond his work. He played the piano all his life and became an avid collector of Swiss art. He was also very involved in theater and for many years was on the board of the Zurich Theatre Association. Walter married Marie-Blanche Halperine. They had four sons: Nicolas Julius, Alfred, Roger Boris, and Ulrich Daniel.

WERNER BAER (1899–1975) — Werner studied electrical engineering at the Swiss Federal Institute of Technology in Zurich. Although his professional interests clearly pointed to a career in electrical engineering, he entered the bank in 1922 on his brother's advice. Werner's greatest passion was the stock exchange, and he was an expert on securities markets. In addition to the stock exchange, organizational matters, and economic issues, another of Werner's great interests was the *Weekly Bulletin of Julius Baer & Co.* Werner married Nelly Theilheimer and they had four children: Peter Julius, Sonja Maria, Beatrice Anita, and Rudolf Erik. Werner and Nelly collected paintings and sculptures.

NICOLAS JULIUS BAER (b. 1924) — Nicolas was the eldest son of Walter Baer. Nicolas joined the bank in 1951. He graduated the same year from Zurich University as a doctor of economics. Being on close terms with his father certainly helped Nicolas find his way at the bank, which had increased to around sixty employees at the time. He became a full managing partner in 1958. Like other members of his family, he is interested in fine art, collecting abstract expressionist works and Latin American art.

PETER JULIUS BAER (1930–1998) — Peter, the eldest son of Werner Baer, joined the bank in 1955. Like his father, Peter was a born securities market expert.

RUDOLF ERIK BAER (b. 1938) — Rudolf graduated from the Swiss Federal Institute of Technology in electrical engineering. He joined the bank in 1969 and was elected to the board of directors in 1990.

THOMAS AUGUST BAER (b. 1937) — Thomas graduated from Zurich University as a doctor of law and gained a master's degree at Harvard Law School. He was a partner in the Zurich-based law office of Baer and Karrer. Thomas served as chairman of the board of Bank Julius Baer from 1996 to 2003.

MONIQUE BAER (b. 1955) — Daughter of Hans J. Baer, Monique graduated from the Swiss Federal Institute of Technology in Zurich as a certified agricultural engineer. Today she is a motivation coach and consultant.

RAYMOND JULIUS BAER (b. 1959) — Son of Hans J. Baer, Raymond has a master of law from St. Gallen University and a master of laws from Columbia University in New York. He previously served on the management committee of the New York branch of the bank. In 2003, he became chairman of the board of Bank Julius Baer. He is married to Gabriele Richner and they have four children: Julian Julius, Jamie Vincent, Timothy Jeremy, and Jean Shari.

PHOTOGRAPH CREDITS

GENEALOGY TREE OF THE BAER FAMILY

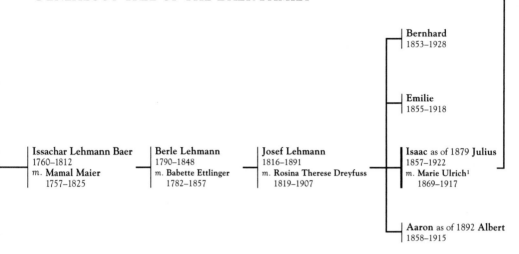

Bernhard
1853–1928

Emilie
1855–1918

Issachar Lehmann Baer
1760–1812
m. **Mamal Maier**
1757–1825

Berle Lehmann
1790–1848
m. **Babette Ettlinger**
1782–1857

Josef Lehmann
1816–1891
m. **Rosina Therese Dreyfuss**
1819–1907

Isaac as of 1879 **Julius**
1857–1922
m. **Marie Ulrich**[1]
1869–1917

Aaron as of 1892 **Albert**
1858–1915

[1]
Marie-Baer Ulrich was the
grandmother of the author
on his father's side and the
great-grand-aunt on his
mother's side.

Richard Josef[2]
1892–1940
m. Ellen Lohnstein
1902–1998

Marianne
1924
m. Jorgen Lykke Olsen
1923–2005

Annette Lykke
1952
m. George Edgar Paltzer
1952

Christian Edgar
1984

Georgine Ellen
1985

Richard Bjørn
1953
m. Helen Gisel
1954

Simon Ferdinand
1983

Eveleen Lucy
1984

Niels David
1989

Hans Julius
1927
m. Ilse Kaelin
1920–2002

Monique
1955

Raymond Julius
1959
m. Gabriele Richner
1960

Julian Julius
1992

Jamie Vincent
1994

Timothy Jeremy
1997

Jean Shari
2000

Ruth Irene
1930
m. David Rudolf Speiser
1926

Irène Elisabeth
1959

Naomi Dania
2001

Daniel Richard
Theophil
1961–1970

Marie Béatrice
1963

Bernhard Andreas
Fortunat Daniel
1971
m. Rahel Foyer
1971

Thomas August
1937
1. m. Heidi Wolff-Limper
1940
2. m. Monika Bettschart
1932

Barbara Birgit
1964
m. Walo Peter Bertschinger
1957

Annabelle Alexandra
1989

Olivia Valentina
1991

Andreas Julius
1967
m. Claudia Lutz
1969

Joel Julius
1998

Lucas Oliver
1999

Florian Tobias Andreas
2002

2
Richard, the father of the
author, was a cousin of his
mother-in-law, Marie
Lohnstein-Kahn.

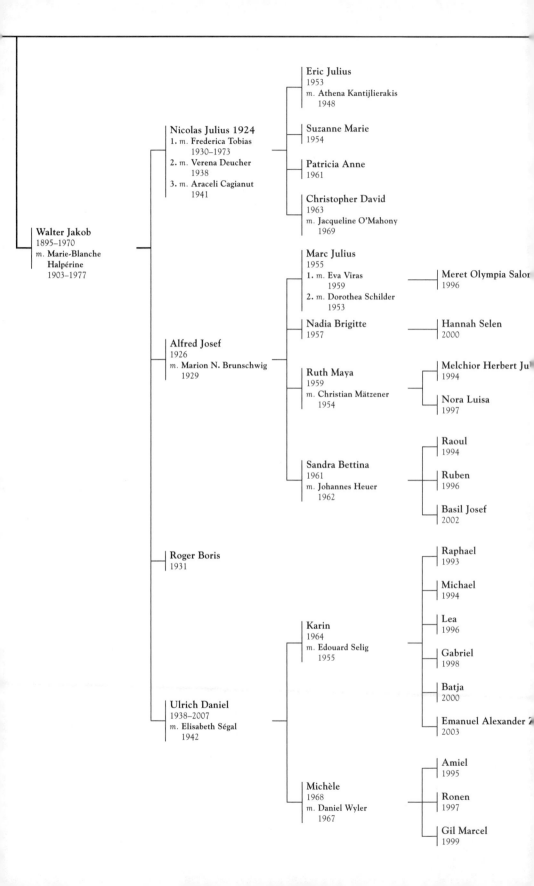

Walter Jakob
1895–1970
m. Marie-Blanche
Halpérine
1903–1977

Nicolas Julius 1924
1. *m.* Frederica Tobias
1930–1973
2. *m.* Verena Deucher
1938
3. *m.* Araceli Cagianut
1941

Eric Julius
1953
m. Athena Kantijlierakis
1948

Suzanne Marie
1954

Patricia Anne
1961

Christopher David
1963
m. Jacqueline O'Mahony
1969

Alfred Josef
1926
m. Marion N. Brunschwig
1929

Marc Julius
1955
1. *m.* Eva Viras
1959
2. *m.* Dorothea Schilder
1953

Meret Olympia Salor
1996

Nadia Brigitte
1957

Hannah Selen
2000

Ruth Maya
1959
m. Christian Mätzener
1954

Melchior Herbert Ju
1994

Nora Luisa
1997

Sandra Bettina
1961
m. Johannes Heuer
1962

Raoul
1994

Ruben
1996

Basil Josef
2002

Roger Boris
1931

Ulrich Daniel
1938–2007
m. Elisabeth Ségal
1942

Karin
1964
m. Edouard Selig
1955

Raphael
1993

Michael
1994

Lea
1996

Gabriel
1998

Batja
2000

Emanuel Alexander ⁊
2003

Michèle
1968
m. Daniel Wyler
1967

Amiel
1995

Ronen
1997

Gil Marcel
1999

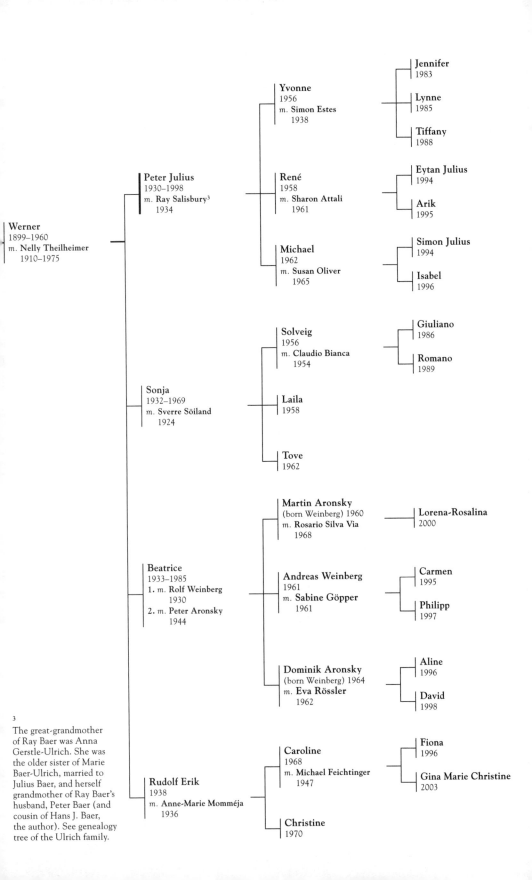

Werner
1899–1960
m. Nelly Theilheimer
1910–1975

Peter Julius
1930–1998
m. Ray Salisbury[3]
1934

Yvonne
1956
m. Simon Estes
1938

Jennifer
1983

Lynne
1985

Tiffany
1988

René
1958
m. Sharon Attali
1961

Eytan Julius
1994

Arik
1995

Michael
1962
m. Susan Oliver
1965

Simon Julius
1994

Isabel
1996

Sonja
1932–1969
m. Sverre Söiland
1924

Solveig
1956
m. Claudio Bianca
1954

Giuliano
1986

Romano
1989

Laila
1958

Tove
1962

Beatrice
1933–1985
1. m. Rolf Weinberg
1930
2. m. Peter Aronsky
1944

Martin Aronsky
(born Weinberg) 1960
m. Rosario Silva Via
1968

Lorena-Rosalina
2000

Andreas Weinberg
1961
m. Sabine Göpper
1961

Carmen
1995

Philipp
1997

Dominik Aronsky
(born Weinberg) 1964
m. Eva Rössler
1962

Aline
1996

David
1998

Rudolf Erik
1938
m. Anne-Marie Momméja
1936

Caroline
1968
m. Michael Feichtinger
1947

Fiona
1996

Gina Marie Christine
2003

Christine
1970

3
The great-grandmother
of Ray Baer was Anna
Gerstle-Ulrich. She was
the older sister of Marie
Baer-Ulrich, married to
Julius Baer, and herself
grandmother of Ray Baer's
husband, Peter Baer (and
cousin of Hans J. Baer,
the author). See genealogy
tree of the Ulrich family.

GENEALOGY TREE OF THE ULRICH FAMILY

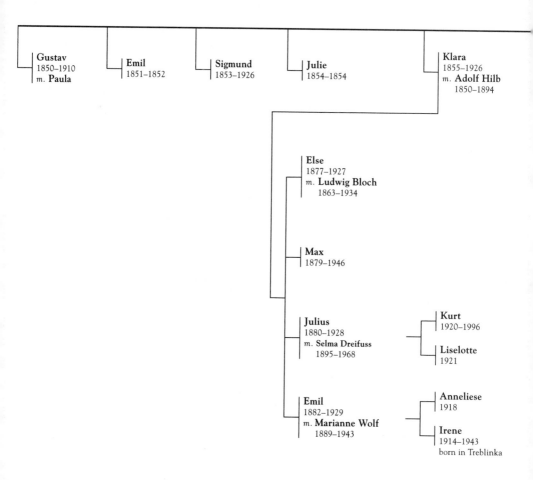

Gustav
1850–1910
m. **Paula**

Emil
1851–1852

Sigmund
1853–1926

Julie
1854–1854

Klara
1855–1926
m. **Adolf Hilb**
1850–1894

Else
1877–1927
m. **Ludwig Bloch**
1863–1934

Max
1879–1946

Julius
1880–1928
m. **Selma Dreifuss**
1895–1968

Kurt
1920–1996

Liselotte
1921

Emil
1882–1929
m. **Marianne Wolf**
1889–1943

Anneliese
1918

Irene
1914–1943
born in Treblinka

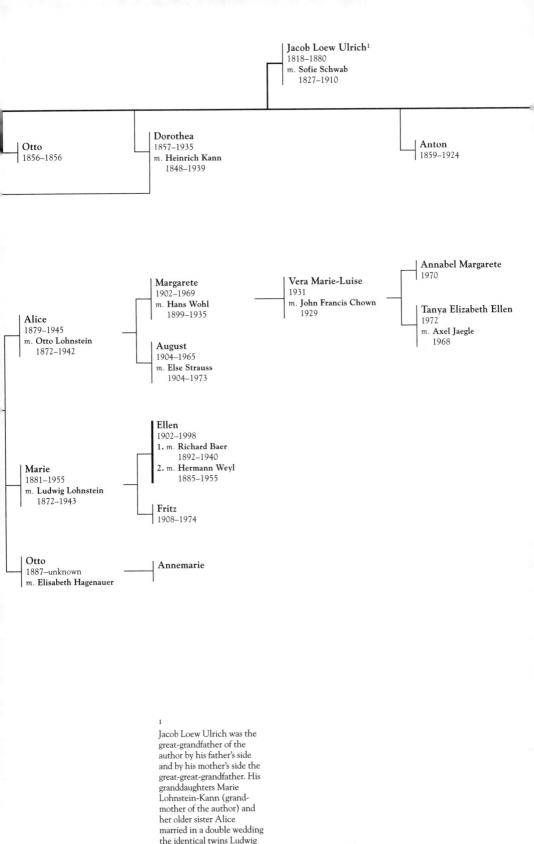

Jacob Loew Ulrich[1]
1818–1880
m. Sofie Schwab
1827–1910

Otto
1856–1856

Dorothea
1857–1935
m. Heinrich Kann
1848–1939

Anton
1859–1924

Annabel Margarete
1970

Tanya Elizabeth Ellen
1972
m. Axel Jaegle
1968

Margarete
1902–1969
m. Hans Wohl
1899–1935

Vera Marie-Luise
1931
m. John Francis Chown
1929

Alice
1879–1945
m. Otto Lohnstein
1872–1942

August
1904–1965
m. Else Strauss
1904–1973

Ellen
1902–1998
1. m. Richard Baer
1892–1940
2. m. Hermann Weyl
1885–1955

Marie
1881–1955
m. Ludwig Lohnstein
1872–1943

Fritz
1908–1974

Otto
1887–unknown
m. Elisabeth Hagenauer

Annemarie

1
Jacob Loew Ulrich was the
great-grandfather of the
author by his father's side
and by his mother's side the
great-great-grandfather. His
granddaughters Marie
Lohnstein-Kann (grand-
mother of the author) and
her older sister Alice
married in a double wedding
the identical twins Ludwig
and Otto Lohnstein.

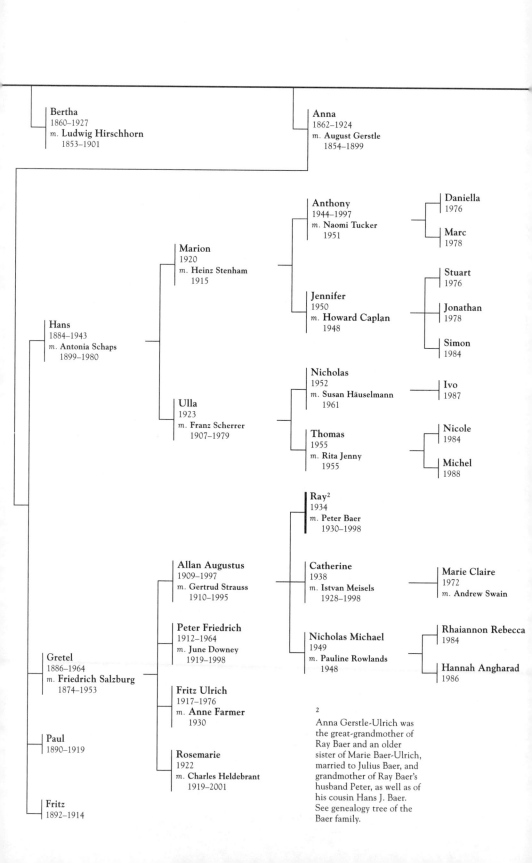

Bertha
1860–1927
m. Ludwig Hirschhorn
1853–1901

Anna
1862–1924
m. August Gerstle
1854–1899

Anthony
1944–1997
m. Naomi Tucker
1951

Daniella
1976

Marc
1978

Marion
1920
m. Heinz Stenham
1915

Jennifer
1950
m. Howard Caplan
1948

Stuart
1976

Jonathan
1978

Simon
1984

Hans
1884–1943
m. Antonia Schaps
1899–1980

Nicholas
1952
m. Susan Häuselmann
1961

Ivo
1987

Ulla
1923
m. Franz Scherrer
1907–1979

Thomas
1955
m. Rita Jenny
1955

Nicole
1984

Michel
1988

Ray[2]
1934
m. Peter Baer
1930–1998

Allan Augustus
1909–1997
m. Gertrud Strauss
1910–1995

Catherine
1938
m. Istvan Meisels
1928–1998

Marie Claire
1972
m. Andrew Swain

Peter Friedrich
1912–1964
m. June Downey
1919–1998

Nicholas Michael
1949
m. Pauline Rowlands
1948

Rhaiannon Rebecca
1984

Hannah Angharad
1986

Gretel
1886–1964
m. Friedrich Salzburg
1874–1953

Fritz Ulrich
1917–1976
m. Anne Farmer
1930

Paul
1890–1919

Rosemarie
1922
m. Charles Heldebrant
1919–2001

Fritz
1892–1914

[2]
Anna Gerstle-Ulrich was
the great-grandmother of
Ray Baer and an older
sister of Marie Baer-Ulrich,
married to Julius Baer, and
grandmother of Ray Baer's
husband Peter, as well as of
his cousin Hans J. Baer.
See genealogy tree of the
Baer family.

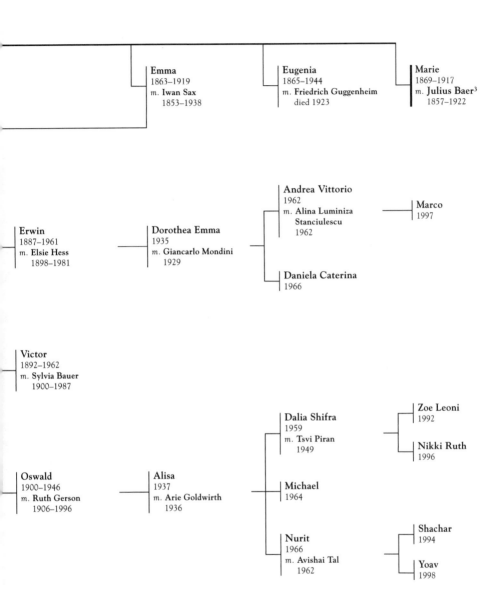

Emma
1863–1919
m. Iwan Sax
1853–1938

Eugenia
1865–1944
m. Friedrich Guggenheim
died 1923

Marie
1869–1917
m. **Julius Baer**[3]
1857–1922

Erwin
1887–1961
m. **Elsie Hess**
1898–1981

Dorothea Emma
1935
m. Giancarlo Mondini
1929

Andrea Vittorio
1962
m. Alina Luminiza
Stanciulescu
1962

Marco
1997

Daniela Caterina
1966

Victor
1892–1962
m. **Sylvia Bauer**
1900–1987

Oswald
1900–1946
m. **Ruth Gerson**
1906–1996

Alisa
1937
m. Arie Goldwirth
1936

Dalia Shifra
1959
m. Tsvi Piran
1949

Zoe Leoni
1992

Nikki Ruth
1996

Michael
1964

Nurit
1966
m. Avishai Tal
1962

Shachar
1994

Yoav
1998

Index